WORDS

that make

a difference

WORDS
that make
a difference

and how to use them
in a masterly way

ROBERT GREENMAN

LEVENGER
PRESS

Delray Beach, Florida

Published by
Levenger Press
420 South Congress Avenue
Delray Beach, Florida 33445-4696 USA
www.levengerpress.com

Earlier editions of this book were published in 1983 by Times Books,
under the title *Words in Action*, and in 1989 by
Farragut Publishing Company

Passages from *The New York Times* are reprinted with permission from
The New York Times Company

"The Purist" is from *Verses from 1929 On* by Ogden Nash and first
appeared in *The Saturday Evening Post*. ©1935 by Ogden Nash.
Reprinted by permission of Little, Brown and Company.

ISBN 1-929154-05-4

Cover and book design by Levenger Studios

To

my beloved aunt

Hilda Grayson

to the memory of

my beloved uncle

Arthur Ehrlich

and

to the memory of

my cherished friend

Seymour Berkowitz

The limits of my language mean the limits of my world.

– Ludwig Wittgenstein

Contents

Publisher's Preface

When it arrived on my desk in early July of 1995, Bob Greenman's package surprised me. Levenger received product prototypes all the time, but not books. But here was this book about *Words That Make a Difference*—an earlier and by then out-of-print version of the one you hold in your hands. The title intrigued me, as did the fact that the words were taken from the pages of *The New York Times*. I flipped it open and read a passage. That's all it took to get hooked.

Here was the mother lode of those words—the ones that come out of the blue like stray gamma rays. And this was how you used them to turn that thing called a sentence into a marvel. Most of the words were familiar—just slightly, maddeningly, out of grasp. *Antipodes*? Yes, I'd heard it, read it, but what exactly did it...ah, that's what it meant, and look how *The Times* used it. I'll remember it now. And this is how I'll introduce the word to my sons.

That kept me reading another passage, and then another and another, like snacking on popcorn, until I don't know how much time passed. The idea began then of what a great book this would be for anyone going into college, and how nice it would be to have this on your shelf after college, too.

Yes, it was a great book—but Levenger didn't publish books.

"Why not?" Bob asked when I called him at his home in Brooklyn. "Aren't you 'tools for serious readers,' and isn't this a book for serious readers?" You could hear it in the voice of this dedicated journalism teacher. He had a passion for his work and for words, and for the fact that using words wisely and creatively did indeed make a difference. Bob had used *The Times* for many years as a teaching tool and had carefully culled its passages to compile the vocabulary builders for his book. He knew in the way good teachers do that students could better master words if they saw how skillful writers used them, and how the words might pop up in daily life.

Absolutely, I agreed. But Levenger wasn't into publishing. Maybe someday.

As the years passed, we came across other books at Levenger that intrigued us and that had either fallen out of print or were searching for a new publisher to breathe fresh life into them. We gradually warmed to the idea of publishing, and in 1999 issued our first books (two rediscovered gems of Lewis Carroll's) under the imprint Levenger Press.

I hadn't forgotten about Bob's book. I put my copy in front of our editor, Mim Harrison. She too was hooked. She was also determined that Levenger would publish this tool for serious readers. And what a delightful learning tool this is that we put in your hands, both for students who are learning these words for the first time and those who are learning them again, in an even better way.

Bob's persistence reminds me of Eleanor Roosevelt's famous words: "The future belongs to those who believe in the beauty of their dreams." Both the author and the publisher have realized one of their dreams with the Levenger Press edition of this book. We hope it performs a similar magic for you, and that you'll use this book to help express yourself and your dreams.

Steven Leveen

Acknowledgments

This book's forebears can be traced to 1979, when Marjorie Longley of *The New York Times* commissioned me to write a book, similar to this one, whose concept and format was mine but whose title she supplied, *The New York Times Captive Vocabulary*. Over a three-year period, approximately 100,000 copies were distributed free to students from elementary school on up who had classroom subscriptions to *The New York Times*. A few years later, I proposed a trade version of that book to Leonard Schwartz at Times Books and *Words in Action* was born.

An earlier paperback of this book, also titled *Words That Make a Difference*, was published by Dan Rapoport's Farragut Press. Paul Dickson, who has written more than forty books, several of them about words, led me to Dan and I remain grateful.

Which brings me to Steve and Lori Leveen, the founders of Levenger. From the first time they opened that earlier paperback edition, they loved this book. Knowing the pride they take in their company and how carefully they select the items in their catalog, I consider *Words That Make a Difference* to be in outstandingly good company.

Mim Harrison, my editor at Levenger Press, guided and reassured me from the moment she told me Levenger had decided to publish this book. She has made excellent choices regarding the contents and format of this edition. My thanks to Mim for her sharp editorial judgment.

My thanks also to Lee Riffaterre, of the legal department at *The New York Times*, and to Mike Levitas, the editorial director of book development for *The New York Times*, for their help in reprising the book and allowing me to bring fresh material to this edition.

For help and advice at points along the way, my thanks to Charles Robinson, director of news information services at *The New York Times*, and to Lana Bezinyan, Leslie Bluestone, Loretta Montagnino and Howard Pollack.

To my wife, Carol, my loving appreciation for sharing the quest for words and passages for this book, for her taste and judgment in selections, and for her continuing encouragement, patience and love.

Introduction

I created *Words That Make a Difference* not simply for people who want to know what words mean, but for people who want to use them effectively in their everyday communication. Any word that increases our ability to express ourselves enriches our lives.

Words That Make a Difference is a gathering of passages from *The New York Times*, each one featuring a useful, vital word that can be part of everyone's working vocabulary. Each featured word appears in the context of an amusing anecdote; a sparkling quote; a vivid description; an informative, witty or provocative statement; or simply a good piece of writing. And each passage provides enough context to readily understand how the word is used.

The New York Times presents, each day, the largest chunk of English language published anywhere. It is from that reservoir of language—a weekday paper averaging more than 250,000 words, a Sunday paper averaging more than 625,000 words—that these passages were gathered, from newspapers published between 1981 and 1999. They provide a twenty-year panorama of American and world history and culture—which for some readers of this book may be a lifetime or more ("Dad, who *were* the Beatles?").

How should you read this book?

If you are planning to use this book to enhance your vocabulary, don't study it; relax and have fun with it. In fact, even if you are familiar with every one of the featured words, you may still enjoy reading the passages and seeing how *The Times* used the words.

Writers, speakers and broadcasters will find hundreds of words here that will add color, vitality and humor to their work. English and social studies teachers from elementary school through college will find this book a rich classroom resource. The passages are models of good writing, and many of them are natural springboards for class discussions and writing assignments. (Consider the word *ignominy*, for example, which appears many times in *The Scarlet Letter* and is presented here in a modern context that provides a history lesson as well.)

If you are a student preparing for the Scholastic Achievement Test (SAT), you'll find many words here that you are likely to encounter on the test. Plop yourself down in a comfortable spot and browse through the book. Check off the words you know. Underline the words that are new to you (yes, if you own this book, please write in it) and say them aloud. Take in the meaning of the passages; consider them little stories, and you'll find yourself effortlessly absorbing new words.

No matter how extensive your vocabulary, *Words That Make a Difference* can help you be more expressive in your thinking and communicating. In addition, you will probably come across words you may be familiar with but that you rarely use. *Words That Make a Difference* reacquaints you with those words, adding variety, precision and life to what you say and write.

Many of the words that come to us new and that we make our own are small steps in coping with life, helping to release us from cords of inexpressiveness that hamper our communication. Being able to describe people as *stoic, quixotic, avuncular, enigmatic* or *puckish* brings us closer to understanding them. Being able to say, write or even think that this person's smile is a *facade*; that her *non sequiturs* make conversation impossible; that the play we've just seen was *insipid*; that I am *contrite*—not just sorry or regretful, but contrite—brings clarity and precision to our language and our thoughts.

The words and their passages

The passages from *The New York Times* that appear in this book were written in the clear, concise and readable style that *Times* staff writers and editors strive for. Certain words are presented in more than one passage to illustrate their literal and figurative uses (*suffuse*); their use in two different parts of speech (*fecund*); two distinctly different senses of the same word (*bourgeois*); or just because the two passages were particularly arresting, even though the featured words in them were used in the same way (*imbue*).

In most cases the definition accompanying a featured word applies only to the word as it is used in the passage. The definition for *vehicle*, for example, says nothing about its being a device for carrying people because that is not the sense in which *vehicle* is used in the passage. In cases where two or more passages illustrate different uses of the same word, a separate definition precedes each passage (see *vacuum*).

Every passage appears here as it did in *The Times*, with two minor exceptions. Where needed, I inserted in brackets the name of the person, place or thing being referred to in the passage, for clarity's sake. And on occasion, I combined several short paragraphs into one.

Many of the passages contain supplementary language notes (indicated by small diamonds)—word histories, linguistic sidelights, background material on news items, quotations from literature and personal comments. I hope you'll find them interesting and enjoyable.

Following the main section of the book are several short chapters of insights into the language that will make this book even more useful in your quest to speak and write more effectively.

The Times, it's been a-changing

If you read this book closely, you will notice that some style points in the passages are not consistent with the style that you see in the daily paper today, or even among other passages in the book. That's because most of the passages appeared in *The Times* prior to November 1999, when the latest edition of *The New York Times Manual of Style and Usage* was published and several new style changes went into effect. Each edition of *The Times's* style manuals since 1895 has set guidelines for the ways things are to be written in the newspaper. Among the changes in the 1999 style guide were the removal of the hyphen in *teenager*; use of the lowercase for *a.m.* and *p.m.*; use of a lowercase in titles, unless they precede a name (President Lincoln, the president); and the use of a semicolon rather than a comma before the final *and* in a series, as you just saw following the close of the parenthesis in this sentence.

A dateline appears at the beginning of a *Times* article only when a reporter has transmitted the article from the datelined place. In the entry for *diminutive*, the dateline "BUENOS AIRES, May 16" means that the reporter transmitted the information from Buenos Aires to *The New York Times* on May 16 (it appeared in *The Times* on May 17). Were the article about Argentina transmitted from Santiago, Chile, that city would have appeared in the dateline. Articles written in The Times building in Manhattan, or transmitted from anywhere else in New York City, carry no dateline, with one exception. Those transmitted from the United Nations building carry a United Nations dateline.

What is it about *The Times?*

In compiling *Words That Make a Difference*, I plumbed every regular section of the weekday and Sunday *Times* (excluding Sunday's book review and magazine sections)—even the capsule movie reviews that appear in the daily television listings, the Corrections and the Editors' Notes that appear on page 2 of the main news section. All contained the kind of inspired writing and conversational tone that make this newspaper so readable.

Among newspapers, *The Times* does not have a monopoly on good writing, but it does have an abundance of it every day, and its writers and editors are supremely concerned with style. Journalism may be "history in a hurry," but for all its attention to deadline, *Times* writing, as you will see here, exhibits precision, elegance and grace.

The words
and
their passages

Index
of
Words That Make a Difference

Pronunciation Key

The pronunciations in *Words That Make a Difference* are presented in a form called respelling, adopted from the *NBC Handbook of Pronunciation*, the bible of pronunciation for radio and television announcers. (The pronunciations of the words themselves, however, are not necessarily those given in the *NBC Handbook*.) If some of the pronunciations sound a bit strange or stilted when you say them aloud, that's because they are not supposed to be spoken as independent units but as they would sound in conversational speech. Try them that way and they will sound natural.

Most pronunciations will be obvious at first glance. The following key will be helpful, however, in distinguishing the way the vowel sounds and several consonant sounds are respelled. Stress the syllables that are printed in uppercase letters.

This sound...	*...is respelled like this*
hat	hat
art	ahrt
bear	bair
fall	fawl
date	dayt
end	end
heat	heet
server	SER ver
phone	fohn
wit	wit
try	trigh
boil	boil
hour	OW er
show	shoh
put	poot
root	roo:t
rouge	roo:zh
thin	thin
then	th:en
above	uh BUHV
face	fays
faze	fayz

If a pronunciation differs from the one you've been using or hearing, check your dictionary; for the purposes of this book, I have provided only one pronunciation per word, but it's quite possible that the pronunciation you're familiar with is equally "correct." I placed quotation marks around that last word because dictionaries do not attempt to dictate correctness in pronunciation; rather, they indicate the way or ways that educated speakers pronounce words. For that reason, dictionaries provide alternate "correct" pronunciations for thousands of words. For example, the pronunciation for *aberrant* in this book is given as *a BAI ruhnt*. However, *A buh rint* is just as commonly heard among educated speakers and will be found in the dictionary as well.

Readers may question why pronunciations for words like *altruism* (*AL troo i zuhm*) and *arduous* (*AHR joo uhs*) do not include colons after the *oo's*, since they would seem to be sounded the way they are in *root* rather than *foot*. The reason is that in relaxed, normal speech, the second-syllable vowel sounds in those words do, indeed, come out shorter and less stressed than they do when we say the words as independent units.

algorithm

The problem of fair division is thousands of years old, but the mathematical theory is still young, according to "Cake-Cutting Algorithms: Be Fair if You Can," a book by Jack Robertson and William Webb that surveys the known methods of cake cutting. These include  moving-knife algorithms (somebody shouts "Stop!" when he thinks a knife that's moving across a cake is hovering over his fair share), dirty-work modifications (for dividing up things nobody wants) and divide-and-conquer algorithms.

see page 25

aberrant   *a BAI ruhnt*
deviating from the normal or the typical

In one of his last articles, "The Social Stress Syndrome," Dr. Kardiner commented on what he termed the violence, fanaticism and aberrant sexual behavior common in contemporary society—qualities that he considered symptoms of decline. He contended that such antisocial behavior, when it affects more than 10 or 15 percent of a society, weakens the pillars that support it.

abhor   *uhb HAWR*
to detest

HIROSHIMA, Japan, Feb. 25—Pope John Paul II today made a strong appeal for peace at the place where the first atomic bomb was detonated on Aug. 6, 1945. "To remember Hiroshima is to abhor nuclear war," he declared. "To remember Hiroshima is to commit oneself to peace."

abjure   *uhb JOOR*
to renounce or repudiate

He abjures drinking and smoking, avoids parties and rarely entertains visitors. "To me, it's a big deal when the mail comes," he says.

◆ *Abjure* means to renounce, repudiate or put aside: She has abjured the company of men. *Adjure* means to command or direct: The judge adjured the witnesses not to talk to reporters until the trial was over.

abomination   *uh bahm uh NAY shun*
anything hateful and disgusting

The deterioration of tea began when bags were substituted for leaf tea. Then came powdered instant tea, a still worse progression, and finally the abomination of ready-to-drink tea from cans or dispensers.

aboriginal   *a buh RI juh nuhl*
native; indigenous

Some 6,000 years ago, aboriginal Americans found their way to the great meadow on Nevada's 11,949-foot Mount Jefferson, hunters from the parched lowlands in pursuit of game. They established a permanent camp, with pit houses and hunting blinds of stone, to which they and their descendants returned many a summer over the centuries.

abortive   *uh BAWR tiv*
failing to accomplish an intended objective; fruitless

Barry Rosen is not likely to forget the moment, months after the event, when he found out about the abortive helicopter attempt to rescue the American hostages in Iran. "It was," he said the other day, "the most depressing moment of the captivity."

abrasive   *uh BRAY siv*
causing irritation; rubbing people the wrong way

On his part, Mike Wallace agreed that Mr. Buckley was indeed inimitable, but differed on the precise nature of his charm. "Bill's such a gentle person," he said. "I think he would find it quite hard to be abrasive and insistent the way I am, but he has a style and it's a style that clearly works."

abrogate   *A bruh gayt*
to abolish or annul by authority

Nuclear specialists note that no signer of the treaty banning the spread of weapons has ever abrogated safeguards. Most of the nations that appear to be developing weapons have refused to sign.

abstain   *ab STAYN*
to refrain from something by one's own choice

A woodchuck, he discovered, cannot be trained with behavior modification techniques to abstain from raiding the author's garden.

+ The American Indian name for the woodchuck was *otchek* or *otchig*. White traders Anglicized the name, which had nothing to do with wood or chucking, through the process known to linguists as folk etymology, a change in spelling or pronunciation to make words look or sound more similar to familiar words, with little regard to similarity in meaning or derivation.

abstemious   *ab STEE mee uhs*
in its strict sense, moderate or sparing in eating or drinking: the word is used here in a broader sense

After Ronald Reagan became the nation's 40th President yesterday, Mrs. Reagan prepared to appear at the inaugural balls in a hand-beaded gown designed by James Galanos. Its cost is estimated by industry experts to approach five figures, and the overall price of Mrs. Reagan's inaugural wardrobe is said to be around $25,000. Limousines, white tie and $10,000 ball gowns are in; shoe leather, abstemiousness and thrift that sacrifices haute couture are out, it seems, as Nancy Reagan sweeps from fete to fete in a glistening full-length Maximilian mink.

abstinence   *AB stuh nins*
voluntary restraint from food, drink or other pleasures; self-denial

To protect her voice, she now leads an abstinent life, having completely given up smoking and drinking.

abstraction   *ab STRAK shuhn*
an idea separated from its physical reality

Proposals for reviving Manhattan's West Side along the Hudson River have been around so long they have become abstractions, even as they continue to be weapons and levers in political tradeoffs.

abstruse   *ab STROO:S*
hard to understand because of being extremely complex; deep

Islamic law, which is so abstruse that algebra must be used to calculate inheritances, may not seem like an especially appealing field of scholarship, but once she caught the bug, Dr. Wakin could not shake it off.

abyss   *uh BIS*
a bottomless pit; often a reference to hell, chaos or the end of the world

If there ever was a playwright who knew exactly what he wanted to do and then did it, it is Sophocles in "Oedipus the King." This tragedy is relentless as it plunges both its hero and the audience into the abyss of a dark and horrible truth. There's no fooling around, no waste. Each character provides the hero with another key to his real identity, his involuntary crimes. Piece by piece, the entire picture comes together with a tidal force that is quick and deadly enough to shake the world.

a cappella   *ah kuh PE luh*
without instrumental accompaniment: Italian, in the manner of the chapel

Revolutionary Tea, a five-member a cappella ensemble, will perform early American music in period costumes in a free concert at 1 P.M. at the Citicorp Market Atrium.

accolade   *A kuh layd*
anything done or given as a sign of great respect, approval, appreciation, etc.

"It's the greatest honor I could ever receive," Tony Bennett said Monday night, and who could argue? After all, Mr. Bennett's Lifetime Achievement Award came from the National Academy of Popular Music, an association of songwriters, and whose accolades could a singer cherish more? As another award winner, Lionel Hampton, put it, "If they didn't make it, we couldn't play it, and if we couldn't play it, we'd have no gigs."

accost   *uh KAHST*
to approach and speak to before being greeted, especially in an intrusive way

Conrad Valanos, owner of the Monocle restaurant on Capitol Hill, once accosted a young woman who was rushing to greet former Senator Jacob K. Javits. "Why don't you wait until he finishes his lunch?" Mr. Valanos admonished sternly, realizing only later that the woman was the Senator's favorite niece. "Boy," he later recalled, "was I embarrassed."

acerbic   *uh SER bik*
sharp, bitter, sour or harsh in temper or language

Hugh Laurie plays another of Austen's more memorable minor figures, the acerbic husband who buries himself in his newspaper except when making lacerating wisecracks.

acolyte   *A kuh light*
an attendant or follower: originally, one who assists a priest in the celebration of Mass

Dressed in a sheet, he plays a holy man seeking acolytes at a shopping mall in New Jersey. "Let's face it," he says with a pseudo-swami accent that could curdle yogurt, "we're all unhappy."

acronym   *AK ruh nim*
a word formed from the first—or the first few—letters of a series of words. To be an acronym, a series of letters must be spoken as a word, not as individual letters: NATO is an acronym, NBC is not.

Richard Nixon's political advisers were eerily prescient when they named his 1972 campaign organization the Committee to Re-elect the President: It wasn't too long before his critics dubbed it CREEP, a moniker that proved hard to shake, especially after the Watergate break-in. Nowadays, when nearly everything in politics is market-tested by polls, focus groups and consultants, it would be unthinkable for a Presidential candidate to blunder into an acronym like CREEP.

Familiar Acronyms

AWOL	M*A*S*H	ROM
CAT scan	Nabisco	SALT
DOS	NAFTA	SWAT
EPCOT	NIMBY	scuba
FEMA	NOW	snafu
Fiat	OPEC	yuppie
HUD	OSHA	ZIP code
laser	radar	
MADD	RAM	

acuity   *uh KYOO: uh tee*
acuteness; sharpness or clarity of thought or vision

If driving at night has recently become more difficult, don't necessarily blame your headlights. Once you move out of your 20's, there's a good chance that the problem has nothing to do with your car's equipment and everything to do with your age. Baby boomers are getting old, and one sign of that is a loss of visual acuity. "When you're 45, you need 50 percent more light to see as well as you did when you were 25," said Jeff Erion, lighting manager for Visteon Automotive Systems in Dearborn, Mich.

adamant   *A duh mint*
unyielding: Greek, adamas, *a hard stone or supposedly unbreakable substance (the same Greek root gives us diamond)*

While video game enthusiasts often concede that some of the games sold in stores have violent content, they are adamant that the games do not encourage players to imitate what they see on screen. To them, fighting animated enemies is merely thrilling competition and no more harmful than football, professional wrestling or a cartoon in which Wile E. Coyote battles the Road Runner with anvils and dynamite.

ad hoc   *ad HAHK*
for a special case only; without general application: Latin, toward this

It takes only a drop of the proverbial hat for solo musicians to join forces in a concert of chamber music these days. When the chemistry is right, no matter how ad hoc the instrumental combination might seem, the musical results can be stimulating for all concerned if the performers are evenly matched and temperamentally in tune.

ad hominem   *ad HAH mi nem*
appealing to one's prejudices rather than to reason, as by attacking one's opponent rather than debating the issue: Latin, to the man

A theory is offered and the students evaluate it for fallacies, circular reasoning and ad hominem arguments.

adjunct   *A juhngkt*
someone who teaches one or more classes at a college or university and is not a full-time member of the faculty

The 70-year-old Mr. Woodcock, a former president of the United Automobile Workers, will become adjunct professor of political science at the University of Michigan at Ann Arbor.

a thing added to something else, but secondary and not essential

Dance has long been offered as an adjunct to university physical-education, music and theater courses. Now these are being expanded into full-scale departments offering programs that lead to bachelor's or master's degrees in art, science, education or fine arts. In many cases, the facilities of the academic programs far surpass those of private studios.

adulation   *a djuh LAY shuhn*
great and widespread admiration or praise, often to excess and sometimes extending to hero worship

According to his friends, Judge Weinfeld is somewhat baffled by the adulation he has received. His attitude toward his life's work appears akin to his feelings about jurors—to whom, he feels, no thanks are ever due. "I happen to believe that one who faithfully and conscientiously discharges his duty neither is entitled to, nor must he or she expect, thanks," he tells jurors before they are discharged. "Your reward must come from the knowledge that you responded to the call of duty as a citizen, and were privileged to play an important part in the administration of justice."

adversity   *ad VER suh tee*
misfortune; poverty; hardship; trouble; tough times

The characters who live in the enchanted never-never land of musical theater have their own special ways of dealing with adversity. Facing an uncertain life in a foreign land, the newly widowed Mrs. Anna simply whistled a happy tune in "The King and I." And the United States Government, dangerously depressed by the Great Depression, learned to accentuate the positive when a plucky little orphan made the Roosevelt Cabinet sing an anthem of optimism in "Annie."

aegis   *EE jis*
sponsorship; auspices: originally, the aegis was the shield of Zeus; it was also carried by his daughter, Athena. It symbolizes divine protection.

Many of those in the arts will take to the streets today at 3 P.M. for a Rally to Save the Arts, one of several in the nation. Not exactly in the streets but in the Lincoln Center Plaza, under the aegis of the American Coalition to Support the Arts, which embraces arts organizations, unions, artists and people who are concerned about the arts.

affable   *A fuh buhl*
pleasant and easy to approach and talk to; friendly; gentle and kindly

In conversation after his Philadelphia Beethoven rehearsal, Mr. Tennstedt, speaking in German, emerged as an affable, almost childlike man, full of a nervous, eager earnestness and a sometimes undisguised pleasure in his own success ("I have received four prizes for my Mahler recordings," he announced out of the blue).

affluent   *A floo uhnt*
wealthy; prosperous; rich

"I'll tell you what's important in fashion today. Clothes for the corporate wife, the businesswoman. Especially because these are poor times, people must look affluent. But the clothes must be understandable. You see all those silly Parisian clothes in the paper, but you don't see them anywhere else." [Halston]

ajar   *uh JAR*
slightly open

Human error led to the sinking of a clam boat off southern New Jersey in January, the United States Coast Guard said yesterday. Investigators have determined that the 84-foot boat, the Beth Dee Bob, sank on Jan. 6 because clam cages had been improperly stacked and a watertight engine room door had been left ajar, said Coast Guard Comdr. Michael Kearney.

akimbo   *uh KIM boh*
with hands on hips and elbows bent outward: Old Norse, kengboggin, *bow-bent*

In "Lion of the Desert" we see Mussolini at the height of his power. This is Mussolini as the world knew him—vain, arrogant, ambitious. There is the outthrust chin, the arms akimbo, the abrupt gestures, the strut.

akin   *uh KIN*
similar; related to

Dr. Samuel Gridley Howe established in Boston in 1832 the Massachusetts Asylum for the Blind—now the Perkins Institute—to provide blind children with an education akin to what public schools were offering.

alacrity   *uh LAK ruh tee*
eager willingness or readiness, often manifested by quick, lively action

There are many ways to catch crabs, but I never progressed much beyond the long-handled net routine. In late summer and fall I visit the ocean end of a salt pond, where, in many places, the sandy bottom shelves slowly away.

Crabs will be foraging for food in the shallows and if one moves with alacrity one will often, in a few hours' scampering, fill a 12-quart bucket.

albeit   *awl BEE it*
although; even though

Even though the scope of the home-office deduction has been drastically limited by Congress and the Internal Revenue Service over the years, it nonetheless remains one of the most cherished—albeit difficult to claim—deductions available to taxpayers.

alfresco   *al FRES koh*
in the open air; outdoors: Italian, in the cool

BALTIMORE, Aug. 6—After the sun has set and he is finished watering his rooftop garden, 89-year-old John Pente beams down upon the fresh crowds that have returned to the aging streets of his beloved Little Italy. They are back for an alfresco specialty from the old country, open-air movies that flash onto the parking lot wall of Da Mimmo's restaurant, proudly projected from a bedroom window of Mr. Pente's row house.

algorithm   *AL guh ri thuhm*
any systematic method of solving a certain kind of problem, or any set of instructions that can be followed to carry out a particular task

The problem of fair division is thousands of years old, but the mathematical theory is still young, according to "Cake-Cutting Algorithms: Be Fair if You Can," a book by Jack Robertson and William Webb that surveys the known methods of cake cutting. These include moving-knife algorithms (somebody shouts "Stop!" when he thinks a knife that's moving across a cake is hovering over his fair share), dirty-work modifications (for dividing up things nobody wants) and divide-and-conquer algorithms.

allay   *uh LAY*
to put fears, etc., to rest; quiet; calm; lessen, relieve or alleviate pain, grief, etc.

In the hope of someday allaying the social and physical handicaps of albinos, scientists at the University of Minnesota are unraveling the intricacies of pigment formation, looking for an understanding that may help them correct the genetic flaws that cause the disorder.

alleviate   *uh LEE vee ayt*
to relieve, reduce or decrease

> Beachgoers who are stung by jellyfish can alleviate the pain by mixing a paste of meat tenderizer and cool water and spreading it over the sting.

allusion   *uh LOO: zhuhn*
an indirect, but pointed or meaningful, reference

> A woman asked about improving "the quality of life for people who use Sydenham Hospital," the recently closed medical facility in Harlem. She never mentioned blacks directly. But the allusion was not lost on the Mayor.

in music, art, etc., some aspect of a work that reveals a debt to, or indicates the influence of, others in the field

> In many respects, "Attila" is the first "pure" Verdi opera, a score that finally consolidates his own unique musical voice and contains few if any direct allusions to the more classically restrained styles of Rossini, Bellini and Donizetti.

aloof   *uh LOO:F*
reserved and cool

> He plays with clarity, intelligence and immense authority. Yet he is a cool pianist. Proportion to him is more important than color. He refuses to make a play for the audience, and he performs miracles of virtuosity in a detached, aloof manner.

altercation   *awl tuhr KAY shuhn*
an angry or heated argument, usually of short duration: it may or may not involve a physical clash

> Andy Kaufman, the zany comedian whose shifting moods and unpredictable confrontations keep his audience off-guard, got into an altercation on national television Wednesday night. Midway through "Late Night With David Letterman," an hour of comedy and talk on NBC-TV, Mr. Kaufman and another guest, Jerry Lawler, a heavyweight wrestling champion, started exchanging insults and accusations. Just before a commercial break, Mr. Lawler rose from his chair and slapped Mr. Kaufman on the cheek, knocking him out of his chair and off the stage. Moments later, Mr. Kaufman repeatedly cursed at Mr. Lawler and threw a cup of coffee at him.

altruism   *AL troo i zuhm*
unselfish concern for the welfare of others; selflessness

Some species of ants studied, for example, have been found to be compassionate toward their nestmates, showing altruistic tendencies that include dying in defense of their fellow workers.

ambidextrous   *am buh DEK struhs*
able to use either hand with ease

Roughly two-thirds of humans are right-handed, according to a current estimate, while the rest are either left-handed or ambidextrous to varying degrees. But why humans should have this preference for one side over the other is a mystery. One clue, known for years, is that most newborn infants tend to lie with their heads turned to their right sides.

ambience   *AM bi uhns*
atmosphere; environment; milieu: also spelled ambiance

For ambience and fine food try the Hotel du Village on Route 32 north of New Hope at Phillips Mill Road. It is a country inn with fireplaces on both ends of the dining room and warm-weather dining on the terrace.

ambivalence   *am BI vuh luhns*
conflicting feelings toward a person or thing

And there was an ambivalence about bees in the Scriptures. The Bible points out that while the bee's honey is a sweet nectar, its sting is a painful thorn.

amenable   *uh MEE nuh buhl*
able to be influenced or controlled; responsive

What problems are you having with your marriage or children? Might these be amenable to therapy? If so, get help, the sooner the better, from a marriage or family counselor, psychotherapist or sex therapist. Similarly, get help if you are very depressed and unable to pull yourself out of it.

amenity   *uh ME nuh tee*
an attractive or desirable feature that makes a situation more pleasant

On the high desert mesas of the Navajo reservation, known for its pedestals of sculpted rock, the amenities of modern life are few. Half of the reservation's declining population, which now numbers 172,000, live in wood-heated houses without indoor plumbing. Roads are unpaved. There are telephones in fewer than a quarter of the homes, which are scattered over an area that takes in portions of four Western states and is roughly the size of West Virginia. Only the tribal government's health service, in Window Rock, Ariz., is on line.

✦ During World War II, Japanese cryptologists were able to decipher every code the Americans used but one—the Navajo language. A group of Navajos recruited by the Marine Corps devised a code that used Navajo words to represent English words and letters. Words with no Navajo equivalent became a code in themselves. Thus, tank was "turtle" and barrage was "iron rain." The Navajos spoke it over radios, one code talker at each end, not only baffling the Japanese, but saving time by eliminating the need to code and decode English.

amuse bouche   *uh MOO:Z boo:sh*
a small, delicate, complimentary dish presented to diners as the prelude to a lunch or dinner: French, please the mouth. Also called amuse-gueule, *gueule being a slang term for throat.*

While you browse the menu at Destinee, on East 61st Street, your napkin is lifted and handed to you and a small white plate is set down on your place setting. If you are lucky, it will hold a precisely cut cylinder of smoked salmon, filled with fresh shredded crab and dabbed with caviar, a glistening stain of pesto oil spooned around it. In the microworld of amuse bouche, it is a generous three bites: cool, salty and creamy but as candid and clean tasting as it looks. Especially between a few sips of Champagne. It may be the perfect first course.

anachronism   *uh NA kruh ni zuhm*
anything that is or seems to be out of its proper historical time: Greek, ana, *against +* chronos, *time*

By removing the hereditary peers—who inherit their titles and are, for the most part, descended from the landed aristocracy that ran England centuries ago—Mr. Blair was dispensing with one of the most extreme symbols of Old World, class-ridden Britain. Most Britons felt that having hereditaries in the House of Lords was an anachronism, if not an embarrassment, said Rodney Barker, a constitutional expert at the London School of Economics, but no one really knew what to do about it. "Nobody talked about it much or took it very seriously," Dr. Barker said. "But once you have a government that is seriously committed to constitutional reform, once you start looking at the second chamber and saying, 'The majority of these people are here because of their great-great-great-grandfathers, and this is absurd,' then everyone sees that the emperor has no clothes."

✦ One of literature's most famous anachronisms is found in Shakespeare's *Julius Caesar*. "The clock has stricken three," says Cassius, after we hear the striking. But clocks were not invented until 1,400 years after Caesar's death.

anathema   *uh NA thuh muh*
a thing or person greatly detested; any strong curse

"Genetic determinism is anathema to Americans, who want to believe everyone is born equal, with an equal chance for a happy life," Dr. Berscheid remarked in an interview here. "It's simply not so. The most important factors governing success in life are genetically determined: appearance, intelligence, sex and height."

Though Horace is the play's sanest and gentlest white man, and though he is ill besides, he is here seen plunging wildly up and down wine-dark staircases while roaring anathemas at his untrustworthy wife.

androgynous   *an DRAH juh nis*
having a blend of male and female characteristics

Eileen Fisher, the president of the clothing stores that carry her name, which this fall introduced a campaign using two models in their late 40's, said she's convinced that there's a consumer backlash to the androgynous young women who have dominated fashion. "I want a new, more realistic image for women to aspire to," Ms. Fisher said. "I'm tired of everyone being so tall, so thin, so young. I want to say, Women have arrived, we have the confidence to be ourselves, we can get old."

anecdote   *A nik doht*
a short, entertaining account of some happening, usually personal or biographical

One Beckett anecdote that I have heard in several variations strikes at the quintessence of the man as a master of uproarious pessimism. On a bright

29

sunny day he was walking through a London park with an old friend, Mr. Beckett exuding a feeling of joyfulness. His friend said, "On a day like this it's good to be alive." Mr. Beckett answered, "I wouldn't go that far."

angst   *ahngst*
a gloomy, often neurotic feeling of generalized anxiety and depression

If Mother's Day arrives Sunday before you have a chance to buy just the right gift, there's no cause for angst. Potential presents will line Park Avenue South from 16th to 32d Streets from 11 A.M. to dusk.

annotated   *A nuh tay tid*
containing critical or explanatory notes, as in a literary work

Nearly a third of the book is devoted to a concise and surprisingly comprehensive sexual encyclopedia (it even includes words like frottage and defloration), an annotated list for further reading and resources for help in sexually related areas.

antecedents   *an tuh SEE duhnts*
one's ancestors, ancestry or past life

Mr. Paton, who has no Afrikaner antecedents and still speaks with a suggestion of his father's Scottish burr, observed in his autobiography in an arresting sentence that "the birth and rise of Afrikaner nationalism is one of the most powerful subthemes of my life story."

antediluvian   *an ti di LOO: vi uhn*
very old, old-fashioned or primitive; colloquially used for anything hopelessly outdated: Latin, ante, before + diluvium, flood—a reference to the Biblical Flood

When Blanda was throwing passes and place-kicking for the Oakland Raiders in 1975, he was celebrated as a geriatric wonder, a graying 48 in a game that counts a man of 38 as an antediluvian relic.

anterior   *an TI ree er*
at or toward the front; forward: opposed to posterior

The prairie sphinx moth has four anterior wings of mottled shades of gray and brown, and its underwings are a pale yellow outlined in black.

Lepidopterists (scientists who specialize in the study of moths and butterflies) prize the moth for its beauty and rarity and sometimes refer to it as the "holy grail" of the insect world.

◆ According to medieval legend, the Holy Grail is the cup or platter used by Jesus at the Last Supper, and by Joseph of Arimathea to collect drops of Jesus's blood at the Crucifixion; the quest for the Grail, which disappeared, is treated in Malory's "Morte d'Arthur," Wagner's "Parsifal" and Tennyson's "Idylls of the King."

anthropomorphic   *AN thruh puh MAWR fik*
appearing to be human in form or characteristics

It is hard to imagine most of the electronic games existing before George Lucas's "Star Wars" in 1977. The exception is Midway's Pac-Man, a relatively gentle game with a sense of humor in which a round, anthropomorphic ball with an enormous appetite gobbles up shining gold beads and an occasional piece of fruit while four fuzzy monsters try to gobble him up.

anthropomorphize   *AN thruh puh MAWR fighz*
to think of, or treat, a nonhuman object as though it were human

And, as everybody in an automated office knows, people end up anthropomorphizing the computer. There is talk of "putting the computer to bed," of "feeding" it programs. There are computer terminals named Chuck, Muffy and John Travolta now processing insurance claims.

antipodes   *an TI puh deez*
two opposite or contrary things; any two places directly opposite each other on the earth: originally, the people on the other side of the earth

King Carl XVI Gustaf of Sweden, whose popularity has increased visibly since his marriage to a young German woman and the birth of their two children, is probably the antipodal figure among European monarchs in relation to Juan Carlos's direct political role. He maintains that his political functions have been reduced more completely than any other monarch's in Europe.

antiseptic   *an ti SEP tik*
preventing infection by inhibiting the actions of microorganisms: figuratively, lacking warmth or vitality; coldly impersonal; barren

Dr. Halsted was the first to put rubber gloves on members of the surgical team in the operating room. His superior results were attributed to his extraordinary antiseptic techniques as well as his meticulous handling of human tissues and control of bleeding during surgery. These were details to which few other surgeons paid attention and were crucial in improving surgical results.

Last summer, "Pirates" vacated the Uris to make room for "My Fair Lady"—only to land in Broadway's *second* most antiseptic house, the Minskoff.

antithesis   *an TI thuh sis*
the exact opposite

In his new book, "Chasing Monarchs," the naturalist Robert Michael Pyle chronicles his efforts to follow the monarchs on their winter migration by tracking them on the ground in a battered old Honda Civic. The book makes an incongruous companion piece to his 1995 book, "Where Bigfoot Walks," which chronicled his pursuit of a creature that seems like the very antithesis of the butterfly: the big, clumping and probably mythological beast known as Bigfoot.

antsy   *AN see*
impatient; fidgety; nervous; anxious: from having ants in one's pants

Antsy and grim-faced, they shuffled into the Brooks Atkinson Theater last night for a performance of "The Iceman Cometh," Eugene O'Neill's four-and-a-half hour epic. But their anxiety had nothing to do with the $100 seats or the extended playing time. It had everything to do with the Knicks. "The timing of this couldn't be worse," said William Nemeth, 38, a commodities broker from New Jersey who would have rather spent the evening cheering and cursing Latrell Sprewell as the Knicks went down in flames. They lost, 96-89, leaving the San Antonio Spurs leading the series, 3 to 1.

apercu   *aper SOO:*
a quick impression or insight: French

"Firing Line," its producer Warren Steibel argues, has never tried to condescend to its viewers, but rather has proceeded on the principle that "if Bill thinks something is interesting, the audience will think so too." The formula has apparently worked. The program won an Emmy Award in 1969, and its host, though frequently controversial for his acerbic apercus, has earned the respect of conservatives and liberals alike.

apex   *AY peks*
the highest point; pinnacle

Raised in conditions so poor that hunger reportedly left her with lifelong stomach problems, Ms. Jiang grew up to become a beautiful actress, then used her marriage to Mao to reach the apex of power in China and help preside over the brutal persecution and chaos of the Cultural Revolution.

aphorism   *A fuh ri zuhm*
a short, pointed sentence expressing a wise or clever observation or a general truth; maxim; adage

Some years ago, Denis de Rougemont wrote a very good book called "Love in the Western World." In "The Lone Pilgrim," Laurie Colwin is writing a fictional anatomy of love that is confined to America now. De Maupassant and Colette come to mind, also La Rochefoucauld and Vauvenargues, for Miss Colwin has a flair for aphorism. "Fulfillment," she writes, "leaves an empty space where your old self used to be." Of two lovers married to other people, she observes: "They would never have love's greatest luxury: time. They would never own anything in common or travel together." "A love affair is like a shot arrow," a character says. "It gives life an intense direction, if only for an instant."

apocryphal   *uh PAH kruh fuhl*
of doubtful authorship or authenticity: given out as true, but probably or definitely not so: said of stories or anecdotes whose truth or accuracy cannot be determined

From 1947 through 1966, the Cubs finished in the second division for 20 straight seasons, a record. A story is told that may be apocryphal but is absolutely symbolic. A broadcaster at Wrigley Field, one version goes, made an urgent announcement over the air. "Would the lady who lost her nine children please pick them up at Wrigley Field immediately," he said. "They are beating the Cubs, 12-0."

✦ Among the most famous apocryphal stories is the one about W.C. Fields' gravestone reading, "On the whole, I'd rather be in Philadelphia." It doesn't.

apolitical   *ay puh LI ti kuhl*
not concerned or connected with political matters

While Mrs. Gouletas-Carey said in a recent interview with The New York Times that she was not interested in politics—"I'm very apolitical," she said—she has made substantial political contributions since 1976, according to public documents. In 1979 and 1980, for example, she donated $17,500 at the national level, Federal campaign records show, and she has served on Senator Kennedy's finance committee.

apostle   *uh PAH suhl*
an early advocate or leader of a new principle or movement, especially one aimed at reform

Also at 8 P.M. on Sunday, WNEW-TV, Channel 5, has its own musical offering in the form of "The Beach Boys 20th Anniversary Special." Yes, the tuneful apostles of youthful innocence and good times have been around for 20 years, selling enough records to put them in the superstar class of the Beatles and Elvis Presley.

append   *uh PEND*
to attach or affix; add as a supplement or appendix

The Islamic Republicans appear to be losing an important base of support among the traditionalist merchants of the bazaar—the original bankrollers of the revolution—who in the past have been thought of as quite religious. Most append "haj" to their names, indicating that they have made the religious pilgrimage to Mecca.

Because the word "charisma" has been carelessly appended to every politician with a good smile and every rock star capable of unnerving adolescents, one hesitates to use it when describing Karol Wojtyla. Until, that is, one reads again the dictionary definition: "An extraordinary power of healing ... a personal magic."

aquifer   *A kwuh fuhr*
an underground layer of sand or porous rock containing water, into which wells can be sunk

Santa Fe, which sits on a 7,000-foot-high plateau at the southern base of the Rocky Mountains, is, like much of the West, dependent on the annual snowfall to the north to recharge the underground aquifers on which the area has so far depended for its water supply.

arbiter *AHR bi ter*
a person fully authorized or qualified to judge or decide

SAN FRANCISCO, May 12—Herb Caen, the columnist for the San Francisco Chronicle who probably comes as close as anyone to being an arbiter of taste in this city, was more or less speechless after visiting the new $7 million Maxwell's Plum restaurant, which officially opened here last night. "The place puts me in mind of W.C. Fields' definition of sex," Mr. Caen wrote, quoting the late comedian: "I don't know if it's good and I don't know if it's bad. All I know is that there's nothing quite like it."

arbitrary *AHR buh trai ree*
not fixed by rules but left to one's judgment or choice; discretionary

Short, bowl-like cuts on older women are still common, perhaps because they remember the days of the Cultural Revolution when Red Guards carried scissors and arbitrarily snipped off locks they deemed too long or fancy.

arcane *AR kayn*
understood by only a few

The behavior of electrified chocolate is the latest discovery in an arcane field of physical chemistry and engineering called electrorheology, which investigates changes in the viscosity of fluids in response to electricity.

archetype *AHR kuh tighp*
a perfect example of a type or group

Stefan Gierasch brings conviction to the role of the malevolent sergeant named Bloody Five, and Kevin O'Connor and James Greene have an archetypal authenticity as earthy soldiers. Grizzled and bedraggled, they look like sad sacks from a timeless army.

✦ "The Sad Sack" was a popular comic strip drawn by George Baker for armed service publications during World War II. *Sad sack* was Army slang for a confused, disheveled, maladjusted and unhappy soldier. He was a well-meaning bungler who consistently got himself into trouble. In the 1930s the word had been used by students to describe an introverted, socially unacceptable person—the same type they might today call a nerd.

archipelago   *ar kuh PE luh goh*
a group or chain of many islands: Greek, archi, *chief* + pelagos, *sea*

The Comoros, a tiny archipelago northwest of Madagascar in the Indian Ocean, has had 18 coups or coup attempts in the 24 years since it won independence from France.

ardent   *AHR duhnt*
intensely enthusiastic or devoted

Blossom Dearie is a jazz singer, pianist and songwriter whose style and choice of material have captured an ardent following in New York.

arduous   *AHR joo uhs*
difficult to do; laborious; onerous; full of hardships

The Mount Evans Hill Climb is an arduous 28-mile bicycle race that ends on the highest paved road in the United States—14,264 feet above sea level.

arguably   *AHR gyoo: uh blee*
that can be convincingly argued

In a country where the reverence for poets, singers and writers often gives them authority rivaling that of officials of the state, Mr. Vysotsky was arguably the most popular of his time. It was a popularity that few Westerners, even those living in Moscow, could fully appreciate, perhaps in part because his ballads rarely dealt explicitly with politics, because the street language he used with such effect is almost untranslatable and because the life he sang about is so alien to the West.

artifact   *AR tuh fakt*
any object made by human work, especially one of archaeological or historical interest

One of the Titanic's bronze whistles, silent for nearly 87 years, blew deep and steady here on Saturday at an exhibition of artifacts from the sunken luxury liner. Thousands of people standing in city streets responded with cheers and whistles after the 10-second blasts, about two minutes apart shortly after 4 P.M. The ceremony was held outside the old Union Depot where other artifacts from the Titanic were on display. "That's great, that's great, that's great," said Thomas Goulding, who said he had been intrigued by the Titanic since he heard stories as a boy in Ireland about its sinking on April 15, 1912. The police estimated the crowd for today's event at 80,000 to 100,000, much higher than the 2,000 to 3,000 organizers had predicted. The whistle, from the forward smokestack, was recovered from the wreck in 1993.

assiduous   *uh SI joo: uhs*
done with constant and careful attention

Instead of celebrating May Day, many local union chapters are mobilizing to commemorate May 3, the 190th anniversary of the Polish Constitution, the first written Constitution in Europe. The date has been assiduously ignored by the Communist governments until now.

assuage   *uh SWAYJ*
to make less severe or burdensome; ease

But is it a valid premise or simply a rationalization used to assuage guilt? Can working mothers truly compensate for the 40 to 60 hours a week they are absent from the home by compressing shared occasions with their children into smaller slices of time?

astute   *uh STOO:T*
keen in judgment

The astutely chosen songs in Ms. McCorkle's new show follow the ups and downs of a romance in delightfully unpredictable ways. Always a supple pop-jazz technician, Ms. McCorkle also broadens her expressive range, drawing everything from the blues to Broadway to Brazilian pop, and adapting her style accordingly.

athwart   *uh THWAWRT*
across; from one side to the other of

They blocked the bridge before dawn with about 15 cars, pickup trucks and campers parked athwart both lanes. A sign at the front of the bridge read: "Crow Reservation Closed to Fishing Today, Tomorrow and Forever." Some fishermen got around the bridge by taking other, unblocked roads.

atrophy   *A truh fee*
to waste away

The idea that the electric guitar was a magical lance and that guitarists were rock-and-roll heroes, began to get out of hand during the late 60's. Guitar solos, which had originally been short breaks in songs, grew long and bloated. The songs atrophied until they were flimsy excuses for endless displays of guitar prowess.

attenuate   *uh TE nyoo: ayt*
to weaken; dilute

The 1980-81 Broadway season reached its official conclusion last night with the opening of "It Had to Be You," the last show to arrive in time to qualify for this year's Tony awards. I'm afraid the season didn't end with a bang or even a whimper—just an attenuated yawn.

atypical   *ay TI pi kuhl*
not typical; not characteristic

Reel life bearing no arithmetically calculable resemblance to real life, Miss Stanwyck is noted for her generosity and modesty. "She's atypical of actresses," says her close friend, Shirley Eder, the columnist. "She has pride in her work, but I don't think she realizes her worth as an actress or as a person. She thinks she's average; she thinks it's an imposition to ask her friends to come help honor her."

au courant   *oh koo RAHNT*
up to date; well-informed; with-it: French

On 68th Street just east of Columbus Avenue and a short walk from Lincoln Center, Simon's was the setting of a farewell party for Walter Cronkite. From that time on, it has been on the must list of the au courant.

au pair   *oh PAIR*
a young person, usually from another country, who does housework, tutoring, etc. for a family in exchange for room and board: French, as an equal

After a few months she became homesick for England and returned to work [there] as an au pair for an American couple and took a course in cooking, the accepted preparation for upper-class English girls raised primarily for marriage.

augur   *AW ger*
a sign of things to come; a portent: from augur, a priest of ancient Rome who interpreted the will of the gods through signs such as the flight of birds

Pokemon has its own story line (as did Power Rangers and Ninja Turtles), but it also taps into the notion of collecting that sustained the Beanie Babies craze. While Power Rangers had the story line without the collecting and Beanie Babies had the collecting without the story line, Pokemon has both. All of this augurs well for the future, Mr. Del Vecchio said. "The principles they are applying indicate it will last longer than the average kid franchise," he said. "Whether it will last 30 years will depend on other factors, like how good they are going to be as marketers and what other franchises may be introduced that will do an even better job. You know, kids are fickle. They will get tired of these kind of properties and dash off to the next one."

aura *AW ruh*
an atmosphere or quality that seems to arise from and surround a person or thing

Husky and agile, gentle and competitive, Valenzuela gives off an aura of immense natural ability and superior athletic intelligence, a sense that he is always doing the right thing. He exhibits no flaws, no insecurities; the people in his own dugout sit and gape at his advanced state.

auteur *oh TER*
a film director with a distinctive, personal style

To the end, Mr. Bresson remained a true auteur who controlled every facet of his work, who worked independent of commercial considerations and who made films that are instantly recognizable as his. Although he was too iconoclastic to inspire a school of filmmakers to follow him, he had a legion of admirers, becoming, as Jean-Luc Godard put it, "to French cinema what Mozart is to German music and Dostoyevsky is to Russian literature."

autocratic *aw tuh KRA tik*
ruling with absolute power, as a dictator; having unlimited power over others

The teamsters' union, chartered in 1899, is an autocratic organization with intense centralized power. It has been marked for decades by secrecy, nepotism, lucrative amenities for union executives and violence.

autonomy *aw TAH nuh mee*
independence

Why are engaged couples so apprehensive? The list seems endless: Getting married means giving up a degree of freedom and autonomy, leaving yourself open to hurt and abandonment, having to reveal the truth about everything, from idiosyncracies to the bank balance you said you had but don't.

avant-garde   *ah vahnt GAHRD*
leading in new or unconventional movements, especially in the arts: French

To say that "Promised Land" is avant-garde theater is putting it mildly. The actors never show their faces (the curtain rises by degrees, but only as high as shoulder level); they speak not a single word, and, oh yes, the lead character is a rock.

avert   *uh VERT*
to turn away; to prevent

Two years ago, as Charles Finnie, an investment banker in San Francisco, was driving home from work, he did what he did nearly every time he got in the car: he picked up his cell phone and started dialing. Eyes averted from the road, he slammed into the car in front of him. No one was injured, but the impact jammed Mr. Finnie's door shut. So he climbed out through the sun roof—still talking on the phone.

avuncular   *uh VUN kyuh ler*
having the qualities of an uncle, especially a benevolent uncle

During commercials for Kraft products ("Good food and good food ideas," Mr. Herlihy would say), audiences heard only his voice, a voice he said he tried to make sound friendly. It was an avuncular, next-door-neighbor, deep, mellow kind of voice, a digestive guide through the preparation of all manner of soufflés, dips, marshmallow salads and fondues.

awash   *uh WAHSH*
flooded

Outside, the handsome buildings along Park Avenue were awash with light in the splendid spring sun.

axiomatic   *ak si uh MA tik*
universally accepted as true

It has become axiomatic that local newscasts celebrate lurid and titillating subjects during the ratings "sweep" periods, but increasingly that preoccupation is spilling into the rest of the year as well.

bandy

The curse is officially over. Or should be. No announcer

should ever fear jinxing a pitcher who is en route to a no-

hitter or perfect game by uttering those words before the

deed is done. Last year, the MSG

Network's Ken Singleton and Jim Kaat

bandied "perfect game" and "no-

hitter" and David Wells suffered no

hex. And yesterday, Channel 5's Tim

McCarver and Bobby Murcer trotted out the terms early,

with no ill effects for David Cone.

see page 44

bailiwick   *BAY luh wik*
specific area of interest, activity, skill or authority

Netscape, founded in 1994, has struggled over the last 18 months under an assault from Microsoft. Its Navigator was the runaway leader in the market for the browser software used to find and view pages on the World Wide Web. Browsing software opened the Internet, which had been the bailiwick of researchers, to anyone with a computer and a modem. But Microsoft, responding to the Internet revolution, entered the market aggressively, bundling the Microsoft browser, Internet Explorer, into its industry-standard Windows operating system and giving it away free.

balk   *bawk*
to hesitate or recoil

With food, as with clothing, the extremes set the direction of fashion, and even if those extremes are not adopted completely at the popular level, they change the way we see and taste. Although the average woman at first may balk at the idea of a drastically raised hemline and vow not to shorten anything, if the style takes hold with fashion arbiters, longer skirts and dresses begin to look dowdy.

balky   *BAW kee*
stubbornly resisting

Voyager 2's balky camera platform failed to respond correctly to commands today as engineers struggled in vain to diagnose and perhaps fix the spacecraft's problem.

ballast   *BA luhst*
anything heavy carried in a ship, aircraft or vehicle to give stability, or in a balloon or airship to help control altitude

At the end of the last century, excavations at Bubastis and other Egyptian sites produced so many mummified cats that they were shipped out by the boatload, either as ballast or to be spread on fields as fertilizer.

banal   *buh NAL*
dull; trite; commonplace

As for Miss Walters, she still combines sharp, edgy questions with banal meanderings. This time around she was asking her guests what kind of tree or flower they would prefer to be.

"Messidor," which opens today at the Lincoln Plaza Theater, is a very beautiful, arid and difficult-to-sit-through movie in which Mr. Tanner, as he has done before, makes further use of Switzerland—small, clean, uptight and landlocked—as the ultimate metaphor for the banality of contemporary existence.

bandy   *BAN dee*
to pass gossip, rumors or remarks about freely and carelessly

The curse is officially over. Or should be. No announcer should ever fear jinxing a pitcher who is en route to a no-hitter or perfect game by uttering those words before the deed is done. Last year, the MSG Network's Ken Singleton and Jim Kaat bandied "perfect game" and "no-hitter" and David Wells suffered no hex. And yesterday, Channel 5's Tim McCarver and Bobby Murcer trotted out the terms early, with no ill effects for David Cone.

bane   *bayn*
the cause of distress, death or ruin

Pets are the bane of a decorator's life. What the decorator has put together—the perfect home—the imperfect pet can tear asunder. There are cats that dig up wood floors, and dogs that shred Naugahyde sofas and rugs.

barfly   *BAHR fligh*
a person who spends much time drinking in barrooms

Mr. Austin, who is a capable director as well as actor, seems to be making a career out of playing crude barflies, lowlife characters that one prefers to encounter on stage rather than in blind alleys.

baroque   *buh ROHK*
fantastically overdecorated; gaudily ornate

There are endless recipes for salmon, and many early ones, perhaps to dress up this poor man's fish, are baroque. Salmon was served garnished with crawfish, quenelles of truffled forcemeat, truffles "fashioned like olives," tiny goujons of sole and small fried smelts. Escoffier, who gives a litany of such dishes in his cookbook, said he liked the fish best served plain.

◆ The term *baroque* is applied to the fantastic and over-decorative in art. The baroque style dominated seventeenth- and eighteenth-century art, sculpture and architecture. *The Oxford English Dictionary* has *baroque* derived from *barroco*, the Portuguese word for a rough or imperfect pearl, but adds, "of uncertain origin." The *American Heritage Dictionary*, alone among all the dictionaries consulted, provides this derivation of *baroque*, and no other: "from Italian *barocco*, after the founder of the style, Federigo Barocci (1528-1612). Barocci, a painter, was an influential figure in seventeenth-century European art."

bastion   *BAS chuhn*
a well-fortified or defended position: often used figuratively

Traditional English sweets, with their reliance on dried fruits, nuts and egg custards, are particularly warming and satisfying in winter. In Britain, the last bastions of these desserts are the dining rooms of grand hotels. And in London, two in particular specialize in English desserts: Claridge's, with its beloved bread-and-butter pudding, and the Dorchester.

bathos   *BAY thahs*
false pathos; sentimentality

"On the Stroll" is about an elderly bag lady, a 16-year-old runaway girl and the young pimp who "turns her out" as a prostitute. If Miss Shulman had not been so skillful, the subject might easily have turned to bathos, or a documentary earnestness.

bedeck   *bi DEK*
to cover with decorations; adorn

WARSAW, Tuesday, Aug. 4—A demonstration against food shortages turned into a confrontation between the Polish authorities and the Solidarity union yesterday when the police halted a column of buses and trucks bedecked with flags and placards.

bedevil   *bee DE vuhl*
to plague or frustrate

Colonial farmers were bedeviled by and indebted to stones. When they plowed, dug wells or excavated for foundations, they struggled with stones. But as the farmers denuded the Northeast's forests, lumber became too valuable to be used in fences, and stone, ubiquitous and cheap, took its place.

beguile   *bi GIGHL*
to charm in a fascinating way

Although origins of recipes are generally difficult to pin down, credit for the invention of Irish coffee usually goes to Shannon Airport in Ireland's County Clare. Its entry into this country in 1952 resulted from the efforts of Stanton Delaplane, a columnist with the San Francisco Chronicle, who was beguiled by the drink at the airport bar and gave the recipe for it to a bartender at the Buena Vista Cafe on Hyde Street, near Fisherman's Wharf.

behemoth   *bi HEE muhth*
any animal or thing that is huge or very powerful: originally used in the Bible—Job 40:15—to describe a huge animal, possibly a hippopotamus

The popular notion of the dinosaur pictures a ponderous, lumbering behemoth whose great hulk and weight and deliberate movements kept it from roaming far from its birthplace.

There will be scheduled stops at Newfoundland's largest wooden church as well as at the St. George cliffs at the peninsula's tip overlooking Iceberg Alley—through which frozen behemoths drift down from the Arctic.

belie   *bi LIGH*
to give a false idea of; misrepresent

Forty years ago Miss Asbury would have been called a chorus girl. Nowadays that title is rarely used. Most find it a demeaning expression that belies their competence as dancers and their status as working women.

Recent studies belie the widespread belief that the stress of retirement often precipitates serious illness and death. And there are unquestionably many happily retired people who are doing just what they want, within the constraints of physical abilities, fixed incomes and rampant inflation.

belittle   *bi LI tuhl*
to make seem less important; speak slightingly of; deprecate

The shingled houses of East Hampton and its neighboring villages sit calmly by the sea. They do not attempt to belittle the ocean or to upstage it as do the palaces of Newport, glorious confections designed with deliberate indifference to the landscape they sit beside.

✦ *Belittle* was coined by Thomas Jefferson. Not everyone was pleased with the invention. H.L. Mencken, in *The American Language*, says that when it first appeared in print in Jefferson's *Notes on the State of Virginia*, published 1781-82, "the 'European Magazine and London Review' let go with a veritable tirade against it." The furor must have existed for decades, for in 1812 John Adams wrote to Benjamin Rush: "I approve Jefferson's word 'belittle' and hope it will be incorporated into our American Dictionaries. We ought to have an American Dictionary: after which I should be willing to lay a tax of an eagle a volume upon all English Dictionaries that should ever be imported." (Indeed, Noah Webster's two-volume *American Dictionary of the English Language* was published in 1828.)

It was not unusual for words coined or used in eighteenth- and nineteenth-century America to be denounced by self-appointed British and American critics who considered themselves guardians of the English language. They urged the eradication of such uncouth or barbaric words as *lengthy, presidential, congressional, influential, bogus, reliable, standpoint, jeopardize, leniency, demean, accountability, Americanize, balance* (remainder), *energize, evoke, nationality, demoralize, stockholder, caucus, census, checkers* (the English call the game *draughts*), and, used as verbs, *advocate, propose, locate* and *progress*, the last of which Benjamin Franklin called "abominable."

belle époque   *bel ay PAHK*
the era of elegance and gaiety that characterized fashionable Parisian life in the period preceding World War I: French

In the legendary belle époque that preceded World War I, Rodin was universally looked upon as an artistic colossus—at once the heir and equal of the great masters of the past and a giant among the artists of the modern age.

bemoan   *bi MOHN*
to deplore or lament

Mr. Vysotsky's ballads, spoofing or bemoaning the harsh realities of Soviet life, captured the hearts of Russians of all ages and from all walks of life. His funeral in Moscow last July developed into a demonstration by tens of thousands of fans.

benchmark   *BENCH mahrk*
a standard point of reference in measuring or judging value and other qualities: from a surveyor's mark, made on a permanent landmark of known position and altitude, and used as a reference point in determining other altitudes

Despite being far surpassed by subsequent films in violence, bloodiness and sexual explicitness, Alfred Hitchcock's "Psycho" remains a benchmark in movie making even 35 years after its original release. Its shower-stabbing sequence is widely considered the most famous scene in cinematic history, studied frame by frame by students of cinematography. Its score, by Bernard Herrmann, featuring those screaming violins, is still played in concert.

benign   *bi NIGHN*
good-natured; kindly

Everyone likes the human way in which the white whales rise on their tails to honk at visitors, and the benign, blissful smiles that stretch over their fleshy faces.

not malignant—i.e., not cancerous

Ted Petersen, the offensive tackle, is out while recovering from surgery to remove a benign tumor on the hip. Is this to be last year all over again, another season with injuries striking all parts of the team?

doing little or no harm

The sea nettle and the moon jellyfish are often seen in the Northeast. The moon, by far the most common in the area, is especially benign; its toxin usually results in no more than a pinprick sensation. The sea nettle can deliver a painful sting that leaves a red welt; however, the irritation is usually gone in a few hours.

berate *bi RAYT*
to scold or rebuke severely

Mr. Saroyan's third play, "Love's Old Sweet Song" in 1940, failed in the view of most critics and at the box office. He insisted it was "one of the best plays in the American theater," and berated audience and critics alike.

bereft *bi REFT*
left at a loss; desolate

"Ultimately the West Side will be bereft of a wholesale meat market," said Benjamin Young, a spokesman for the Meat Purveyors Association. "It's just a matter of time before it will be driven out, because this property has greater value for other purposes."

best
to win out over, defeat or outdo

By willing his own death, Bobby Sands has earned a place on Ireland's long roll of martyrs and bested an implacable British Prime Minister. It is a bitter and joyless victory, but it was predictable.

✦ *To best* and *to worst* mean exactly the same thing.

bestial *BES chul*
brutal or savage

No, the United States does not have the wisdom or the power to right all the wrongs of the world. But the experience of Hitler surely taught us the danger of pretending that bestial governments can safely be ignored while they operate only at home.

bibelot   *BI bloh*
a small object whose value lies in its beauty or rarity; trinket: French

On Bleeker Street near Abingdon Square, Scott Hamilton and his partner, Ed Hyre, continue to offer such wares as 19th-century French faux-bamboo furniture and assorted bibelots at their antiques shop, much as they have for 15 years.

bibliomania   *bi blee uh MAY nee uh*
a craze for collecting books

Edward Robb Ellis lives contentedly with his bibliomania in the space people normally allow for their bookshelves. The rest of his Chelsea apartment is given over to his books—more than 8,000 of them lining shelves, resting on chairs, tables and sofas, stacked waist-high all over the living room, dominating the kitchen, the hallway and the bedroom, forming aisles between rooms.

bibliophile   *BI blee uh fighl*
a person who loves or admires books; a collector of books

WILMETTE, Ill., May 31—From Maine and Arizona and points between, ready with shopping carts and guided by maps, on the lookout for first edition classics and pulp tear-jerkers, 25,000 bibliophiles descended last week on the Brandeis Used Book Sale, billed as the largest in the world. The first customer arrived at 2:30 A.M. last Saturday, 15½ hours before the gate opened on 300,000 used books spread under two circus tents in a shopping center's parking lot.

Bildungsroman   *BIL duhngz roh muhn*
a novel, like David Copperfield, *that portrays the growth of a young person toward maturity: German,* bildung, *formation* + roman, *novel*

Like so many first novels, "Stranger" is a Bildungsroman that traces the coming of age of its hero, and it begins in the tiny English village of Great Much, where Horace Littlefair, an orphan who has grown up with his grandfather, is about to leave home to seek his fortune in faraway London.

blanch   *blanch*
to turn pale

Many Parisian purists blanch at the thought of eating Provence's food in which olive oil replaces butter, just as Yankees express contempt for the grits and "greasy" fare of our own South.

✦ In its broadest sense, *Yankee* means *American*. In its strictest modern sense, it means *New Englander*. *Yankee* is from the Dutch *Jan Kees* (John Cheese), and was first a disparaging nickname for any Hollander, then for Dutch pirates. During the 1700s it was used by Dutch New Yorkers to describe the English settlers of Connecticut, whose commercial practices they found morally questionable. Eventually, New Englanders adopted it themselves and even converted it into a complimentary adjective (Yankee ingenuity, Yankee craftsmanship). During the Civil War, it was a Southern term of contempt for Northerners (some Southerners still maintain the tradition), but since World War I it has come into worldwide use as a synonym for an American.

bland   *bland*
tasteless; insipid; dull

I have also found that the initial reaction to some no-salt dishes is that they are boringly bland at first bite. But with the second and third bites I find that the depth of flavor increases severalfold.

blasé   *blah ZAY*
having a casual and unexcited attitude toward something because of habitual or excessive exposure to, or experience with, it: French

Even blasé Bloomingdale's was thrown into a flutter recently when Carmen Romano de López Portillo, wife of the President of Mexico, bought $1,600 in Madeleine Mono products, including the tester display.

blatant   *BLAY tuhnt*
glaringly conspicuous or obtrusive

If an entire party has not finished a course, it is blatantly rude to remove plates from those who have finished, thereby rushing slower eaters.

blemish   *BLE mish*
a flaw, defect or shortcoming

The battle pits the afternoon Times with its cool, professional approach and detached reporting, against the morning Trentonian, a lively tabloid that rarely points out this aging industrial city's blemishes and cheers it with photographs of children having birthday parties and the vacation snapshots of anyone who sends them in.

blitz   *blits*
a sudden, overwhelming attack, effort or campaign; referring literally to a military action, and figuratively to any stormlike assault

In its latest drug-fighting measure, his Administration has budgeted $195 million for an advertising campaign on television and radio and in print to discourage adolescents from using illegal drugs. The national blitz will get under way next month. "Our goal," Mr. Clinton said, "is to make sure that every time a child turns on the TV, listens to the radio or surfs the Internet, he or she will get the powerful message that drugs can destroy your life."

✦ *Blitz* is a short form of the German *blitzkrieg* (lightning war), a term originated by the Germans and used to describe World War II military tactics, involving high-speed, coordinated attacks of tanks and planes. Blitzen (Lightning) is one of Santa's reindeer.

bluff   *bluhf*
a high, steep, broad-faced bank or cliff

Coastguardsmen who stand watch at the station here, high on a bluff near Northport, say that nonfatal accidents—capsizings, groundings and collisions—have increased in what F. Scott Fitzgerald called "the most domesticated body of salt water in the Western Hemisphere, the great wet barnyard of Long Island Sound."

blurb   *blerb*
a publisher's note on the dust jacket of a book

"Important" books were those books they forced you to read in high school because they were good for you, the ones that felt 20,000 pages long. When I open a book and read a jacket blurb that says it is an "important" book, I drop it as gingerly as a pit viper.

✦ *Blurb* was coined about 1914 by Gelett Burgess, the American humorist (1866-1951), who defined it as "self-praise, to make a noise like a publisher." It was among the more than 100 words he made up, defined and gave usage examples of in *Burgess Unabridged: A New Dictionary of Words You Have Always Needed* (1914), but the only one to survive the dictionary—although another word he coined (which is not in the book), *bromide*, is now standard English and means a trite saying. Burgess originally defined a bromide as a boring person who utters trite sayings.

Among the words Burgess hoped would fill a need in the English language but didn't make it out of his dictionary were *cowcat*, a person whose main function is to occupy space; *gefoojet*, something one ought to throw away but doesn't; *oofle*, to try to find out a person's name without asking; *tintiddle*, a witty retort, thought of too late.

boldface   *BOHLD fays*
a type with a heavy, dark face, **like this**

Hundreds of New Jersey physicians may be violating a rule of the State Board of Medical Examiners that says doctors may not put their names in boldface in the Yellow Pages.

bolster   *BOHL ster*
to support, strengthen or reinforce

Along with astronauts and Olympic gold medal winners, few things bolster the pride of the ordinary Russian like the Bolshoi Ballet. Throughout the world, the company is synonymous with dance.

bombast   *BAHM bast*
talk or writing that sounds grand or important but has little meaning; pompous language

In the process of guiding the N.A.A.C.P., Mr. Wilkins traveled more than half of each year, visiting branches of the organization and giving lectures in which he espoused civil rights causes. His sparse gray hair and gray mustache and his slim figure clad in conservative suits were familiar to millions of Americans who saw him on television as he argued, literately and eloquently but without bombast, for the emancipation of his people.

bona fide   *BOH nuh FIGHD*
authentic; genuine

Each year there are fewer bona fide outdoor eating places in New York because owners put roofs over their gardens so they can realize profits from the space regardless of the weather.

bonkers   *BAHNG kers*
crazy: a slang word

I don't know what this actor is up to in "Macbeth," and I doubt that he does, either. In the early scenes, he is so shifty-eyed and bonkers that one expects him to be arrested for suspicion of murder before he actually commits one.

boor   *boor*
a rude or ill-mannered person

This is not to suggest that boorishness on the courts is an American monopoly. John McEnroe and Jimmy Connors can be as coarse as goats, and they are American, but Ilie Nastase has scaled peaks of vulgarity in his time, and he is a Rumanian.

✦ *Boor* was originally a Dutch word meaning *peasant*, and meant that in English, too, until about the end of the sixteenth century, when it took on its present meaning. This type of semantic change is called "pejoration" (a change of meaning for the worse), and the resulting word is a "pejorative." Other pejoratives are *lewd*, once *layman*; *vulgar*, once *the common people*; *knave*, once *boy*; *silly*, once *simple*. In recent times, *politician* has taken on a pejorative shade.

bourgeois   *boor ZHWAH*
middle-class in beliefs, attitudes and practices: French

There was a sense, of course, in which Pissarro was quite literally an outsider among the French painters of his time. He was born into a bourgeois Jewish family in the Virgin Islands, then a Danish possession to which his father had emigrated from Bordeaux in 1824. And although he spent five years (1842-47) at boarding school in a suburb of Paris, Pissarro did not settle in France until the age of 25. His family had intended for him to go into the family business, but he seems to have acquired a sense of his true vocation early on, and his distaste for the conventions of bourgeois life—later abetted by his devotion to anarchist doctrine—was, in any case, said to be intense.

They closed all the flower shops in China in 1966 and ordered people who kept goldfish to dump them into sewers and rivers. These and other tiny items of beauty were deemed bourgeois, so they became targets when Mao Zedong opened his Great Proletarian Cultural Revolution against, among other things, the "four olds"—old ideas, culture, habits and customs.

bowdlerize   *BOHD luh righz*

to alter, reword or remove parts of a book, play, etc. that are considered offensive; expurgate. Thomas Bowdler, an English editor, published The Family Shakespeare *in 1818, having removed or altered the parts "which cannot with propriety be read aloud in a family."*

For a year, Mr. Davies interviewed the Beatles and their friends and relatives and sat in on composing and recording sessions. But his book was published two years before the breakup. And the Beatles had bowdlerized the manuscript, tearing out indiscreet stories of life on tour.

brash   *brash*

insistently and often admirably aggressive, as in this example; but also used disapprovingly to criticize hasty or reckless behavior or judgment

At her peak, Billie Jean King performed a great service to any female athlete. By her brash aggressiveness, she made it more acceptable for women to push themselves, to release anger with themselves for a bad play, to want openly to beat their opponents, to question the officials or even the financial structure of their sport. She gave most women a sense of leadership and pride during vital years of the women's movement.

bray   *bray*

the loud, harsh cry of a donkey, or a sound like this

In the Sinai Desert, a crew filming a difficult sequence for the television series nervously eyed a grazing donkey that luckily waited until the shot was done before emitting an ear-splitting bray.

Kai Winding, the Danish-born trombonist who made his first major impression in jazz as the lustiest of Stan Kenton's braying trombonists in the late

40's and later teamed with J.J. Johnson in the trombone duo known as Jay and Kai, is making his first club appearance in New York in almost a decade this week at Sweet Basil.

brazen *BRAY zin*
showing no shame; bold; open; audacious

FORD HEIGHTS, Ill., Oct. 11—Just about everybody in this desperately poor Chicago suburb could see the illegal drug trade flourishing brazenly on street corners. They wondered why the local police did not see it. Federal prosecutors on Thursday charged that six current and former Ford Heights officers were taking bribes and looking the other way, allowing about 20 drug dealers to sell cocaine, including crack, and heroin.

breach *breech*
to break through

The Vermont Supreme Court has been asked to breach the practice of secrecy in juvenile court by letting the public attend the trial of a teenager accused of torturing and killing a 12-year-old girl.

brio *BREE oh*
vivacity; zest: Italian

The slow and sad middle movement was sustained wonderfully well, and the finale, "Theme Russe," went off with tremendous brio.

Brobdingnagian *brahb ding NA gee uhn*
gigantic: from Brobdingnag, a land in Swift's Gulliver's Travels *inhabited by giants about 60 feet tall*

Approaching, for example, his [Chuck Close's] most recent large-scale acrylic work, "Mark," completed in 1979, the viewer is taken aback by the scale of the eyeglasses, as big as two tennis racquets; the stubble beard with hair follicles the size of ant holes; the freckle on the nose as large as a quarter. On such Brobdingnagian terms, the image is both a face and a startling abstraction of one.

brunt *bruhnt*
the main force or impact

Mrs. Kudukis has become head of Clevelanders for 100,000 Families, a new organization that will, she said yesterday, "take to task anyone who makes a negative remark about Cleveland." "No person or city should be continually the brunt of a joke," said Mrs. Kudukis.

brusque   *bruhsk*
rough and abrupt in manner and speech; curt

Decades of success never entirely mellowed Mr. Shumlin, a Colorado rancher's son with a booming voice, who could be as brusque as a drill sergeant.

bubeleh   *BOO buh luh*
a term of endearment, particularly for children, meaning dear child, honey, darling: Yiddish, an affectionate diminutive of grandmother—literally "little grandmother," although Jewish mothers call both female and male babies bubeleh

Like the rest of the new Children's Zoo, the appeal seems universal. A pair of hulking teen-aged boys talked earnestly to a goat on a recent members' preview day, while four women bent over a nearby ducklings' enclosure, crying, "Hello, bubeleh," to a mass of peeping yellow fuzz.

bubkes   *BUHB kis*
something trivial, worthless, insultingly disproportionate to expectations: in Russian the word's literal meaning is beans, but as a Yiddish word it is used only as below

As is common in many industries, Hollywood often bestows titles in lieu of raises. "There are vice presidents in this industry who make $800 a week and vice presidents who make $800,000 a year," says Charles Powell, who went from "senior vice president worldwide advertising, publicity and promotion" at Universal to chairman of his own marketing firm. "There are 22-year-old vice presidents who aren't earning bubkes. But the title is the new negotiating ploy, the major perk."

bucolic   *byoo: KAH lik*
relating to country life; rustic

EAST FISHKILL, N.Y.—The picture-postcard rolling hills and valleys along the Hudson River near here are no longer just bucolic backdrops for travelers between New York City and the upstate resorts and cities—they now make up the fastest-growing area in New York State.

buffalo
to confuse; baffle; intimidate: a slang word

No one who has spent so many years in public life is likely to be buffaloed by any reporter's news conference question.

buffoonery   *buh FOO: nuh ree*
clowning around

The carefree buffoonery of the 27 clowns, three of them women, who perform acts and entr'actes in the Ringling Bros. and Barnum & Bailey Circus unit playing Madison Square Garden through May 31, is a series of infinitely varied capers.

burgher   *BER ger*
a solid citizen: originally a middle-class inhabitant of a European town, but used today in English usually in a humorous or facetious way

After lunch, the Hall of Famers were driven a few blocks to Doubleday Field, named after Abner Doubleday, who either invented the game of baseball here in 1839 or never visited here or never played baseball, depending on whom you read. The burghers of Cooperstown prefer the first version, which gives them the chance to sell a lot of hot dogs, homemade pies and sun visors two days every August.

burnout   *BERN owt*
a loss of drive, motivation or incentive, resulting from the demands of a particular job that have taken an emotional or spiritual toll on a person

When I looked into the eyes of a friend of mine, a burned-out social worker, I couldn't get an accurate reading on whether she had just lost her Title XX funding or forgotten to defrost something for dinner. All zones of pain and disappointment are equally pressing during burnout. The judgment blurs.

✦ *Burnout* was coined by Herbert Freudenberger, a psychologist, in his 1974 book, *Burnout: The High Cost of High Achievement.* Apparently he never suffered from it. Dr. Freudenberger, his son said, worked fourteen or fifteen hours a day, six days a week, until three weeks before his death in 1999 at the age of seventy-three.

bush league *boosh leeg*

second-rate: in its original sense, bush league describes a second-rate or small minor league

It has always seemed obvious to me that the millions who settle for the bush-league trash on television do so only because they are unaware of the truly top-notch junk available in other forms.

C

copious

He was able to reconstruct conversations with people long

dead because he had kept copious notes. Mr. Hoving said,

"I'm a compulsive writer, and I habitually keep

a daily journal in which I note even the

shade of a person's complexion

when I speak with them."

see page 87

cache *kash*
anything stored or hidden, especially in large numbers

Recently, the antiques shop called the Place Off Second Avenue came upon a cache of 1940's tin pails in a toy store that was going out of business and bought up the entire stock.

cachet *ka SHAY*
distinction; prestige: originally, an official seal or stamp on a letter or document

"There are literally hundreds of attempts weekly to break into the computers," a Pentagon spokesman said. "It's constant because there's a certain cachet to getting into the Pentagon system."

cacophony *kuh KAH fuh nee*
harsh, jarring sound; a noisy jumble of sounds

Above all, you feel the perfect marriage of restaurant and neighborhood in the cavernous main dining room, where middle-aged couples, young singles, groups of young women, a sprinkling of older diners and the occasional couple with small children create a joyous cacophony that rises to ear-splitting levels on a Saturday night.

cadence *KAY duhns*
a rhythmic flow of sound

There was laughter in the poet's weathered eyes. How did it feel to receive a foundation award of $60,000 a year for the next five years simply to go on living the life he loves? "Walll," drawled Robert Penn Warren in a voice soft and husky with the cadences of his Kentucky boyhood, "how do you feel about just stumbling on a piece of money on the pavement and it's yours?"

cadenza   *kuh DEN zuh*
an elaborate instrumental passage in a concerto played alone by the featured instrument near the end of a movement: it is either improvised by the soloist or written out by the composer or someone else

When did you last see a conductor perch on the edge of the piano, peering benignly at the soloist, during the cadenza of a Mozart piano concerto? On Saturday evening, if you attended the New York Philharmonic concert at Avery Fisher Hall. Kurt Masur and Alfred Brendel? No, Bobby McFerrin and Chick Corea, and informality prevailed.

cadge   *kaj*
to beg or get by begging; sponge

Marjorie Gross, for example, travels to and from all of her around-Manhattan gigs on her secondhand bicycle because she cannot afford taxicabs, and she carries her minuscule wardrobe with her in shopping bags and plastic luggage as she cadges places to stay from sister—and brother—performers.

cajole   *kuh JOHL*
to coax, influence or persuade by soothing words

It was Roy Wilkins's painstakingly orchestrated legal strategy that ultimately persuaded the Supreme Court in 1954 to outlaw school segregation. And he was a leader in the civil rights coalition that cajoled and pressed and persevered until Congress finally banned discrimination in the great civil rights enactments of the 1960's.

callous   *KA lis*
insensitive: callous and callus, a hardened, thickened place on the skin, derive from the Latin callum, *hard skin*

"We've become so callous," Ms. White said. "You see a bum on the street and immediately you think, 'Why don't they go to work?' But you don't know what they went through."

candid   *KAN did*
honest or frank

BOSTON, July 3—Apologies to organized religion, but surely any candid clergyman would concur: The most widely revered shrine in Boston is Fenway Park.

candor   *KAN der*
sharp honesty or frankness in expressing oneself

"A Prince of Wales has to do what he can by influence, not power," he once explained with characteristic candor. "There isn't any power. There can be influence. The influence is in direct ratio to the respect people have for you."

canny   *KA nee*
careful and shrewd in one's actions and dealings; clever and cautious

They called Carl Vinson the Swamp Fox, a tribute to his canny flair for running the Pentagon from his seat in the United States House of Representatives. Admirals quaked and generals quavered when the tall Georgian called them before the House Armed Services Committee, which he ruled like a potentate for 14 of his 50 years in the House before retiring from Congress at the age of 81.

canon   *KA nin*
a body of rules, principles or criteria

"Another block not often included in tours is West 81st Street, also between Columbus and Amsterdam," Mr. Zito said. "These houses were built in the age of individuality. This is where design really takes off, defying all architectural canons. There is such an exuberance here. They used every kind of device: cherubs, lyres, every kind of ornament you can imagine."

works or authors accepted as essential

During his extended and extraordinarily prolific prime, Sinatra did more than anyone to establish the canon of American popular standards. He was famous, observes Mr. Comstock, for rescuing and shining a brilliant light on "orphan songs," among them "These Foolish Things," "When Your Lover Has Gone," and "I've Got You Under My Skin."

cantankerous   *kan TANG ker uhs*
bad-tempered; quarrelsome; perverse

Barring the unlikeliest of mathematical surprises—the French electoral system is a complex and highly cantankerous piece of machinery—the Socialists will control the National Assembly without needing to seek allies.

canvass   *KAN vuhs*
to conduct a survey on a given subject; poll

If you were to canvass any group of serious cooks and ask the name of the one basic ingredient best suited to no-salt cookery, you would doubtless receive more answers than the components of a Macedonian salad. I would answer without pause: mushrooms.

capricious   *kuh PREE shuhs*
tending to change abruptly and without apparent reason; erratic; flighty

Farmers are at the mercy of nature's capriciousness: it can kill off a year of tender nurturing in a single day; it can cause the buds of one orchard to freeze and drop off while not bothering the trees on a hill a few miles away.

career   *kuh REER*
to move at full speed; rush wildly

The car injured 27 pedestrians when it careered into the crowd while the driver and two passengers were trying to elude a pursuing police car.

caricature   *KAR uh kuh choor*
an imitation that is so distorted or inferior as to seem ludicrous

"I did research," the dark-haired, dark-eyed actress said the other day. "An actor friend and I drove around to places where hookers hang out, and I watched them. I saw the way they approached the cars, the businesslike way they handled themselves. I also talked to a hooker I knew in Boston. My goal was to make Gloria a real person and not a caricature of a hooker."

✦ Among several purported origins of *hooker*, a prostitute, is that when Joseph Hooker, a Civil War general, ruled Washington, D.C.'s red-light district off-limits to his men, they retaliated by nicknaming the women there "hookers." Another theory has hookers named for the Hook of Holland, where the clientele were sailors from the ships that traded between there and British ports. But *hooker* may have originated in New York City before the Civil War, when a number of brothels flourished at Corlear's Hook. Marian Touba, currently a reference librarian at the New York Historical Society, located Corlear's Hook on an old map, placing it just south of where the Williamsburg Bridge now stands, and on a piece of land that jutted into the East River but that no longer exists.

carriage   *KA rij*
the manner of carrying the head and body; posture; bearing

When they first met in late 1979, he was the prince in "Swan Lake." She remembers his regal carriage and his dark, curly hair.

cash cow   *kash kow*
a profitable asset or resource

Outlets started as a much-needed way for manufacturers to rid themselves of excess inventory. As they turned into cash cows, however, manufacturers that did not have enough seconds began manufacturing some merchandise especially for the outlet stores, much of it of lower quality.

cataclysm   *KA tuh kli zuhm*
a great upheaval that causes sudden and violent changes, as an earthquake, war, etc.

The Mount St. Helens volcano, called Loowit, or Lady of Fire, by the Indians of the Pacific Northwest, erupted with cataclysmic force on the sunny Sunday morning of May 18, 1980. The explosion, which tore 1,300 feet off the 9,607-foot peak, was calculated by geologists to have released the equivalent of 500 times the energy that was unleashed by the atomic bomb dropped on Hiroshima.

catalyst   *KA tuh list*
a person or thing acting as the stimulus in bringing about or hastening a result

Perhaps the most dramatic example of how Presidential attention influenced a book, and of how a book influenced public policy, occurred with Michael Harrington's "The Other America: Poverty in the United States" (Macmillan), which is generally credited with being the catalyst of the Kennedy-Johnson "war on poverty."

catechism   *KA tuh ki zuhm*
a handbook of questions and answers for teaching the principles of a religion

In catechism lessons, nuns used to ask, "Why did God make the world?" and the answer was "For His glory." Samuel Johnson might be said to have made the first great English dictionary in the same way.

✦ A few selections from Samuel Johnson's (1709-1784)
Dictionary of the English Language, published 1749:
Net. Anything reticulated or decussated at equal distances,
with interstices between the intersections.
Oats. A grain, which in England is generally given to horses,
but in Scotland supports the people.
Patron. Commonly a wretch who supports with insolence, and
is paid with flattery.

caterwaul   *KA ter wawl*
to make a shrill, howling sound like that of a cat in heat; screech; wail

Prince sings exclusively in a falsetto, which he pushes at times to an eerie
caterwauling intensity.

catharsis   *kuh THAHR sis*
a release of emotional tensions through a real or vicarious experience that
allows one's pent-up feelings to flow freely or be purged

Mr. Simon's first wife, Joan, died of cancer in 1973. Later that year he married the actress Marsha Mason. ("I'm a person who must be married," he
says.) Out of that second marriage, and presumably out of a feeling for guilt
for having entered into it, Mr. Simon wrote "Chapter Two." " 'Chapter Two'
shows you how I'm always using my life in my work," he said. "It was
extremely painful writing it. It's my favorite play for many reasons. It was
cathartic for me."

✦ In its literary sense, *catharsis* had its origin in Aristotle's *Poetics*,
where it referred to the purging of the audience's emotions of
pity and fear aroused by the actions of the tragic hero. It has
never been established with certainty just what Aristotle meant
when he wrote, "Tragedy through pity and fear effects a pur-
gation of such emotions," but the concept remains basic to the
idea of what a tragic play ought to effect among audiences.

catholic   *KATH lik*
wide-ranging in tastes or interests; liberal

Mr. Neville, who is 46 years old, traces his catholic taste back to childhood.
The Neville household echoed with sounds of Gene Autry, Nat (King) Cole,
Sam Cooke and Clyde McPhatter—for starters. "I liked opera, spirituals,
whatever sounded good," Mr. Neville said. "I was just a music kid."

caucus   KAW kuhs
a private meeting of a committee to decide on policy, pick candidates, etc.,
especially prior to a general, open meeting

Ignoring a review that should have warned us off, we exposed ourselves to
a tasteless film called "The History of the World, Part I." I was proud of my
children when a family caucus produced a 4-0 vote to walk out.

caustic   KAW stik
cutting or sarcastic; biting; literally, a substance that can burn or eat away,
like acid

But the crackling on-air chemistry between Mr. Siskel and Mr. Ebert, their
sometimes spirited, even caustic, disagreements and, ultimately, their opinions that consistently reflected broad public tastes, quickly made them such
powerful persuaders that movie ads routinely included their thumbs up
endorsements.

cavalier   ka vuh LEER
casual or indifferent toward a matter of importance; offhand

Certainly, the evidence presented by Mr. Rayfield suggests that Chekhov was
both wildly attractive to women—he seems to have had admirers trailing
after him wherever he went—and cavalier with their affections, moving from
one mistress to another and then back again, all the while annotating their
reactions in his fiction.

caveat   KA vee at
a warning

Want an oil company credit card? A few caveats are in order. Make sure you
answer all questions on the application. Be careful about estimates of how
much gas you expect to use. Take pains to see that your previous credit performance is up to par. And be accurate—a tough computer is watching and
scoring you.

cavort   kuh VAWRT
to romp about happily; frolic

Remarkable-looking animals will cavort at the Bronx Zoo on Saturday and
Sunday, and some of them may resemble your children.

cede   *seed*
to give up one's rights to; yield; grant

Congress is the special preserve of print reporters, and television cedes them the field while it concentrates on the President and the Cabinet.

celerity   *suh LE ruh tee*
swiftness in acting or moving; speed

Perhaps the most admirable aspect of "The Laundry Hour" is the celerity of the actors. During each blackout, one or both of them quickly change costume—from clerical black to Las Vegas glitter. Despite these frequent switches in attire and the talk about samsara, "The Laundry Hour" remains singleminded—60 minutes spinning on one cycle.

> ✦ *Samsara* is the Hindu and Buddhist concept of the eternal cycle of birth, suffering, death and rebirth.

celibacy   *SE luh buh see*
the state of being unmarried, especially that of a person under a vow not to marry and to practice complete sexual abstinence

Father Wagner, in his letter, questioned the meaning of celibacy, and the tone of his letter was considered by the Church leaders to question the vow. "I suggest that for many priests," his letter said, "the lack of physical intimacy, which is supposed to assure their availability to loving service, is in fact an exhausting, debilitating privation which makes them less healthy, less creative and less giving."

cenotaph   *SE nuh taf*
a monument or empty tomb honoring a dead person whose body is somewhere else

The 60-year-old Pope spoke before the memorial cenotaph in Hiroshima's Peace Park, close to the epicenter of the blast from a bomb dropped by a United States B-29 in the final days of World War II.

centrist   *SEN trist*
one taking a position in the political center

Mr. Timerman started La Opinión in 1972 with a group of leftist writers, but moved the paper to a more centrist position as it encouraged the coup that overthrew President Isabel Martinez de Perón in 1976.

cerebral   *suh REE bruhl*
intellectual

Mr. Sahl is a cerebral humorist who enjoys working along the cracks of contradiction in society and in jabbing its institutional faces. He has recently completed his autobiography, "Heartland," and is writing a screenplay for Sidney Lumet, the director.

cessation   *se SAY shuhn*
a ceasing, or stopping, either forever or for some time

WASHINGTON, July 9—A Presidential commission recommended today that the states endorse the concept that human life ends when the brain stops functioning. It urged all 50 states to adopt a simple uniform law defining death as the "irreversible cessation of all functions of the entire brain, including the brain stem."

chanteuse   *shahn TOO:Z*
a woman singer, especially of popular ballads: French

The incomparable—Hildegarde! That introduction has been as much a trademark as her long white gloves and dainty handkerchief. And the chanteuse, who has been in show business for "54½ years" by her reckoning, will appear, gloved fingers dancing on the piano keys, at Marty's in a two-week engagement starting tonight.

charade   *shuh RAYD*
a pretense that continues even though both sides in a controversy or relationship see its transparent falseness: after charades, *a game in which words or phrases to be guessed are acted out in pantomime*

When angry baseball players and club owners broke off their latest meeting, Mr. Moffett said he would not call them back together until he heard "something positive" from both sides. "It's kind of futile and sort of stupid," Mr. Moffett commented, "just to be going through a charade of getting together on a regular basis when there's no movement as far as the parties are concerned."

charisma   *kuh RIZ muh*
a strong personal appeal or magnetism

And Mr. Vidnovic, who made his mark in the recent revivals of "Brigadoon" and "Oklahoma!," is more than simply professional. He is every inch a star. With his flashing eyes, commanding baritone and bursting physical exuberance, he exudes more charisma than any Broadway leading man in years.

charismatic   *ka riz MA tik*
the designation of various religious groups or movements that stress divine inspiration, manifested by speaking in tongues, healing by the laying on of hands, etc.

Many sat barefoot on the floor and held Bibles. For the first half hour, they sang Jesus songs, raising their hands in the air in the charismatic invoking of the Holy Spirit, and many spoke in tongues.

chauvinism   *SHOH vi ni zuhm*
fanatical patriotism; jingoism; unreasoning devotion to one's race, sex, etc., with contempt for other races, the opposite sex, etc.

Food chauvinism is among the most virulent of all prejudices, and perhaps the most dogmatic of all food chauvinists are clam chowder devotees. In New England, where the American version of clam chowder originated, the three warring factions (clear broth, cream broth and Rhode Island-style pale tomato broth) have planted their respective flags over the territory, and woe to anyone who challenges them.

◆ Nicolas Chauvin was a soldier in Napoleon's army who, even after the final defeat at Waterloo, retained such enthusiasm for Napoleon, and so often sang out his praises, that he made a ridiculous figure of himself. Characters based on Chauvin were written into several French plays of the time, and that helped to spread his name as a synonym for excessive patriotism.

◆ *Chauvinism* is one of the many thousands of eponyms in our language, words that have sprung from the name of a person, place or thing. Some others are: aphrodisiac, hector, mentor, pander, dunce, babel, mecca, maudlin, chimera, guy, lynch, boycott, quisling, quixotic, tantalize, macadamize, vandal, assassin, malapropism, bowdlerize, panic, stentorian, sandwich, shrapnel, derrick, guillotine, silhouette, dahlia, wisteria, ohm, volt, ampere, watt, champagne, cognac, sherry, cashmere, mesmerize, bedlam, damask, cynical, serendipity.

cheek by jowl   *cheek bigh jowl*
close together; side by side

Cheek by jowl were tabletop flea markets, health-care information desks, a live honeybee display, block association stands, a Shetland pony ride and the Knights of Columbus booth.

chef d'oeuvre   *she DER vruh*
a masterpiece: French

"S.O.B.," Blake Edwards's hilarious chef d'oeuvre of bile, slapstick, ill will and hurt feelings, is set in a paranoid's vision of a Hollywood populated entirely by people double- and triple-crossing each other.

+ *Bile* has come to mean anger, or bitterness of spirit, through the ancient theory that yellow bile was the body fluid, or humor, that in excess produced choler, or rage. The three other major humors, any of which, when predominating, were believed to determine one's health and disposition, were black bile, responsible for sadness or depression (*melancholy* is from the Greek *melas*, black, and *chole*, bile); blood, which caused cheerfulness (the English word *sanguine*, from the Latin *sanguinis*, blood, means cheerful or optimistic), and phlegm, which caused sluggishness or dullness. The English word *phlegmatic* means unemotional, unexcitable or apathetic. A proper balance of the fluids meant "good humor" and an imbalance, "ill humor."

chichi   *SHEE shee*
very smart or sophisticated: usually used in a somewhat derogatory sense, suggesting affectation, showiness, effeteness, etc.: French

"Neil Simon writes exactly the way I talk," Mr. Matthau notes. "That is, the more serious the situation, the funnier he gets. His humor is ironic, sardonic, sweetly sarcastic, just like mine. I know the chichi critics say that Simon is shallow, but that's because they feel something has to be incomprehensible to be profound."

chivvy   *CHI vee*
to nag; manipulate

The late Jean Monnet, who imagined and chivvied into existence what is now known as the European Community, was insistent about institutions. Their creation is the one way people can apply the lessons of experience and escape the raw repetition of collective follies, he felt. In another fashion, the late President de Gaulle also stressed institutions as the key to coherent society.

chockablock   *CHAHK uh blahk*
crowded or jammed

When news programs produced no profits, audience ratings didn't matter. Now, the primary goal for a local newscast is generally no different than it is for a prime-time series: achieving the largest possible audience. And the method is often the same too: aim for the lowest common denominator. "Live at Five," for example, is chockablock with five-minute celebrity interviews.

chronicle   *KRAH ni kuhl*
to tell or write the history of; record; recount

The film, which is none too frank about Elvis's problems, nonetheless closely chronicles his decline. The polite, bashful fellow who beams with pride when Ed Sullivan pronounces him "a real decent fine boy" becomes flashy, bloated and crude. The Elvis whose face is so fresh and unguarded, whose expression reveals so much when the press asks him about his sweetheart or his mama, becomes a glassy-eyed wreck.

chutzpah   *KHOOTS puh*
defined by Leo Rosten in The Joys of Yiddish *as gall, brazen nerve, effrontery, incredible "guts"*

"Anybody who has got the chutzpah and the gall," Mr. Berger said, "to try and convince us that, in an election year, saying that we don't need a fare increase is not political, has got to be taking us all for fools." Deputy Mayor Robert F. Wagner Jr. objected to Mr. Berger's remarks by shouting, "That's a cheap shot."

More and more, maîtres d'hôtel and restaurateurs say, people will do just about anything to get a table at the hottest restaurants in the nation's most competitive foodie town. They lie. They cheat. And yes, they steal. "The chutzpah was incredible," said Jeffrey Toobin, a writer for The New Yorker who arrived at Bouley Bakery on West Broadway last month only to discover that a party of six had, well, fibbed about their name so they could take the table from Mr. Toobin's party of six. The impostors seemed to have read the reservation book upside down and backward. "The restaurant people asked them to give up the table. They refused." He sighed. "It was one of those possession-is-nine-tenths-of-the-law situations," said Mr. Toobin, a legal analyst who wrote a best-selling book on the O.J. Simpson trial. "We didn't want to make a scene, and finally the restaurant improvised a table for us. All we wanted to do was eat dinner."

Cinderella   *sin duh RE luh*
a person or thing whose merit, value, beauty, etc. is for a time unrecognized

If the oboe ever manages to rival the flute as a popular solo instrument, Heinz Holliger will probably be regarded as the musician who started it all. The 41-year-old Swiss oboist, in New York for a recital at the Metropolitan Museum of Art tomorrow night at 8, has been acclaimed all over the world for his virtuosity and compelling musicianship on this Cinderella of instruments.

cinéma vérité   *si nay MAH vay ri TAY*
a type of documentary film or film making that attempts to capture the sense of documentary realism by spontaneous interviews, the use of a hand-held camera and a minimum of editing of the footage: French

"Best Boy," a documentary by Ira Wohl, was first shown at the 1979 New York Film Festival and then shown again in New York a year later. It is about Philly, a 52-year-old retarded man, and his elderly parents, and whereas the most common criticism of cinéma vérité is that it exploits, distorts and ridicules, there was general agreement among film critics that "Best Boy" was done with the best of intentions. They said it was moving, intelligent and full of love.

circuitous   *ser KYOO: i tuhs*
taking a roundabout, lengthy course

The livery car turned west across Allen Street's two-way traffic and rushed into Rivington Street, with the police car in pursuit. A circuitous chase went south on the next street, Eldridge, then east on Delancey, and back north on Allen, amid light Sunday traffic.

circumscribe   *SER kuhm skrighb*

to limit; confine; restrict

To eyes uninitiated into the subtleties of traditional Buddhist dance and music, the dance was fairly circumscribed ritual movement and gesture built on slow pivoting turns, hops and wreathing of hands and arms, performed at a stately, gracious pace to the deep roar of long horns, low-voiced drums, trumpets, cymbals and muted chants.

circumvent   *SER kuhm vent*

to overcome by artful maneuvering; prevent from happening by craft or ingenuity

More than 20 years ago Mr. Kavanagh made headlines when he painstakingly hand-printed a work called "The John Quinn Letters." The letters of Mr. Quinn, deceased, who was a distinguished patron of the arts, were available only to scholars at the special-manuscripts room of the New York Public Library, provided they were read but not copied or quoted from directly. Mr. Kavanagh circumvented these caveats by memorizing parts of the letters, dashing repeatedly out to Bryant Park, jotting those parts down and eventually printing his book. A court brouhaha ensued, ending when Mr. Kavanagh destroyed most of his printing.

clamber   *KLAM buhr*

to climb with effort or clumsily, especially by using the hands as well as the feet

The five-and-a-half-foot, 45-pound Florida alligator was recaptured in two brief escape attempts earlier this summer before it got loose last month by clambering over a fence separating the zoo's outdoor alligator pen from an adjacent pond in Denver's City Park.

clandestine   *klan DE stin*

kept secret or hidden, especially for some illicit purpose; done without the knowledge of those who would regulate or punish such actions

Mr. Mercer said there are no open slave markets [in Mauritania] but that men, women and children are bought and sold clandestinely, traded from one master to another. He did not know the going price for a slave but said a young woman had been sold to a suitor by her owner, an Islamic judge, for 2,000 British pounds, the equivalent of $1,870. The biggest trade is in children, the report said.

claque   *klak*
a group of admiring or fawning followers; also, a group of people paid to go to a performance and applaud

Miss Scotto is hailed by some as the successor to Maria Callas (as in a non-musical sense, Jacqueline Kennedy Onassis was) but is damned by others as "Renata Screecho." Miss Scotto has a fiercely loyal claque who will follow her to hell, but she also has a group of growling standees who profoundly distrust her talent. One claque wildly applauds the least laudable of her performances while the anti-claque claque comes ready to hiss and boo at her slightest off-key note.

class action   *KLAS AK shun*
a legal action brought by one or more persons on behalf of themselves and a much larger group, all of whom have the same grounds for action

Now local white fishermen and the Klan have been accused in a lawsuit of conspiring to threaten and intimidate the Vietnamese into leaving. The case pits two longtime courtroom enemies against each other—the Klan and the Klanwatch organization, an arm of the Southern Poverty Law Center in Birmingham, Ala., that filed the class action lawsuit on behalf of the Vietnamese fishermen.

classicist   *KLA si sist*
one whose attitudes or principles adhere to the traditional or standard methods and pursuits of a field, rather than to the acceptance of new or experimental directions

Classicists believe that botanical research should be confined to the systematic exploration and analysis of the plant world. More and more botanists, however, have come to believe that they are failing in their obligations to society if they do not apply their knowledge to solving global problems such as hunger and energy shortages.

cliché   *klee SHAY*
a word, expression, architectural style, fashion, etc. that has been overused or overdone to the point of having lost its effectiveness and originality

The Los Angeles he depicts in these pages is a complete cliché: a city obsessed with youth, beauty and power, a city indistinguishable from the one depicted in the novels of Judith Krantz and Sidney Sheldon and in dozens of television movies. We learn—surprise!—that there are people in Los Angeles who spend a lot of time driving around town in their expensive cars, who like being seen at trendy restaurants, who pay attention to their tans, their muscles and their sunglasses.

cloying *KLOI ing*
having an excess of a quality, as sweetness, richness or sentimentality, to the point of arousing distaste or disgust

Like so many restaurants with an expressionist chef who free associates, [it] falls down on main courses, primarily because intricate and complicated flavorings and food combinations that can be diverting in appetizer-size portions become cloying in larger amounts.

coalesce *koh uh LES*
to unite or merge into a single body, group or mass

In the beginning, circa 1975, "Saturday Night Live" offered a kind of outrageous sassiness that served as a refreshing antidote to the normal blandness of television entertainment. In a year or two, the program had reached its peak, coalescing in a superb ensemble that included Chevy Chase, Gilda Radner, John Belushi and Dan Aykroyd.

coalition *koh uh LI shuhn*
a temporary alliance for some specific purpose

A coalition of six local unions is scheduled to meet this morning with negotiators for The News and The Times to discuss the wage pattern set by the deliverers. The coalition includes mailers, photoengravers, paper handlers, electricians and two machinist locals.

cockamamie *kah kuh MAY mee*
ridiculous; ludicrous, silly; nonsensical: slang, said to have derived from decalcomania, the process of transferring decals to glass, metal and other materials

A man as traveled and sophisticated as George Bush knows the importance of population control. So do his friends and relatives. But he announces that he will veto any Congressional effort to restore the paltry United States contribution to the United Nations population fund, because of some cockamamie excuse that some of the money may help abortion in China—which it will not.

✦ Cockamamies are pictures on tissue-like paper that come off as inked impressions when pressed against wet skin, leaving a temporary tattoo. The impermanence and piddling value of a single cockamamie on paper probably gave rise to the word's current use.

cocksure   *kahk shoor*
sure or self-confident in a stubborn or overbearing way

Teamster leaders have long rejected complaints against the union. From Daniel J. Tobin, who guided the union almost 50 years, through Mr. Fitzsimmons, they have been tough-minded and cocksure. "Problems have a way of solving themselves," Mr. Hoffa was quoted as telling Ralph C. James and Estelle D. James for their 1965 book, "Hoffa and the Teamsters." "If you stall long enough, the troubles, or troublemakers, will disappear." He also said: "I don't trust anybody; everybody has his price."

coffer   *KAW fer*
a treasury; funds: a coffer is a chest or strongbox in which money or valuables are kept

Alaska's coffers were so bulging with oil and other mineral royalties, that the state announced a treasury giveaway in April 1980. The Legislature voted to end the income tax for most residents, refund all income taxes paid in 1979 and 1980 and distribute a cash dividend every year to each resident 18 years or older.

✦ Doublets like *coffer* and *coffin* are two or more words derived from the same original word but reaching English through different routes and currently used with different meanings. *Dish* (from Old English) and *disk* (from Latin) stem from the Latin *discus*. Other doublets: frail/fragile; gentle/genteel; amicable/amiable; major/mayor; particle/parcel; potion/poison; secure/sure; balsam/balm; adamant/diamond; scandal/slander; whole/hale; no/nay; from/fro; shirt/skirt; liquor/liquid; guarantee/warranty; channel/canal; shatter/ scatter.

cognoscenti   *kag nuh SHEN tee*
people with special knowledge in a field, especially the arts; expert: often used with a flavor of irony

It used to be that only the cognoscenti knew about the New York City Ballet-affiliated School of American Ballet's annual spring workshop performances, which will take place tomorrow night and Monday afternoon and evening at the Juilliard Theater at Lincoln Center.

colloquy   *KAH luh kwee*
a conversation, especially a formal discussion; conference

LOS ANGELES—Last Sunday morning, as millions of people were leisurely celebrating Easter, 60 men and women from several continents met in a hotel conference room for an intense three-hour colloquy entitled "The Behavior of Large Corporations."

combative   *kuhm BA tiv*
ready or eager to fight; pugnacious

A good way to get rid of a resting bee, without panic, Mr. Auditore says, is to blow on him. "They're susceptible to wind and more often than not if you blow on them they'll fly away. I would go so far as to say that they are friends," he says. "They're very docile. You never find two bees fighting over a blossom, for example. They never fight. They're not combative. And always remember, if there weren't any bees, nothing in the city would be green."

comely   *KUHM lee*
pleasant to look at; attractive; fair

Several times since he started punching people for pay in 1972, Bobby Chacon lost his enthusiasm for the Sweet Science. For anyone watching on television Saturday while Cornelius Boza-Edwards took fungo practice on Bobby's comely head, it was not difficult to understand why. There are many pleasanter ways to earn a living, including being shot out of a cannon at county fairs.

comity   *KAH muh tee*
civility; courtesy

Mr. Carter, the historian from Emory, said he refused to believe that anybody who defended the flying of a Confederate flag was necessarily racist. But, he said, the flag's defenders "show an insensitivity to one of the great Southern values, and that is politeness." "If you really care about comity in a society,"

Mr. Carter said, "it means you have to look at symbols from the point of view of the people who are most hurt by them, and that's African-Americans."

commensurate   *kuh MEN shoo rit*
proportionate

The treasure to be found on the sunken British warship Edinburgh probably far exceeds that recently retrieved from the liner Andrea Doria, and the risks are commensurate.

commonplace   *KAH muhn plays*
everyday; usual; common

The "doing two things at once" syndrome is so commonplace that few people are aware they're engaging in it. They riffle through magazines while watching television, compose letters in their minds as they walk, dictate as they pedal the exercise cycle, and use laptop computers as they listen to music on airplanes.

compatriot   *kuhm PAY tree uht*
a person of the same country

One of the more consistent and perplexing prejudices encountered in traveling around the world is the feeling of superiority northerners of almost any country have for their southern compatriots; if, in fact, they even consider them as such. ("It is really another country down there," one often hears them say.)

compendium   *kuhm PEN dee uhm*
a brief compilation derived from a total field of knowledge

Across town, the Museum of Broadcasting at 1 East 53d Street has dipped into its collection of television programs to put together "Satire in the Air," a compendium of television programs from 1961 to now. It includes "That Was The Week That Was," "Saturday Night Live" and "Laugh-In," as well as programs with Jack Benny and the Smothers Brothers.

complacent   *kuhm PLAY sint*
self-satisfied; feeling no need to change; content; smug

Although Japan's unemployment is low compared with the rate in many other countries, full employment, or close to it, is a key clause in the social contract that has kept the public complacent and one political party in power almost consistently since World War II. Now, for the first time since the lean years after Japan's defeat in the war, most people here know someone who is out of a job—and fear that they could be next.

complement   *KAHM pluh ment*
something that completes, makes up a whole or brings to perfection

The two men respect each other, and they speak of how they complement each other—Mr. Perella with his intuitive approach to closing deals and Mr. Wasserstein with his strategic thinking.

composure   *kuhm POH zher*
calmness of mind or manner; self-possession

Mrs. Harris reacted with the composure that has become her hallmark during the often-agonizing testimony about the shooting death of Dr. Herman Tarnower, the author and physician who for most of 14 years had been her companion and lover: chin up, eyes clear, blinking slightly.

compound   *kahm POWND*
to intensify by adding new elements

Sleep researchers dream of a world where high school starts at 9:30 or 10, instead of the more typical 7:30 or 8. They say the sleep patterns of teenagers shift when they are moving through high school, a biological change that is compounded by school days that begin earlier than when the students were in middle and elementary school.

compromise   *KAHM pruh mighz*
to weaken, endanger or place in jeopardy

An estimated 600,000 to 1.2 million cases of shingles occur every year, in the elderly or in people whose immune systems are compromised. "It can be very painful because it pinches the nerve cells," said Dr. Abbas Vafai, chief of biologics at the Centers for Disease Control and Prevention in Atlanta.

conceit   *kuhn SEET*
a small, imaginatively designed item

Candied violets are used in my home to decorate custard desserts, such as an English custard, white and yellow ice creams, yellow puddings and so on.

They are, as I have stated often, my favorite conceit where dessert garnishes are concerned.

concomitant   *kahn KAH muh tuhnt*
accompanying; attendant

Your eyes are small, red and runny; your nose is large, red and runny; and your sneezes rock the room. "Nobody ever died of hay fever," your friends say. A lot they know. Thanks to a spring drought, however, and a concomitant drop in the production of ragweed, this year promises to be less of a misery than any since the mid-60's.

concrete   *kahn KREET*
specific, not general or abstract

GDANSK, Poland, Sept. 6—Solidarity leaders said today that the union must expand its role and come up with a concrete program to lead Poland out of its economic crisis.

concurrence   *kuhn KER uhns*
a happening together in time or place

The 52 Americans were freed only minutes after Ronald Reagan was sworn in as the 40th President of the United States. The concurrence in timing held millions of Americans at their radios and television sets, following the pageantry of Inauguration Day and the news of the hostages' release.

condominium   *kahn duh MI nee uhm*
a joint rule by two or more states

Until Vanuatu gained independence last July, Paris and London ruled the archipelago, formerly the New Hebrides, whose romantic beauty was celebrated by James A. Michener in his "Tales of the South Pacific." The Anglo-French condominium set up two of everything on the island: school systems, police forces, courts, languages, currencies and more.

✦ A condominium, in its popularly known American sense, is an apartment house held by joint ownership: Each apartment is bought and owned individually as if it were a house. The land the building is on is usually held by a corporation.

configuration   *kuhn fi gyuh RAY shuhn*
arrangement of parts

Architects who specialize in children's rooms stress simple, floor-oriented spaces that are flexible enough to provide for changing configurations as children's ages change and to accommodate children's own creativity in arranging their environments.

confluence   *KAHN floo: uhns*
a flowing together of two or more streams, ideas or traits

The Robbers Roost Ranch, five miles from town, is the classic Western ranch. It has 26,000 acres, almost twice as many as the island of Manhattan. The ranch buildings, some of the cabins 60 years old, are at the confluence of the two rivers that run through its dry land, Rock Creek and the Medicine Bow.

Mr. Perahia's music is irresistible. He sits down to play, and Schumann, Mozart, Beethoven somehow appear fresh and whole. In him, the confluence of passion and restraint, of spontaneity and carefully laid proportion is so natural that one cannot imagine these separate ingredients ever having existed apart from one another. Any hint of falseness, of calculation, any rude gesture or inelegance are unthinkable.

conglomerate   *kuhn GLAH muh rit*
a large corporation formed by the merger of a number of companies in unrelated, widely diversified industries

Working out of paper-strewn offices here on busy Burbank Boulevard, Steve Allen is a virtual one-man media conglomerate. His versatility qualifies him as a personal hedge against the uneven nature of the sundry entertainment businesses. If a television series is out of favor with the Nielsen ratings, there's always songwriting. If the book business is sluggish, there's always the nightclub act.

conjurer   *KAHN jer er*
a magician

The 52-year-old Mr. Schindler put himself through Brooklyn College with magic and now makes a living with it at conventions, bar mitzvahs, theaters, industrial shows and the other stopping places of practicing conjurers.

consecrate   *KAHN suh krayt*
to make or declare sacred for religious use

Current Catholic theology teaches that only ordained celibate men may consecrate the bread and wine that symbolize the body and blood of Christ.

consort   *KAHN sawrt*
an ensemble of musicians or musical instruments

The ear-tickling sounds of shawms, recorders, krummhorns, dulcians, racketts, cornettos, sackbuts, lutes and viols in consort can be festive enough to suit almost any occasion.

consternation   *kahn ster NAY shuhn*
great fear or shock that makes one feel helpless or bewildered

Twice a day the twin towers of New York's World Trade Center rise and fall about 14 inches. They also tilt about two inches, first to the west and then to the east. Such behavior by the city's tallest structures might cause consternation were it not for the fact that all of New York responds in the same way to the passage of earth tides, the terrestrial counterpart of ocean tides, as do all land masses, to a greater or lesser degree.

consummate   *KAHN suh mayt; KAHN suh mit*
to bring to completion or fulfillment; accomplish

Other Administration officials said they were aware of reports that China was selling missiles in the Middle East and elsewhere. While expressing concerns over those reports, several officials said there was conflicting information about what weapons might be for sale. They said they had no evidence that a deal had been consummated.

complete or perfect in every way; supreme; very skillful; highly expert

Mr. Sinatra can phrase a conversational song or a standard pop ballad like nobody in the business. Those teasing hesitations, those dramatic asides that only rarely lapse into melodrama, those gruff percussive attacks—they add up to a consummate stylist.

contentious   *kuhn TEN shis*
involving or characterized by dispute; controversial

The active ingredients in marijuana appear to be useful for treating pain, nausea and the severe weight loss associated with AIDS, according to a new study commissioned by the Government that is inflaming the contentious debate over whether doctors should be permitted to prescribe the drug.

contiguous   *kuhn TI gyoo: is*
touching along all or most of one side

Another big way in which humans have increased the coyote's fortunes is by exterminating wolves, which historically kept the coyote bottled up, ecologically speaking. The demise of the wolf in most of the contiguous 48 states liberated coyotes in two ways: deer populations exploded, providing more prey, and the most important predator of coyotes disappeared.

contingent   *kuhn TIN jint*
a group forming part of a larger group

Mr. Ibarra traveled to the capital without the contingent of eight bodyguards that accompanied him at all times in Tijuana, justice officials said. The assassins seemed to know details of Mr. Ibarra's travel plans, suggesting they acted on information from inside the police.

dependent on something else; conditional

Getting composers to come onstage to chat about their music during a concert can be a good thing at times, and organizations like Meet the Composer, which made some of its grants contingent upon such involvement, have used these talks to create bridges between composers and listeners.

contrapuntal   *kahn truh PUHN tuhl*
relating to counterpoint: *the art of adding a related but independent melody or melodies to a basic melody, in accordance with the fixed rules of harmony, to make a harmonic whole*

No one knows precisely what instrument or instruments Bach had in mind for his Art of Fugue, a monument of contrapuntal composition he left unfinished at his death. It can be performed on harpsichord and organ and by ensembles of various kinds and, in any case, must always be given in a practical arrangement devised by someone other than the composer. Chances are that this would not have bothered Bach at all.

contrite   *kuhn TRIGHT*
feeling remorse for sins or wrongdoing; repentant

Romanowski said today that he remains contrite over the most notorious incident of his career, one that has overshadowed the fact that he has played on two Super Bowl winners in San Francisco and a third in Denver. The incident occurred last season, during a Monday night game against the 49ers, when Romanowski spit at receiver J. J. Stokes. The action was spotted on instant replay, and Romanowski was fined $7,500 by the league.

co-opt *KO ahpt*

to persuade or lure an opponent to join one's own side

Mr. Mobutu is a master of co-opting would-be opponents. Diplomats say he has systematically let his enemies feed at the state trough, rotating them in and out of office and encouraging many to become wealthy in order to neutralize them.

copious *KOH pee uhs*

plentiful; abundant

He was able to reconstruct conversations with people long dead because he had kept copious notes. Mr. Hoving said, "I'm a compulsive writer, and I habitually keep a daily journal in which I note even the shade of a person's complexion when I speak with them."

✦ Why does Mr. Hoving refer to the person whose complexion he notes as "them," when there is only one person? To be grammatically correct, a singular antecedent—"person's"— must be followed by a singular pronoun—"him," "her" or "him or her." Did Mr. Hoving say "them" out of carelessness, or did he say it intentionally, to include both sexes while avoiding the awkwardness of "him or her"? We don't know. But the use of "they," "them" or "their" to follow singular nouns or pronouns is becoming more common and acceptable. In the attempt to keep writing both nonsexist and graceful, this is a vexing problem, for no English word embraces the singular of both sexes. Options are to recast the sentence or make both parts plural. Mr. Hoving might have said that in his daily journal he will note "the shade of complexion of a person I have spoken with" or "the shades of people's complexions when I speak with them."

cornerstone *KAWR ner stohn*

the basic, essential or most important part; foundation

Historically the British have passionately protected their privacy, the cornerstone of their manners and morals. When the idea of a census was first raised here in 1753 it provoked heated debate. William Thornton, a Member of Parliament, charged that it was "totally subversive of the last remains of English liberty."

corniche   *kawr NEESH*
a roadway that winds along a cliff or steep slope: French, cornice

There were still scores of strollers and picnickers along the corniche overlooking the Mediterranean, as is usual on Sundays, but they shied away from the usually crowded corner near the American Embassy.

corpulent   *KAWR pyuh luhnt*
stout; obese; fat

For years, this weight-obsessed nation has considered fatness and slimness matters of willpower. The corpulent are blamed—by others or by guilty conscience—for a disgusting inability to turn down dessert. And the verdict is surely just in some cases. But more and more evidence suggests that many fat people may be in the grip of biochemical forces that are indeed hard to control.

corpus   *KAWR puhs*
a complete or comprehensive collection

Hundreds of symphonies in a dizzying variety of styles have been written since 1911, but the one corpus of work that seems to be entering the standard repertory is the set of 15 written by Dmitri Shostakovich.

corrode   *kuh ROHD*
to eat into or wear away gradually; to cause to deteriorate

Of the many little things that corrode the quality of life in New York, surely those little things that pets leave behind on sidewalks, in gutters, near trees and underfoot are among the most egregious. And the worst of it is, they are not always so little, and their numbers are growing. Fourteen years after the City Council passed the so-called pooper-scooper law, demanding that dog owners either pick up after their pets or risk a fine that is as high as $100, many owners seem to view the law as an amusing anachronism, as readily flouted as the law against excessive honking.

cosset   *KAH sit*
to treat like a pet; pamper

As the producer who persuaded Elizabeth Taylor to make her Broadway debut in "The Little Foxes," Zev Bufman knows how to cosset, pamper and otherwise please his star. He is said to have spent more than $20,000 to redecorate Miss Taylor's dressing room in her favorite color, lavender, and, on opening night last Thursday, to have given her a small, perfect diamond.

coterie   *KOH tuh ree*
a close group of people who share a common interest

For almost 30 years El Charro on Charles Street in Greenwich Village has had a loyal coterie that has come to rely on certain dishes.

coterminous   *koh TER muh nuhs*
having a common boundary; contiguous: same as conterminous

There will be no total eclipse next year, and none visible from the coterminous United States until the next century.

countervail   *kown ter VAYL*
to counteract; be successful or useful against

The church has become the principal countervailing power in Brazil to the governing military because of its involvement in social issues, but it has not drawn the same support from the Brazilian public in matters of social morality. Divorce and civil weddings have come to Brazil despite the church's opposition, and about six million Brazilian women, 90 percent of them Catholic, are believed to be using birth-control pills.

courtly   *KAWRT lee*
suitable for a king's court; dignified; polite; elegant

The Wimbledon championships are under way, that courtly gathering of knights and ladies, the beauty and chivalry of the All England Lawn Tennis and Croquet Club with its strawberries and cream, its white gloves and flowery hats, meticulously manicured lawns and impeccable manners. It is also the stage on which a spoiled brat like John McEnroe can demonstrate how ugly an ugly American can get.

couture   *koo TOO:R*
women's clothes in new or specially designed fashions

Designers in the United States no longer flock to couture shows to copy line for line what Paris designers are doing. They have developed their own confidence to the point where they feel they know better what their customers want to wear.

covet   *KUH vit*
to want ardently, especially something that another person has

For just about as long as there has been a border with the United States, some Canadians have believed that Americans covet their country and the resources it contains. A few conspiracy subscribers still believe Washington harbors ambitions about northern expansion similar to those that provoked the first armed incursion into what is now Canada in the 18th century. And a certain type of Canadian is sure that free-trade agreements are a plot to make Canada a commercial colony of the United States.

crass   *kras*
vulgar; tasteless; coarse; ill-mannered

[Malcolm Forbes's] chums all arrived with packages, because although the host would never be crass enough to ask for gifts, he did put a postscript on his invitations that read, "Since it's a surprise party, don't tell me what you're bringing."

creature comforts   *KREE cher KUHM ferts*
anything providing bodily comfort, such as food, clothing or shelter, as opposed to comforts for the soul

"Americans were spoiled by the muscle cars," Mr. Bishop said, referring to the powerful American cars produced during the 1960's. "Those cars had huge road performance, as well as air-conditioning and all the other creature comforts you could want."

✦ *A very strong smell of brandy and water forewarned the visitor that Mr. Squeers had been seeking in creature comforts a temporary forgetfulness of his unpleasant situation.*

– Charles Dickens, *Nicholas Nickelby*

crescendo   *kruh SHEN doh*
in music, a gradual increase in the volume or intensity of sound; but also used figuratively, to describe a gradual rise to a peak

Indian classical music, an improvising tradition with an age-old repertory, embraces extremes. It can serenely contemplate a single note suspended in time, and it can flaunt high speed and dramatic crescendos.

The prime minister is at the lectern, struggling to field a series of increasingly challenging questions from the leader of the opposition. Jeers are rising in crescendo from the Parliament floor, and the few spectators allowed in are on the edge of their seats, fairly straining for a view. The scene, known as question time, has been adopted straight from British politics. On the surface, just two weeks into its existence, it still may seem like a jolting innovation to some in the often soporific world of the Japanese Parliament.

crestfallen   *KREST faw luhn*
dejected, dispirited or depressed

An American woman who is a resident of Peking and who enrolled her 5-year-old son in the Peking No. 1 kindergarten this fall was crestfallen when she was told that her child was the only one in his class who misbehaved.

criterion   *krigh TI ree uhn*
a standard, rule or test by which something can be judged

The criterion for insanity in criminal trials here is the standard formulated by the American Law Institute. It states that "a person is not responsible for criminal conduct if at the time of such conduct, as a result of mental disease or defect, he lacks substantial capacity to appreciate the wrongfulness of his conduct or to conform his conduct to the requirements of the law."

crossover   *KRAWS oh ver*
in music, crossing over in style, as from jazz to rock, or in appeal, as from a jazz to a rock audience

The success of projects like the Three Tenors—crossovers that sell beyond the usual classical market—stunned recording executives more used to selling recordings by the thousands than the millions. Other crossover releases were tried, some with astonishing results, like the sensation Andrea Bocelli, the darkly handsome, blind Italian tenor, who sings arias, lighter classical works and pop songs, and has sold some 14 million records worldwide on the Philips label.

cull   *kuhl*
to select and gather

More than 110 distinguished collections of American, Asian and European antiques culled from 16 states and overseas will be on display.

culpable   *KUHL puh buhl*
deserving blame

When the Watergate investigations began, serious doubts existed about President Nixon's culpability. "What did the President know, and when did he know it?" Senator Howard H. Baker Jr. kept asking. It took more than a year and required testimony from the President's top aides (though not the President himself) and Nixon's own tape-recorded comments in the Oval Office to answer that basic question.

cum   *koom*
with: used chiefly in hyphenated compounds with the general meaning
"combined with" or "plus"

Five months ago, Havana Village, a Cuban restaurant-cum-bar, moved from University Place to 68 Fifth Avenue, at 13th Street, where its spare but attractive Hispanic formality contrasts with the easygoing Sun Belt style of the Lone Star Cafe just across the border on the other side of the avenue.

cynosure   *SIGH nuh shoor*
any person or thing that is a center of attention or interest

On the night of Oct. 2, 1979, as Pope John Paul II was paraded in triumph from the right-field bullpen at Yankee Stadium, elevated in clear sight of 80,000 people, the latest of two dozen threats on his life that day was being received by the largest security operation in New York history. The moment was harrowing. Shimmering in white, moving ever so slowly, reaching out for the crowds, the Pope was as much a target as a cynosure.

> ✦ *Cynosure* is from the Greek *kynosoura*, dog's tail, and was the old name for Polaris, the North Star, and its constellation, now called Ursa Minor. Because the North Star was essential to navigation, and was carefully observed, its name passed into use as meaning anything that is the center of attention.

doughty

Rising toward 5 in the morning, when the desert stars are

just starting to pale, the doughtier visitors

make their way back up to the

hermitage to watch the dawn.

see page 113

dais   *DAY is*
a platform raised above the floor at one end of a hall or room, as for a throne, seats of honor, a speaker's stand, etc.

> Burgess Meredith squinted under the glare of the television lights, looked out from the dais across the shimmering pool surrounded by 224 wine enthusiasts crammed into the Four Seasons restaurant and declared: "I'm not here because I'm in the trade. I'm here because I buy more wine than anybody else. So I deserve to be here!"

dalliance   *DA lee uhns*
amorous play; flirting

> Eva Perón came to Buenos Aires from the provinces at the age of 14, an aspiring actress who through her wits and dalliances rose to become mistress and then wife of the populist strongman Juan Domingo Perón.

daunting   *DAWN ting*
making one afraid or discouraged; intimidating; disheartening

> I would say that in most kitchens, professional or otherwise, pastry making is and has been over the centuries the most daunting aspect of cooking. Many a home cook who may be a master of casseroles or a perfectionist when it comes to pastas and pâtés cringes inwardly at the thought of blending flour, fat and liquid to produce a crust for pie.

deadlock   *DED lahk*
a standstill resulting from the action of equal and opposed forces, as when both

sides in a strike refuse to budge, or when the members of a jury cannot agree on a verdict; stalemate

> A Federal jury declared yesterday for the second time that it was deadlocked in the mail-fraud and extortion trial of Joseph M. Margiotta, the Nassau County Republican chairman, and that "further deliberation is pointless."

dearth   *derth*
a scarcity or lack

> Mr. Simpson said the Transit Authority had been forced to hire people lacking stated minimum qualifications because of a dearth of qualified applicants.

debacle   *di BAH kuhl*
an overwhelming defeat or rout: a word borrowed from French in the nineteenth century, originally meaning the breaking up of ice in a river

> In his one try for elective office, his race for Governor on the Republican ticket in 1934, he [Robert Moses] was defeated by 800,000 votes, the largest margin in New York State history. After the debacle, his administrative power continued unabated, but he never again considered running for office.

debilitating   *di BIL uh tay ting*
making one weak or very tired by sapping one's energy or health

> Having labored mightily to get there, is she [Blair Brown] happy as a movie star? Yes and no. "I find the movies I've done to be debilitating. I end up physically weaker. I can't deal too well with the stress. Whereas on stage, I usually end up stronger. I've been working, my voice is strong, my body's strong."

debonair   *de buh NAIR*
suave; nonchalant

> Before his arrival in Liverpool, Colm knows so little about everything from sex to urban life that he makes John Merrick of "The Elephant Man" look as debonair as Fred Astaire.

debunk   *di BUNGK*
to expose the false or exaggerated claims of

Though the notion of a "male menopause" comparable to the hormonal changes that women experience has been soundly debunked, there is considerable evidence that many—if not most—men undergo an unsettled and often life-disrupting period sometime between the ages of 35 and 50.

> ✦ *Bunk*, as a synonym for nonsense, had its origin around 1820, when Congressman Felix Walker made a long, tedious and irrelevant speech to Congress, the only purpose of which was to impress the voters back home in Buncombe County, North Carolina. He later explained that he had felt bound to "make a speech for Buncombe." *Buncombe* or *bunkum* (and since 1900 the shortened form, *bunk*) soon became a synonym for empty political claptrap.

deciduous   *duh SI joo: is*
shedding leaves annually (as opposed to evergreen)

Eastern deciduous woodlands are famous, of course, for their bright fall yellows, oranges and russets. Now red is coming to the fore, and not only in autumn; much of the forest is acquiring a pervasive rosy blush in the spring as well. The reason is that the soft green springtime hues of hardwoods like oaks and hickories, and the darker greens of northern conifers like pines, are being replaced by the blazing red buds, flowers and fruits of another, more adaptable and aggressive species of native tree: the red maple.

decipher   *dee SIGH fuhr*
to translate a coded message or interpret something; to make out the meaning of

Scientists report today that they have completed the first major step in deciphering the secrets of one of the deadliest viruses ever known, the influenza virus of 1918. Though their work answers some questions about the origin of the virus, the scientists say it leaves the most fundamental question dangling: What made the virus, which killed 20 million to 40 million people worldwide, so lethal?

decorum   *duh CAW ruhm*
conformity to social conventions

Japan is a nation enormously attached to formality, decorum and to a politeness that verges on the exquisite. There is a way to do things and a way not to. Anyone who steps out of line is likely to get into trouble. "The nail that sticks out shall be hammered down," a proverb says.

decry   *di CRIGH*
to speak out against strongly and openly; denounce

Reggae developed in the slum areas of Kingston and other Jamaican cities and towns, and the island's poor have always been its core audience. Its lyrics decry racism and economic oppression, and its rhythms are derived from Afro-Jamaican folk sources.

deface   *di FAYS*
to spoil the appearance of; disfigure; mar

A team from the National Geographic Society reported last month that magnificent Maya drawings they found in a remote Guatemalan cave had been defaced by thieves trying to saw them off.

definitive   *di FI nuh tiv*
complete and authoritative on a certain subject, said of certain scholarly works

When it was rumored some years ago that my much admired colleague Waverly Root was engaged in compiling a definitive encyclopedia of food, there were loud huzzahs from my end of the table. Mr. Root is the American-born expatriate now living in France who wrote the definitive English-language book on French gastronomy, "The Food of France" (Knopf, 1958).

defoliate   *di FOH lee ayt*
to strip of leaves

Gypsy-moth caterpillars did a record amount of damage in the Northeast in 1981, eating the leaves off trees covering at least nine million acres from Maine to Maryland, according to estimates by forestry experts. That was twice the area defoliated last year, they say.

deft   *deft*
skillful in a quick, sure and easy way; dexterous

There are few tricks more difficult than picking up a raw scallop with chopsticks. At Woo Lae Oak, the waiter was trying to move a dozen onto the gas-fired grill on our table, and for an American, he was showing a deft hand. Still, by scallop No. 10, the strain began to show. "Why don't you just flick them, like a hockey puck?" I suggested. He shot a slick white scallop straight from its plate onto the grill, where it began sizzling happily. The waiter was pleased, but not too pleased. "You guys made me cheat," he said.

defunct *di FUNGKT*
no longer living or existing; dead or extinct

Woodchucks hibernate in winter, although not too deeply, and they some-times pop out of their dens during warm spells. This tendency probably helped create the now nearly defunct custom in certain areas of this nation to attribute weather-forecasting abilities to the creatures.

✦ *Woodchuck* is among the more than 100 American words bor-rowed from the Algonquian Indian languages, most during the seventeenth and eighteenth centuries. Among the survivors, and the dates of their first recorded use, are:

caribou, 1610	porgy, 1775
caucus, 1745	powwow, 1624
chipmunk, 1841	quahog, 1799
hickory, 1634	raccoon, 1608
hominy, 1629	skunk, 1634
mackinaw, 1827	squash, 1643
moccasin, 1612	squaw, 1634
moose, 1613	terrapin, 1672
opossum, 1610	toboggan, 1829
papoose, 1634	tomahawk, 1612
pecan, 1778	totem, 1609
persimmon, 1612	wampum, 1647
Podunk, 1666	wigwam, 1628
pone, 1612	woodchuck, 1674

dégagé *day gah ZHAY*
free and easy or unconstrained in manner, attitude, etc.: French

In the day clothes, hemlines run from knee to calf lengths, though skirts can be artfully draped or full. Mr. Blass has a tendency to tie a knot at the hem of overblouses, tunics and skirts to contribute to the dégagé spirit.

deify *DEE uh figh*
to make a god of; glorify, exalt or adore in an extreme way; idolize

"Eno is God," says the graffiti spray painted on the walls of Greenwich Village and SoHo. Why Brian Eno? In the past, rock musicians were consid-ered worthy of deification only if they were powerfully sensual singers like

Elvis Presley or virtuoso instrumentalists like the guitarist Eric Clapton. But Brian Eno sings only occasionally and self-consciously, and he is not a virtuoso on any instrument.

déjà vu   *DAY zhah voo:*
the illusion that one has previously had an experience that is actually new to one: French, already seen

"'Send in the Clowns' was two years old when I first heard it," Miss Collins recalls, "and Sinatra had already recorded it. But as soon as I heard it, I knew it belonged to me. I have that feeling of déjà vu sometimes about a song. It's almost as though I knew it from another life."

demise   *di MIGHZ*
death, often connoting a gradual decline before dying, or a disappearing into the past, as in the demise of an art form, a neighborhood, a way of life. Demise rarely appears in The New York Times *as a synonym for the death of a person, except in the newspaper's paid death notices.*

Mr. Brown, now director of professional development for the National Association of Elementary School Principals in Virginia, squarely places the blame for the demise of handwriting, and its cousins, grammar and syntax, on computers and E-mail. "I'm quite frankly appalled when I get E-mail where the first letter of the sentence isn't capitalized and sentences are filled with spelling mistakes," he said. "All matter of rules and courtesy seem to have vanished."

denounce   *di NOWNS*
to accuse publicly; inform against

The former Soviet Union had Pavlik Morozov, the child who was said to have denounced his own father to the authorities for hoarding grain; the modern United States has a sixth-grade boy who, responding to an anti-drug program at school, reported his own parents to the police after discovering a small amount of drugs at home.

condemn strongly

With bitter speeches and vitriolic chants, more than 1,000 demonstrators gathered at a rally in Union Square yesterday to denounce Mayor Rudolph W. Giuliani and his plans to force people in city shelters to work in exchange for their beds and to stop people from sleeping on city streets by threatening to arrest them.

depressant   *di PRE suhnt*
an agent that lessens functional activity

Taken black, iced coffee is a perfect appetite depressant, and so is a pleasant help to dieters. Iced tea, on the other hand, seems to induce hunger.

deride   *di RIGHD*
to ridicule; make fun of

France has tended to mock America's increasingly draconian attitude toward cigarettes in much the same way it derides Washington's interest in the sexual mores of politicians—that is, as the puritanical preoccupations of a country still in its infancy. About a third of adults in France smoke, compared with about a quarter of Americans.

de rigueur   *duh ree GER*
required by etiquette; according to good form; fashionable: French, in strictness

Keeping a gun for self-defense is still a private, even furtive matter; it is not yet de rigueur to exchange home-gun stories at dinner parties.

desecrate   *DE suh krayt*
to abuse the sacredness of; subject to sacrilege; profane

Surely there are better ways for Congressional lawmakers to demonstrate their love of country than to dilute Americans' free-speech rights. This simple truth continues to elude the House of Representatives. For the third time in four years, the chamber has approved a constitutional amendment that would undermine the right of free expression by allowing Congress to prohibit the physical desecration of the American flag. Once again, it is up to the Senate to block this assault on the Bill of Rights.

desolate   *DE suh lit*
uninhabited; deserted

Here, among the greasewood, black lava buttes and abandoned silver mines of southwestern Idaho, southeastern Oregon and northeastern Nevada, the country is so desolate and so remote that, as recently as the early 1900's, maps described portions of it as unexplored.

despise   *di SPIGHZ*
to look down on with contempt and scorn

"All Night Long," a comedy starring Gene Hackman and Barbra Streisand, has joined the select group of movies that audiences actively despise. "For most pictures, we'll have a full house, and maybe one person will ask for his money back," a Bruin [Theater] usher says. "For this movie, there will hardly be anyone in the theater, and five or six of them will ask."

destitute   *DES ti too:t*
lacking the necessities of life; living in complete poverty

Offering tax credits, loan guarantees and other incentives to encourage private businesses to create jobs and housing, President Clinton swept into the destitute Oglala Lakota Sioux reservation today, by many measures the sickest, most hopeless, most squalid corner of America.

desuetude   *DE swi too:d*
the condition of not being used anymore; disuse

She has been thrown away by her husband and by the world. Poking in trash cans with the shaft of a broken umbrella, she tries to reverse the tide of desuetude, to salvage things and put them back into their places.

detachment   *di TACH ment*
the state of being disinterested or impartial

Having gone through 444 days of captivity in Iran, Kathryn Koob was able to look with some detachment upon an incident at a college in Iowa in which a speech she was giving was interrupted by shouting Iranian students. "I almost felt at home, if you will," Miss Koob said, "because Iranians love political discussions, particularly Iranian men. When they discuss something, they become very active and it was a very typical Iranian political discussion."

detractor   *di TRAK ter*
one who disparages the worth or reputation of something

Social scientists have long encountered difficulty proving their work worthwhile enough to warrant Government support. Detractors have included both political conservatives who say the Government has no business poking into people's personal and sexual lives, and natural scientists who have cast doubt on the scientific quality of much social research.

detritus   *di TRIGH tuhs*
an accumulation of debris

He made a printing press from oddments and scraps, the detritus of secondhand shops and the lucky find on the street.

deus ex machina   *DAY uhs eks MA kee nuh*
anyone or anything that unexpectedly intervenes to change the course of events

Now, with corporate leadership diminished and the city struggling to cope with the recession, local business and community leaders have started what they call the Vision Project to chart new directions. One example is consideration of a proposal to ask the state to legalize casino gambling for Hartford. "We are in such difficult times that people would like a deus ex machina, they would like a god to pop up out of the box and say, 'Your problems are solved,'" said Hartford's Mayor, Carrie Saxon Perry. "But that's gone. It's a new day."

> ✦ *Deus ex machina* is a Latin phrase meaning *god from a machine*. In ancient Greek and Roman plays, a deity was sometimes brought in by stage machinery to intervene in the action and resolve problems. It was lowered into the stage action, and then raised out of it, by a hoist.

devoid   *duh VOID*
empty; completely without

Even though he was one of the most famous men of this century, DiMaggio's funeral this morning at SS. Peter and Paul Roman Catholic Church, where he had made his first communion and married his first wife, was astonishingly small, devoid of the celebrities of his vanishing era or, for that matter, of this one.

devotee   *de vuh TEE*
one ardently attached or devoted to anything; enthusiast; fan

Few devotees of fine wines would disagree that the chardonnay grape produces the greatest dry white table wines made in North America.

dexterity   *dek STER uh tee*
skill in using one's hands, mind or body; adroitness

Whether in the unadorned but orderly Chinatown dining room or in the somewhat more gracious uptown outpost, the one dish not to be missed is the marvelous duck—available on no more than 20 minutes' notice and carved at the table by a chef who wields a scalpel-sharp cleaver with a dexterity that Dr. Christiaan Barnard might envy.

diametrically   *digh uh ME trik lee*
completely; absolutely; utterly

Louella Hatch, who rents an apartment in the Bronx, and Louise Henry, who owns apartments in Brooklyn, have diametrically opposite views on most aspects of rent stabilization. But in one thing they agree: Each feels it has been administered unfairly.

diminutive   *duh MIN yuh tiv*
of small size

His diminutive height and small frame distinguished him from most of Mr. Safir's other bodyguards, who are tall and muscular.

a word or name formed from another by the addition of a suffix expressing smallness in size and, sometimes, endearment or condescension

BUENOS AIRES, May 16—She is a legend, the subject of television shows and Broadway musicals, known the world over by her diminutive, Evita. And here, in the country that both bore her and reflects her, she is not dead. Eva Perón lives. She lives in memories so powerful that the former country girl who rose to be a willful ruler continues to tug at the nation, still dividing those who adore her and despise her.

dint   *dint*
force; exertion: now chiefly in "by dint of"

As the Associated Press reporter at City Hall until he retired last December after 47 years in the business, Schroeder was not often read by people in this city. But by dint of knowledge and personality, he guided colleagues through the many mazes of government. Inevitably, his perceptions—and they were perceptions, not biases—were those absorbed by newspaper readers and television viewers.

diocese   *DIGH uh sees*
the district under a bishop's jurisdiction

The Pittsburgh diocese, which has negotiated four successive contracts with its teachers, is a leader among Catholic school systems in collective bargaining.

dire   *digh er*
dreadful; terrible

If it does nothing else, "Richard's Things" illustrates what dire trouble an actress can land in when she works with a director with no understanding of her talents. Liv Ullmann, who can be so very sensitive and authentic, is this time called on to play a preposterous soap-opera queen.

disabuse   *dis uh BYOO:Z*
to correct a false impression; to rid of false ideas

In "Russia Under the Bolshevik Regime," Richard Pipes attempts to disabuse his readers of any lingering notion that the early years of Communist leadership in Russia were somehow more benign and well-intentioned than the later ones were or that there was a fundamental change in the regime following the transition from Lenin's leadership to Stalin's.

disarray   *dis uh RAY*
an untidy condition; disorder; confusion

In the confusion following the revolution, the Iranian caviar business was said to be in disarray, with a flourishing black market, unhygienic products and risky delivery. Christian Petrossian, the exclusive importer of Russian caviar in Europe, said his company stopped buying Iranian caviar.

disavow   *dis uh VOW*
to deny having any connection with; disclaim; renounce

Miss Keough has been something of a rebel among the families of the former hostages because she developed an affection for Iranians in a three-month visit to Iran while her father was the head of the American school there. It was a feeling she refused to disavow, even after her father had become a prisoner of Islamic militants.

discerning   *di SER ning*
having or showing good judgment or understanding

Stores such as Macy's, Dean & Deluca, Bloomingdale's and Zabar's are competing so hard for the attention of the discerning olive oil user that they dispatch buyers to Europe to scout the small groves for the finest oils.

disclaimer   *dis CLAY mer*
a disavowal, as of pretensions, claims or opinions

According to a careful opening disclaimer, the four young men who star in "Beatlemania" are "not the former members of the musical group known as the Beatles." This laughable announcement is made for legal reasons, not esthetic ones, because anyone fond of the real Beatles will immediately spot the fraudulence of the enterprise.

discord   *DIS kawrd*
disagreement; conflict; quarreling

The Prime Ministers of India and Pakistan pledged to take immediate steps to reduce the risk of nuclear war and seek solutions to a half century of raging disputes, including their most volatile discord, the conflict in Kashmir.

disdain   *dis DAYN*
to regard or treat as unworthy or beneath one's dignity; look down upon

DiMaggio glided across the vast expanse of center field at Yankee Stadium with such incomparable grace that long after he stopped playing, the memory of him in full stride remains evergreen. He disdained theatrical flourishes and exaggerated moves, never climbing walls to make catches and rarely diving headlong. He got to the ball just as it fell into his glove, making the catch seem inevitable, almost preordained. The writer Wilfrid Sheed wrote, "In dreams I can still see him gliding after fly balls as if he were skimming the surface of the moon."

disenchantment   *dis in CHANT muhnt*
a loss of belief in an illusion; disillusionment

Mr. Cronkite is exceptional primarily in light of the awesome power and responsibility that prolonged national television exposure has thrust upon him. His disenchantment with the Vietnam War was instrumental in shifting public opinion to the side of the peace movement. Lyndon Johnson is reported to have concluded, "If we've lost Walter, we've lost the country."

disgorge   *dis GAWRJ*
to pour forth, empty out, as though from a throat or stomach; eject; expel

Hour by hour, cars and trucks back up to the Salvation Army's warehouse loading dock on the edge of the prosperous East Side here and disgorge clothing. Skirts and parkas, neckties and tank tops, sweat pants and socks, a polychromatic mountain of clothes is left each week, some with price tags still attached.

disingenuous   *dis in GEN yoo uhs*
insincere

"Beatlemania" was a horror on the stage, and it's even more of a horror at close range, where the seams really show. This isn't a loving impersonation, or even an honest one. It's cheap, disingenuous and loathsome.

dismember   *dis MEM ber*
to cut or tear off arms or legs

In film as in other media, violence has long since become commonplace, with people dismembered, impaled, incinerated, blown up, machine-gunned or otherwise annihilated with numbing regularity.

disparate   *DI spuh rit*
essentially not alike; widely different

The Sudan is Africa's largest and probably most culturally disparate nation, with 18 million people scattered over nearly a million square miles. It has more than 1,000 languages and tribal dialects.

dispel   *dis PEL*
to cause to vanish; to scatter and drive away

Trying to paint a more realistic picture of drug users, the Government said today that out of every 10 people who used illegal drugs in 1997, 7 had full-time jobs. Officials said they hoped the data would dispel the notion that most drug users are burned out and disconnected from the mainstream. "The typical drug user is not poor and unemployed," said Gen. Barry R. McCaffrey, Director of the Office of National Drug Control Policy. "He or she can be a co-worker, a husband or wife, a parent."

dispiriting   *di SPIR uh ting*
lowering the spirits of; making sad, discouraged or apathetic

Although Winfield's good nature has not been tested by a personal slump, he has not sulked after Yankee losses. After a dispiriting defeat in Oakland, he was one of only a few New York players who signed autographs on the way to the bus.

disport   *di SPAWRT*
to indulge in amusement; play; frolic

While much of the city disported itself yesterday in a sunny start to the holiday weekend, several hundred professional magicians spent an afternoon without illusion at an East Side auditorium talking with one another about the secrets of the conjuring art.

✦ From *disport* we get *sport*, through the linguistic process known as apheresis, the dropping of an unaccented syllable or vowel at the beginning of a word. That process gave us *though* from *although*; *squire* from *esquire*; *fender* from *defender*; *cute* from *acute*. "'Scuse me" and "Morning" (for "Good morning") are examples of the same process.

disquieting   *dis KWIGH uh ting*
disturbing to one's usual way of thinking; causing unease

If kids don't run up against ideas that are disquieting, or challenging, or different from what they've always believed, or different from what their parents believe, how will they ever grow as human beings?

dissident   *DI suh duhnt*
one who disagrees or dissents, as from an established church, political system or school of thought

A former dissident priest of the Episcopal church who vigorously opposed that church's decision to allow female priests has been ordained by Terence Cardinal Cook for service in the Roman Catholic Archdiocese of New York.

dissipate   *DIS uh payt*
to drive away; make disappear; to break up and scatter

"You know what I do when I'm angry? I hit a pillow. Try that," suggests the psychiatrist, played by Billy Crystal, to his New York gangster client (Robert De Niro) in the Warner Brothers movie "Analyze This." But it is bad advice, according to new research by social psychologists. Though pop psychology books and articles perpetuate the notion that "getting your anger out" is cathartic and can help dissipate hostility, the researchers have found just the opposite: Venting anger on inanimate objects—punching a pillow or hitting a punching bag, for example—increases rather than decreases aggressive behavior.

dissonance   *DI suh nuhns*
a lack of harmony; discord

Though most couples spend a lot of time talking to each other, many lack the skills needed to get their messages across effectively, to express their feelings or resolve conflicts without hurting each other or provoking anger and dissonance.

distended   *di STEN did*
swollen

Scrawny dogs scampered through the dirt. A few cows stood in the background. Hundreds of crying, filthy, half-naked children with distended bellies and women waiting to be evicted sat on heaps of clothes and other possessions in rope bags.

ditty   *DI tee*
a short, simple song

"We don't want to fight,/ But, by Jingo, if we do,/ We've got the ships, we've got the men,/ We've got the money, too." Ships, men and money have been considered the essential ingredients of military preparedness since long before that music hall ditty became popular at a moment of tension between the British and Russians in the 1870's.

♦ From the British music hall ditty referred to in the passage arose the term *jingoism*, meaning aggressive or warmongering patriotism, the equivalent of the French *chauvinisme*. The song was popular during the Russo-Turkish War (1877-1878), when Prime Minister Benjamin Disraeli ordered the British fleet to Constantinople, where it prevented a Russian takeover. The lines that follow those in the passage are: *We've fought the Bear before,/ and while we're Britons true,/ The Russians shall not have Constantinople.* "By Jingo!" is a euphemism for "By Jesus!"

diva   *DEE vuh*

a leading woman singer, especially in grand opera: Latin, goddess

Miss Mills made her name playing Dorothy in the Broadway production of "The Wiz." But since then she has grown from an adolescent wonder into a pop-soul diva peddling adult eroticism in steamy numbers like "Two Hearts" and "Feel the Fire."

dive   *dighv*

a cheap, disreputable, low-class establishment, especially a bar, gambling place, dance-hall or the like: a slang word

Some spoke with nostalgia of the poolrooms of the past. "They were all dives," said Jake LaMotta, the former middleweight champion known as the Bronx Bull, who was a spectator at the tournament. "The only home you had was the poolroom. What else you had to do in the Bronx? After we came back from work, we always went there," the 60-year-old Bull recalled of his youth. "By 'work' I mean stealing. Not that we stole anything, just stuff beginning with A—a truck, a car, a bike."

divest   *duh VEST*

to strip

Like all crustacea, crabs must, in order to grow, periodically divest themselves of their bony exterior skeletons, which have no growth cells. This molting takes place from 21 to 23 times for the male and 18 to 20 for the females.

The Swarthmore College board of managers divested itself of nearly $2.4 million in stock from corporations that deal with South Africa, saying American concerns should be "responsible agents for progressive social change in South Africa." The board voted to divest itself of stock in Citicorp and the Newmont Mining Corporation, both of New York, and the Timken Company of Canton, Ohio.

docile   *DAH suhl*

easily managed or handled; tame

Albino animals also tend to be docile and are preferred subjects in laboratory research.

docudrama   *DAHK yoo drah muh*
a television dramatization based on facts, often presented in the style of a documentary to impart a sense of authenticity

For three hours this evening, beginning at 8 o'clock, CBS-TV is offering "The Bunker," a dramatization of the final days of Hitler and his Third Reich. John Gay's script is based on a book by John O'Donnell, who was on assignment for Newsweek in the Berlin of 1945. Mr. O'Donnell, played by James Naughton, is seen entering Hitler's underground hideout. He explains: "I can't guarantee that what you are about to see is historical truth. I do believe the stories present a kind of psychological truth," referring to the accounts of survivors. We are, once again, in the murky twilight world of the "docudrama." Conversations are reconstructed, personalities are transformed into performances and reality is adjusted, however slightly, in the interest of dramatic construction. The pitfalls of the genre are by now familiar. The dangers remain undiminished.

dog
to follow close by untiringly and persistently

Snacks containing it are required to carry what is arguably the most unappealing food product label in history: "Olestra may cause cramping and loose stools." And the manufacturer has been dogged by a consumer advocacy group, the Center for Science in the Public Interest, that has reminded consumers at every turn of the possible ill effects from munching olestra snacks.

doldrums   *DAHL druhms*
sluggishness or complete inactivity; stagnation

Although seasonality is becoming less important in selling wedding gear, the peak season remains January through March, with an eye to summer weddings. The people doing the alterations are busiest from April to July. And by all accounts December is the doldrums for the bridal industry. Nobody shops for wedding gowns at Christmas.

doleful   *DOHL fuhl*
full of sorrow or sadness; mournful; melancholy

Yesterday was the 77th birthday of Vladimir Horowitz. "I'm an old man and I don't know if I can play any more," he dolefully said, looking out at an interviewer from the corner of his eyes. He wandered over to the piano. "But perhaps." The Horowitz hands began to play pearly Scarlatti, crashing Liszt, songful Rachmaninoff, the coda of Chopin's F minor Ballade. "Maybe," he admitted, "the reflexes are not so bad, after all."

✦ In music, a coda is a passage at the end of a movement or composition that brings it to a formal close. The word is Italian for tail.

dollop   *DAH luhp*
a lump or blob of some substance; a measure or amount

Imagination and invention have infinitely extended the list of possible cold soups. Fruit, vegetables, seafood and chicken, in delectably pale pastel tones and crowned with a dollop of whipped cream or sour cream, are the rule.

The traditional Democratic approach, represented by Mr. O'Neill, calls for "targeted" tax cuts, giving special attention—an extra dollop of tax relief—to those with low or middle incomes.

dominion   *duh MIN yin*
control; rule

Since 1947, when India and Pakistan were carved from the British Empire, dominion over the storied Himalayan area of Kashmir has been in dispute, and was the direct cause for two of the three wars between the two nations.

✦ The name *Pakistan*, for the country created as a separate Muslim nation in 1947 from parts of British India, came both from a combination of the names of the then Muslim parts of India—Punjab, the Afghan Northwestern Frontier, *Kashmir*, Sind and Baluchi*stan*—and by combining the Urdu words, *pak* (pure) and *stan* (country).

dormant   *DAWR mint*
asleep or lying as if asleep; inactive

A one-day wonder is a long-dormant stock that leaps from a low price to a very high one in the course of a single day, or at most two. There is talk that a new product is a killer that will soon dominate a hot industry. The trading volume can be huge, perhaps several times the number of shares in existence. Internet chat rooms and cable television shows focus on the stock. Analysts are found to explain its attraction. The chief executive may turn up to discuss his high hopes for his new product. Then, just as suddenly, the price collapses.

double entendre   *DOO: bluh ahn TAHN druh*
a term with two meanings, especially when one of them has a risqué or indecorous connotation: French, double meaning

When rock-and-roll enjoyed its initial surge of popularity in the mid-50's, many fundamentalist Christians recoiled in horror. To them, rock's "savage rhythms," and the thinly concealed double entendre of many rock-and-roll lyrics, made it "the Devil's music."

double take   *DUH buhl TAYK*
a delayed reaction to some remark, situation, etc., in which there is at first unthinking acceptance and then startled surprise or a second glance, as the real meaning or actual situation suddenly becomes clear

When the tough narcotics detective named Gus Levy first appears on the screen in Sydney Lumet's "Prince of the City," some unsuspecting members of the audience are likely to do double takes. Is it? Could it be? Yes, it is Jerry Orbach, the song-and-dance man, star of the current "42d Street" and other Broadway musicals.

doughty   *DOW tee*
valiant; brave: now used humorously with a somewhat archaic flavor

Rising toward 5 in the morning, when the desert stars are just starting to pale, the doughtier visitors make their way back up to the hermitage to watch the dawn.

dour   *DOW er*
gloomy; sullen

Knick executives have addressed Coach Jeff Van Gundy about his glum demeanor and critics have questioned whether his dour style has affected his team. In a sarcastic aside, Van Gundy said he will put on a happy face. "This is the new me," Van Gundy said. "I am not dour. I am upbeat. I want you guys to document each of my smiles, which will be plenty."

dowager   *DOW uh jer*
an elderly woman of wealth and dignity

In the old days, Opening Night of New York's Metropolitan Opera was a grand occasion when dowagers could show off their jewels, singers could sing out their hearts and opera lovers could thrill to the return to the state of America's claim to world-class culture.

A Wilshire Boulevard landmark, the hat-shaped building of the Brown Derby restaurant, is being torn down to make way for an office building. But across the street, another landmark is still in business, the dowager Ambassador Hotel, where movie stars of the 1930's and 40's celebrated in the Coconut Grove, and where Senator Robert F. Kennedy was gunned down by an assassin in 1968.

doxy   *DAHK see*
a woman of low morals, specifically a prostitute or mistress: obsolete British slang

The playwright's third character is Janet, a doxy from Illinois who arrives at the cafe one night on her way to seek stardom in Hollywood, but ends up staying as a waitress.

doyenne   *daw YEN*
the senior member, or dean, of a group, especially one regarded as an authority because of superior knowledge and long experience; the masculine equivalent is doyen

For those who wish they could be Martha Stewart, now at least they can own a piece of her company. Ms. Stewart, the doyenne of domestic details, plans to sell $100 million in stock in her company, Martha Stewart Living Omnimedia Inc., according to documents filed yesterday with the Securities and Exchange Commission.

draconian   *dray KOH nee uhn*
extremely severe or cruel

In 1784, Benjamin Franklin, then the American Ambassador to France, calculated that because Parisians liked to stay up late and sleep mornings, they burned 64,050,000 needless candles each summer, at a cost of $19 million. His proposal was draconian: "In the mornings, as soon as the sun rises, let all the bells in every church be set ringing. If that is not sufficient, let cannons be fired in every street to wake the sluggards effectively."

✦ Draco, a seventh-century B.C. Athenian statesman, drew up a code of laws in 621 B.C., nearly every violation of which was punishable by death, even petty theft and laziness. Hence, his name has become synonymous with harsh and merciless laws. Draco was the first to put Greek laws into writing, but those he chose to codify were, for the most part, the ones that benefited the rich and powerful.

dry   *drigh*
humorously intended, but said matter-of-factly

Sipping orange juice, the Prince of Wales stood studying a modernistic bronze sculpture titled "Icarus" at the National Air and Space Museum. Finally, he turned away from the oddly misshapen work of art. "I'd love to have seen it," he remarked drily, "before it melted."

ducal   *DOO: kuhl*
in the fashion of a duke; condescending; imperious

Interviewed on television, Mr. Chirac displayed the ducal manner toward journalists that, to one degree or another, all the candidates use. He repeatedly informed his principal questioner when it was time to change the subject, and at one point, sensing resistance, scolded him for impoliteness.

dumbfounded   *duhm FOWN did*
made speechless through shock, amazement or astonishment

"Harvey's mother explained that the only bed available was Harvey's and he was in it. The young lady agreed to sleep with Harvey and got in bed with him. When Harvey, who was about 14 years old, awoke and saw this voluptuous blonde next to him, he was dumbfounded. The blonde opened one eye and said: 'Don't worry, young man, I won't hurt you.'"

dun   *duhn*
to ask a debtor insistently or repeatedly for payment

Many of the former students who are being dunned by the Federal Government for unpaid student loans in southern Ohio are making the same plea that brought them to the student loan officer in the first place—they don't have the money.

E

epitome

Escoffier thought strawberries a sufficiently royal delicacy to
name a dessert he invented—strawberries macerated in

orange juice and curacao, served in a crystal

bowl with creme chantilly—after the

Russian royal family, the Romanovs.

In England, brimming bowls of

strawberries during the Wimbledon tennis matches still

epitomize the summer social season.

see page 129

earmark   *EER mahrk*
to set aside or reserve for a special purpose or recipient

New York's lottery was started in the early 1970's. The state keeps 45 percent of the sales from the lottery as revenue, which state officials say is earmarked for education. Forty percent is paid out in prizes, and the remainder is used to pay for administration.

ebullient   *i BUH lyuhnt*
overflowing with enthusiasm or high spirits; exuberant

The versatile talents of Leonard Bernstein were omnipresent during the Lincoln Center Chamber Music Society's final Haydn-Stravinsky concert, held in Alice Tully Hall on Sunday night. His ebullient musical presence as both conductor and pianist gave the occasion a distinctly buoyant character—as Stravinsky himself reportedly remarked after hearing his "Rite of Spring" conducted by Mr. Bernstein: "Wow!"

ecclesiastical   *uh KLEE zee AS ti kuhl*
relating to the church or the clergy

A United Methodist Church minister in Chicago was suspended after being found guilty yesterday of breaking church law by having blessed the union of two gay men, in an ecclesiastical trial that drew national attention to an increasingly controversial issue among many Protestants.

echelon   *E shuh lahn*
a level of command, authority or rank

Adri, the sportswear designer who has always had her special following, has catapulted into the top echelon of fashion makers.

eclectic   *i KLEK tik*
composed of material or ideas gathered from a variety of sources

Live artillery shells, a dead sea turtle half the size of a Volkswagen Beetle, a drowned giraffe, antique crockery, pocketbooks, chemical sludge, raw sewage and about 5,000 cords of driftwood a year—the waters of New York Harbor yield a strange and eclectic bounty.

✦ A cord is 128 cubic feet of wood cut for fuel, and usually arranged in a pile 8 feet long, 4 feet wide and 4 feet high.

eclipse   *i KLIPS*
to overshadow or make dim by comparison

The brief remarks of a mother whose daughter had been murdered eclipsed speeches by politicians and officials at a City Hall ceremony yesterday marking the opening of National Victim Rights Week. "It is not just the pain of losing a loved one," Diana Montenegro said. "I buried my daughter, but I cannot bury my anger and my pain. Time and again we see short-term sentences given to the criminals while we, the victims, serve lifetime sentences of fear, grief and violation."

efficacy   *E fi kuh see*
power to produce effects or intended results; effectiveness

Dr. Peter J. Hauri, director of the sleep disorders center at Dartmouth Medical School, says that while most sleeping pills "are initially effective, most lose efficacy when used chronically."

egalitarian   *i gal uh TAIR ee uhn*
treating or considering all classes of people as equals

An organization called Parents for Public Schools, with a membership of 1,000 whites, was formed 18 months ago. Its president is a businessman, Walter Smiley, who has two children in public elementary schools, and who says: "I'm not a liberal. I don't think I'm anything unusual. I'm not egalitarian in the sense that you can take my money and give it to somebody else, but I'm egalitarian about the first grade. I think they're all alike at that age, and they all deserve the same chance."

egregious   *uh GREE jis*
outstandingly bad: Latin, standing out from the herd

In an atmosphere of sober formality, the impeachment trial of President William Jefferson Clinton began in earnest today in the United States Senate, with the Republican prosecution asserting that he should be removed from office because of "egregious and criminal conduct." "No man is above the law and no man is below it," said Representative F. James Sensenbrenner Jr. of Wisconsin a few moments after the gavel fell, quoting President Theodore Roosevelt.

elect   *i LEKT*
persons belonging to a specially privileged group

Watching various reviewers trying to avoid saying anything unkind about Kurt Vonnegut's new book, "Palm Sunday," one realizes that, contrary to public opinion, a literary reputation is the hardest thing in the world to lose. Once among the elect, a novelist is as difficult to impeach as a President. Again and again, he is given the benefit of the doubt, and since literary criticism is such a doubtful business, this is all the margin he needs.

elephantine   *EL uh fuhn teen*
huge; ponderous; clumsy

Rhododendrons grow rapidly, and the longer they grow without discipline, the larger they get. Sometimes these evergreen shrubs become elephantine and block light from the front windows of a house or dwarf everything else in the garden.

elicit   *i LI sit*
to draw forth; evoke

Some of the hunger strikers have elicited pledges from their families not to order food or medical treatment in their behalf after they lose consciousness in the final stages as death nears.

elliptical   *uh LIP tuh kuhl*
in the shape of an elongated circle; an oval having both ends alike

Kepler's discoveries that planetary orbits were elliptical and that planets speed up when they get closer to the Sun laid the groundwork for Sir Isaac Newton's theory of gravity a half-century later.

omitting a word or words to avoid directness; ambiguous; unclear

When Prime Minister Paavo Lipponen delivered a report on Finland's security and defense policy to Parliament on Monday, his wording about Finland's relationship to NATO was far more elliptical than it was two years ago. He spoke of a "military alliance," but avoided the word NATO. He omitted the word "reconsider" and said, "Military alignment is always a question that has to be evaluated as a part of the whole security policy."

elusive   *i LOO: siv*
difficult to find or locate; avoiding, or seeming to avoid, being found; evasive

Officials of the World Wildlife Fund, which has sought to preserve the giant panda in the mountains of China and the humpbacked whale in the seas off Hawaii, visited the lost colony of the rare and elusive prairie sphinx moth today at a secret site on the high plains of northeastern Colorado.

PHILADELPHIA, Jan. 31—It was a day like hundreds that had gone before in the life of Debra Adams. Along snow-banked streets, she tramped from door to door, from store to store, seeking the elusive warmth of a smile and two words that she had not heard for more than two years: "You're hired."

emancipated   *i MAN suh pay tid*
released legally from control and supervision

Now 17, Mr. Brown is legally emancipated from his parents. His mother, who has a drinking problem, lives in a small town in upstate New York, Mr. Brown said, and his father works in Saudi Arabia for an oil company.

embargo   *im BAHR goh*
a prohibition of trade in a particular commodity

The Carter Administration made a point of going beyond the requirements of the United Nations embargo on arms sales to South Africa, ruling out the sale of equipment of any description to the armed forces or the police.

embellish   *im BE lish*
to beautify through ornamentation or adornment

Instrumental music of the late Renaissance tends to be fairly simple and straightforward compared with the more complex vocal forms of the period, and its primary purpose was to entertain or add embellishment to ceremonial events.

emblematic   *em bluh MA tik*
representing something else; serving as an emblem; symbolic

In front of a red backdrop on a brightly lit stage, everything is emblematic: a small red flag represents a chariot, two chairs become a bed chamber.

emeritus   *uh ME ruh tis*
retired from active service, usually for age, but retaining one's rank or title

Harrison R. Steeves, professor emeritus of English at Columbia College, where for many years he had been chairman of the English department, died Saturday at his home in Kingston, R.I. He was 100 years old. Professor Steeves was an impressive and highly respected figure at Columbia, where he had been on the faculty from 1905 until his retirement in 1949.

eminence grise   *ay mee nahs GREEZ*
a person who wields great power and influence secretly, unofficially or behind the scenes; the power behind the throne; often used incorrectly for anyone in charge: French, gray eminence

Oded Aboodi has two visiting cards. The first describes him as chairman of the investment firm Alpine Capital Group. The second identifies him as an employee of Time Warner. Both can be ignored. Mr. Aboodi's real role is to act as the eminence grise for Steven J. Ross, the ailing chairman of the world's largest media and entertainment company. Despite having no formal title at Time Warner, Mr. Aboodi leads negotiations, structures important deals and offers financial advice.

✦ Cardinal Richelieu (1585-1842), Louis XIII's chief minister, had the French king completely under his control, actually directing the foreign and domestic policies of France. From the title given cardinals and the color of his robe, Richelieu was known as *L'Eminence Rouge*, red eminence. The power behind Richelieu, however, was said to be his secretary, a Capuchin monk named Père Joseph, from whose gray attire arose *his* nickname, *L'Eminence Grise*, gray eminence.

emulate   *EH myuh layt*
to try, often by imitating or copying; to equal or surpass

Correction: An article in the House & Home section on Oct. 29 about home improvement experts who are seeking to emulate the success of Martha

Stewart in publishing and on television misidentified one who plans to start a magazine within a year. She is Barbara Smith, not Chris Casson Madden.

enclave   EN klayv
a minority culture group living as an entity within a larger group

ISELIN, N.J., Nov. 22—On a crisp November Sunday, Oak Tree Road here was the picture of a thriving South Asian immigrant enclave. The windows of gold jewelers sparkled with 22-karat necklaces. Shoppers went in and out of the markets, arms loaded with sacks of vegetables and spices from home.

a distinctly bounded area enclosed within a larger area

Mr. Kaplan is one of millions of elderly people in Florida and one of about 15,000 residing in the Century Village retirement community, one of the scores of Florida's sprawling, sunwashed enclaves designed for living out the golden years.

encroach   in KROHCH
to intrude by gradual steps upon another's domain

Half of the world's 6,000 languages are considered by linguists to be endangered. These are the languages spoken by small societies that are dwindling with the encroachment of larger, more dynamic cultures. Young people feel economic pressure to learn only the language of the dominant culture, and as the older people die, the non-written language vanishes, unlike languages with a history of writing, like Latin.

endemic   en DE mik
constantly present in a particular area

Colombia's endemic poverty made the disaster even worse. Buildings made of decaying cement and cinderblock were no match for the might of the quake. Only the northern section of Armenia, where the wealthy live, was left largely intact. Here, authorities set up headquarters for the relief effort.

endow   in DOW
to provide with some talent, quality, etc.

A visitor to my vegetable garden might wonder why two-thirds of it is given over to Hubbard squash, butternut squash, potatoes and tomatoes. I grow those particular squashes because nature endows them with a protective rind that keeps them good in a cool, walled-off part of the cellar most of the winter.

endowment   *in DOW muhnt*
a bequest or gift that provides an income for an institution or person

The Richard Rodgers Production Award was set up in 1978 with a $1 million endowment from the composer to bring the work of promising new composers and librettists to the New York stage. The award, which comes from income generated by the endowment, is turned over to the theater producing the winning musical.

engulf   *in GUHLF*
to swallow up; overwhelm

CARTAGENA, Colombia, July 6—Pope John Paul II knelt today before a bare cement cross planted in the desolate sea of dried mud that was once the town of Armero and prayed that "through the solidarity, work and willpower of the people of this land, there should arise, as if out of the ashes, a new city." A vast expanse of soil covers virtually all of the once-prosperous market town, which was engulfed eight months ago by a huge avalanche of water, ice and gravel after the eruption of the Nevado del Ruiz volcano.

enhance   *in HANS*
to raise to a higher degree

Early in his presidency, Mr. Sadat enhanced his popularity by eliminating many of the police-state controls that Nasser had relied on to keep himself in power in the years after the officers' revolt that brought down the monarchy in 1952.

enigma   *i NIG muh*
a perplexing, baffling or seemingly inexplicable matter

In some ways, Mr. Agca remains as much an enigma as when bystanders grabbed him moments after two bullets struck the Pope. The suspect's precise motives, beyond a distaste for authority and a desire to shock, are not clear. It is not known how he paid for his extensive travels, although there are hints that the money may have come from drug sales or from robberies.

enigmatic   *e nig MA tik*
perplexing; baffling

SUNSPOT, N.M.—Astronomers have found that the sun is ringing like a bell, reverberating in a manner that enables scientists at this solar research community near Alamogordo to explore for the first time the interior of that enigmatic star.

> ✦ Is there a music of the spheres? Yes, according to Pythagoras, the sixth-century B.C. Greek philosopher and mathematician. From his knowledge that the pitch of notes depends on the speed of vibrations, and that the planets rotate at different speeds, he concluded that each planet must make its own sound. And, he reasoned, since all things in nature are harmoniously made, the sounds made by the rotating planets must harmonize.

enmity   *EN muh tee*
the bitter attitude or feelings of an enemy or of mutual enemies; a strong, settled feeling of hatred, whether displayed or concealed

The enmity between the Croatians and the Yugoslav Government is long-standing. It dates to 1918, when the Austro-Hungarian Empire was broken up and Croatia became part of Yugoslavia.

ennoble   *i NOH buhl*
to give a noble quality to; dignify

Philosophers have sometimes suggested that pain is ennobling to the human spirit. However, it is safe to say that most of those who share this view in the abstract would seek relief in the face of actual pain.

ensconced   *en SKAHNST*
placed or settled comfortably, snugly or securely

Trevor Howard and Celia Johnson. Rarely have two names been so inextricably linked by a single production, in this case a film. "Brief Encounter" was made in 1945 and its Noel Coward story of bittersweet love in a suburban English railway station has ensconced itself in the "Casablanca" category of movie classics.

entice *in TIGHS*
to attract by offering hope of reward or pleasure; tempt

> LITTLE ROCK, Ark., Sept. 12—This city's boosters have just made a film designed to entice industry here. Entitled "One in a Million," it is a handsomely mounted 17 and a half minutes of fresh-faced Southerners at work and at play in central Arkansas.

entomologist *en tuh MAH luh jist*
a zoologist who specializes in the study of insects

> Though it may seem like a sick joke to those whose vacations are now being ruined by the persistent and painful bites of black flies, Edward Cupp, an entomologist at Cornell University, spent five years and about $150,000 figuring out how to mass-breed the pesky creatures in his laboratory.

entrenched *in TRENCHT*
securely or solidly established

> Hawaii is no stranger to monopolies. This former island kingdom is still a place where a handful of landlords own vast tracts, where entrenched business interests dominate civic affairs and where the Democratic Party, which has held sway since statehood, controls the governorship, the entire Congressional delegation and roughly 80 percent of the Legislature.

entrepreneur *ahn truh pruh NOOR*
a person who organizes and manages a business undertaking, assuming the risk for the sake of the profit

> But Cincinnati missed what may have been its biggest economic opportunity. At the turn of the last century, it was the world's biggest manufacturer of carriages; when a couple of entrepreneurs named Henry Ford and J. W. Packard came looking for capital to start their auto factories, the local bankers turned them down. So they went to Detroit instead.

environs *in VIGH ruhnz*
the districts surrounding a town or city; suburbs or outskirts; surrounding area; vicinity

> Everyone agrees that loss of the commuter trains would be a heavy blow to Philadelphia and its environs. The trains run on 13 lines fanning out like

veins in a maple leaf to the north and northwest, with two extending like a split stem to the south and southwest.

ephemeral   *uh FE muh ruhl*
short-lived; transitory

Visiting a remote lake for a few days is something like glimpsing the face of a lovely woman in a crowd: the encounter, albeit ephemeral, quickens the heart with wonder and delight.

Television, for all its awesome reach, has an ephemeral touch. Even the best programs rarely leave footprints in libraries, archives, indexes or books. It is harder to retrieve the transcript of a documentary seen by millions than to unearth an obscure magazine article read by thousands.

epicenter   *EP i sen ter*
a focal or central point: usually, a geological term, meaning the point on the earth's surface directly above the focus of an earthquake from which the shock waves radiate

For the French, who have made Cannes the epicenter of the film world for two weeks every year, there is new competition from the American Film Market in Los Angeles, a similar film festival.

epicure   *E pi kyoor*
a person who enjoys and has a discriminating taste for fine foods and drinks

There is also, for the first time since 1975, a hunting season for American brant on the East Coast. These small geese—an epicure's delight if the birds have been eating the right fare—nest farther north than do the Canada, snow or blue geese.

> ✦ The Greek philosopher Epicurus (c. 341-247 B. C.) taught that the goal of women and men should be a life of quiet pleasure, governed by self-discipline, morality and cultural development. One of the meanings of epicure that has come down to us—someone devoted to luxury and sensual pleasure—is, therefore, a gross distortion of what Epicurus taught.

epigram   *E puh gram*
a short poem with a witty or satirical point, or any terse, witty, pointed statement

OAKLAND, Calif., Jan. 26—The story is told that Gertrude Stein, who spent her girlhood in Oakland, once said that the problem with Oakland was, "When you get there, there isn't any THERE there." Like most such acid-etched epigrams, the assessment is more clever than true.

epilogue   *E puh lahg*
a closing section added to a novel, play, etc., providing further comment, interpretation or information

In a strange epilogue to the suicide last December of the novelist Romain Gary, a relative of Mr. Gary's, Paul Pavlowitch, says in a new book that Mr. Gary was the author of a 1975 Goncourt Prize-winning novel attributed to a writer named Emile Ajar.

epiphany   *uh PI fuh nee*
a realization that changes one's life; a moment of sudden intuitive understanding; a flash of insight; originally, an appearance of some divine being

Mr. Riese was born in Harlem. A high school dropout, he and his brother went to work as dishwashers in 1936. By 1940, they had scraped together the $500 down payment for an $8,500 luncheonette at 15 East 40th Street. When they sold it four years later for $38,000, including a $10,000 cash payment, Mr. Riese had an epiphany: "Why sell a sandwich for a 10-cents profit when you can sell a restaurant for $10,000?"

epithet   *E puh thet*
an abusive or contemptuous word or phrase used to describe a person

Of all the scornful epithets hurled at Government regulators in recent years, none was more telling than "national nanny." Don't drink saccharin, you'll probably get cancer. Don't eat candy bars in school, you need your vitamins. Be careful of sugared cereal, it may cause cavities. Nanny knows best.

epitome   *uh PI tuh mee*
the ideal expression of something; the perfect representation of a whole class

The Hindenburg was the epitome of 1930's luxury; passengers rode in state-rooms equipped with beds, desks and washstands, and they dined at tables overlooking picture windows, under which whales and icebergs floated past, only a few hundred feet below the zeppelin. Passengers could even sing to the accompaniment of an aluminum grand piano.

Escoffier thought strawberries a sufficiently royal delicacy to name a dessert he invented—strawberries macerated in orange juice and curacao, served in a crystal bowl with creme chantilly—after the Russian royal family, the Romanovs. In England, brimming bowls of strawberries during the Wimbledon tennis matches still epitomize the summer social season.

> ✦ Georges-Auguste Escoffier (1846-1935) was chef to the staff of Napoleon III in the Franco-Prussian War. He gained an international reputation in London after the war as chef at the Carlton and Savoy hotels. At the Savoy he invented peach Melba for the opera singer Dame Nellie Melba. (The singer, born Helen Porter Mitchell, took the name Melba from her birthplace of Melbourne, Australia.) The dessert is made with poached peach halves, vanilla ice cream and raspberry sauce.

equanimity   *ee kwuh NI muh tee*
the quality of remaining calm and undisturbed; evenness of mind and temper; composure

Professor Cunningham said that when he lectures in parishes and someone in his audience raises the subject of hell, he replies that the church believes that it means estrangement from God, just as heaven is the ultimate union with God, rather than a geographical location. "That reflection is taken with great equanimity," he said. "It's not like it shocks people terribly."

equivocal   *i KWI vuh kuhl*
uncertain; undecided

Many doctors use many drugs for uses that are not approved by the Food and Drug Administration. Many times those uses are being investigated and are later approved. However, in many other cases, scientific proof of efficacy is equivocal or lacking.

ergonomics   *er guh NAH miks*
the study of the problems of people in adjusting to their environment, especially the science that seeks to adapt work or working conditions to suit the worker

Ergonomic chairs, which have proliferated in Germany in the last few years, are meant to conform and adjust to the sitter's body on the job. They have pneumatic and hydraulic mechanisms, operated by levers or buttons, that adjust the backs and seats to varying heights and angles; their signature is usually a five-pronged base and a molded back.

errant   E rint
erring or straying from the right course or from what is right

When NATO bombed residential areas of Belgrade for the first time early this morning, two errant missiles, meant for military office buildings, hit houses instead. Dejan Filipovic, 26, was in his upstairs bedroom on Miruliceva Street when a missile nearly blew him out of the window.

erratic   i RA tik
having no fixed course; irregular; wandering; unpredictable

According to several witnesses, the Acura was driving erratically when it drove up a grassy median, hurtled through the air and landed on the north-bound side of the roadway near 100th Street.

ersatz   ER zahts
a substitute, especially an inferior imitation; artificial

Many of the restaurants on Monterey Bay are seeking to convince customers that squid, when flattened, tenderized, breaded and sautéed, tastes very much like abalone. To purists the ersatz abalone is not like the real thing, having a more "fishy" flavor.

erudite   ER yoo: dight
having or showing wide knowledge gained from reading; learned; scholarly

Lincoln Kirstein, a co-founder of the New York City Ballet and a visionary who never wavered in his belief that ballet could flourish in America, died yesterday at his home in Manhattan. He was 88. A poet, novelist, historian, art collector and critic, the erudite Mr. Kirstein was an expert in many fields. But it was as a ballet director that he made his greatest contributions to American culture.

escalate   E skuh layt
to grow or increase rapidly, often to the point of becoming unmanageable, as prices or wages

Quilts, which have been in revival since the early 1960's, have escalated in price at an astounding rate in recent years. Last November an appliquéd and trapunto cotton quilt awash with flowers, stitched probably in Pennsylvania around 1850, sold at Sotheby Parke Bernet's York Avenue galleries for

$7,750, the auction record for a quilt—five times the price paid for such bedcoverings a decade ago.

eschew   *es CHOO:*
to take conspicuous care to avoid; shun

Though Mr. Scheinman spent years on Wall Street he never looked the part, eschewing pinstripes for turtlenecks and cowboy boots and, in later life, drawing his graying hair back into a ponytail.

esoteric   *e suh TE rik*
understood by or meant for only the select few who have special knowledge or interest

The language gap is not too serious if one orders from the standard menu, but it results in considerable frustration for those who want to try more esoteric specialties offered only on the Japanese menu.

espouse   *i SPOWZ*
to embrace, support or advocate a cause, idea, etc.

The Moral Majority is a Christian fundamentalist political movement founded in 1979 by a television evangelist, the Rev. Jerry Falwell. It espouses conservative views on a wide range of social, religious and political issues and has lobbied against the proposed equal rights amendment, abortion and civil rights for homosexuals.

ethereal   *i THI ree uhl*
delicate; heavenly; sublime; exquisite: Greek, like the heavens

The patisserie and cafe closed six years ago in a rent dispute. On the day it reopened this month in the same space, I hurried to see whether Mr. Pascal was still making his fantasy dessert, Le Delice cake, an ethereal combination of ganache, chocolate mousse, coffee butter cream, creme chantilly and toasted almonds piled between layers of almond meringue.

ethnic stew   *ETH nik STOO:*
a mixture of ethnic groups living within a particular boundary: it implies the harmonious coexistence of groups that maintain their separate identities, and is replacing the term "melting pot," which suggests assimilation or a loss of separate identities

In the ethnic stew of New York, the Eskimo flavor has been lacking. Now the Eskimo, represented by art rather than in person, has a center in town, the Alaska Shop, a gallery at 31 East 74th Street that sells and exhibits objects made in northern Canada and Alaska.

eulogy *YOO: luh jee*
a formal speech praising a person who has recently died

At a funeral service yesterday attended by 500 people, including notables from the literary and theatrical worlds, Paddy Chayefsky, who died Saturday at the age of 58, was eulogized as a family man and friend, and as a writer who used his pen with passion to expose the injustices of ordinary life.

euphemism *YOO: fuh mi zuhm*
a mild or inoffensive word substituted for one that is more direct or blunt

One of the things that persuaded Mr. Matthau to do the film was his respect for the play. "When you left the theater after seeing 'First Monday,' you felt good because you hadn't been taken. That play isn't escapist entertainment. 'Escapist entertainment,' by the way, is a euphemism for junk."

euphonious *yoo: FOH nee is*
melodious; pleasant sounding

Some scholars say the euphonious quality of Irish names makes them song-like. It has become so common for American parents to use Irish last names like Ryan, Shannon and Kelly for their children's first names that a Harvard researcher is studying the trend.

evanescent *e vuh NE suhnt*
fading as quickly as it appears; transitory; short-lived; ephemeral: Latin, e, out + vanescere, to vanish

Every July, in northern Westchester County and dozens of other places around North America, hordes of butterfly lovers fan out to spend a day counting species and individuals of the insect families that start life as creepy caterpillars, but then, often for just a week or two, transform into evanescent winged wonders, seeking nectar and mates before expiring.

evocative *uh VAH kuh tiv*
vivid and seemingly realistic, as in the artistic representation of a particular time or place

MIDNIGHT (55) * CROSS CREEK (1983) Mary Steenburgen, Rip Torn, Peter Coyote. Atmospheric, beautifully evocative drama of Florida writer Marjorie Kinnan Rawlings in backwoods. (PG) (2hrs.)

exacerbate *eks A ser bayt*
to intensify; aggravate

Paul Auster's novel "City of Glass" is set in a cold, forlorn New York. But his sense of the city is more complex. He takes great pleasure in the fleeting encounters that occur on subway platforms, in bank lines and in Laundromats. "New York is a weirdly friendly town and I always find myself having conversations with complete strangers," said Mr. Auster, who lives in Brooklyn. "On the other hand, if you're feeling lost and alone, the city can exacerbate your loneliness."

excise *ik SIGHZ*
to remove by cutting out

The new version of "Trade Wind" consists of the original opening chapter as well as several other chapters that were excised in the earlier version.

execrable *ek SE kruh buhl*
abominable; detestable; very inferior; of poorest quality

Serious tasters smell a group of wines several times before actually tasting them, and only rarely does tasting change their opinions. And that's the secret to getting through an important tasting in which the quality of the wines can range from superb to execrable. Plenty of wines need not be tasted at all: they can be eliminated by smell alone.

exegesis *ek suh JEE sis*
an explanation, critical analysis or interpretation of a word, work of art or literary passage, especially of the Bible

Mr. Johnson recalled how Mr. Barr had persuaded the Modern's collections committee to buy a triptych of Marilyn Monroe, painted by James Gill. "He was intensely interested in the Monroe mythology, the symbolism," Mr. Johnson said. "He harked back to Aphrodite and even the White Goddess. By the time he finished his exegesis, there wasn't a dry eye in the house."

✦ A triptych (Greek, three folds) is a set of three panels with pictures, designs or carvings, often hinged so that the two side panels may be folded over the central one. Triptychs are usually religious in nature and often used as altarpieces.

exemplar   *ig ZEM plahr*
a model worthy of imitation

Bob Marley, who had become the world's best-known reggae artist before his death this year, was more than a leading pop songwriter and musical innovator; in Jamaica, he was looked up to as a spiritual and moral exemplar.

exhume   *ig ZYOO:M*
to dig out of the earth; disinter; bring to light; revive or restore after a period of neglect or forgetting

Twenty-five bodies have been exhumed in Los Angeles and Riverside Counties so far in an investigation into the mysterious deaths of more than 50 patients in five southern California hospitals.

Jose Quintero's unwarranted exhumation of Eugene O'Neill's 1924 "Welded" at the Horace Mann Theater at Columbia University succeeds in proving that this is one of O'Neill's most dreadful plays.

exodus   *EK suh duhs*
a going out; a departure of a large number of people

Shortly after noon, a tremendous exodus takes place during Ramadan in downtown Cairo as people leave for home. By 3 in the afternoon, a street like Kasr el-Nil is as deserted as an old American mining town that went bust. The shops are closed, the restaurants are shuttered, everyone is gone except for clusters of men praying in corners of buildings and sidewalks where they have laid down straw prayer mats.

✦ Ramadan is the Moslem month during which the faithful fast from sunrise to sunset. It is the month when Allah sent down the Koran to earth.

exonerate   *ig ZAH nuh rayt*
to free from a charge of guilt; declare blameless; exculpate

Capt. Alfred Dreyfus, a French army officer, was court-martialed on espionage charges in 1894. He was eventually exonerated, and most historians believe the charges arose because he was Jewish.

exorcise   *EKS awr sighz*
to drive out from within one something that has been troublesome, tormenting or oppressive: originally, to drive an evil spirit out or away by use of a holy name or magic rites

Was young Rudolph Giuliani, at whatever age, beaten up, shoved around, picked on, harassed, humiliated or otherwise bullied by his peers? Was there some terror, some childhood trauma that he has been unable to exorcise, that might help to explain his exceedingly dangerous compulsion, as Mayor of a huge and fractious city, to disdain the role of statesman and rule as a bully himself?

expansionism   *ik SPAN shuhn i zuhm*
the policy of expanding a nation's territory or its sphere of influence, often at the expense of other nations

Answering repeated Greek charges of "Turkey's expansionist aims," the Defense Minister declared, "Since the establishment of the republic, no war has been engaged by Turkey." He said Turkey had no desire to acquire land outside its own territory but would not "give one inch to anybody."

expeditious   *ek spuh DI shuhs*
efficient and speedy; prompt

The sea robin, the various puffers or blowfish, the horned pout or the catfish all present a problem to those preparing them for the table: they have to be skinned, deheaded and gutted in the most expeditious manner possible.

expiate   *EK spee ayt*
to make amends for; atone for

Mr. Speer (the name is pronounced shpair) was the only Nazi leader at the Nuremberg war-crimes trials in 1945-46 to admit his guilt. There were those who thought he spent the rest of his life trying to expiate the horrors of the concentration camps and slave factories, and others who found his memoirs self-serving, showing the pure technician unmoved by human misery.

expletive   *EKS pluh tiv*
an exclamation or oath, especially a profanity or obscenity

McEnroe, the left-hander from Douglaston, Queens, who is seeded second, left England last summer as a hero after having battled Borg in a memorable five-set final. Today, he smashed two racquets, lost two points on penalties, called the umpire, Edward James, an "incompetent fool" and then uttered a four-letter expletive during a final confrontation with Fred Hoyles, the referee.

✦ Among the evidence implicating President Richard M. Nixon criminally in the Watergate scandal that resulted in his resignation from office in 1974 were tapes of conversations he had secretly recorded in the Oval Office. In the publicly-released transcripts of those tapes, the White House replaced the obscenities spoken by the President and others with the parenthesized phrase "expletive deleted." So frequently did "expletive deleted" appear in the transcripts that it became a catch phrase still popular today, used not only in print but in conversation, as when someone says "expletive deleted" rather than uttering an obscenity.

explicit   *ik SPLI sit*
clearly stated and leaving nothing implied; distinctly expressed; definite

Both you and John Updike are longtime New York writers. What is the difference between John Cheever and John Updike? "Well, I'm 20 years older than John. I'll be 67 on May 27. Updike writes far more explicitly about sex, for one thing. Explicit sexual scenes don't particularly interest me. Everybody knows what's going on. I can't think, in the whole history of literature, of an explicit sex scene that was memorable, can you?"

exponent   *eks POH nint*
a person who is an example, type or symbol of something; someone who explains, advocates or represents

Harry Stanley, a vaudevillian turned lecturer who was such a subtle master of philolillogical orotundity and frammatical linguistation that when he got wound up it took a while before it became apparent that nobody had the foggiest idea what he was talking about, died on Feb. 15 at the Actors Fund Home in Englewood, N.J. He was 100 and had been a leading exponent of double talk for the better part of a century.

✦ "But I for one feel that all the basic and sadum tortumise, all the professional getesimus and tortum kimafly will precipitously aggregate so that peace shall reign. I want to make that perfectly clear." [From Mr. Stanley's obituary.]

expound   *ik SPOWND*
to set forth or explain in detail

The Secretary seemed to go out of his way to woo the Western governors, most of whom are Democrats. Wearing a cowboy hat and an open-neck plaid shirt, he expounded on his own Western roots—he grew up on a ranch in Wyoming—and the West's natural beauty. And he paid enthusiastic compliments to the Governors, each of whom he addressed by their first name.

extant   *EK stuhnt*
still existing; not lost or destroyed

The elaborately carved ivory cross, still tentatively attributed to Master Hugo, a lay artist working at the English monastery of Bury St. Edmunds, is considered one of the finest works of medieval art extant.

extemporaneous   *ek stem puh RAY nee uhs*
spoken without preparation; improvised

"Life is unfair," said President John F. Kennedy when asked about the resentment that reservists, who had "done their time," felt about being called up for Vietnam service. In his most philosophical extemporaneous comment, he ruminated aloud: "There is always inequity in life. Some men are killed in a war and some men are wounded, and some men never leave the country. . . . It's very hard in military or personal life to assure complete equality. Life is unfair. . . ."

extol   *ek STOHL*
to praise highly; applaud

Let the meek extol the virtues of mild-mannered cultivated leeks. Real cooks forage for ramps. The leafy, bulbous, aromatic plants, the wild cousins of leeks, sprout in rich forest soil from Canada to Georgia, and as far west as Minnesota. Ramps have more heat and bite than leeks or scallions and, when cooked, a soft nutty taste rarely found in either garlic or onions.

In the 1960's, when gasoline was cheap and high-performance cars ruled the roads, songs were written about Pontiacs. In fact, a tune by Ronnie and the

Daytonas extolling the engine of the Pontiac GTO rose as high as No. 4 on the pop music charts in 1964.

extradite   *EK struh dight*
to turn over an alleged criminal, fugitive, etc. to the jurisdiction of another country, state, etc.

Although his extradition was immediately demanded by the Iranian Government, Mr. Bani-Sadr, 48 years old, will be permitted to stay in France so long as he refrains from political activity.

extricate   *EK stri kayt*
to set free; disentangle

At breakfast, the beautifully bright and fresh grapefruit is so badly cut that fork and knife are needed to extricate the fruit.

exude   *ig ZOO:D*
to send out gradually in drops through pores or small openings; ooze out

This butterfly lays its eggs in the flowers of thyme. The caterpillars feed there for a period, but are then picked up by ants that are attracted by the sweet fluid that the caterpillars exude. They are carried back to the ant's nest, where they complete their development, feeding on the young ant brood while the ants, in turn, feed on the caterpillar secretion.

In addition to skill and steadiness, Winfield, at age 29, exudes a childlike joy in playing and in his own celebrity. He has a contagious, gap-toothed smile, like Magic Johnson's, that television cameramen have learned to zoom in on after he reaches base on a hit or makes an especially satisfying catch.

F

fecund

Just what is it about Shakespeare's work that accounts for

his enduring ability to engage the popular imagination, his

accessibility to so many eras and cultures? The usual

reasons offered for his

greatness—the richness of

his language, the range and

depth of his characterizations, the

fecundity of his imagination—do not explain why he, rather

than, say, Dante or Chaucer, has become and remained a

household name. Nor do paeans to his storytelling gifts:

after all, he lifted most of his plots from pre-existing works.

see page 145

fabrication   *fa bri KAY shuhn*
a falsehood

The Washington Post said today that an article it printed about the life of an 8-year-old heroin addict in the slums of Washington, for which the author won a Pulitzer Prize this week, was a fabrication.

facade   *fuh SAHD*
a superficial appearance or illusion of something; in its literal sense, the front of a building

There was no Joe Louis behind any facade. He was the same slow-spoken, considerate person in a close social group as he was to the vast crowds that surged in on him to clutch his every word when he was at the apogee of the boxing world.

facetious   *fuh SEE shuhs*
not meant to be taken seriously or literally

On a wall of the National Cattlemen's Association office in Denver hangs a bumper sticker urging: SUPPORT BEEF—RUN OVER A CHICKEN! Facetious, of course, but the slogan reflects a new disquiet among America's cattle ranchers and cattle feeders as they struggle to survive in one of the most expensive and risky of farm industries.

fallible   *FA luh buhl*
liable to err or make a mistake

The quality of orchestral playing, both soloistic and ensemble, that Sir Georg Solti drew from the Chicagoans last night at Carnegie Hall was so consistently high that an air of unreality settled over the entire evening. The listener could virtually forget that mundane, fallible instruments and musicians were mediating between him and the music; direct contact of a rare sort was made possible.

fastidious   *fa STI dee uhs*
careful in all details; exacting; meticulous

Parisians, fastidious in many things, do not hesitate to toss their used yellow Metro tickets on the station platforms and corridors.

✦ Paris's subway system is the Metro. So is Moscow's. London's is the Underground. In London, pedestrian passageways under crowded intersections are called subways.

fatalist   *FAY tuh list*
one who accepts every event as inevitable

For three hours the 10 National Guardsmen stationed in the town were pinned inside their barracks by rifle fire as the rebels shot up houses and looted stores. An 11-year-old boy was killed and eight townspeople were wounded. From inside the barracks the soldiers' desperate call for help went unanswered. "We have become used to it," José Osnel Colato, a 25-year-old soldier, said later. "We are all going to die sometime." His was the fatalistic attitude of the Salvadoran peasant, in and out of uniform, for as the world debates the fate of El Salvador it is in small communities such as San Agustin that the brunt of the war is being felt.

fatuous   *FA choo: is*
silly; foolish; complacently stupid or inane: Latin, fatuous, foolish (also the root of infatuation)

"The Prince of Egypt" touches biblical bases from Moses' adoption to his receiving the Ten Commandments and manages to have different personalities for each stage along the way. As a young scamp (with the voice of Val Kilmer), Moses seems dangerously close to the standard-issue Disney adventurer, right down to that fatuous ballad about what to do with his life. ("Here among my trappings and belongings I belong/ And if anybody doubts it, they couldn't be more wrong!") The film works best when it stops relying on easy fluff and lets what is, after all, a mighty strong story, speak for itself.

fawn   *fawn*
to show favor or attention by servile, flattering or obsequious behavior

From the start, the "21" strategy has been to make good customers part of its extended family. Regulars are greeted by name at the door, seated at their usual table and fawned over by their customary waiter.

feckless   *FEK luhs*
weak; ineffective: a clipped form of effectless *through the linguistic process known as apheresis (see* disport *for more examples)*

Although he was dismissed by many as a somewhat feckless interim leader when he became President after the death of Gamal Abdel Nasser, Mr. Sadat gradually showed that he had staying power, political skill and an ability that transformed him into a world statesman when he paid his historic visit to Jerusalem in the search for peace.

fecund   *FEE kuhnd*
fertile; fruitful; prolific

And Mr. Behler said that unlike snapping turtles, which can lay 50 eggs at a time, Egyptian tortoises lay only one egg at a time. "They are not very fecund," he said.

Just what is it about Shakespeare's work that accounts for his enduring ability to engage the popular imagination, his accessibility to so many eras and cultures? The usual reasons offered for his greatness—the richness of his language, the range and depth of his characterizations, the fecundity of his imagination—do not explain why he, rather than, say, Dante or Chaucer has become and remained a household name. Nor do paeans to his storytelling gifts: after all, he lifted most of his plots from pre-existing works.

felicitous   *fuh LI suh tuhs*
aptly chosen; suitable; appropriate

The all-male cast has been felicitously chosen, and what might have passed as stereotypes in a less-sensitive production become fully-fleshed human beings.

festoon   *fe STOO:N*
to adorn by suspending strings of flowers, ribbon, fabric, etc. between two points

In Mr. Buatta's English sitting room, the walls are glazed dark red and the windows majestically festooned with an elaborate curtain. "The special lining is essential," he explained, "but most clients wouldn't pay extra for it." The chintz—a gorgeously rich Chinoiserie pattern with birds, flowers and pagodas—is also used for some of the upholstery. "I'm in my Chinese period," he said.

✦ Chintz is a printed and glazed cotton fabric, usually of bright colors and with flower designs or other patterns. Because of the cheap quality of some chintz fabrics, chintzy came to mean cheap, stingy, petty or gaudy. Chinoiserie is an ornate style of decoration for furniture, textiles, ceramics, etc. based on Chinese motifs.

fiasco   *fi A skoh*
a complete failure, especially an ambitious project that ends as a ridiculous failure

Mr. Silverman's impatience for success at NBC led him to rush series on the air—and then off again at the first hint of ratings failure. The biggest fiasco was "Supertrain." Put on the air six months before its producers felt it was ready, and then extravagantly promoted, the show was a failure. It cost NBC $5 million and Mr. Silverman a lot of credibility.

figuratively   *FI gyuh ruh tiv lee*
not literally or actually, but in a manner of speaking; using an image or exaggeration to make a point

Michael Jordan remains head and shoulders above all the others, figuratively and literally. Not only does he spend much of his time on the court soaring over it, like a capeless Captain Marvel, but when his Chicago Bulls team confronts the barest threat, he nearly singlehandedly takes charge, as he did against Portland in the N.B.A. finals, and for the Olympic team, both of which, to be sure, won the world titles in 1992.

fin de siècle   *fah(n) duh see EK luh*
originally referring to the advanced and modern ideas and customs of the nineteenth century's closing decade in Europe and America, its sense shifted to mean sophisticated, overly elegant and decadent in that era, especially in art, literature and upper- and middle-class social life. (Having experienced our own fin de siècle, it will be interesting to follow the attributes that become associated with it.) French, end of the century.

146

Day trading is, first and foremost, an outgrowth of the almost decade-long bull market in stocks. Because most day traders try to ride stocks that are rising, the practice would be ludicrous if shares were falling. But day trading is much more than a bull-market phenomenon. Indeed, its popularity is very much a fin de siècle happening. Day trading has at its heart two very current American loves: technology and the promise it holds, and the do-it-yourself-investing craze. Who wouldn't like to think that she could beat the professionals at their own game?

finesse   *fi NES*
to avoid by adroit maneuvering; get around

Bertrand Russell was quite certain that his telegrams to Nikita Khrushchev at the time of the Cuban missile crisis managed to finesse World War III.

firebrand   *FIGH er brand*
a person who stirs up others to revolt or strike

A calm and reasoning man, Mr. Wilkins did not avoid the limelight, and Presidents and governors sought his counsel on racial matters. But Mr. Wilkins did avoid both words and deeds that would seem to cast him in the role of a firebrand.

> ✦ The original stage lighting device called the limelight was invented by Thomas Drummond in 1826. Its low heat and brilliant light were produced by the combustion of oxygen and hydrogen on a surface of lime. The limelight's shortcoming was that its powerful beam was limited to only one player or section of the stage at a time. Being in the limelight, then, was to be in full public notice.

fishmonger   *FISH mahng ger*
a dealer in fish

Fish bargains can be found in fishmongers along Ninth Avenue between 38th and 42d Streets, where whole large bluefish big enough to serve four to eight people are selling for 99 cents a pound. They are good wrapped in foil and baked with slices of lime or lemon, garlic, and dill or parsley.

flaccid   *FLAK sid*
soft and limp; flabby

The concluding Brahms Symphony No. 3 was less happily done. Mr. Mehta had the orchestra playing truly; some of the lyrical moments were ravishing. But Brahms is not really about ravishment. His music prospers with more firmness. Mr. Mehta's Brahms Third was a flaccid affair.

flagrant   *FLAY gruhnt*
outrageously glaring, noticeable or evident

Until recent years, banks refused to count working wives' salaries, alimony or child support in establishing credit, and there were many other instances of flagrant sex discrimination in lending.

flak   *flak*
criticism, especially as a widespread reaction to some public action or statement

Cher has taken flak over the years for her husky tone and limited dynamic range, but as she moved through a medley of early hits like "Gypsies, Tramps and Thieves," through 80's ballads like "After All," and into her current neo-disco material, that voice asserted its outstanding qualities. It is a quintessential rock voice: impure, quirky, a fine vehicle for projecting personality. Even the computer manipulations it endures in "Believe" can't make it sound like anyone else's.

> ✦ *Flak* is a World War II German acronym for anti-aircraft gun: *fl(ieger)a(bwehr)k(anone)*. The word was used by all nations in the war for the bursting shells (seen as puffs of smoke) fired from such artillery, whose fragments could pierce nearby aircraft.

flamboyant   *flam BOI int*
overly showy; extravagant

No one ever said Elton John was understated, but the singer may have hit a high note for flamboyance at his 50th birthday celebration in London. His costume was so elaborate that he had to be transported to the 600-guest party at the Hammersmith Palais in a trailer truck decorated to resemble an 18th-century French drawing room, The Times of London reported yesterday. The costume, which cost more than $80,000, included a 15-foot train of white ostrich feathers and a silver wig three and a half feet high, topped with a silver ship under full sail. The singer had to be lowered from the truck with a pneumatic lift. At the party he was seated on a golden throne.

fledgling　　*FLEJ ling*
just getting started; almost ready to take flight, as a baby bird would be

Producing opera is a notoriously expensive undertaking. The biggest budget item, especially for smaller companies, is hiring union orchestra musicians for rehearsals and performances. Many fledgling companies have been sunk by the expense.

flotsam and jetsam　　*FLAHT suhm and JET suhm*
the wreckage of a ship or its cargo found floating on the sea or washed ashore: specifically, flotsam is goods found floating on the sea, and jetsam is cargo thrown overboard to lighten a ship in danger

In addition to the Columbia, there are 1,156 other spacecraft orbiting the earth, as well as 3,419 pieces of debris, including spent rocket bodies, nuts, bolts—the flotsam and jetsam of space shots conducted not just by the United States and the Soviet Union, but by everybody else, too.

fluke　　*floo:k*
a result, especially a successful one, brought about by accident; stroke of luck: a slang word

Mr. Moriarty's entry into the fireworks business at age 15 was a fluke. When the government began auctioning off the belongings of interned Japanese-Americans during World War II in Washington State, Mr. Moriarty bid $15 for what he thought was a handful of fireworks. To his surprise, however, the $15 purchased an entire truckload.

flux　　*fluhks*
continuous change

New York often seems a city in perpetual flux, with change the only constant. One morning, with a small belch of explosives and a puff of plaster dust, the building around the corner is reduced from a sum to its parts. The next day, the grocery down the street becomes a gourmet shop. Once thriving businesses are abandoned. Abandoned buildings are transformed into cooperative lofts.

foible　　*FOI buhl*
a minor weakness or failing of character

According to its producers, the difference between "Another Life" and major network soap operas is that the new serial will have an underlying religious theme and present positive answers to moral perplexities. Otherwise, viewers can look forward to the usual array of human foibles and miseries.

foment *foh MENT*
to stir up; instigate; incite

Bosnia's media, especially radio and television, hold a particular place of infamy in that country. Broadcast propaganda helped foment the ethnic hatred that led to war, and today it is impeding peace and reconciliation.

forage *FAW rij*
to search for food; to feed

Left on their own after their mothers are killed, usually in an illegal hunt or sometimes by a passing truck on a remote highway, young bears will almost surely die, because they cannot forage or otherwise fend for themselves in the first months of life. Some are brought to Ms. Maughan so young that she has to bottle-feed them every two hours.

forebear *FAWR bair*
an ancestor

Diana, a former kindergarten teacher whose forebears include the first Duke of Marlborough, is now formally styled Diana, Princess of Wales—not Princess Diana, because only someone born a princess may use that style.

✦ *To forbear* is to avoid or shun: "Remember your diet and forbear the dessert." However, *forbear* is also a variant and acceptable spelling for *forebear*, an ancestor.

formidable *FAWR mi duh buhl*
difficult to surmount or undertake

Obviously, the production problems surrounding "Khovanshchina" are formidable, not the least of which is the fact that Mussorgsky died before orchestrating the opera. What exists is the piano-vocal score with the Fifth Act only sketched in.

forthrightly   FAWRTH right lee
directly; frankly

A musical about Charlie Chaplin, called, forthrightly, "Charlie Chaplin," will open on Broadway next April.

The gate of the tall green bullpen fence in right field in Shea Stadium swung open, and Mike Marshall appeared. Marshall, the Mets' 38-year-old relief pitcher, took one skipping step, like a boy on a lark, and then trotted forthrightly across the outfield to the mound, like a man on a mission.

fractious   FRAK shuhs
hard to manage; unruly; rebellious

In signing the treaty with Israel, Mr. Sadat alienated most of the fractious Arab world, which broke relations with Egypt.

Francophile   FRAYNG kuh fighl
a person who admires or is extremely fond of France, its people, customs, etc.

Comparisons between California wines and French wines inevitably invite howls of protest, often from Francophiles who object to the suggestion that California producers may be capable of making a superior product. No matter how scientific the tasting nor how sophisticated the tasters, a finding that a California wine has vanquished a renowned French wine in a blind competition is always challenged.

fraught   frawt
filled; charged or loaded down

The term black art is fraught with problems. It doesn't describe a style, a period or a fixed set of ideas. It can serve equally well as political statement and sales pitch. It has been used to carve out a valuable power base for artists excluded from the mainstream, but it has also insured that the mainstream continues to flow along without them. All of these factors jostle around in the National Black Fine Art Show, now in its third year. In fact, they are one of the exhibition's chief attractions.

frenetic   fruh NE tik
frantic; frenzied

Pudgy's style is to "work a room." The frenetic comedian, whose other name is Beverly Cardella, stalks the tables of a nightclub, insulting guests in a style somewhat reminiscent of Don Rickles but with less reliance on name calling or criticism of people's appearances.

frisson   *free SAW*
a shudder, tingle or shiver, as of excitement, fear or pleasure

Yesterday's Bill Blass show was supposedly his swan song, though he hasn't officially announced the sale of his business. So, there was a frisson of excitement tinged with nostalgia among the faithful waiting in the Bryant Park tent yesterday morning for what might be his final fashion statement.

fritter   *FRI ter*
to waste bit by bit on petty things, usually used with "away"

Barrymore, his great "Hamlet" behind him, would eventually bring about his own destruction by frittering away his talent and psyche in Hollywood.

frugal   *FROO: guhl*
not wasteful; thrifty; economical

As a bride, a long time ago, I pored over the newspaper advertisements on Thursday and spent most of Friday driving from market to market buying the specials. My husband thought that was so wonderful that he told his mother how frugal I was. It certainly beat staying home and cleaning house.

fruition   *froo: I shuhn*
a coming to fulfillment

Construction of the mall, to be known as Broadway Plaza, would bring to fruition an idea that has been discussed since the early 1970's as a way to revitalize a shabby area.

frumpy   *FRUHM pee*
dull, plain and unfashionably dressed, said of girls or women

Looking doughy and frumpy, wearing a perpetual hit-me expression, Miss Ullmann is cast as a widow who does little but sulk and tremble.

fudge *fuhj*
to refuse to commit oneself or give a direct answer; hedge

What do you call a jazz ensemble that consists of eight to 10 musicians and combines the loose agility of a small combo with the density and firepower of a big band? Jazz musicians and critics have never been sure, and they have usually fudged the issue by referring to such groups as octets, nonets, or tentets, or, more informally, as "little big bands."

furbelows *FER buh lohz*
showy, useless trimming or ornamentation

Dressed in a lavender gown with amazing furbelows and a frumpy bonnet, Mr. Ohno has made himself up like a glittering old hag.

furor *FYOOR or*
uproar; fury; rage

During the post-publication furor over "Lolita," Nabokov himself, who died in 1977, dismissed charges of pornography as "foolish" and called his book "just a story, a fairy tale, as all stories are." He patiently informed another interviewer, "My knowledge of nymphets is purely scholarly, I assure you. In fact, I don't much care for little girls."

> ✦ A nymphet is a sexually precocious young adolescent or preadolescent girl. In *Lolita* (1955), Vladimir Nabokov applied the term to his twelve-year-old title character.

furtive *FER tiv*
done in a stealthy manner to avoid observation; surreptitious

BELA CRKVA, Kosovo, July 5—This ruined little village buried its dead today in a bitter, tearful ceremony. Reburied them, actually. Most of the 64 people laid to their final rest on a sun-baked hilltop this afternoon had been hastily, furtively buried at night by other villagers near where they were reportedly shot dead by Serbian forces early on the morning of March 25, hours after the NATO bombing began.

fusion   *FYOO: zhuhn*
a blend of jazz and rock or other popular musical styles

A few of fusion music's pioneers, the members of the group Weather Report, for example, have continued to make challenging music out of rock, Latin and ethnic rhythms, electronics, and elements of the jazz tradition.

G

gallimaufry

That glorious gallimaufry, the Ringling Brothers and Barnum & Bailey Circus, is back in Madison Square Garden with a spectacle that celebrates the 200th anniversary of circuses in America. The country's first circus was a  one-ring presentation in Philadelphia in April 1793. The show that continues through May 2 at the Garden is a three-ring event, a heartwarming hodgepodge that justifies the traditional billing of "The Greatest Show on Earth." A performance on the morning of March 26 revealed it to be a bold production filled with parades, pageantry, pachyderms and ponies. Lions roared, acrobats soared and clowns and chimpanzees made mischief.

see page 157

gaffe   *gaf*
a social blunder; faux pas; saying the wrong thing: French, blunder

In foreign commercial dealings, Representative Simon lists these embarrassing gaffes: A major American fountain pen manufacturer inadvertently suggested in Latin American advertisements that its product would prevent unwanted pregnancies; "Body by Fisher" in Flemish came out "Corpse by Fisher"; the first Chinese version of "Come alive with Pepsi" promised that "Pepsi brings your ancestors back from the grave"; Chevrolet's Nova told potential Latin American customers that the car "doesn't go"—"no va."

gall   *gawl*
to irritate; annoy; vex

"All we want is to print the truth," said Witold Slezak, head of the printers' union in Warsaw. "We feel that we have a moral responsibility for the information that we provide to society through our work." This position has led, inevitably, to a clash with the censors, whose heavy red-pencil markings on page proofs have long galled the printers, who were in a position to read the information that was denied to the rest of Poland.

gallimaufry   *ga luh MAW free*
hodgepodge; mixture; medley; jumble: French, a dish made by hashing up odds and ends of food

That glorious gallimaufry, the Ringling Brothers and Barnum & Bailey Circus, is back in Madison Square Garden with a spectacle that celebrates the 200th anniversary of circuses in America. The country's first circus was a one-ring presentation in Philadelphia in April 1793. The show that continues through May 2 at the Garden is a three-ring event, a heartwarming hodgepodge that justifies the traditional billing of "The Greatest Show on Earth." A performance on the morning of March 26 revealed it to be a bold production filled with parades, pageantry, pachyderms and ponies. Lions roared, acrobats soared and clowns and chimpanzees made mischief.

galvanize *GAL vuh nighz*
to arouse to awareness or action; to stimulate as if by electric shock; stir

Nguyen Ngoc Loan, the quick-tempered South Vietnamese national police commander whose impromptu execution of a Viet Cong prisoner on a Saigon street in the Tet offensive of 1968 helped galvanize American public opinion against the war, died on Tuesday at his home in Burke, Va. He was 67 and had operated a pizza parlor in nearby Dale City.

gambol *GAM buhl*
to jump and skip about in play; frolic

In the Northeast, most of those who visit the seashore in summer are there to sail, to gambol in the waves or to lie like slowly ripening squashes in the sun, while, through much of July and August, the surf caster languishes.

gamely *GAYM lee*
in a plucky or courageous manner

"I'm here, I have been all the intervening years," says William Saroyan's entry in "Who's Who in America." Yesterday the 72-year-old author was reported hanging in gamely following a stroke that felled him Monday at his home in Fresno, Calif.

gamut *GA muht*
the entire range or extent

As the latest in a long line of distinguished "Peter and the Wolf" narrators, a group that has run the gamut from Eleanor Roosevelt to David Bowie, Mr. Koch was not to be outdone, and he gave his all to the job.

gargantuan *gahr GAN choo uhn*
of immense size; huge; colossal

The showiest pieces for the gargantuan, fully developed symphony orchestra come from the late 19th century and the early years of our own century.

✦ Gargantua, a giant of medieval legend, was adopted by Francois Rabelais (c. 1494-1553) in his epic satire *Gargantua and Pantagruel*. The giant's most famous attribute was his colossal appetite: 17,913 cows supplied him with milk in his infancy, and in one of his exploits he swallowed five pilgrims in a salad. *Gargantuan* is usually found in reference to someone's appetite. Indeed, the original character got his name from *garganta*, the Spanish word for gullet.

garish   *GAI rish*
gaudy; showy

Some of the best dyed furs around are in the collection by Anne Klein & Company for Michael Forrest. Colors—wine, navy, olive green, mustard— are not garish and very wearable.

garner   *GAHR ner*
to collect or gather

At another bait site, Dr. Lynch pointed to a group of ants that seemed to fear a piece of food they had garnered might be stolen by other species. To prevent this, they had camouflaged the bit of tuna by covering it with forest debris so it would not be recognized by their competitors.

gastronomic   *ga struh NAH mik*
of the art or science of good eating

"Pudding" is a vague term in English gastronomic history, originally applied to sausages and later to desserts wrapped in cloth and boiled. Today, "pudding" can mean desserts in general, or it can mean that category of baked, steamed or boiled gastronomic finale that has ended meals in England since the Middle Ages.

gauche   *gohsh*
lacking social grace; crude; awkward; tactless: French, left [hand]

Mrs. Scherrer, a cool blonde and one of Paris's most elegant hostesses, will as usual be breaking the rules with a buffet where everything can be eaten with fork only and even with one's fingers, considered gauche in French society, where even sandwiches are eaten with a knife and fork.

gazebo   *guh ZEE boh*
a roofed but open-sided pavilion from which one can gaze at the surrounding scenery

The setting is a breeze-swept, seaside gazebo that belongs to a dilapidated tourist guesthouse in Tobago.

gel   *jel*
to become a solidified whole

Adapted from Wim Wenders's 1987 poetic cult film, "Wings of Desire," "City of Angels" tells the story of a droopy sad-sack angel who falls in love with a mortal and in a supernatural leap of faith turns himself into a human who can taste, smell, bleed and, of course, die. So why don't the ingredients gel into a melt-in-your-mouth tear-drenched pudding of palpitating heart and flowers?

> ✦ *Gel* is an example of a back-formation, a word actually formed from, but looking as if it were the base of, another word. In this case, the noun, *gelatin*, came first, and the verb, *gel*, was derived from it. Similarly, while the noun *burglar*, meaning "one who burgles," may seem to be the child of the verb *to burgle*, the opposite is true: *burgle* has been used since the nineteenth century, *burglar* since the sixteenth. Other examples of back-formations are *beg* from *beggar*, *opine* from *opinion*, *enthuse* from *enthusiasm*, *edit* from *editor*, *peddle* from *peddler*, *orate* from *orator*, *reminisce* from *reminiscence*, *gloom* from *gloomy*, *upholster* from *upholsterer* and *peeve* from *peevish*.

gemütlichkeit   *guh MOOT li kight*
having a feeling of warmth and congeniality; coziness: German

Describe an interior as glowing with gemütlichkeit and you summon up images of velvet, lace, painted furniture and antique porcelain stoves. At Vienna '79 warmth and snugness are achieved in a suave, gray modern interior that suggests a smart supper club, Northern European style.

genealogist   *jee nee A luh jist*
a specialist in the field of tracing family histories

A genealogist is on hand to explain that Lady Diana's famous family tree includes everyone from Winston Churchill and Bertrand Russell to Humphrey Bogart and Lillian Gish. The branches have obviously been stretched.

genesis   *JE nuh sis*
origin; beginning

Country clubs, it is easy to forget, had their genesis in the decades after the Civil War, when America discovered organized sport, and a new generation of young men—those with the money and time to be sporting—took to the country to play.

genre   *ZHAHN ruh*
a category or type of literature, such as poetry, novel or short story or, more specifically, mystery, western or science fiction: French. There are also genres in film, painting and other arts.

Traditional British mystery writers remind us that at heart their stories are nothing less than novels, with memorable characters, engaging backgrounds and incidental information conveyed palatably. To place superior mysteries only on the genre shelf is to diminish their value as serious fiction that has the nerve to be fun.

genteel   *jen TEEL*
belonging or suited to polite society

Although their cool three-part harmonies evoke a genteel placidity that is very different in spirit from the emotion-charged gospel-oriented style of most contemporary black groups, the Mills Brothers are regarded as the founders of modern-day black harmony singing.

geriatrics   *je ree A triks*
the study of the physical process and problems of aging

Well past retirement age, Mr. Strunck and Mr. Bayer stay on year after year as their contracts are renewed. And each year, according to their superiors, they defy all the geriatric rules by coming through with steadily higher sales and profits in one of the most keenly competitive areas in retailing.

ghoulish   *GOO: lish*
deriving pleasure from loathsome acts or things

Just what did the voters of Northern Ireland mean by electing an imprisoned nationalist guerrilla to the British Parliament? To some, the victory of Robert

Sands constitutes an endorsement of the Irish Republican Army and its bloody ways. Some bitter-enders may even hope, ghoulishly, that Mr. Sands will persist to the death in his 53-day prison hunger strike. But his death would be a tragedy serving no worthy purpose, and to view his election as a mandate for violence is a shallow distortion.

gingerly   *JIN jer lee*
cautiously, carefully or warily

Though Mr. Kelly, 69 years old, claims he no longer dances, he gingerly executed several steps to the audience's delight.

✦ *Gingerly* has nothing to do with ginger. Its derivation is not precisely known, but it is thought to have originated more than 400 years ago from a French word, *gensour*, meaning delicate or dainty.

glower   *GLOW er*
to stare with sullen anger; scowl

Gossage has long been recognized as the most intimidating late-inning reliever in baseball, with a blazing fastball and a glowering expression that menaces opposing batters. "Hitters always have that fear that one pitch might get away from him and they'll wind up D.O.A. with a tag on their toe," said Rudy May.

gnomic   *NOH mik*
wise and pithy; saying a great deal in a minimum of space

The seven symphonies of Sibelius show us a composer working out his own destiny, nowhere more uncompromisingly than in his terse, gnomic and expressively severe Fourth Symphony.

goad   *gohd*
to prod or urge to action; incite; spur; arouse; egg on

Three years ago, Jim Everett, then the Rams' quarterback, was sitting for a television interview in a studio and the broadcaster, a known provocateur, goaded Everett by calling him "Chris Evert." Everett took umbrage, flipped over a table and pounced on the interviewer and wound up wrinkling both their suits.

gratuitous   *gruh TOO: uh tuhs*
without cause or justification; uncalled for; unwarranted

A spokesman for SmithKline also said that the president of the company, Henry Wendt, wrote to the three networks last month to express concern about the level of "gratuitous violence and sex on primetime shows." SmithKline advertises such products as Contac and Dietac.

gravitate   *GRA vuh tayt*
to be attracted or tend to move toward

Episcopalians tend to gravitate toward professions and the business world, and a significant amount of Episcopal money can be found in the nation's finest museums and universities. But the percentage of Episcopalians actually involved in producing art or pursuing purely intellectual matters does not appear to be anywhere nearly as great as the percentage in business and the professions.

gravity   *GRA vuh tee*
importance; seriousness; earnestness; dignity

But to me, Petrossian offers the ultimate caviar experience. In this dark, hushed cathedral to caviar, solemn waiters approach their work with reverence. There is gravity in the way they take your order and begin setting out the ritual objects—the special spoons and plates for caviar—and even more gravity in the way they carry the caviar in on its silver stand.

gregarious   *gri GAI ree uhs*
fond of the company of others; sociable

Milanov was gregarious. She liked to talk to colleagues on stage during a performance. Here is George London getting ready to pour his soul out in the Nile scene. Just as he starts, Zinka whispers, "How's the baby, George?"

grimace   *gri MAYS*
a twisting or distortion of the face, as in expressing pain, contempt, disgust, etc.

We had dined well, no doubt about that, and on some extraordinary combinations of flavors. There had been, for example, a marriage of baked lobsters with a savory, silken, vanilla-flavored sauce. Lobsters? Vanilla? It would seem to be one of the least compatible flavor liaisons conceivable. If the reflexive reaction to such a dish was a grimace, it was quickly dispelled. The combination not only worked, it was a triumph of taste over logic.

grouse *grows*
to complain; grumble

A lot of people who are busy growing old right now are just going to have to stop it. I lunched the other day with a fellow who spent the hour grousing about how retirement was going to drive him into poverty. It was hard to sympathize with him. "You wouldn't have to retire if you hadn't gone ahead and gotten old," I was tempted to tell him, but didn't.

grudgingly *GRUH jing lee*
with reluctance or unwillingness

LONDON, April 26—The centuries-old English belief that a man's home is his castle was cited here again this month as Britons grudgingly completed their 1981 census forms. "As a nation we don't like it," conceded a spokesman for the Office of Population Censuses and Surveys. "It's simply part of the British character to be suspicious of personal questions."

guffaw *guh FAW*
a loud, coarse burst of laughter

While reading H. L. Mencken, he recalled, he once broke the library calm with loud laughter. It was a Saroyan hallmark: he was frequently ejected from class for guffawing, was removed under guard from a San Francisco courtroom and, to his puzzlement, was shushed by an usher at a performance of James Thurber's "The Male Animal."

guile *gighl*
slyness and cunning in dealing with others; craftiness

The footage of Elvis's early press conferences makes it even more abundantly clear why his fans fell in love with him. In those days, Elvis was so guileless that his every thought registered clearly on his face. When he met with the press, he was trusting and sweet. He grew to be more oddly comfortable with all of these inquisitive strangers, in fact, than he may have been in private. In any case, it must have been easy for his fans to imagine that Elvis was someone they really knew.

guise *gighz*
outward appearance; semblance

Miss Pascoe, an adult actress, with her hair in pigtails and her socks drooping, effectively conceals herself within the guise of an adolescent.

gung-ho   *gung hoh*
enthusiastic, cooperative, enterprising, etc. in an unrestrained, often naïve way

Remembering his rookie year with the Lions, he said: "I was really gung-ho for the team. But a vet took me aside one day and said, 'One day you'll learn. This is a business. A cold business. If you're of no use to them, you're gone.' "

◆ *Gung-ho* was the motto of Lt. Col. Evans F. Carlson's Marine Raiders in World War II. Impressed by the zeal of the Chinese Industrial Cooperatives Society, which he had witnessed in China, Carlson adopted the Chinese name of the group as an example to his men of the spirit and dedication of the Chinese Communists during the war. *Gung-ho* is a shortening, with some linguistic liberties, of the Society's name, which means "work together."

H

harbinger

According to the Kodansha Encyclopedia of Japan, which

covers the nation's culture, the dragonfly was believed in

mythology to be the spirit of the

rice plant and a harbinger of rich

harvests. It was a symbol of the power

of the Yamato court in the eighth

century and was mentioned in later poems set to music.

see page 171

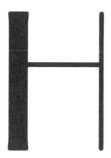

habeas corpus   *HAY bee uhs KAWR puhs*
in law, a writ, or order, requiring that a detained person be brought before a court at a stated time and place to decide the legality of that person's detention or imprisonment. The right of habeas corpus safeguards one against illegal detention or imprisonment: Latin, that you have the body

> With the exception of The Buenos Aires Herald, a small but influential English-language paper, all Argentine papers have steered away from reporting on disappearances and allegations of torture, usually consigning occasional small articles on habeas corpus suits to the back pages.

habitué   *huh BI choo ay*
a person who frequents a particular place: French

> A swing through the museums and galleries just outside New York City can hold a number of happy surprises for even the most sophisticated habitué of the salons of SoHo and upper Madison Avenue, and a day or a weekend in the country may be just the tonic for the late-summer doldrums.

hackneyed   *HAK need*
made trite and commonplace by overuse

> This hackneyed melodrama sets its tone in the first few minutes with talk about home and families being "the heart of this heartland" and about people having a "heavy heart." The heaviest thing about "Heartland" is the burden of the actors and of the audience.

haggard   *HA guhrd*
having a worn look, as from sleeplessness, grief or illness; gaunt

The Yankees straggled off their plane from Chicago at 3:30 A.M. yesterday, and seeing his haggard players, manager Joe Torre canceled last night's batting practice—before the first game of a four-game series against Boston. Don't bother showing up until 6 P.M., he told them. Get some rest.

haggle   *HA guhl*
to argue about terms, price, etc.; bargain; wrangle

Despite the heat, the business of Cairo continues. At the Khan el Khalil, the city's huge maze of stalls and shops that stretches for about two miles, Egyptians in long robes haggle over copper and brass items with tourists in shorts.

halcyon   *HAL see ahn*
calm; peaceful; happy; idyllic: halcyon days are the best of times, the days looked back on with nostalgia

Back in the West's halcyon days, spring 1991, when Saddam Hussein had just been vanquished in the gulf war and Eastern Europe had apparently jettisoned Communism for good, few Americans had even heard of the Serbian leader, Slobodan Milosevic. Mr. Milosevic was cultivating ethnic hatreds and threatening war, but in a seemingly isolated corner of Europe known to few outsiders and apparently of little concern to Washington.

✦ In Greek myth, Halcyone was the daughter of Aeolus, the keeper of the winds. When her husband Ceyx drowned in a shipwreck, the grieving Halcyone threw herself off a cliff into the sea. But as she fell, the gods changed her and Ceyx into kingfishers. Legend says that kingfishers nest upon the ocean's surface, which Aeolus calms during their breeding season.

hallmark   *HAWL mahrk*
a mark or symbol of genuineness or high quality: from the official mark stamped on gold and silver articles at Goldsmith's Hall in London as a guarantee of their purity

Strawberries and raspberries are familiar favorites, but how many Americans know the taste of blackberries, gooseberries and red or black currants? These berries are the hallmarks of a summer in England. There, they are made into unusual ice creams, jellies and pies, or stewed and served with crème fraîche.

◆ Currants are named for Corinth, the Greek island where the dried seedless grapes were originally grown and exported from during the fourteenth century as *raisins de Corauntz*.

hanker   *HANG ker*
to crave, long or yearn for

Compared with other nationalities such as South Americans, who have a hankering for orange drinks, "the American consumer is in love with the cola taste," said Lawrence Adelman, first vice president of Dean Witter Reynolds.

haphazard   *hap HA zerd*
casual, unplanned; random

Still, supervision is so haphazard around the country that fighters not fully recovered from concussions are allowed to box again only a few days later, of course after a physical examination that would approve a corpse. In many cases, to get around the unenforceable rules, they merely have to change their names.

happenstance   *HA pin stans*
a chance or accidental happening

Making perfect iced coffee is an art, not happenstance. Pouring hot coffee over ice cubes just won't do it. The melting ice cubes will quickly dilute the coffee, producing yet another example of bad delicatessen coffee.

harbinger   *HAR bin jer*
a person or thing that comes before to give an indication of what follows, or to announce the approach of a change: in medieval times the harbinger was the person sent ahead of an army or royal party to arrange for its lodging and other comforts

According to the Kodansha Encyclopedia of Japan, which covers the nation's culture, the dragonfly was believed in mythology to be the spirit of the rice plant and a harbinger of rich harvests. It was a symbol of the power of the Yamato court in the eighth century and was mentioned in later poems set to music.

hardscrabble   *HAHRD skra buhl*
providing little in return for much effort: scrabble means to scratch or paw as though looking for something

The Agca family lives a hardscrabble life, as it always has, in the Boztepe, or Gray Hill, area of Malatya, a slum where most of the houses, like theirs, are made of mud bricks and roofed with tile.

haughty   *HAW tee*
having or showing great pride in oneself and disdain or scorn for others; proud; arrogant

In its first year, Ammirati & Puris Inc. took a rather haughty approach for a fledgling advertising agency with no clients whatsoever: It turned down business representing $3 million in billings.

haunt   *hawnt*
a place often visited

"Downtown is dead without the Indians this summer," said Buddy Spitz, manager of the downtown Theatrical Restaurant, a haunt of visiting ballplayers that has been hurt by the strike.

haunting   *HAWN ting*
making a deep, unforgettable impression; not easily forgotten; so deeply affecting as to keep returning to one's mind

One of the most haunting of all war films features only a single casualty, and that of a man who dies in bed. Yet Jean Renoir's classic 1937 "Grand Illusion," an oasis of subtlety, moral intelligence and deep emotion on the cinematic landscape this summer, remains an implicitly devastating indictment of battle.

haute couture   *oht koo TOOR*
the leading designers and creators of new fashions in clothing for women, or their creations; high fashion: French, high sewing

When she took over La Côte Basque, Mrs. Spalter stuck to the Soule traditions and standards, and proved to be a highly competent restaurant operator. She was charming, beautifully dressed and demanding. She wore haute couture dresses at dinner, and refused tables to women who wore pants suits. She explained in an interview that some pants suits had "chic" and others did not, and that she did not want to discriminate between women.

haute cuisine   *oht kwi ZEEN*
the preparation of fine food by highly skilled chefs, or the food so prepared: French, high cooking

Also on the menu is an item called friande, the ultimate marriage of haute cuisine and fast food: a hot dog in puff pastry.

haven   *HAY vin*
a place of safety; refuge; shelter or freedom. Although "safe haven," as it is used in the first entry below, seems a redundancy, it serves to distinguish havens sought for protection (whether from tax collectors or an invading army) from havens having other benefits.

Western diplomats, human rights advocates and Balkans specialists say much of Bosnia has become a virtual safe haven for war crimes suspects, especially southeastern Bosnia, which is under the command of French peacekeeping troops and is a stronghold of the Bosnian Serbs.

Dr. Marvin C. Goldstein, an orthodontist and businessman who defied the segregationist sentiments of the mid-1960's by opening Atlanta's first integrated hotel, died on Saturday at his Atlanta home. He was 80. Dr. Goldstein's hotel, the American, opened in 1964 and became a haven for black people turned away by other establishments and for civil rights workers. Among them was the Rev. Dr. Martin Luther King Jr., who held meetings there with his top aides even before the hotel formally opened.

hawk   *hawk*
to advertise or peddle goods in the street by shouting

Since there is no worldwide patent on Rubik's Cube, it is not surprising to find copies (Wonderful Puzzler, Magic Cube) from Taiwan and Hong Kong replacing "designer" T-shirts as the hottest-selling item on the streets. They are also being hawked on the sands of Coney Island, where, according to one entrepreneur, they are outselling cold beer and inflatable green frogs imprinted with "Kiss Me"; but they are not outselling the hot knishes.

hegira   *hi JIGH ruh*
a journey made for the sake of safety or as an escape; flight: Arabian, to leave,

from the forced journey of Mohammed from Mecca to Medina in A.D. 622, from which the Moslem era dates

In the Northeast, the angler who is unable to spend the time or money for a winter hegira south tries to throttle the lust for angling until March. To overindulge in daydreams of breaking surf or purling mountain streams for months on end is like waiting too long in a crowded bar for one's sweetheart to arrive.

heinous   *HAY nuhs*
outrageously evil or wicked; abominable

On the theory that evil sells, the Pearl Brewing Company of San Antonio began last October to market J.R. Ewing's Private Stock, a beer named for the heinous star of the television show "Dallas." "People today buy an image, not a beer," a brewery official said. He added: "This beer will do well as long as the television show does well."

herculean   *her KYOO: lee uhn*
requiring the strength of a Hercules; calling for great strength, size or courage

"Ready!" shouted the judge, raising his arms to the sky. And the eight thick men in shorts on either side of the long rope thumped down their hiking boots for a foothold and the earth shuddered. "Take the rope!" called the judge. The rope straightened as the 16 heavy hands gripped it. "Toll!" Groans, herculean in depth, rent the air. Muscles strained and bodies swayed in unison. The coach for each team ran up and down the line beside his squad, shouting, urging, hopping, crawling, pleading with his mates to pull with all their heart.

heresy   *HE ruh see*
any opinion opposed to official or established views or doctrines: originally, a religious belief opposed to the orthodox doctrines of a church or the rejection of a belief that is a part of church dogma

Seven members of the Baha'i faith, which Iran's Moslem Shiites consider heretical, were also executed on charges of spying for Israel.

Last month the members of the New York Drama Critics Circle committed what could be taken for an act of theatrical heresy; they elected not to give an award to a "best new musical" of the 1980-81 season.

hermetic   *her ME tik*

completely sealed, especially sealed against the escape or entry of air; sealed off from outside influence or interference: from Hermes Trismegistus, *the Greek name for the Egyptian god Thoth, among whose supposed inventions was a magic seal to make vessels airtight*

Born in Sighet, a small town in the Carpathian mountains of Rumania, Mr. Wiesel grew up in a Hasidic community, studying the Talmud and the mysteries of the cabbala. It was a hermetic life devoted to study and prayer, a life devoted to God.

heterogeneous   *he tuh ruh JEE nee uhs*

composed of unlike or unrelated parts; varied; widely different: the opposite of homogeneous, *meaning similar, identical or uniform*

One of the better-kept secrets of recent art-book publishing has been the appearance of "Marcel Duchamp, Notes" in a bilingual French and English edition. The book consists of a heterogeneous quantity of lately discovered handwritten notes, every last one of which is reproduced in facsimile original size, in as noble a production as any artist could desire.

hiatus   *high AY tuhs*

a break or interruption in the continuity of something; gap

Now, after a hiatus of 28 years, the author of "Cry, the Beloved Country" is waiting with all the anxiety and hopes of a literary unknown for the publication of his first novel since "Too Late the Phalarope."

hinterland   *HIN ter land*

an area far from big cities and towns; back country: German, back land

RISODH, India, April 21—This tiny settlement astride a railway line in Bihar state is typical of India's 850,000 villages, except that it is quite a bit poorer than most. Life here has not changed much since Mohandas K. Gandhi walked India's hinterland, proclaiming the most downtrodden of the poor, the so-called untouchables, to be "the children of God."

◆ *Hinterland* originated with German colonial expansion in the nineteenth century. Although it may now be used to describe any out-of-the-way area, it then referred to the area lying behind an occupied coastal district, which the occupier claimed belonged to it by right of its possessing the coast, even if the inland region was as yet unexplored or unoccupied.

homily   *HAH muh lee*
a sermon, especially one about something in the Bible

ILOILO, The Philippines, Feb. 20—In the region of these islands where the contrast between those who labor in the fields and those who live in luxury is the starkest, Pope John Paul II delivered an impassioned homily today on the unjust division of the world's riches.

hook   *hook*
an arresting or catchy section of a song that "grabs" the listener or gives the song a more singular identity

Mr. Hadley's cavernous, Bowie-esque singing contributes to the melodrama. But the real impact comes from the hook-filled songs and the richness of their textures.

hoopla   *HOO:P lah*
showy publicity; ballyhoo

Amid tributes, telegrams, yet another award and a healthy dose of pomp and hoopla, Walter Cronkite yesterday closed out his 18-year career as anchor of "The CBS Evening News."

horse trading   *HAWRS tray ding*
bargaining marked by shrewd calculation by both sides

The reasons for budget decisions are seldom committed to paper. Final figures often reflect complex horse trading among the White House, the budget office and the agencies.

hubris   *HYOO: bris*
excessive pride or self-confidence that brings down the wrath of the gods for such insolence

The fabricated story that won a Pulitzer Prize has made newspaper people think about their business as nothing else has for years—and not just on the paper that printed it, The Washington Post. There is a sharpened concern about the responsibility of reporters and editors: the standards we impose on ourselves. But the episode points to a deeper problem, and I wonder how many in the press will face it. That is the danger of hubris, the overweening pride that leads to a fall. In our case, it is a constitutional hubris, a belief that the First Amendment gives journalism an exalted status. It is in particular a belief that the Constitution gives us a right to use anonymous sources without being called to account.

✦ Hubris is the insolence or self-pride in Greek tragic heroes that leads them to ignore warnings from the gods. In Greek tragedies it is this lack of wisdom that proves the "tragic flaw" leading to the hero's fall. At the end of Sophocles' *Antigone*, after Creon has rejected the prophet Tiresias's warnings and suffered the death of Antigone, whom he ordered executed, and the self-destruction of his wife and son, the leader of the chorus says: "Wisdom is the supreme part of happiness; and reverence toward the gods must be inviolate. Great words of prideful men are ever punished with great blows and, in old age, teach the chastened to be wise."

hullabaloo   *HUH luh buh loo:*
loud noise and confusion; hubbub; commotion; uproar; clamor

It was the kind of hullabaloo reserved for coronations, or when Elvis or a spacecraft is sighted. Michael Jordan, His Airness, the World's Greatest Hoopster, was returning to basketball and the Chicago Bulls, and much of the nation seemed transfixed. And it was here in this relatively tranquil Midwestern city today that Jordan, after 18 months of baseball and some 10 days of rumors, began his comeback against the Indiana Pacers. Hordes of reporters converged on Market Square Arena. National television was on hand. Scalpers reportedly were seeking as much as $680 for $42 tickets.

humanities   *hyoo MA nuh teez*
the branches of learning concerned with human thought and relations—as distinguished from the social and natural sciences—especially literature, philosophy, history, languages, art, theology and music

"Our students get an excellent education not just in dance but in the humanities as a whole," said Carolyn Brown, dean of the dance program at the State University College at Purchase. "The more you know, the more you are able to give."

hunky-dory   *HUHNG ki DAW ree*
all right; fine: a slang word

"Unleash greed and everything will be hunky-dory," was Mr. Stone's brief analysis of the Reagan economic theory.

hyperbole   *high PER buh lee*
exaggeration for effect, not meant to be taken literally, as in "He's as strong as an ox," or "I'll love you till the end of time"

"At the time," Mr. Slatkin said, "considering the President was in the audience, I indulged in some hyperbolic praise of the Mozart symphony, even calling it a 'mini masterpiece.' It is not that terrific, of course, but considering that it was written by Mozart when he was only 9 years old, I would call it amazing and a very pleasant piece of music, but not a great one."

hyphenate   *HIGH fuh nayt*
a title, name or designation whose parts are connected by a hyphen, such as Irish-American, actor-director or poet-politician

Tossing a tennis ball up and down in one hand, Michael Davis says, "It's not what you do, but how you do it." Mr. Davis is joking, but he is also clearly a man of style. He is an inspired juggler-comic—a distinguished hyphenate once worn by W.G Fields.

incongruous

It was an incongruous sight, the white-haired priest in black shirt and white collar, standing in an immense poultry house filled with thousands of clucking birds and  the acrid stench of manure. The priest, the Rev. Jim Lewis, was in this unlikely place because the Episcopal Church has assigned him an unlikely mission: to improve the lives of Delaware's chicken farmers and poultry plant workers.

see page 188

I

iatrogenesis   *ee a truh JE nuh sis*
the creation of illnesses and injuries in patients as a result of medical treatment:
Greek, iatro, *doctor* + genic, *produced by.* Iatro *is seen also in* pediatrician,
psychiatrist *and* podiatrist.

There is a long list of iatrogenic diseases—those induced by physicians and
by the drugs, vaccines and other new therapies they use. Certain anemias
have resulted as a complication of the surgical insertion of artificial heart
valves, for example. Such diseases are essentially diseases of medical
progress. They would not have occurred in the days when doctors could do
little beyond prescribing worthless medications and holding the hands of
patients as they died. Today many therapies actually work, but their unde-
sired effects make them double-edged swords.

icon   *IGH kahn*
a revered person; someone regarded as embodying to the highest degree the
essential characteristics of an era, a group, a profession or an art: from
the Orthodox Eastern Church's images of Jesus, Mary, a saint (considered
sacred objects)

DiMaggio was one of those rare sports stars, like Babe Ruth, Muhammad Ali
and Michael Jordan, who not only set new standards of athletic excellence
but also became a distinctive part of American culture. As stylish off the field
as on, DiMaggio was an icon of elegance and success, a name as recognizable on Broadway and in Hollywood as at the ball park. Millions of baby
boomers who never saw DiMaggio play instantly understood the reference
in the Paul Simon song of the 1960's—"Where have you gone, Joe
DiMaggio? A nation turns its lonely eyes to you."

iconoclast   *igh KAH nuh klast*
a person who challenges, attacks, rebels against or seeks to overthrow accepted traditions, ideas, beliefs or styles

Frank Zappa, a composer, guitarist, band leader and producer who was rock's most committed iconoclast, died Saturday evening at his home in Los Angeles. He was 52 years old. The cause was prostate cancer, The Associated Press reported. Mr. Zappa was a quintessential 20th-century American composer, a maverick within popular music and an outsider among classical composers. His huge body of work—more than 60 albums since 1966—embraces doo-wop, big-band suites, heavy metal, jazz-rock, blues-rock, orchestral music and every pop fad he decided to mock.

ideology   *igh dee AH luh jee*
the body of ideas reflecting the social needs and aspirations of an individual, group, class or culture

"He is a psychopath with no defined ideology," the Istanbul security chief said today of Mehmet Ali Agca, the 23-year-old Turk who is under arrest in Rome on charges of shooting Pope John Paul II.

idiom   *I dee uhm*
a characteristic style, as in art or music

Mr. Darnell's most impressive accomplishment is his blending of a wide variety of contemporary musical idioms: his songs for "Fresh Fruit in Foreign Places" combine reggae rhythms, the funk style of James Brown and a melodic sensibility that recalls the show tunes of bygone days. But these elements blend so smoothly that one tends not to notice how disparate they are.

idiosyncrasy   *i dee uh SING kruh see*
a peculiarity, habit or mannerism of an individual

Great singers are an amazing species. Fairly early in life they discover that their lungs and throats can do certain things better than anybody else in the world. As such they are irreplaceable, and Lord! how they know it. They grow up, most of them, vain, spoiled, pampered, rich, accustomed to having things their own way. They have idiosyncrasies that would simply not be tolerated in a normal society. Olive Fremstad, she of the sumptuous voice and equally sumptuous figure, insisted on being paid in cash before every performance. No cash, no Fremstad.

idyllic   *igh DI lik*
having a natural charm and picturesqueness; simple, pleasant and peaceful

The setting is idyllic: 70 acres of rolling meadows, lawns and formal gardens; daffodils, tulips, primroses and lots of blue forget-me-nots; a secluded path winding around a lake past geese, wildflowers and ferns.

ignominy   *IG nuh mi nee*
public shame or humiliation

Paying tribute to Richard M. Nixon on the day after his death at the age of 81, American and world leaders today emphasized the 37th President's epochal achievements in reconciling the United States with Communist powers, rather than the ignominy of his resignation from office.

> ✦ In *The Scarlet Letter*, Roger Chillingworth confronts his wife after seeing her standing in punishment before the townspeople, holding her illegitimate infant. "I might have known that, as I came out of the vast and dismal forest, and entered this settlement of Christian men, the very first object to meet my eyes would be thyself, Hester Prynne, standing up, a statue of ignominy before the people."

illiteracy   *i LI tuh ruh see*
lack of education or culture, especially an inability to read or write

The report says bluntly that "from the preoccupations of the popular culture with the paranormal, the psychic, the mystic, and the occult, it is apparent that an alarming number of American adults cannot tell sense from nonsense." Scientific illiteracy in a world in which science and technology play so great a part seriously undermines the citizen's capacity to understand society and to help keep it prosperous and strong.

illusory   *i LOO: suh ree*
deceptive; unreal; illusive

Many prominent scientists in the past described ball lightning as illusory. In 1839 the great physicist Michael Faraday announced his conviction that ball lightning was nothing more than an afterimage on the retina of the eye, produced by the nearby flash of ordinary lightning.

imbue   *im BYOO:*
to permeate; pervade; saturate

The current popularity of sex therapy is poignant testimony to the fact that many of us were not allowed as children to express ourselves in sexually healthy ways, that many were imbued with feelings of guilt, inhibition and restricted beliefs about what "normal" sexual thoughts and behaviors are.

In all countries, and especially in new ones, school is typically viewed as a place not just to learn but also to be imbued with civic and patriotic spirit.

impassive   *im PA siv*
not feeling or showing emotion; unmoved

At the chilling moment in the film "Apollo 13" when Tom Hanks tries to maneuver the crippled spacecraft on an exact course toward Earth, the audience at the Ziegfeld Theater held its collective breath. But Jim Lovell, the real-life commander of Apollo 13, watched the drama impassively while he munched buttered popcorn in the last row.

impeccable   *im PE kuh buhl*
without defect; faultless; flawless

In an institution that runs on comity and tradition, Senator John W. Warner has mastered the art of fitting in. With his impeccably tailored suits, silver-gray hair and associations with Elizabeth Taylor and Barbara Walters, the gentleman from Virginia looks, at first glance, like the senator from central casting.

impede   *im PEED*
to hinder the progress of; obstruct or delay

South African drivers characteristically assume that they have the right of way in nearly all circumstances. They pass impartially on the left or right. They indicate their desire to pass by driving as close as possible to the car that is impeding their progress, sometimes coming within half a car length at speeds of over 60 miles an hour, and they seldom slow down as a courtesy to another driver.

imperceptible   *im per SEP tuh buhl*
so slight, gradual or subtle as not to be easily perceived

> Swirling in for a landing at La Guardia, the pilot banked into a 90-degree turn, dropped the helicopter down 200 feet and made an imperceptible touchdown.

impervious   *im PER vee uhs*
incapable of being penetrated or affected by

> The armor—stainless steel jackets designed to fit around the money box at the bottom of each phone, making it impervious to knives, fists, hammers, fireworks and even explosives with a force of a quarter stick of dynamite— has already been placed on the 5,000 most vandalized phones in the city and will be put on the rest during the summer.

imprimatur   *im pruh MAH ter*
sanction or approval; originally, an official license to print or publish a book or pamphlet, especially such permission granted by a censor of the Roman Catholic Church: Latin, let it be printed

> Representative Tom Lantos, born a Hungarian, long since naturalized as an American, could scarcely contain his joy as he flew west this morning for the ceremony here marking the accession of Poland, Hungary and the Czech Republic to the North Atlantic Treaty Organization. "After a thousand years of desperate craving to be part of the West, today it's official—we're in, we get the imprimatur of NATO," the silver-haired, 71-year-old California Democrat said.

> Introduced yesterday at a news conference in Manhattan, a booklet, "The Bible and Public Schools: A First Amendment Guide" published by the National Bible Association and the First Amendment Center, has the imprimatur of groups that have been on opposite sides of several divisive religious issues. The groups range from People for the American Way, an organization that tries to combat the influence of the religious right, to the National Association of Evangelicals, a group that has supported school prayer.

impromptu   *im PRAHMP too:*
without preparation or advance thought; unplanned; spontaneous

The Governor, his mother, four aides, two state troopers, several Italian guides and five reporters jumped into taxis and formed an impromptu motorcade, with the two motorcycles leading the way. Rushing headlong into the peak of the Roman rush hour, the taxi careered through the city's winding streets, running red lights, weaving around oncoming traffic and forcing cars off the road.

impudent   *IM pyoo duhnt*
shamelessly bold or disrespectful; saucy; insolent

Improvisational comedy is essentially impudent madness. Because virtually all of it is created at the moment, often out of current experience and usually at the suggestion of audiences, it has little time for such niceties as taste and taboos. Improvisational comics must be fast on their feet and quick with their tongues. Inventiveness and situations count, not gags.

impugn   *im PYOO:N*
to oppose or challenge as false or questionable

In 1933, Shawn founded his Men Dancers company at the 75-acre farm he owned in the Berkshires, now the site of the dance school and festival. His aim was to convince the world that men could dance without impugning their virility, and to that end the group of nine male dancers—"God's gift to the women's colleges of America," as one reporter put it—crisscrossed the country performing in dances choreographed for them by Shawn and members of the company. It was a happy day for Ted Shawn when an Atlanta newspaper ran a review on its sports page.

impunity   *im PYOO: nuh tee*
exemption from punishment, penalty or harm

"It's time for honest talk, for plain talk. There has been a breakdown in the criminal justice system in America. It just plain isn't working. All too often repeat offenders, habitual lawbreakers, career criminals, call them what you will, are robbing, raping and beating with impunity and, as I said, quite literally getting away with murder. The people are sickened and outraged. They demand that we put a stop to it." [Ronald Reagan]

in absentia   *in ab SEN shuh*
although not present: Latin, in absence

Two men who were convicted in absentia of international trade in weapons with terrorist organizations were each sentenced yesterday to 17²/₃ to 53 years in prison. They are believed to be out of the country.

inadvertent *in uhd VER tuhnt*
unintended

Culinary history is peppered with instances of inadvertent genius, those blunders and miscalculations that turned into winners. One of the most famous is the Toll House cookie, first made in 1933 by Ruth Wakefield, who owned the Toll House Inn in Whitman, Mass. Having assumed that pieces of chocolate added to the batter for a butter cookie would melt and result in chocolate cookies, she was surprised to discover that the chocolate pieces kept their shape. And a new cookie was born.

incarnate *in KAHR nit*
in human form; personified

It's no secret that Mr. Hines may be the best tap dancer of our day, but he's never had a chance to show himself to quite the advantage that he does here. Wearing slick-backed hair, a series of sleek evening outfits and a raffish smile, he's more than a dancer; he's the frisky Ellington spirit incarnate.

incensed *in SENST*
very angry; enraged

Bill Gleason knew what he was doing when he raised three of his daughters to be lawyers. When the Chicago Hustle of the Women's Pro Basketball League tried to dismiss Gleason as coach last weekend, he had a phalanx of legal help that was as incensed as he was.

incessant *in SE suhnt*
constant

In a misguided effort to impart a sense of service (or perhaps because they are Aquarians), some waiters become incessant water pourers, reaching across tables with pitchers every time a sip is taken.

> ✦ Aquarius, the eleventh sign of the Zodiac (January 21 to February 18), is symbolized by a man pouring water from a vessel. *Aquarius* is Latin for *waterbearer*.

inchoate   *in KOH it*
not organized; lacking order

At two hours and 40 minutes, the production seems unduly long, and there are inchoate passages in the staging, as there are in the play itself. However, "Jungle of Cities" offers the Brooklyn Academy of Music company a fertile environment for exploration. For the first time this season, with Americanized Brecht, the company has found a general compatibility between actors and characters.

incisive   *in SIGH siv*
keen; penetrating; acute

"The school systems are now dealing with a population that does not think that language is the primary means of thinking," said Leon Botstein, the president of Bard, a liberal arts college in Annandale-on-Hudson. "The major instrument of thinking—language—is no longer taught in a coherent relationship with thinking. Language becomes ritualistic, even with the best of students, rather than being used to think incisively."

incognito   *in kahg NEE toh*
with true identity unrevealed or disguised: Italian, unknown

Supreme Court Justices Lewis F. Powell Jr. and Byron R. White dine incognito among out-of-towners at the Supreme Court cafeteria. Once, a tourist, not recognizing Justice Powell, asked him to take a picture of his family.

incommunicado   *in kuh myoo: ni KAH doh*
detained, residing or imprisoned without communication with the outside world: a Spanish term introduced at the time of the Spanish Civil War, 1936-39

The romance toppled a crown, shook an empire and titillated the world. It is history now. The Duke of Windsor is dead, the Duchess ill and incommunicado in Paris.

incongruous   *in KAHNG roo: is*
out of keeping; out of place; unexpected in a particular setting

It was an incongruous sight, the white-haired priest in black shirt and white collar, standing in an immense poultry house filled with thousands of clucking birds and the acrid stench of manure. The priest, the Rev. Jim Lewis, was in this unlikely place because the Episcopal Church has assigned him an unlikely mission: to improve the lives of Delaware's chicken farmers and poultry plant workers.

incredulous   *in KRE dyuh lis*
showing doubt or disbelief

The boy liked parties, girls, the accordion; so when, at age 17, he told Piotr and Emilia of his desire to become a priest, they were incredulous.

incursion   *in KER zhuhn*
a sudden, brief invasion or raid

The French are not particularly receptive to foreigners on their fashion turf. But since they are convinced that they are the leaders, they will tolerate some incursions from outsiders who want to take advantage of the huge audience of buyers from throughout the world that the French fashion shows attract. The operating rule, however, is that visitors maintain a low profile and do not try to seize center stage.

indefatigable   *in di FA ti guh buhl*
not yielding to fatigue; untiring

Actors are indefatigable, even as fate and casting agents buffet them into assuming alternate occupations. There are actor-waiters, bartenders, typists, cabdrivers, housecleaners and salesmen. One actor-waiter zoomed from serving up fettuccine Alfredo to playing opposite Richard Burton in "Equus" on Broadway.

indelible   *in DE luh buhl*
unforgettable; unerasable; permanently fixed

President Kennedy's funeral was held on his son's third birthday. In one indelible moment of family heartache and American history, the boy stood outside St. Matthew's Cathedral in Washington with his mother and sister, raising his hand in a salute as he squinted into the sun while his father's coffin rolled by. His mother, Jacqueline Bouvier Kennedy, had leaned down and whispered to him in advance to salute, a gesture the boy had seen many times as military escorts greeted the Commander in Chief.

indigenous   *in DI ji nuhs*
native to a place

The three Americans who were killed while on a mission to help the Uwa people of Colombia had distinguished themselves in the United States and in international organizations as passionate defenders of the environment and of the rights of indigenous people, associates said yesterday.

indigent   *IN di juhnt*
in poverty; poor; destitute

Last year, Mr. Buchbinder and his 399 colleagues in the Legal Aid Society's criminal defense bureau represented 162,656 indigent defendants in New York City assigned to them by the courts.

indisputable   *in di SPYOO: tuh buhl*
that which cannot be disputed or doubted; unquestionable

Rosa Ponselle, indisputably one of the greatest operatic talents this country has ever produced, died of a heart attack yesterday in her Baltimore mansion, Villa Pace, at the age of 84.

indissoluble   *in di SAH lyoo buhl*
undissolvable; lasting; permanent

A great sadness, however, has intruded on Mr. Menuhin's sunlit world—the death early in January of his sister, Hephzibah. Four years his junior, Hephzibah Menuhin began playing the piano publicly with her brother at 13. It was an association, both musical and personal, that remained indissoluble; and several generations of music audiences will remember them as they came out on stage together hand in hand.

ineffable   *in E fuh buhl*
too overwhelming to be expressed or described in words; inexpressible

By the end of the play, the apparently passionless character, a woman without biography, has communicated to us a feeling of ineffable loneliness. There is no solace or interruption in her regimen—no friends, phone calls or even solicitors or burglars. She does not have the grace of music, literature or self-indulgence. Through an accumulation of details and objects, we arrive at a point of complete empathy with the woman as she heads toward her inevitable conclusion.

inept   *in EPT*
awkward; clumsy; incompetent; unskillful

The Time-Life production of "The Search for Alexander the Great," currently running on WNET/13 on Wednesday evenings at 10, offers four hours of generally inept drama. With James Mason reading lengthy narrations while strolling around the ruins of a Greek amphitheater, the production rarely becomes more than an illustrated lecture.

inextricable   in EK stri kuh buhl
incapable of being disentangled, untied or removed from

You can quickly come up with half a dozen nominees or more for the show-stoppers' hall of fame from the ranks of Broadway musicals, some of them inextricably linked to a legendary performance, others less so: Barbra Streisand's "Don't Rain on My Parade" in "Funny Girl," Ethel Merman's rendition of "Rose's Turn" ("Gypsy"), "The Rain in Spain" ("My Fair Lady"), "Sit Down, You're Rocking the Boat" ("Guys and Dolls"), Elaine Stritch delivering "The Ladies Who Lunch" ("Company"), "Gee, Officer Krupke" ("West Side Story") and surely, Carol Channing, serenaded and celebrated in the "Hello, Dolly!" production number.

infallible   in FA luh buhl
incapable of error; never wrong

It has been observed here before now that no matter how deficient an umpire may be in physical beauty, personal charm and social grace, he is infallible on balls and strikes and matters of faith and morals.

infighting   IN figh ting
intense competition or conflict, often bitterly personal, as between political opponents or within an organization or group

Iran's bitter political infighting has grown even fiercer since the release of the American Embassy hostages, casting doubt on the future course of the revolution, which is two years old this week.

influx   IN fluhks
a flowing in; a continual coming in of persons or things

The American shrimpers contend that the influx of Vietnamese fishermen has overcrowded the bay, threatening both their livelihoods and the shrimp crop.

inform   *in FAWRM*
to give form or character to; be the formative principle of

Dickens's earliest aspirations, in fact, were focused on the theater, and his passion for drama would unconsciously inform all his later work.

infuse   *in FYOO:Z*
to put into as if by pouring; instill; fill

One of the most common safety tests for cosmetics and other consumer products—and one heavily criticized as inhumane—was developed by the United States Food and Drug Administration. It measures irritation in the eyes of albino rabbits that are infused with an array of products ranging from perfumes to oven cleaners.

Society is infused with the vain idea that now is best, or worst or most important. If medieval society was geocentric, believing that all else revolved around the earth, we might be called neocentric—obsessed with now.

innate   *i NAYT*
existing naturally, rather than acquired

The four foods that seem to lend themselves most naturally to no-salt cookery are tomatoes, onions, mushrooms and eggplants. These vegetables have an innate flavor that is more pronounced when they are cooked, and if treated properly their flavor gratifications need not be enhanced by salt.

innocuous   *i NAH kyoo uhs*
harmless; inoffensive; dull and uninspiring

There is also a special "Bionic Briefcase" that is bulletproof and theftproof, contains both a bug and tape-recorder detector, and a device to sniff out bombs. "It's an innocuous-looking briefcase, but it can be made to do most things in a security field," Mr. Jamil said. "You just pack your bomb sniffer, your homing device and pajamas and you're ready to go."

insatiable   *in SAY shuh buhl*
constantly wanting more; unsatisfiable

The destruction, both vocal and personal, came about partly owing to Miss Callas's own insatiable desire for celebrity and a need to be close to power. But the chief instrument of ruin most certainly was the late Mr. Onassis, who from this book's detailed testimony was a remarkably crude, trivial and nasty man.

insipid *in SI pid*
without flavor; tasteless; dull; lifeless

Under the mistaken impression that American country-pop music is "serious" concert fare, Miss Mouskouri also performed recent pop hits like "When I Dream" and "The Rose" with the same elocuted politeness with which she delivered the pop adaptation of the "Costa Diva" from Bellini's "Norma." It was all terribly insipid. Miss Mouskouri should have devoted more energy to exploring her Greek heritage and less time aspiring to American kitsch.

insouciance *in SOO: see ins*
freedom from concern or care; indifference or unconcern, especially to the impression one is creating: French, without care

In moments, the women had polished off a few hundred dollars' worth of caviar. They did it with enormous insouciance, as if this were no more than a coffee shop they were stopping into for a snack. Having finished, they wiped their mouths, paid their bill, picked up their shopping bags and sauntered out. Their attitude made it clear that caviar, to them, is an everyday occurrence.

insular *IN suh ler*
like an island; detached; isolated

The impoundment of the livestock represents the latest step in the Federal Government's efforts to move thousands of Navajos off their rugged ancestral homelands in northeast Arizona, one of the most insular and physically isolated regions of the country.

insuperable *in SOO: puh ruh buhl*
impossible to overcome; insurmountable

The staggering death toll in Turkey may lead some people to conclude that there is no preparing for a force as abrupt and unpredictable as a major earthquake, that nature, in some forms, is simply insuperable and human means inadequate. That would be the wrong conclusion. It is not a question of stopping earthquakes or preventing death altogether. It is a question of preventing needless death, of keeping a city from killing itself when an earthquake strikes. Nature may be insuperable in some forms, but human neglect is not.

intangible   *in TAN juh buhl*
an asset that cannot be seen, such as a character trait

There have been few defensive ends who could match Willie Davis in the physical attributes of speed, agility and size, plus the intangibles—intelligence, dedication and leadership.

integral   *IN tuh gruhl*
necessary for completeness; essential; an inseparable part of

Perhaps complacent about its brand's place in the popular culture, Levi Strauss has not responded well to a wave of aggressive competition in recent years, and its jeans have lost some of their cachet. While Levi Strauss stayed committed to its five-pocket button-fly 501 jeans, which until recently were an integral item in any high school wardrobe, high-end designers like Ralph Lauren and Tommy Hilfiger carved out market share with fashionable bell-bottom and cargo-pants styles.

internecine   *in ter NEE sin*
pertaining to conflict within a group; mutually destructive

For years the hospital, founded in the last century by Protestant missionaries, had treated the injured from all sides of Lebanon's internecine bloodletting with fine impartiality.

interpolation   *in ter puh LAY shuhn*
to insert between or among others; interpose

Except for a couple of interpolations designed to expand dancing opportunities, the ballet sticks fairly close to the traditional fairy tale.

intimidate   *in TI mi dayt*
to make timid; make afraid; overawe

The most pervasive confusion exists on menus printed entirely in French or

Italian, generally in upper-class establishments where a certain air of intimidation prevails with staff as well as on the menu. The idea in such cases must be that those who have to ask what dishes are do not belong there anyway, a hint that customers might well consider taking.

intone   *in TOHN*
to utter in a singing tone or in prolonged monotones

BELFAST, Northern Ireland, Sept. 9—The judge, resplendent in a scarlet robe, sits facing the defendant, who is guarded by two policemen. The lawyers wear curly gray wigs and starchy white dickeys, and the crier opens the trial by intoning, "God Save the Queen."

intractable   *in TRAK tuh buhl*
stubborn; obstinate; resisting treatment or cure

Widespread hunger remains intractable throughout the world and is exacting a high human toll. About half a billion individuals are still crippled by hunger, and a billion or more others should have a more varied diet, according to nutritionists. The great majority of the undernourished—some 80 percent, by World Bank estimates—are women and children.

intransigent   *in TRAN si juhnt*
uncompromising; inflexible

Improvisation of that kind is what Mr. Matthau enjoys most about film acting. "When you get an intransigent director and writer who complain if you change a single comma, that is very unconducive to doing comedy. Shakespeare never described what happens in a scene. He just put the words down, like a good playwright, and then he died."

✦ Many words found in Shakespeare's works are now obsolete: for example, *accite* (to summon), *bollen* (swollen), *coistrel* (knave), *shunless* (inevitable) and *twire* (twinkle). On the other hand, Shakespeare provided the language with more currently used words (either coined by him or found in his works for the first time) than any other writer. They include:

accommodation	gull (dupe)
apostrophe	gust
aslant	heartsick
assassination	hint
barefaced	hot-blooded
baseless	hurry
call (visit)	impartial
control (the noun)	import (the noun)
countless	inauspicious
courtship	indistinguishable
dawn (the noun)	lackluster
denote	laughable
disgraceful	leapfrog
dislocate	lonely
distrustful	lower (the verb)
dress (the noun)	misanthrope
dwindle	monumental
educate	needlelike
eventful	obscene
excellent	pedant
exposure	premeditated
fitful	reliance
fretful	submerged
frugal	summit
grovel	

intrusive   *in TROO: siv*
intruding; coming unbidden or without welcome

Some of the waiters affect a style that they seem to think is breezy but which is really intrusive and insolent. There is also a tendency to use the kindergartenish "we." Spilling wine on a cloth and menu, the waiter soothed an annoyed patron with, "We're not going to let that spoil our evening, are we?"

inundate   *I nuhn dayt*
to flood; cover with water

Last year, heavy snows in the western mountains and torrential rains in central China resulted in flooding along the Yangtze. To prevent the river cities of Wuhan, Nanjing and Shanghai from being inundated, dikes and levies were opened or broke under pressure, flooding millions of rural residents out of their homes.

Since she appeared in last month's three-part television adaptation of John Steinbeck's "East of Eden," Jane Seymour has been inundated with scripts, according to the actress, who said most of the offerings called for her to play "evil women."

inure   *in YOOR*
to make accustomed to; toughen or harden through exposure to; habituate

In 1977, attorneys for a 15-year-old Florida youth argued that six to eight hours' worth of daily television viewing had so inured him to violence that he had lost the ability to distinguish right from wrong, and therefore should not be convicted of fatally shooting his next-door neighbor, an 82-year-old woman, during a robbery attempt. Elements of one episode of the boy's favorite television show, "Kojak," were said to resemble the actual slaying.

inveigh   *in VAY*
to make a violent verbal attack; talk or write bitterly

The novel, "The Book of Ebenezer Le Page," was begun in the 60's by G.B. Edwards. It is a story told by a bandy-legged, crotchety old bachelor who inveighs against any signs of change on the Channel Island of Guernsey, where he has lived his entire life.

inventory   *IN vuhn taw ree*
the store of goods on hand

The Salvadoran Navy lists 11 boats in its inventory. Two are capsized hulls, four have been stripped for parts, and of the rest, only three are operational.

to make an appraisal, as of one's skills, personal characteristics, etc.

In an interview a couple of months ago, I was reported to have said that burnout can be a productive time for people, a time to inventory life's satisfactions. My interview with the reporter sounded actually enthusiastic about the benefits of burnout. I hope I didn't leave anyone with the impression that depression can be fun.

invertebrate   *in VER tuh brit*
an animal without a backbone, or spinal column; any animal other than a fish, amphibian, reptile, bird or mammal

Instead of working on all endangered species simultaneously, the department will concentrate on higher species. This means that mammals will be given top priority and such invertebrates as insects and mollusks lower priorities.

invidious   *in VI dee uhs*
causing animosity, resentment or envious dislike

In 1979 the Senate Judiciary Committee adopted a policy statement declaring it "inadvisable for a nominee for a Federal judgeship to belong to a social club that engages in invidious discrimination."

invoke   *in VOHK*
to resort to or put into use, as a law, ruling, penalty, etc.

But golf has a history of conscience. Golfers often have invoked penalties against themselves for a violation that only they saw or knew. The late Babe Didrikson Zaharias once disqualified herself from a tournament for having hit the wrong ball out of the rough. "But nobody would have known," a friend told her. "I would've known," Babe Didrikson Zaharias replied.

ire   *IGH er*
intense and usually openly displayed anger; fury

While car makers are still capable of rousing the ire of environmentalists, notably by increasing their output of gas-guzzling but high-profit sport utility vehicles, attitudes within the industry are slowly but perceptibly changing. A new generation of auto executives is taking charge, one that views environmental values as part of mainstream American life.

irredeemable   *i ri DEE muh buhl*
impossible to reform; hopeless

"Nickleby" as a novel is rich in Dickensian sentimentality, and it is if anything intensified on the stage. The good characters are angelic, the evil irredeemably bad.

irrepressible   *i ri PRE suh buhl*
incapable of being repressed or restrained

The "Popemobile," an open vehicle such as the one he was riding in when he was shot yesterday, has become a symbol of his mobility. Before his weekly audiences in the square, he stands in the vehicle as it winds through the crowds. The act is a byproduct of his instinctive showmanship and his irrepressible desire to bring the church to the people.

J

joie de vivre

It was 1953, and Paris was inexpensive and romantic, and

it was possible then, as it had been possible in

Hemingway's time, to make writing not only a

vocation but an entire way of life. And so a

group of young Americans went to Paris,

where they wrote and drank and played

tennis and sat up all night at cafes, and where they started

a little magazine that ran on talent and enthusiasm and

youthful joie de vivre.

see page 202

jaded   *JAY did*
unimpressible or unexcitable from having indulged in something so much; blasé

"BROOOOOOOCE!" So went the cries of nearly a dozen police officers as Bruce Springsteen walked past the 18th Precinct station house on West 54th Street. As he strolled through midtown Manhattan on a sunny weekday afternoon, no other pedestrians stopped him or yodeled his first name. They just looked at him as he passed by, trying to quietly absorb his presence with their gaze in the jaded way that New Yorkers respond to fame. It was only the police officers who reacted, pulling out their summons pads for Mr. Springsteen to sign and yelling, "You're the best!" as he complied.

jerry-built   *JER ee bilt*
built poorly, of cheap materials; unsubstantially built: a mid-nineteenth century British slang word of uncertain origin

The majority of the fresh fruit and vegetable markets in eastern Long Island are relatively small and vary in structure and produce. Some are on wagon beds, some in jerry-built shacks that seem to be put together with a few boards, hammers and nails.

jettison   *JE tuh suhn*
to throw away as useless or a burden: originally, to throw overboard to lighten a ship in an emergency

The Americans managed to withdraw their army to Manhattan, but the British crossed the East River, landed in the area of the East 30's and pushed crosstown, slicing through demoralized rebel troops. Near Lexington Avenue and East 42d Street, where people still rush about, Washington was outraged by the behavior of his troops, who jettisoned their arms and fled. It was here that he threw his hat on the ground and cried, "Are these the men with whom I am to defend America?"

When last heard from in September, Anita Bryant, having ended her marriage of 20 years, had left Miami and returned to her native Oklahoma. She jettisoned her religious crusade against equal rights for homosexuals and said she had decided she believed in "live and let live."

jocular *JAH kyoo ler*
joking; humorous; full of fun

Mr. Young's high spirits showed time and again in an understated jocularity that caused laughter in the audience of reporters and Johnson Space Center employees. Once Captain Crippen was asked if his pulse rate of 130 at liftoff, against Mr. Young's 90, meant he was more excited. "You betchum I was excited," he said. Mr. Young added, "What you don't understand is, I was excited too. I just can't make it go any faster." Mr. Young is 50 years old, seven years older than his partner.

joie de vivre *zwah duh VEE vruh*
delight at being alive; enjoyment of life: French, joy of living

It was 1953, and Paris was inexpensive and romantic, and it was possible then, as it had been possible in Hemingway's time, to make writing not only a vocation but an entire way of life. And so a group of young Americans went to Paris, where they wrote and drank and played tennis and sat up all night at cafes, and where they started a little magazine that ran on talent and enthusiasm and a youthful joie de vivre.

josh *jahsh*
to tease good-humoredly: colloquial American since the 1880s; origin uncertain

The droll, witty Harvard Lampoon staff, the prime joshers of the Ivy League, have selected People magazine for their next parody effort.

journeyman *JER nee min*
a competent, experienced but not brilliant worker or performer

Asbury Park has long been famous for its journeyman musicians, hardworking rock-and-rollers who produced an earnest, bluesy type of music that perfectly matched the noisy, summertime rhythms of the local board-walk. When the Stone Pony first opened here in 1974, it was no more than another roadhouse in a town that teemed with jukebox bars. But within three years, the club became ground zero for a blend of rhythm and blues and denim-jacket rock known as the Jersey Shore sound.

juggernaut   *JU gurh nawt*
an unstoppable force

McDonald's, it's safe to say, has changed the world, imprinting cookie-cutter standardization on the global psyche. Now Joan Kroc, the widow of Ray Kroc, who made McDonald's into a golden-arched juggernaut, is using a few of her millions to try to change one corner of the world, donating $80 million to the Salvation Army for a community center in inner-city San Diego.

✦ At a centuries-old annual festival honoring the god Vishnu, in the Indian town of Puri, thousands of worshippers drag a wagon, 45 feet high and 35 feet square, through the streets. In the wagon, whose 16 wheels are 7 feet in diameter, is a statue of Vishnu in his incarnation as Jagganath, the Lord of the Universe. Through the centuries, stories have persisted of celebrants throwing themselves under the wagon's wheels in order to die in the god's sight. While some people have done that, most deaths under the Jagganath wagon have been accidents. *Juggernaut*, adapted from *Jagganath*, was first used metaphorically in the nineteenth century to mean an irresistible, massive crushing force. Today it may describe any force that is, or seems, unstoppable.

juxtaposition   *juhk stuh puh ZI shuhn*
the placement or location of things side by side or close together

The juxtaposition of old and new is widespread in Africa. But in Nigeria, oil wealth has burnished the glitter of new things in an obvious sort of way: The man who wears the traditional robes is just as likely to be sporting Gucci loafers and a gold Rolex.

K

ken

Thomas Hart Benton, the American regionalist painter who

was Jackson Pollock's teacher and Harry S. Truman's

favorite artist, has long been associated

in the public ken with the earthy art

and people of his native Missouri

and Middle West. The muralist

depicted farmers scything hay, gaunt

Ozark hillbillies, black sharecroppers, soldiers in

honkytonks, miners hunched over from years in the pits and

riverboats on the Mississippi.

see page 207

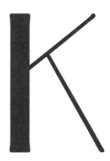

kamikaze   *kah mi KAH zee*

a suicide attack by a Japanese airplane pilot in World War II; the airplane or pilot in such an attack: thus, a reckless act of suicidal proportions

"I Won't Dance," which was unveiled at the Helen Hayes yesterday afternoon, can take its place alongside such other recent Broadway kamikaze missions as "Animals" and "Inacent Black."

✦ *Kamikaze*, the name applied to Japan's World War II suicide air squadrons, originated in thirteenth-century Japan. In 1274, Kubla Khan, the first Mongol to rule all of China (his grandfather was the warrior Genghis Khan) attempted an invasion of Japan but was stopped by heavy losses. His second attempt, in 1281, failed when 1,000 of the 4,400 invading warships were destroyed by typhoons. The Japanese called the seemingly God-sent storms kamikaze, or divine winds.

ken   *ken*

mental perception

Thomas Hart Benton, the American regionalist painter who was Jackson Pollock's teacher and Harry S. Truman's favorite artist, has long been associated in the public ken with the earthy art and people of his native Missouri and Middle West. The muralist depicted farmers scything hay, gaunt Ozark hillbillies, black sharecroppers, soldiers in honkytonks, miners hunched over from years in the pits and riverboats on the Mississippi.

kerfuffle   *ker FUH fuhl*
disorder; flurry; stir; agitation

Jeffrey Toobin caused a kerfuffle when he wrote in The New Yorker this week that Bill Clinton was interested in running for the Senate from Arkansas in 2002. If Mr. Clinton won in his home state and Mrs. Clinton won in somebody else's home state, they would make history as the first connubial Senate team. When the President called the story "crazy," I knew it could be true.

✦ *Kerfuffle* is a combination of Gaelic and Scots, from *car*, to twist about, and *fuffle*, to become disheveled or mussed up. It has a rustic lilt and charm to it, and it may catch on in American speech. But it may also become overworked and lose its novelty.

kinetic   *ki NE tik*
pertaining to motion

This is one of the best performances by any dancer in recent memory, both sensitively shaped and kinetically exciting. As Mr. Parsons keeps dancing with beautifully bright flair, Miss York attempts to run after him. But the speedy pirouettes and distorted barrel turns in the air—the total virtuosity—stop her, as they do the hearts of the audience.

kiosk   *KEE ahsk*
a small structure open at one or more sides, used as a newsstand, bandstand, subway entrance, etc.

There are lines for almost everything in Poland. Lines at kiosks for newspapers in the morning become lines for cigarettes later in the day. There are lines for bread, lines for vodka, lines for plane tickets, linoleum and detergents. Lately, lines for gasoline have meant waits of one to two hours.

klutz   *kluts*
a clumsy, graceless or awkward person: Yiddish, klots, *a log or block of wood*

Mr. Chappelle said he agreed that most comedians are troubled people. "A lot of comedy comes from pain and insecurity, and that's what drives you to the stage," he said. "You're loved and accepted up there onstage. Comedians are guys who couldn't get dates in high school. I still feel a little bit like Clark Kent," he said. "When I was performing in Washington, at night women would sometimes throw themselves at me. I felt like Superman. But the next day in school I was like a bumbling klutz. Clark Kent."

2:50 A.M. (DIS) * GEORGE OF THE JUNGLE (1997). Brendan Fraser, Leslie Mann. A klutz raised by apes wins the heart of an heiress. Swinging comedy. (PG) (1 hr. 40 mins.)

L

locus

The year's striking musical moments often came during events ostensibly about other things. James Levine's Met Orchestra concert at Carnegie Hall in mid-November advertised Milton Babbitt's new piano concerto, but it was a performance of Dvorak's G major Symphony that made the jaw drop and the heart beat faster. Here was a locus of points: the sophistication of a big-time orchestra, the dead-on contact with late 19th-century style, and a simple sympathy with the dancing and singing of rural Central Europe.

see page 221

lace   *lays*
to add a dash of alcoholic liquor to

Don't pass up the torta De Medici, which has a layer of sponge cake topped by a frothy cloud of chocolate mousse laced with rum—it melts in your mouth.

lackluster   *LAK luh ster*
dull; uninspired; unimaginative

The Philadelphia Orchestra played a peculiarly frustrating concert at Carnegie Hall on Monday evening. With Franz Welser-Most on the podium, the orchestra sometimes played stunningly and sometimes was so lackluster that it was difficult to believe this was the Philadelphia. Conducting the most vividly picturesque and emotionally searing of Shostakovich's wartime scores, the Eighth Symphony, Mr. Welser-Most vacillated between moments of high-tension direction and long stretches in which he allowed the music to meander.

lagniappe   *LAN yap*
an item given free to a customer when something else is bought

Ms. Davidson is the author of five culinary whodunits with names like "The Cereal Murders," "Dying for Chocolate" and "Killer Pancake." Sales of each book have surpassed the last, according to Bantam Books, her publisher, and there are now almost a million copies of them in print. And for lagniappe, each book features up to a dozen recipes, all original and all created by the former dud-in-the-kitchen.

✦ *Lagniappe* is among the words of French origin that came into English through French-speaking settlers in Canada and Louisiana. Others are:

bayou	parlay
butte	picayune
caribou	portage
chowder	prairie
chute	praline
crevasse	pumpkin
depot	rapids
flume	rotisserie
gopher	sashay
jambalaya	shanty
levee	toboggan

laid back   *layd bak*
calm, cool and relaxed; nonchalant; low-keyed: a slang term

One of the more colorful and lively places offering the limited but entertaining range of Texas dishes is the Cottonwood Cafe on Bleecker Street, just east of Bank Street. The style here is so laid back that you'll feel overdressed in anything more elaborate than a cotton shirt and jeans, but after one of the huge and marvelous frozen tequila and lime juice margaritas, you would be likely to feel at home in anything, even white tie and tails.

languish   *LANG gwish*
to undergo neglect; live under distressing conditions

After years of languishing in small, chilly arenas, figure skating has become hot stuff as a spectator sport. The world championships are a sellout, a 15-city North American tour after the world event will play the largest indoor facilities, and ice shows and skating exhibitions now are regularly seen on network television.

lapidary   *LA puh de ree*
jewel-like in construction; exquisitely fashioned; elegant and precise: Latin, lapidarius, of stones: as a noun, it is a person who creates jewels from precious stones

Ms. McPhee shares her father John McPhee's gift for fine, lapidary prose, and in this novel, her carefully controlled language is the perfect counterpoint to her story of divorce and dissolution. Blessed with a poet's ear for language and a reporter's eye for detail, she proves with this volume that she is also a gifted novelist, a writer with the ability to surprise and move us.

But if the narrative here never coheres into an organic novel in any conventional sense, the reader never really minds, so beautifully does Ms. Mukherjee write. Indeed, her lapidary prose combines with the multi-layered narrative to produce an effect reminiscent of those jewel-toned miniature paintings created by Mogul artists to commemorate Hannah's life: small, exquisite canvases teeming with people and festivities and disasters, canvases that meld together history and folklore into a harmonious if chaotic work of art.

lares and penates   *LAI reez and pi NAY teez*
the treasured belongings of a family or household: Latin

The shelterless people are visible all over the West Side. They sit on the benches of the Broadway malls. They sleep in doorways, often surrounded by the bulging shopping bags that are filled with the lares and penates of their homeless existence. Many talk to themselves. Some are abusive. Most look gentle and vacant.

✦ *Penates* were the personal gods of each Roman household that watched over the family's welfare and prosperity. *Lares* were also household gods, but they were the deified spirits of ancestors who watched over and protected their descendants' homes. The *lar familiaris* was the spirit of the founder of the house that never left it. There were also public lares—guardian spirits of the city, the fields, the highways, the sea, etc. Each home had a shrine in which stood images of its lares and penates, and to which the family prayed. On special occasions offerings were made to them of wine, cakes, honey and incense.

largess   *lahr JES*
a generous bestowal of gifts; liberality in giving

A million-dollar jury verdict for an injured client is a trial lawyer's Oscar, his laurel wreath, his grand slam, his jackpot and his badge of success. It commands the respect of his fellows and entitles him to tell them how he coaxed such largess from the jury.

215

lassitude   *LA suh too:d*
a state of being tired or listless; weariness

Fever and lassitude are the symptoms to look for when checking for tick bites, but physicians in the Hamptons sometimes begin treatment before they have a definite diagnosis.

latent   *LAY tuhnt*
lying hidden and undeveloped within a person or thing, as a quality or power

The secret of chess is that it's a killer's game, requiring above all the will to win. It brings out latent aggression even in the mildest of people, and turns grown men into children when a blunder leads to defeat.

latitude   *LA tuh too:d*
freedom from narrow restrictions

In 1952, Mr. Sauter joined forces with Bill Finegan, who had been chief arranger for Miller and Dorsey, to form an orchestra that would carry out their innovative writing ideas. "We agreed that it would not be brass and saxes all over again," Mr. Sauter explained. "We'd had that. We wanted a different combination of instruments. We came up with one that gave us lots of latitude—from piccolo to tuba. It gave us space to make the lines come out so you don't always have a wad of sound thrown at you."

laudable   *LAW duh buhl*
commendable; praiseworthy

The Administration's plan to provide free vaccinations for all youngsters would put childhood immunization on a par with clean water and a public school education—something government guarantees to every child, rich, poor and in between. That's a laudable goal, with as much appeal for the head as for the heart.

lax   *laks*
loose; not strict; careless; negligent

Security around the gleaming black and white missiles is lax. A Syrian soldier yawns as he glances at the documents of some travelers in cars. It is possible to take pictures.

layman   *LAY muhn*
a member of the laity; a person not of the clergy: any profession can also refer
to those outside it or not skilled in it as lay persons

The word came from the Vatican: "Politics is the responsibility of laymen, and a priest should be a priest." So after 10 years in the House of Representatives, Robert F. Drinan, the liberal Jesuit priest from Massachusetts, gave up his seat last Jan. 1.

leery   *LEE ree*
on one's guard; wary; suspicious

Wall Street has always cherished its eccentrics and been leery of them at the same time: It is hard to tell, after all, what an off-beat individualist with a lot of hustle might be up to. Take an outspoken, Budapest-born securities analyst and stock promoter named Andrew G. Racz.

legalese   *lee guhl EEZ*
the language of legal forms, documents, etc., often thought of as
incomprehensible to anyone but lawyers

The back of a typical auto rental contract contains the conditions, but they are usually in legalese that virtually defies comprehension by anyone but a lawyer.

✦ Legalese: "If the insured is a mortgagee, this company's right of subrogation shall not prevent the insured from releasing the personal liability of the obligor or guarantor or from releasing a portion of the premises from the lien of the mortgage or from increasing or otherwise modifying the insured mortgage provided such acts do not affect the validity of priority of the lien of the mortgage insured. However, the liability of this company under this policy shall in no event be increased by any such act of the insured." [From the Title Insurance Policy for the author's home.]

legion   *LEE juhn*
a large number; multitude

Excitement or preoccupation with an activity may block perception of pain. Stories are legion of athletes who do not realize until the end of the game that they have broken bones.

lethargy *LE thuhr jee*
a great lack of energy; sluggishness

Winter depression, also known as seasonal affective disorder, afflicts as many as 20 percent of the population. The disorder causes many people in northern latitudes to spend the winter beset by blues and lethargy. They tend to sleep more, eat more, crave carbohydrates, gain weight, think slower, concentrate poorly and feel fatigued, irritable and unhappy.

leviathan *luh VIGH uh thuhn*
a whale; anything of immense size and power, as a huge ocean liner: originally, a biblical sea monster, thought of as a whale or crocodile

There are whales in the waters off Long Island, and there are whalewatchers, too—a weekend navy that scouts the still-chilly ocean for descendants of the leviathans whose oil and skin were the most precious products of Long Island's economy early in the 19th century.

lexicon *LEK si kahn*
a dictionary; the vocabulary of a particular author, subject, profession, language, etc.

Love and forbearance figure high in the lexicon of Baptist virtues, but at this year's annual convention of Southern Baptists, held in Los Angeles last week, some serious rifts disrupted the mood.

liaison *LEE uh zahn*
a close relationship

Rarely in France are you served pâtés, terrines and sliced cold meats, such as salamis, without the pickles known as cornichons—and often mustard—as an accompaniment. In this country, sauerkraut is a perfect liaison for a frankfurter on a bun, and cole slaw in many places is the inevitable side dish with hamburgers.

libidinous *li BI duh nuhs*
full of lust: from libido, the sexual urge or instinct; Latin, lubet, it pleases

When Ned Racine (William Hurt), the libidinous, slightly down-at-the-heels lawyer, who is the movie's hero, meets Matty Walker, she drives him wild. Matty (Kathleen Turner) is a rich and unhappily married beauty in a clinging white dress, and she means to arouse in Ned a sexual longing so powerful it will make him absolutely ruthless.

Lilliputian *li luh PYOO: shuhn*
tiny: from Lilliput, a land in Swift's Gulliver's Travels *inhabited by people six inches tall*

Rose growers are learning that small is beautiful. In the last six or seven years sales of Lilliputian rosebushes have increased from limited production for hobbyists to a booming multimillion-dollar business.

limpid *LIM Pid*
perfectly clear; transparent; not cloudy or murky

Some of the calm, limpid coves are perfect for snorkeling among Mediterranean fish in a rocky submarine landscape.

lineage *LI nee ij*
descendants from a common ancestor

Paleontologists in the 19th century kept digging up fossils of early horses no bigger than a diminutive mouse deer. Over the expanse of evolutionary time, they came to see, the horse lineage showed tendencies to increase in body size, leading to the sole surviving genus Equus, which includes such imposing animals as Kentucky thoroughbreds and Clydesdales capable of pulling wagons heavy with beer barrels.

lingua franca *LING gwuh FRAHNG kuh*
a standard language that is widely used as a general medium of communication; a hybrid language used for communication between different peoples, as pidgin English

DENVER, Feb. 21—In the old days, when Ute was the lingua franca of what is now Colorado, Indian bands would travel the Old North Trail, skirting the Rocky Mountains to camp and trade in cottonwood groves here at the confluence of Cherry Creek and the South Platte River.

✦ The original lingua franca (Italian, Frankish language) was a hybrid language of Italian, Spanish, French, Greek, Arabic and Turkish elements, spoken in certain Mediterranean ports beginning in the seventeenth century for the purpose of facilitating business and trade. It consisted mostly of Italian words without their inflections.

lionize   *LIGH uh nighz*
to treat as a celebrity, especially someone unaccustomed to being one

With the Orioles leading the Yankees, 4-3, in the eighth inning of the first game of the American League Championship Series, Tarasco replaced Bobby Bonilla in right field in what was his third appearance in five months. When Derek Jeter clubbed a high shot to right, the 6-foot-1-inch, 205-pound Tarasco was poised to catch it until the 12-year-old Maier leaned over the fence and helped pull the ball into the seats. Umpire Richie Garcia ruled it a home run instead of interference and Maier was lionized by the news media after the Yankees won, 5-4.

> ✦ *Lionize* came into use in the early 1800s, after an exhibit of lions at the Tower of London attracted people from far and wide who had never seen a lion. In Britain, *lionize* also means to sightsee or show someone the sights.

listless   *LIST lis*
feeling no inclination toward or interest in anything; spiritless; indifferent

When Michael is briefly estranged from his wife, he is too listless to do anything but watch the game show "Family Feud" on television.

litany   *LI tuh nee*
a repetitive and almost predictable recital of things, as in a ritual: originally, a form of prayer in which the clergy and the congregation read responsively in a fixed order

At Maybe's recent meeting, the litany of children's problems today was recited: drugs and drinking, alcoholic parents, split homes, abortions, schizophrenia, vandalism, shoplifting and burglary, among other things.

literally   *LI tuh ruh lee*
actually; in fact

The Mayor of Norwalk, Conn. is running again, this time literally, and has offered to take on about half the town in the race. Anyone who beats him does not take the Mayor's job, but gets an official certificate saying the Mayor was defeated.

literati   *li tuh RAH tee*
persons of literary attainment; scholarly or learned people: Latin, learned

Northern New Mexico has been an oasis for writers, artists and photographers since D.H. Lawrence and Georgia O'Keefe settled here in the 20's. The literati have been well established for decades, but now the glitterati are moving in and, much to Santa Fe's dismay, the town is fast becoming an open secret. The most notable new arrivals are probably the Duke and Duchess of Bedford, who have purchased a home in the nearby village of Tesque that was listed for $1.1 million, according to Lee Head, a real estate agent.

lithe   *lighth:*
limber; supple

At 54, Mr. Belafonte is lean, lithe and as strikingly handsome as he was when he first appeared in the 1950's and helped give folk music a period of mass appeal.

litigation   *li ti GAY shuhn*
the process of carrying on a lawsuit; a lawsuit

Damage claims by workers exposed to asbestos and by their families now constitute the largest, and potentially most costly, block of product liability litigation ever to confront American industry. About 25,000 people who believe they are victims have already filed 12,000 suits against 260 companies that manufacture, use or sell asbestos products, according to Michael Mealey, editor of the Asbestos Litigation Reporter.

lobotomized   *loh BAH tuh mighzd*
dulled or deadened, suggesting the aftereffects of a lobotomy, in which part of the brain is surgically removed in order to blunt the emotions of a severely disturbed psychotic

"The Best of Friends," which will be shown Sunday night at 8 on Channel 5, is billed as a screen adaptation of an Ernest Hemingway short story titled "The Three Day Blow." In fact, it bears no resemblance to the story, which is just as well. "The Best of Friends" is Hemingway lobotomized for dopes, something straight out of the "Bad Playhouse" parodies on "Saturday Night Live."

locus   *LOH kis*
a place; a center of activity or concentration; location

The year's striking musical moments often came during events ostensibly about other things. James Levine's Met Orchestra concert at Carnegie Hall in mid-November advertised Milton Babbitt's new piano concerto, but it was a performance of Dvorak's G major Symphony that made the jaw drop and the heart beat faster. Here was a locus of points: the sophistication of a big-time orchestra, the dead-on contact with late 19th-century style, and a simple sympathy with the dancing and singing of rural Central Europe.

loggerheads *LAH guhr hedz*
in a head-on dispute; quarreling (loggerheads is always preceded by at)

Ruling in a dispute that has kept New York and New Jersey at loggerheads for 200 years, an arbitrator appointed by the United States Supreme Court recommended yesterday that Ellis Island be divided between the two, drawing the line largely where New Jersey wanted it. The recommendation, which invited inevitable comparisons to King Solomon's ruling dividing the baby, leaves the museum and the major monuments of the famous immigration station in New York's hands. But New Jersey would gain control over about 22 acres of landfill added to the island, starting in 1890, for the construction of hospital and administration buildings.

> ✦ The earliest use of *loggerhead* was in the sixteenth century to describe a stupid person, a blockhead. Shakespeare used it that way in *The Taming of the Shrew*, when Petruchio, scolding his servants, says: "You logger-headed and unpolish'd grooms! What, no attendance? no regard? no duty?" In the seventeenth century, *The Oxford English Dictionary* says, a loggerhead was an iron instrument with a long handle and a ball or bulb at the end, which was heated in a fire to melt tar and heat liquids and kept at the ready on sailing ships. At about the same time, the current meaning of loggerheads arose, possibly as a metaphor for the heavy and hot loggerheads that sailors may have used as weapons at sea.

lollygag *LAH lee gag*
to waste time in trifling or aimless activity; fool around: a slang word of obscure origin

If you don't have to rush around making a living today, Bryant Park, that often abused greensward between West 40th and 42d Streets just behind the Public Library on Fifth Avenue, is bursting with opportunities for musical lollygagging.

longueur *lahn GER*
a long, boring section in a novel, play, musical work, etc.: French

After some longueurs, the weight of Mr. Wise's expertise helps build a head of steam that rushes the reader along, past implausible parts and bits of clumsy writing, as the conflict between Travis and Black moves to a cosmic Washington showdown.

lug *luhg*
a fellow, especially a stupid or dull one: a slang word

Mr. Caan is most convincing as a none-too-bright lug with a talent for thievery and a desire for the conventional life that is forever beyond his reach.

◆ Calling a dull or stupid fellow a lug may be our unwitting homage to the stereotype of the caveman's brutish treatment of his woman. Lug derives from the Scandinavian *lugga*, which literally means *to pull by the hair*.

lumber *LUHM buhr*
to move heavily and clumsily, as if burdened

For a decade, thousands of children and their families have made pilgrimages to Xcacel each year to experience the wonder of the summer nesting season, when on any evening scores of 400-pound loggerheads glide through the surf, lumber up the sloping beach and burrow into the dune to lay eggs. Turtle rangers protect the nests from the poachers who sack beaches elsewhere in Mexico.

luminary *LOO: muh ne ree*
a famous person

In 1980 the City Council passed 73 measures that became law. Twenty of them name some piece of New York City—a park, a street, a traffic island or a playground—after a local or national luminary or foreign leader.

luminosity *loo: muh NAH suh tee*
brightness

Janacek's orchestra scores are notoriously tricky, but the orchestra played with taut discipline and dazzling luminosity.

luxuriant *luhg ZHOO ree uhnt*
growing in great abundance; lush; rich

In recent seasons, Rosalind Elias, the Metropolitan Opera mezzosoprano, has spent considerable time wearing a luxuriant beard as Baba the Turk, the bearded lady of Stravinsky's "The Rake's Progress."

M

meander

As a child growing up on the Jersey Shore, I channeled my

wanderlust through my 10-speed

bicycle. The terrain was flat

and the traffic almost

nonexistent as I headed inland

and meandered for miles along the country roads, whizzing

past cow pastures, horse farms and wooded parks.

see page 233

macabre   *muh KAH bruh*
gruesome; grim and horrible; ghastly

Soon after the suicide or murder of 913 men, women and children on Nov. 18, 1978, James Reston Jr. visited Jonestown and found the tapes. U.S. officials confiscated them, but Reston got most of them back under the Freedom of Information Act: more than 900 macabre hours.

> ✦ *Macabre* came into English in 1842 from the French *danse macabre*, which was an allegorical representation of Death (in the form of a dancing skeleton or corpse) leading all sorts and conditions of humanity to the grave. It is first found in the fourteenth century, and there is a series of woodcuts on the subject by Hans Holbein the Younger (1497-1543). W.H. Auden's poem "The Dance of Death" was published in 1933. And what music appreciation teacher would be without Camille Saint-Saëns' "Danse Macabre" (1875), that quintessential piece that conjures up images of graveyard frolics?

machination   *ma kuh NAY shuhn*
an artful or secret plot or scheme, especially with evil intent: usually plural

As Miss Swit sees it, people do not have to be knowledgeable about the film industry to enjoy "S.O.B." "It could be about any big business, like General Motors," she said. "They all have the same machinations and the same wheeling and dealing and the same big egos. It's not just our industry that's like this."

magnate   *MAG nit*
a powerful or influential person, especially in business or industry

One film magnate flew his favorite caterer over from New York on the Concorde for a party last Saturday at the Hotel du Cap in Antibes.

magnitude   *MAG nuh too:d*
greatness of size, extent or importance

ZARQA, Jordan, March 7—In cramped, unheated rooms on the outskirts of Amman, the relatives of Mohammed A. Salameh, the man charged in the bombing of the World Trade Center, gathered today and pondered the magnitude of the crime and the infamy that has befallen their name.

magnum opus   *MAG nuhm OH puhs*
a person's greatest work or undertaking

In 14th-century Yemen, then a thriving place along trade routes to the Orient, there was a king with an intellectual bent. He wrote numerous scientific tracts, including one dealing with the cultivation of grains, and was knowledgeable in health and astronomy. But his magnum opus was a six-language dictionary, a work of impeccable scholarship.

makeshift   *MAYK shift*
built for temporary, immediate use; a thing that will do for a while; improvised

For more than a mile, they line the hillsides of this narrow gorge in the heart of Kosovo: makeshift shelters put together from tree branches and plastic sheeting that gave shelter to more than 5,000 Albanians fleeing Serbian attacks during the last three months. Faik Thachi came here in late March with his wife and five children thinking that his stay would last just a few weeks. It would be uncomfortable and cold, but they would be safely out of range of Serbian artillery. They ended up staying three months.

malapropism   *MA luh prah pi zuhm*
the ludicrous misuse of a word through confusion caused by its resemblance to another word: after Mrs. Malaprop, a character in Richard Brinsley Sheridan's play The Rivals *(1775), who makes comical blunders in her use of words: French,* mal à propos, *unsuitable, out of place*

Whether over grits and eggs at his favorite diner or before a jury, Wendell H. Gauthier is so self-effacing that he would be the first to admit the many malapropisms that pop out of his mouth, like the time he lamented a cattle investment because so many cows died of "amtraks." Or the time he characterized another lawyer's argument as the height of "epitome."

✦ "She's as headstrong as an allegory on the banks of the Nile."
— Mrs. Malaprop

malinger   *muh LING ger*
to pretend to be ill or otherwise incapacitated in order to escape duty or work; shirk

All pain is real, whether caused by a tumor pressing on a nerve or by tension that tightens muscles or by fear that constricts arteries. Gastrointestinal cramps triggered by anxiety can be just as painful—and are just as real—as those due to amoebic dysentery or colitis. The only "fake" pain is not pain at all; it is a deliberate lie told by a malingerer.

malleable   *MA lee uh buhl*
capable of being changed, molded, adapted, etc., as metals can that are hammered or pressed into various shapes without breaking

"Democracy in our part of the world is a portmanteau word malleable enough to take all shapes and postures," Chanchal Sarkar, an Indian columnist said this week, applying the lesson in India to the problem in Bangladesh.

✦ A portmanteau word is an artificial blend of two words in order to convey the combined meanings of both. We get *smog* from *smoke* and *fog*; *motel* from *motor* and *hotel*; *greige* from *grey* and *beige*. Lewis Carroll coined the term in *Through the Looking-Glass*, where Humpty Dumpty describes how two meanings get "packed up into one word," like a portmanteau, a valise that opens up like a book into two compartments. Carroll used several portmanteau words in *Jabberwocky*, among them *slithy* (slimy + lithe), *mimsy* (flimsy + miserable) and *chortle* (chuckle + snort). Only *chortle* remains in use. Portmanteaus that have become standard English are *dumbfound* (dumb + confound), *splurge* (splash + surge) and *twirl* (twist + whirl). And of course there are *slimnastics, Exercycle, urinalysis, stagflation, beautility, Instamatic, sexploitation* and *broasted*.

mandatory *MAN duh taw ree*
authoritatively commanded or required; obligatory

Jefferson believed in the mandatory teaching of science to all American citizens, and wrote, "Science is important to the preservation of our republican government and it is also essential to its protection against foreign power."

manifest *MA nuh fest*
evident; obvious; clear

Mohammed Anwar el-Sadat was born Dec. 25, 1918, in Mit Abul Kom, a cluster of mud-brick buildings in Minufiya Province between Cairo and Alexandria. He was one of the 13 children of Mohammed el-Sadat, a Government clerk, and his part-Sudanese wife, a heritage manifest in the boy's skin, darker than the average Egyptian's.

manifesto *ma nuh FE stoh*
a public declaration of motives and intentions by a government or by a person or group regarded as having some public importance

The Russian-born painter Wassily Kandinsky (1866-1944) has long been acknowledged to be one of the central figures, if not indeed the central figure, in the creation of abstract painting. His treatise called "On the Spiritual in Art," published in Munich in 1911, was the first major manifesto of the movement, and the paintings themselves initiate a tradition that can be seen to embrace the work of Miro, Gorky, Pollack and the whole Abstract Expressionist School.

manifold *MA nuh fohld*
having many and various forms, features or parts

"Being here in Alaska, so richly endowed with the beauties of nature, one so rugged and yet so splendid, we sense the presence of God's spirit in the manifold handiwork of creation." [Pope John Paul II]

mantra *MAN truh*
a word or phrase said again and again to reinforce an idea in oneself or others, often in the hope that repeating it will make it come true, or that others will believe it will come true; a watchword: Sanskrit, speech, hymn, incantation

Ms. Li, a 41-year-old entrepreneur, swept past the bevy of nurses at the Beijing Yingdong Sanitary Weight Loss Center, removed the jacket of her gray Chanel suit, primped her perfectly curled hair and stepped nervously onto the scale, all the while repeating what has become a mantra for many Chinese women: "I'm too fat. I'm too fat. I'm too fat."

marathon   *MA ruh thahn*
a long contest or task with endurance as the primary factor: after the 26-mile, 385-yard racing event held at the Olympics and elsewhere

John Bickford, president of the sales group for the Westmorland Coal Company, recalled the marathon sessions during which he and officials of the Israeli Electric Company sat bleary-eyed trying to agree on a 30-year contract to deliver steam coal to the utility.

◆ I will not bore you with yet another retelling of how the Olympic marathon was instituted to memorialize the victory of the Greeks over the Persians at Marathon in 490 B.C., the result of which was announced at Athens by a courier who fell dead on arrival, having run nearly twenty-three miles. I will inform my readers, however, that an *apophasis* is the mentioning of something by saying that it will not be mentioned.

marshal   *MAHR shuhl*
arrange; organize

"American culture is a business culture," said Barry J. Kaplan, an urban historian at the University of Houston. "We have marshaled our resources to create a business culture. If that's true, Houston is the epitome of what America can do."

masochist   *MA suh kist*
one who derives pleasure from suffering physical or psychological pain, either self-inflicted or caused by others

"I was running when marathon running was not fashionable. Maybe part of the reason my first wife divorced me was that I was obsessed with running. To be great in anything, not just the marathon, you've got to have compulsive, obsessive tendencies and a little bit of the masochist. Maybe it's more so for marathon runners. You really have to hurt yourself to run, not only physically but also psychologically."

maudlin   *MAWD lin*

foolishly and tearfully sentimental; mawkish: derived from Mary Magdalene—
her English name was Maudlin in the 1500s—who appeared in paintings and
statuary with eyes red or swollen from weeping at the tomb of Jesus

His [E.Y. Harburg's] first successful song was "Brother, Can You Spare A Dime," written with Jay Gorney in 1932, in the Depression. "I thought that work out very carefully," he told an interviewer, Max Wilk. "I didn't make a maudlin lyric of a guy begging. I made it into a commentary. It was about the fellow who works, the fellow who builds, who makes railroads and houses—and he's left empty-handed. This is a man proud of what he has done but bewildered that his country with its dream could do this to him."

mausoleum   *maw suh LEE uhm*

a large, imposing tomb: after Mausolus, a fourth-century king of Caria (now a
part of Turkey), whose huge, marble tomb was one of the Seven Wonders of the
Ancient World

"It depends on what you go to a restaurant for," Dr. Harris said. "Anyone going out for a quiet evening wants a restful place. But those who want to go to a really in spot to be seen want to feel they are in the thick of the action. If the restaurant were as quiet as a mausoleum, they would walk right out."

maven   *MAY vin*

an expert or connoisseur, sometimes a self-proclaimed one, and often an
amateur: Yiddish

My daughter, the grilled cheese maven, fixed her eyes on mine as her favorite lunch was placed before her. The chirpy Bahamian waiter suggested ketchup. The guy, I thought, had guts, interjecting himself between Lizzie and the one meal this heart-rendingly finicky eater would gladly step over my lifeless body for. Lizzie took a mouthful. I couldn't bear to watch. If the food did not meet her exacting standards, this trip to the tropics would melt down faster than you can say American cheese. With one last wistful gaze out the window at the shimmering marina, I turned to face my daughter, who was suddenly bathed in an angelic glow. "Dad," she said, beaming, "I ate the crust." Allow me to translate. In 7-year-old-speak, "ate the crust" meant "four-star dining experience."

mayhem   *MAY hem*
the offense of committing violent injury upon a person; any deliberate
destruction or violence

There must be hoodlums who attend the theater or opera or ballet as well as baseball, football and hockey games, but they never throw things at the actors, and only certifiable crackpots try to slash the Mona Lisa or take a hammer to Michelangelo's Pieta. Generally speaking, it is only at sports events that violence is done. Customers who wouldn't dream of jeering at Barbra Streisand or Luciano Pavarotti seem to feel that a ticket to the grandstand or the bleachers is a license to commit mayhem on the entertainers.

With a n'yuk, n'yuk here and a woo, woo there and here a slap and there a poke, the Three Stooges will embark on a long day's journey into mirth and mayhem at noon on Monday when The Family Channel serves up a seven-hour Three Stooges Marathon. Starring Moe, Larry, Curly and Shemp, the event will tap 21 of the 190 shorts the slapstick zanies churned out between 1934 and 1965.

meander   *mee AN duhr*
to follow a winding course; wander aimlessly or casually: the Maeander River
in Turkey, now called the Menderes, is noted for its twisting course

As a child growing up on the Jersey Shore, I channeled my wanderlust through my 10-speed bicycle. The terrain was flat and the traffic almost nonexistent as I headed inland and meandered for miles along country roads, whizzing past cow pastures, horse farms and wooded parks.

SAIPAN, Northern Mariana Islands—No place on this entire island, a tropical teardrop of land in the Pacific Ocean, has an address. There are no names on the roads that meander alongside the lazy palm trees, nor on the streets that crisscross the island's modest capital city. No house has a number—not the humble shacks up on the hilly inland roads nor the fancy estates that stretch out beside a lengthy beachfront, not even the modern office buildings.

mecca   *ME kuh*
a place that attracts many visitors: from Mecca, the birthplace of Mohammed in
Saudi Arabia, a holy site that Moslems throughout the world are expected to
make a pilgrimage to at least once

For a week, I have been unable to find a single word in the London papers on the Women's World Cup. I know England isn't represented, but they tell me this is the mecca of soccer. What gives?

meld *meld*
to blend, merge, unite

As the former hostages gradually meld back into American life, more details of their long ordeal are emerging, bringing into sharper focus a picture of deprivation, humiliation and terror, spiked with occasional physical attacks.

melee *may LAY*
a noisy, confused fight or hand-to-hand struggle among a number of people:
French, a mixing

"What saved us was the passengers and crew on the airplane. When they rushed the gunmen, there was a big mad scramble, and everyone was all over the place; it was a melee." One terrorist fired several shots before he was subdued. Five hostages were reported wounded—three Turks and two Japanese.

melisma *muh LIZ muh*
a succession of different notes sung upon a single syllable

In her brief solo, Miss Marie proved to be the most powerful white female soul singer that this observer has ever seen. Capable of executing great whooping melismas in perfect pitch, this tiny red-headed woman passed one of the ultimate tests for a pop singer in being able to deliver a ballad—Donny Hathaway's "Someday We'll All Be Free"—in a large arena and keeping the audience riveted.

memorabilia *me muh ruh BIL yuh*
things saved or collected that relate to a particular event, era, place or person;
mementos; souvenirs

For 50 years, Barry Halper has built a baseball memorabilia empire so vast that his 984 historic uniforms move on dry cleaning racks for viewing in his New Jersey house. He has tens of thousands of items, including a baseball signed by Joe and Norma Jean DiMaggio, the contract that sold Babe Ruth from the Red Sox to the Yankees, an autographed 1936 Lou Gehrig uniform, two rare Honus Wagner tobacco cards and Shoeless Joe Jackson's 1919 White Sox uniform.

ménage à trois   *may NAHZH ah TWAH*

an arrangement by which a married—or unmarried—couple and the lover of one of them live together: French, household of three

There we were, we panda fans, our eyes fixed on Washington's National Zoo and last spring's unfortunate ménage à trois: Ling-Ling, Chia-Chia and Hsing-Hsing. We hoped for progeny; what we got was the spectacle of one female (L-L) being brutalized by one male (C-C) and ignored by the other (H-H).

✦ Three pandas? A ménagerie à trois, perhaps.

mensch   *mench*

an honorable, decent, responsible and humane person—you know, the kind of person we want our children to grow up to be: Yiddish, person

The popular image of Anton Chekhov that has come down to us is that of a saintly man: not only the "nicest" and most approachable of the great Russian writers, lacking Tolstoy's ego and Dostoyevsky's torment, but also the very model of a mensch, that rare thing, a selfless writer who expended much of the energy in his short life caring for others—for his large, importunate family and for the patients he tended to as a doctor. The wisdom of his stories, his sensitivity as a writer, his plays' nuanced insights into human nature—all, we've been encouraged to assume, attest to his own humanity and compassion. Even Tolstoy called him "a beautiful, magnificent man."

mentor   *MEN tawr*

a wise, loyal adviser; a teacher or coach

When he was 10 years old, he was apprenticed to a medicine man, or traditional healer, in his native Ghana. Yesterday, at the age of 29, he graduated from the Cornell University Medical College. Dr. Atta-Mensah still has respect for the techniques he learned as a child, helping his mentor gather roots and herbs for curative potions.

✦ In Homer's *Odyssey*, Mentor was the loyal friend and adviser of Odysseus and the teacher of his son, Telemachus.

meretricious   *me ruh TRI shuhs*

lacking sincerity; alluring by false, showy charms

At her best, Edna St. Vincent Millay expressed a "passion for identification with all of life which few poets of her generation have possessed; she made ecstasy articulate and almost tangible," wrote Louis Untermeyer, poet and critic. But the passing years have not been kind to her reputation, as critics have noted her many borrowings and the meretricious posturing of much of her verse.

✦ Edna St. Vincent Millay got her middle name from St. Vincent's Hospital in New York City. Her uncle, as a young man journeying to America from England, became locked in the hold of his ship. Not discovered until the vessel docked in New York, he was rushed, near death, to the hospital. Her family, in appreciation of the hospital's care that saved his life, used its name as the middle name of the new baby girl in the family.

mesmerize   *MEZ muh righz*
captivate; engross; spellbind; enthrall

Claire Messud's mesmerizing new book, "The Last Life," is a novel, her second it turns out, but the portrait it draws of a family and its disintegration is so vivid, its rendering of the conflicting claims of memory and denial so fraught with felt emotion, that the reader might easily mistake it for a memoir.

messiah   *muh SIGH uh*
any expected savior, liberator or leader: in Judaism, the promised and expected deliverer of the Jews; in Christianity, Jesus, regarded as the realization of the Messianic prophecy

In general, Mr. Springsteen is less than convincing when he seems to be buying the image admiring critics and fans have created for him, the image of the rock messiah whose songs are eternal verities carved in stone. No rock artist can afford to take himself that seriously and, in any case, Mr. Springsteen's writing is too uneven and too musically limited to bear up under the sort of scrutiny that is routinely lavished on holy writ.

metamorphose   *me tuh MAWR fohz*
to change in form or nature; to undergo metamorphosis: Greek, meta, *over +* morphe, *shape*

At the end of the fifth stage, the larva becomes a pupa and then metamorphoses into a moth, which lays egg clusters on trees in the fall. The eggs hatch in the spring.

to undergo a marked or complete change of character, appearance, condition, etc. as figuratively radical as that undergone literally by animals such as butterflies and frogs

The metamorphosis of Chinese women this summer, from being wrapped in cocoons of baggy trousers and formless shirts to wearing colorful and relatively revealing dresses and skirts, even miniskirts, has transformed China into a land not only of beauty but also of beauties.

metaphor   *ME tuh fawr*

a figure of speech in which one thing is said to be another, although in a literal sense it is not, as with "My love is a rose." A figure of speech that employs "like," as in "My love is like a red, red rose," is called a simile. (Note the simile in the second passage under miscreant.*)*

Flame is indeed a reasonable metaphor for Shakespeare's language. It heats, it consumes, it shapes and reshapes itself and everything it touches, and it seems both tangible and intangible, as vaporous in appearance as its effects are real. One time you find yourself reading Shakespeare for the imagery—the occasions of metaphoric transcendence—and the next time, the next line, for words of irreducible simplicity, like the ones Lear speaks as his sanity flickers back to him in Cordelia's presence: "Pray, do not mock me. I am a very foolish fond old man."

meticulous   *muh TIK yoo luhs*

extremely or excessively concerned with details; scrupulous or finicky

First drafts of his books consist of black loose-leaf binders filled with lined white paper, meticulously covered with peacock-blue script—no blots, no scratchings-out.

miasma   *migh AZ muh*

an unwholesome or befogging atmosphere, influence, etc.: literally, a vapor rising from marshes, formerly supposed to poison and infect the air, causing malaria and other diseases

In neighborhoods all around this blossoming metropolis, thousands of families, black and white, have been experiencing an agonizing, unwanted change in their daily lives. A common thread underlies the new living patterns: fear. It rises like a miasma from the 16 unsolved cases of Atlanta's missing and murdered children, in defiance of a generally declining crime rate.

microcosm   *MIGH kroh kah zuhm*
a world in miniature; a community, village or other environment regarded as a
miniature or epitome of a larger world or of the world

In a "touch tank," set up as a microcosm of the Great South Bay, children can
handle horseshoe and hermit crabs, sea stars (which destroy scallops),
urchins and other salt-water invertebrates.

mien   *meen*
appearance

A man of sharp features and severe mien that is not softened by his black
turban, thick spectacles or dark beard, Hojatolislam Khamenei is known to
acquaintances as Vajabi, which roughly translates as "Tom Thumb."

milieu   *meel YOO*
environment, especially a social or cultural setting: French, middle

Frontiers traditionally attract two kinds of people: the enterprising and energetic, and those escaping from somewhere else. This is the milieu that produced Ronald Reagan. He was among millions of people who emigrated to
California in the Depression with little more than their ambition, and he was
among the enterprising and energetic who made their fortune here.

When we enter water we enter an alien milieu. As a child and a teen-ager, I
always had a vague sense of foreboding when swimming in bay, sound or
ocean. Dark shapes—some still, some moving—were below me and tendrils
of seaweed or the soft, undulating forms of jellyfish touching me often
brought a spurt of fear.

ministrations   *mi ni STRAY shuhnz*
the act of giving help; service

Having undergone the ministrations of three different directors, and as many
choreographers, before it finally reached Broadway, "Sophisticated Ladies" is
the kind of show that costume designers are apt to view with something akin
to horror. Willa Kim, the musical's Tony Award-winning costume designer,
agrees. "It was a pain in the neck," she says. "All the directorial changes,"
explained Miss Kim, "meant that numbers, and therefore costumes, were
constantly being cut and added."

minutiae   *mi NOO: shuh*
small, unimportant details

Bits, pieces, minutiae, the commonplace all go into the journal because "someday they'll be of interest," he says. "I always include the price of things, the names and addresses of restaurants. I write routine stuff because I never know what will interest the historians, and it's often the obvious stuff that gets lost."

miscreant   *MIS cree int*
a criminal; an evildoer or villain, as in the first example here; often applied, though, with a wink by the writer, as though to indicate that the accuser is going a bit overboard with his or her condemnation, as in the second example

It is the high-tech computer thieves who get nearly all the attention: the hackers, cyberpunks and industrial spies who delight in slipping past firewalls and penetrating seemingly impenetrable systems for fun and profit. But another type of miscreant is wreaking havoc in the computer world: the burglar. As laptops become smaller and lighter, they also become easier to pinch.

Passengers were still filing down the aisle. The American Airlines flight attendant had to scoot around them to pounce on the miscreant like a hall monitor cornering a school scofflaw. "Sir, you put that away immediately!" he barked. The passenger, who had just completed a quick cell phone call to check his office voice mail, was already putting the phone away.

misgivings   *mis GI vingz*
a disturbed feeling of doubt, fear or apprehension

Despite his misgivings about the nation's state of preparedness, General Doolittle has hope. "America," he said, "seems to have gotten lazy, selfish and immoral, but is in the process of correcting it."

mishmash   *MISH mash*
a hodgepodge; jumble

The playwright has merged the most memorable scenes from James Whale's 1931 Hollywood version with random scraps from the 1816 Shelley novel only to end up with a talky, stilted mishmash that fails to capture either the gripping tone of the book or the humorous pleasure of the film. This "Frankenstein" has instead the plodding, preachy quality one associates with the lesser literary adaptations of public television.

misogyny   *mi SAH juh nee*
hatred of women, especially by a man

"Cheaper to Keep Her," which opened yesterday at the Criterion Center and other theaters, has a strain of misogyny that's part of a larger cynicism it displays. Miss Lopez, though she does it with delicious animation, plays a scheming woman who won't bed down with Mr. Davis until he buys her an expensive dinner. And the alimony plot offers plenty of opportunity for similar observations about women and their motives.

> ✦ *Misogyny* derives from the Greek *miso* (hatred) + *gyno* (woman), and is one of a number of English words prefixed with *miso* or *mis* and meaning the hatred of something. Those likely to be encountered in general reading are *misanthropy*, hatred of people (*anthropos*, a man), and *misogamy*, hatred of marriage (*gamy*, marriage).

mogul   *MOH guhl*
a powerful or important person, especially one with autocratic power: the Moguls were the Mongol conquerers and rulers of India who held power from the 16th to early 18th centuries

What young pianist does not secretly hope that a great mogul in the management world will hear him, realize that the next Rubenstein or Horowitz has appeared, and rush to him with fat contracts and a promise of unending fame?

monastic   *muh NA stik*
characteristic of monastery life; ascetic; austere

To write, William Faulkner said, the tools he needed were "paper, tobacco, food and a little whisky." The question is, what sort of food? Should it be severe and monastic, a meal of canned tuna and tea? Should he pick at dishes such as Alice B. Toklas's Salade Aphrodite, yogurt, apples and celery, "for poets with delicate digestions"? Or, like Balzac, is he nearly killing himself with black coffee, ground at frequent intervals from a grinder attached to the desk?

monotheism   *MAH nuh thee i zuhm*
the doctrine or belief that there is only one God

CAIRO, March 8—The fate of the contents of the Royal Mummy Room at the Egyptian Museum continues to spark discussions among Government officials, museum personnel and antiquities experts. President Anwar el-Sadat ordered the museum exhibit closed in early October because, he said, Egypt's monotheistic creed is against the public display. The museum's gallery of 30 or more mummies of Pharaohs, on public view since 1958, was immediately put under lock and key, and a committee was appointed to study the problem of the future of the mummies.

montage   *mahn TAHZH*
the art, style or process of making one pictorial composition from many pictures or designs, closely arranged or superimposed upon each other: French, mounting

Condon's has a long bar, at the end of which is the bandstand that faces the row of tables that lines the other wall, beneath a montage of photographs of greats that have blared and muted in the annals of jazz.

moot   *moo:t*
open to debate; unresolvable

It is a moot point as to whether blondes have more fun, but millionaires certainly do, especially Malcolm S. Forbes, who is the chairman of Forbes magazine. Mr. Forbes is not what one would call a reticent type. He enjoys himself smack in the public eye, and balances such unmillionairelike activities as ballooning and motorcycling with the more genteel pursuits of collecting Faberge and yachting.

mordant   *MAWR dint*
biting; cutting; caustic or sarcastic in speech or wit

In one famous if possibly apocryphal story, Fritz Kreisler had a memory slip while playing a Beethoven violin sonata with Sergei Rachmaninoff. As Kreisler improvised in search of the thread, he whispered, "Do you know where we are?" Rachmaninoff's mordant reply was, "Yes, we're on the stage of Carnegie Hall."

moribund   *MAW ruh buhnd*
having little or no vital force left; stagnant

Whitney Young was one of the leading figures on the American scene as executive director of the National Urban League from 1961 to 1971. The league, founded in 1910 by white and black social workers and philanthropists, had become moribund. Under his leadership, the league grew tremendously and its activities, power and influence were revitalized.

mortified   *MAWR tuh fighd*
stricken with embarrassment; humiliated as the result of an unpleasant experience

Embarrassment infected Bernie Williams as he walked back to home plate in the second inning of Monday night's game against Oakland. Williams had taken a pitch out of the strike zone and started running to first, pleased at drawing a bases-loaded walk—until he realized the count was actually three balls and two strikes. With teammates using caps to cover their faces and hide their laughter, a mortified Williams returned to the plate, picked up his bat—and bashed a grand slam against Mike Oquist, capping an eight-run rally. The Yankees went on to win, 12-8.

mosaic   *moh ZAY ik*
a picture or decoration made of small pieces of inlaid stone, glass, etc.; something resembling this kind of construction

Best of all, Boston is a superb walking town. Compact and convenient, a mosaic of distinctive neighborhoods, it is a baby London.

motif   *moh TEEF*
a dominant or recurring theme, idea, feature, element, etc.

Many of the plays and stories of that celebrated esthete Oscar Wilde shared a dominant motif—the exposure of a secret sin, followed by humiliation and disgrace.

Amsterdam Avenue, for all its distinguished architectural pockets, is a tribute to the tenement, and its continuing motif from one end to the other is the fire escape, mostly in standard, straightforward metal, but occasionally displaying a coquettish bellying out to relieve the uniformity.

mot juste   *moh ZHOOST*
the right word: French

Miles Davis, in the words of Gil Evans, the arranger who collaborated in the creation of five important recordings, "was the first man to change the sound of the trumpet since Louis Armstrong." As early as the 1950's, critics vied among themselves on his album liners and in magazine articles for the mots justes to describe the Davis sound.

muckrake   *MUK rayk*
to search for and publicize real or alleged scandal, or corruption by public officials, industrialists, etc.

Virtually alone among Indian journalists, Mr. Shourie, an editor of The Indian Express, the nation's largest circulation daily newspaper, has organized and written muckraking exposés on such scandals as the blinding by policemen of 31 suspects awaiting trial, the selling of women and the detention for years of poor people awaiting trial on minor charges.

✦ The term muckraker—a crusading journalist whose goal is to uncover corruption in business and politics—originated with Theodore Roosevelt. In a 1906 speech, he said, "The men with the muckrakes are often indispensable to the well-being of society; but only if they know when to stop raking the muck." The source of Roosevelt's muckrakers appears to be a character in John Bunyan's 1684 allegorical novel, *Pilgrim's Progress.* In it, those who seek only worldly treasure, while oblivious to life's spiritual riches, are symbolized by "A man that could look no way but downwards, with a muckrake in his hand."

mundane   *MUHN dayn*
ordinary; everyday; commonplace; also, practical, routine or dull

LHASA, Tibet—Yaks may roam the streets outside, and pilgrims may crawl and kowtow along the roads to win divine favor, but inside the Lhasa Holiday Inn there is a more mundane concern: Why are 600 teaspoons missing, and how can the hotel get more? "We don't know if it's the staff or the guests, but as soon as we put a teaspoon on the table, it disappears," said Alec Le Sueur, the hotel's sales and marketing manager, one of 10 expatriates struggling to run an international hotel on the roof of the world.

✦ In its original Chinese usage, *kowtow* means to bow and touch the forehead to the ground to show great respect, as by a young person to someone of an older generation or by anyone to a revered figure. Western ambassadors who refused to kowtow to Chinese emperors as a condition of meeting with them were refused audience.

murky   MER kee

unclear; clouded; confused; obscure: like water in which sediment has been stirred up

Mr. Ocalan, whose followers have waged a long separatist war in southeastern Turkey in which more than 30,000 people have died, was seized in Nairobi, Kenya, in circumstances that remain murky. Turkish agents flew him to Turkey where he faces a possible death sentence on charges including treason and murder.

myriad   MI ree id

countless; innumerable; an infinitely large number: used as an adjective in the first passage and as a noun in the second

KIGALI, Rwanda—This is a land of plenty: plenty of folks tending plenty of crops that grow in myriad small plots, quilted green across the slopes and ravines and summits of a nation that calls itself the land of a thousand hills.

All animals, from frogs to rodents to elephants to humans, begin as single fertilized eggs. Then, during the species' allotted days or months of gestation, the single fertilized cell differentiates into a vast, close-knit community, a myriad of different specialized cells all functioning in harmony. How does this process of differentiation proceed? No one knows. It is one of the central puzzles of modern biology, hotly pursued in laboratories everywhere because answers would almost certainly give clearer understanding of the nature of life and of many human health problems that arise through faults in development.

nosh

In the old days we had only the blue and orange umbrellas

denoting the hot dogs of Sabrett, plus pretzel and ice cream

vendors. Today the peripatetic nosher can choose from

Mexican tacos, Middle Eastern

felafel, Greek souvlaki, Chinese

Fu Manchu stew, Japanese tempura,

so-called New York-style steak sandwiches and true New

York-style hot dogs and egg creams, Afghanistan kofta

kebabs and Caribbean beef or chicken curry.

see page 252

nabob   *NAY bahb*

a very rich or important person: originally, a European who made a large fortune in India or another Eastern country

> Joseph Wharton (1826-1909) was a man of wealth who, like many of the nabobs of his time, was also a philanthropist and a supporter of causes—in his case education and a protective high tariff.

nadir   *NAY der*

the lowest point; time of greatest depression or dejection: Arabic, opposite the zenith

> "It was the nadir of my life," Mr. Vickery recalled. "Paris, 1971. Broke. A string of stupid jobs. A tortured love affair. I was getting nowhere. I asked myself. 'What do I know how to do?' I had done plays in college, and it was really what I liked to do. So, I decided to be an actor."

naïveté   *nah EEV tay*

the state of being naïve; artlessness; ingenuousness: French

> A wide-eyed, strawberry blonde, with a marvelous deadpan quality, Miss McArdle sings such classics as "Blue Skies," "White Christmas" and "They Say It's Wonderful" with a purposeful naïveté that underscores the songs' innocence.

narcissism   *NAHR si si zuhm*

self-love; excessive interest in one's own appearance, comfort, importance, abilities, etc.

Changing seats three times so that a photographer can shoot his "good" side, Mr. Vidal arranges his face—a face he once described as that of one of Rome's "later, briefer Emperors"—in a mirror, turns sharply to a visitor and offers another definition. "I suppose you'll call me a narcissist," he says. "Well, a narcissist is someone better looking than you are."

✦ Because she chattered incessantly, Echo, a wood nymph, was rendered voiceless by Juno, except to repeat what others said to her. When she fell in love with beautiful Narcissus, she could not convey her feelings, but only mimic his words. One day, however, hearing Narcissus call, "Let us join one another," she repeated it, then rushed to his arms. Narcissus recoiled. Crushed, Echo sulked in caves and on cliffs, fading away till only her voice remained (remained, remained, remained). Soon another rejected nymph prayed that Narcissus, too, might know the pain of unrequited love. Vengeance was hers. Narcissus, stooping over a river's brink, fell in love with his image in the water. He talked to it, tried to embrace it, languished over it, pined away and died. Even on its way to Hades, his shade leaned over the boat to catch one last glimpse of itself in the river Styx. The local nymphs prepared a pyre on which to burn the youth's body, but it was gone. In its place a flower grew, purple and white, called to this day—narcissus.

nascent   *NAY sint*
coming into existence; being born

Mr. Youle, who became known in Chicago as The Weatherman and nationally as Mr. Weatherman, was one of several World War II veterans who parlayed their meteorological skills into jobs in the nascent field of television in the late 1940's. During the war, he joined the Army Air Forces, was trained in meteorology and served as an intelligence officer in Panama.

ne'er-do-well   *NAIR doo wel*
an irresponsible and unsuccessful person; good-for-nothing

Nita Longley looks like a child herself, with her big eyes and skinny body and pale freckled face. But she is a mother: she has two small sons, and her handsome, ne'er-do-well husband has left her to raise them alone in a small Texas town.

neophyte   *NEE uh fight*
a beginner; novice

Becoming an inspector for the Guide Michelin is not easy. The apprentice-ship lasts five years because the neophyte must work in every corner of France and visit virtually every restaurant listed in the guide, and all his reports are checked by senior staff members. "It's a long time," said Mr. Trichot, "but we must be sure of the man and he must become one of us."

niche   *nich*
a place or position particularly suitable to the person or thing in it; any small, specialized business market

Robin Fuller was overseeing the financial affairs of clients for a Tucson law firm specializing in the elderly when she realized there was a niche to be filled and reinvented herself as a geriatric care manager.

the particular role of a species in its environment, including its position in the food cycle and its behavior

Roughly the size and shape of a German shepherd, the coyote (the name comes from the Aztec word coyotl and is typically pronounced kai-OH-tee in the East but KAI-oat in most of the West) fills an ecological niche between that of the wolf and the fox.

nirvana   *ner VA nuh*
a place or state of great peace or bliss: from the Buddhist belief that the state of perfect blessedness is achieved by the extinction of all desires and passions

An umpire works about 130 regular-season games and has four one-week vacations, so he is away from relatives and friends for long periods. Despite the incessant travel, however, Hirschbeck called the job nirvana. "I work six months a year," Hirschbeck said. "I don't even count spring training. Plus you get four weeks off. It's easy to look at the negatives, but I look at the positives. I thank God every day for my job. Everything I have in my life is from baseball. How can I not be grateful?"

> ✦ *Umpire* should really be *numpire*. The original French term for a third party who settles disputes was a *noumpere* (not equal), but in English the term became *an umpire* through the incorrect separation of the article and the noun. By the same

process we have *an adder*, from *a nadder*, *a newt* from *an ewt*, *an apron* from *a napron*, and *a nickname* from *an eke name* (an "also" name).

nomadic   *noh MA dik*
wandering from place to place, in the manner of a nomad, a member of a tribe or people having no permanent home, but moving about constantly in search of food, pasture, etc.

A dollar, tip included, is what the nomadic bootblacks who ply their trade in office buildings are paid by most of their customers.

nom de guerre   *nahm duh GUHR*
a fictitious name taken by someone involved in military or political activities who, for safety's sake, must conceal his or her real name; often used by revolutionaries to keep their identity secret in their own country: French, war name

Ricardo Ramírez, the Guatemalan guerrilla commander turned peacemaker, who was better known to his countrymen by his nom de guerre, Rolando Morán, died on Friday in a hospital in Guatemala City. He was 67 and had lived in the Guatemalan capital since a peace accord that ended the country's long civil war was signed in December 1996.

> ◆ Vladimir Ilich Ulyanov (1870-1924) changed his last name to Lenin, Iosif Vissarionovich Dzhugashvili (1879-1953) became Joseph Stalin, and Lev Davidovich Bronstein (1879-1940) became Leon Trotsky. All chose noms de guerre when they were revolutionaries against Russia's czarist rule.

nom de plume   *nahm duh PLOO:M*
a pseudonym assumed by a writer: French, pen name; pseudonym defines any fictitious name used in place of a person's actual or legal name, while nom de plume is reserved for writers

Even by Victorian standards, Charles Lutwidge Dodgson was a considerable eccentric. When the shy Oxford University lecturer veered away from his academic interest in mathematics to publish "Alice's Adventures in Wonderland" and "Through the Looking Glass," he hid behind the nom de plume of Lewis Carroll and, even late in life, refused to acknowledge that he was the author of the best-selling children's classics.

✦ *Nom de plume* is a French term…and yet it is not a French term. It was coined by English-speaking people to give themselves a French term for "false name." The French themselves don't use it. They use *nom de guerre*, a term that originated in the days when every entrant into the French army assumed a name.

Herewith, a short list of writers and others who used noms de plume, noms de guerre, pen names or pseudonyms during part or all of their careers, with their real name first:

Sholom Yakov Rabinowitz	Shalom Aleichem
François-Marie Arouet	Voltaire
Eric Arthur Blair	George Orwell
William Sydney Porter	O. Henry
David Cornwell	John le Carré
Mary Ann Evans	George Eliot
Aleksey Maksimovich Peshkov	Maxim Gorky
Neftali Ricardo Reyes Basoalto	Pablo Neruda
Declan McManus	Elvis Costello
Doris Kappelhoff	Doris Day
Issur Danielovitch Demsky	Kirk Douglas
Nguyen That Thanh	Ho Chi Minh
Ivo Levi	Yves Montand
Joe Yule Jr.	Mickey Rooney
Isabella Van Wagener	Sojourner Truth
Stephen Judkins	Stevie Wonder
Alphonso D'Abruzzo	Alan Alda
EhrichWeiss	Harry Houdini
Ellas Bates	Bo Diddley
Gorden Sumner	Sting

nomenclature   *NOH muhn klay cher*
the act or process of naming

The nomenclature of various dishes is fascinating, for things are, to borrow a phrase, seldom what they seem. There is a crisp puff-pastry dessert called pig's ears; a Mont Blanc is a "mountain" of puréed chestnuts; and eggs in the snow, or les oeufs à la neige, are poached meringues floating in a vanilla custard.

nonchalant   *nahn shuh LAHNT*
coolly unconcerned; casually indifferent

"We talked and laughed for 10 hours. He got to know me, the person, and apparently liked what he heard. When it was time to become intimate, I very nonchalantly mentioned: 'By the way, I just had both my breasts removed. Does that matter to you?' I knew I was taking the biggest chance of rejection of my life," she continued, "but it was now or never. His mouth dropped, his eyes dilated. He was absolutely silent for a minute. Then he said, 'So what.'"

nondescript   *nahn duh SKRIPT*
a person or thing with no outstanding or distinguishing features

FOUR SEASONS, 2800 Pennsylvania Avenue, N.W., (202) 342-0444. A nondescript brick box on the outside, a festival of fine fabrics and fresh flowers on the inside, this is Washington's premier hotel.

nonpareil   *nahn puh REL*
someone or something of unequaled excellence: French, without equal; usually (but not always) spelled as one word

The nearly 80,000 items of baseball memorabilia—from the gorgeously historic to the madly esoteric—that filled the comfortable home of Barry Halper in Livingston, N.J., have mostly been packed up and shipped out. About 20 percent of his collection was sent to the Baseball Hall of Fame, where a wing named for this collector non pareil has been built. Most of the rest of the collection will be sold at a weeklong auction at Sotheby's in Manhattan, beginning on Sept. 23, which, according to Sotheby's, has a chance to break the house record of $34.4 million set by the sale of the Jackie Kennedy Onassis estate.

non sequitur   *nahn SE kwi ter*
a remark having no bearing on what has just been said: Latin, it does not follow

Dr. Harvey A. Rosenstock, a Houston psychiatrist, suggests ending arguments with teen-agers by deliberately introducing a non sequitur that, being irrelevant and unanswerable, usually provokes a smile. For example, when you've reached an impasse, suddenly say, "What do you think of the Australian Government?"

nosh   *nahsh*
a snack; Yiddish, from the German, nachen, *to eat on the sly*

In the old days we had only the blue and orange umbrellas denoting the hot dogs of Sabrett, plus pretzel and ice cream vendors. Today the peripatetic nosher can choose from Mexican tacos, Middle Eastern felafel, Greek souvlaki, Chinese Fu Manchu stew, Japanese tempura, so-called New York-style steak sandwiches and true New York-style hot dogs and egg creams, Afghanistan kofta kebabs and Caribbean beef or chicken curry.

notoriety *noh tuh RIGH uh tee*
fame gained through bad deeds

Theodore J. Kaczynski won notoriety as the Unabomber, the evil genius who mailed deadly pipe bombs to scientists and corporate targets from California to New Jersey.

novel *NAH vuhl*
new and unusual

When John and Carilyn Redman had trouble finding a buyer for their $113,000 home in northern Virginia earlier this year, they hit on a novel solution to beat the high mortgage rates: They decided to raffle it off.

novice *NAH vis*
a person new to a particular activity; beginner

Last October, Salazar predicted he would run 2 hours 9 minutes in the New York City Marathon, his first race at that distance. To the astonishment of many who had dismissed him as a naïve novice, he won in 2:09:41.

nullify *NUH luh figh*
to make valueless or useless; remove the effectiveness of

Whatever his age, it's beginning to show on Ken Norton's face and in the hint of a bald spot. But in order to get a title shot against either Larry Holmes, the W.B.C. champion, or Mike Weaver, the World Boxing Association champion, he must first nullify Gerry Cooney's left hook, the punch that has produced a 24-0 record with 20 knockouts.

numinous *NOO: muh nuhs*
having a deeply spiritual or mystical effect

One of the very few things about African art on which everyone is agreed is that, at its best, it has a numinous quality. It was not meant for collectors and dealers or even for disinterested enjoyment. It was meant, as Miss Vogel reminds us, to give exalted pleasure, but [also] "to express and support fundamental spiritual values that are essential to the survival of the community."

opaque

It is a cloud of pollution that smears the crisp, desert sky

above Phoenix with a puffy,

opaque crown of dirty air

reminiscent of a giant chef's cap.

On many days it can be seen more

than 40 miles from the city.

see page 259

obfuscate   *AHB fuh skayt*
to muddle; confuse; make unclear or obscure

If I seem hypersensitive to recipe obfuscations, it is probably because I was scarred at an early age, when my mother gave me a recipe for one of her coffeecakes. For baking time it said, "The longer it bakes, the better." When I asked her if she meant an hour, a week, or a year, she answered, "A sane person can't have a decent conversation with you." To this day I have not made the cake, wondering just how much time I must set aside for its baking.

oblique   *oh BLEEK*
not straight to the point; indirect

The only reference Maureen Reagan made to her father in a commercial she filmed for a mail-order acne lotion was oblique. "Let me tell you," she said, "it certainly made my life easier during that frantic election campaign."

obstinate   *AHB stuh nit*
stubborn

A teen-ager may be warm and loving one minute, hostile and rejecting the next, flexible and cooperative today, obstinate and self-centered tomorrow.

ocher   *OH ker*
dark yellow: ocher is an earthy clay colored by iron oxide, usually yellow or reddish brown, and used as a pigment in paint

From an airplane, Egypt appears to be a ribbon of water, girded by green and placed in an endless expanse of parched, ocher desert.

257

odious   *OH dee uhs*
arousing or deserving hatred or loathing; disgusting; offensive

Mrs. Shields is also given, like many stage mothers, to odious comparison. In a single breath, she will compare her daughter to Elizabeth Taylor and Natalie Wood, saying that her daughter "has more appeal than Liz had or has," that her daughter's voice cracks "just like Natalie Wood's," and taking her daughter's hand, kissing it three times, concludes with, "I know you'll marry the men you go to bed with, just like Liz did."

officious   *uh FI shuhs*
pretentiously managerial; offering unasked for and unneeded assistance— usually to strangers

Mr. Zane is white, short and chunky, with a buoyant, strutting walk and the very funny look of an officious floorwalker in a second-rate department store.

offshoot   *AWF shoo:t*
something that branches off or derives from a main stem

Bluegrass music, with its commercialized offshoots, is a thriving American subculture, not just in the South, where it originated, but in the New York area as well.

ominous   *AH muh nis*
serving as an omen; indicating the possibility, but not the certainty, of future misfortune or calamity. An omen can be good or bad, but ominous is always used in a negative sense.

When Wal-Mart Stores proposed in 1990 building its first outlet in Vermont, in the village of Williston, it started a fight that turned ugly quickly. The Burlington Free Press ominously editorialized about the "New Jerseyification" of the scenic vacation town of 6,000 residents. The National Trust for Historic Preservation declared the entire state of Vermont and its little white-steepled towns "endangered" by suburban sprawl. It took seven years of expensive battling before the store finally opened.

omnivorous   *ahm NI vuh ruhs*
eating both animal and vegetable food

Why not, we reasoned, learn all we could about what lures a sea robin likes? We quickly discovered that the fish's omnivorous eating habits lead it to hit virtually everything. Sinking plugs, spoons, metal jigs, bucktail jigs—even a weighted fly—all were seized with alacrity.

onus   *OH nuhs*
responsibility; burden

The onus is on the restaurant to have sufficient expertise to recommend a likable wine and to have the grace to take it back if the recommendation is rejected.

opaque   *oh PAYK*
not letting light pass through; not transparent or translucent

It is a cloud of pollution that smears the crisp, desert sky above Phoenix with a puffy, opaque crown of dirty air reminiscent of a giant chef's cap. On many days it can be seen more than 40 miles from the city.

opulent   *AH pyuh luhnt*
rich; abundant

Seven of the Copeland songs were sung by Marilyn Horne, as one more observance of the composer's 80th birthday season. She seemed to be trying to subdue her opulent operatic voice by adopting a quasi-folk approach, and that produced lovely results at times, as in "Long Time Ago."

osmosis   *ahz MOH sis*
a gradual absorption of knowledge or a skill by contact with it rather than through formal study or training

Nell Dorr's father was a photographer, and she learned the craft from him by osmosis and by direct instruction.

ostensible   *ah STEN suh buhl*
given out as such; seeming; professed; supposed

After his evening appearance in "Fifth of July," the actor [Richard Thomas] was lured by his wife, Alma, to La Méditerranée, a Second Avenue restaurant, ostensibly to meet a couple of out-of-town friends. What he found was about 60 mostly in-town friends who had gathered for a surprise party that he insisted was truly a surprise. Mr. Thomas, it turned out, had a surprise of his own. The baby his wife is expecting in September, he confided to some of the guests, is actually twins.

ostentatious   *ah stuhn TAY shuhs*

show-offy, as with knowledge, material possessions, etc.; pretentious; meant to impress others

No one who watched the embarrassing spectacle of Maria Callas in her declining years could fail to see that the soprano was being slowly but certainly eaten alive by the ostentatiously wealthy and vulgar society that surrounded her.

ostracize   *AH struh sighz*

to bar; exclude

I.F. Stone has rejoined the pack. Mr. Stone, the premier loner and dedicated maverick of American journalism, was welcomed back into the National Press Club yesterday after having been ostracized by that section of the journalism Establishment for trying to take a black friend to lunch at the club 40 years ago.

> ✦ Ostracism was originally the method of banishing citizens of ancient Greece whose power was considered dangerous to the state. In a secret ballot taken in the Assembly, the accused's name was written on a piece of pottery, called an ostrakon. In Athens, a majority of at least 6,000 voting members of the Assembly had to vote "yes" for someone to be sent into exile, which was usually a period of ten years. During the ninety years this practice existed in Athens, only ten persons were banished.

overweening   *oh ver WEE ning*

exaggerated; excessive; arrogant

Mrs. Shields also possesses the overweening attention of all stage mothers and managers, commenting, with some concern, that her daughter's face is beginning to change, to look a "little sculpted." "You mean square," said Brooke.

progenitor

Just as human parents produce children of very different

character, pinot and gouais turn out to be the progenitors of

16 very different wine grapes. Three are known throughout

the world. Chardonnay is perhaps the

leading variety of white wine.

Gamay is the grape from which all

Beaujolais is derived. And melon, a

third pinot-gouais offspring, is the

source of all Muscadet.

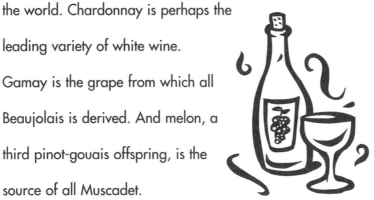

see page 286

pacesetter   *PAYS se ter*
a person, group or thing that leads the way or serves as a model

While explicit honor systems exist only on relatively few campuses, they are generally viewed as pacesetters of undergraduate ethics.

paleontology   *pay lee uhn TAH luh jee*
the science that deals with prehistoric forms of life through the study of fossils

"But Jefferson virtually founded the science of paleontology," Mr. Bedini said. "He collected fossil bones, sometimes failing to identify them correctly. But he stimulated other investigators and lent respectability to the fledgling science."

pallid   *PA lid*
pale or deficient in color; lifeless; dull

A daily special of chicken breast stuffed with vegetables and cheese was also overpowered by its wine sauce, and the pallid version of the garlic-sautéed chicken scarpariello lacked flavor.

palmy   *PAH mee*
flourishing; prosperous

The palmy days of the cowboy lasted only from about 1865, when the big cattle drives north from Texas to the Rocky Mountain grasslands began, until the late 80's, when famous blizzards, barbed wire, overgrazing and plunging cattle prices ended the great days of the open range.

palpable   *PAL puh buhl*
tangible; perceptible

In the 60's, new albums from the Beatles, the Rolling Stones, Bob Dylan, and a few other performers were genuine cultural events. These albums seemed to fuse the rock audience into a palpable coherent community. They were messages from the community's seers, to be savored and probed for hidden meanings and listened to again and again, with joy and reverence, until the group's next album came along.

panache   *puh NASH*
an air of spirited self-confidence or style; dashing elegance of manner

"That's about $185,000," Philip B. Miller, the president of Neiman-Marcus, observed coolly as a voluminous skin-on-skin sable wrap was modeled with appropriate panache. Other six-figure sables, with scalloped edges, were tossed dramatically over leather pants. That's the new order of fashion: ultimate luxury worn as casually as a sweater.

panoply   *PA nuh plee*
magnificent array

All the panoply of monarchy was deployed on this, one of the great days in the history of the House of Windsor: the stirring music of Handel and Purcell and Elgar; the Household Cavalry, in their burnished breastplates and helmets with red plumes; the stately royal horses, caparisoned in silver; almost all the reigning sovereigns of Europe, come in their finery to share in the happy occasion, and the royal bride herself, resplendent in a gown of pale ivory, with puffy sleeves and a train 25 feet long.

pantheon   *PAN thee ahn*
all the gods of a people; the major heroes in a particular category

DiMaggio burst onto the baseball scene from San Francisco in the 1930's and grew into the game's most gallant and graceful center fielder. He wore No. 5 and became the successor to Babe Ruth (No. 3) and Lou Gehrig (No. 4) in the Yankees' pantheon. DiMaggio was the team's superstar for 13 seasons, beginning in 1936 and ending in 1951, and appeared in 11 All-Star Games and 10 World Series. He was, as the writer Roy Blount Jr. once observed, "the class of the Yankees in times when the Yankees outclassed everybody else."

✦ The first Pantheon—Greek for *all the gods*—was a circular temple in Rome that was completed in 27 B.C. and dedicated to all the gods. Later pantheons have been public buildings, the best known of which is the Pantheon in Paris, built as the church of Sainte Geneviève by Louis XV to fulfill a vow he made in 1744 during a serious illness. Begun in 1758, it was completed in 1789. In 1885 it became a secular temple where many of the great people of France are buried, among them Victor Hugo, Jean Jacques Rousseau, Voltaire, Emile Zola, Louis Braille, and many of France's military heroes and political figures.

paparazzo   *pah puh RAH tsoh*
an aggressive freelance photographer who pursues celebrities to take their pictures wherever they go: Italian

Ron Galella, the party paparazzo, was seated much of the evening: "When he's sitting down, you know there's nobody around," someone said.

paradox   *PA ruh dahks*
a seeming contradiction

"The real reason why the monarchy survives," wrote Lord Blake, Provost of The Queens College, Oxford, in The Financial Times last week, "is because the British people want it to survive. In that sense it is not only the oldest, but also, paradoxically, the most democratic of our institutions."

It's a simple dish; yet, minor variations in ingredients and technique can provoke passionate arguments. Its origins are most likely noble, yet its heights were reached after years of peasant refinement. It's the epitome of home cooking, yet can be the pride of a restaurant. This paradoxical dish is ragù, a sauce atomically bound by meat and tomatoes, and for Italians all over the world it's a food that signals the warm, secure embrace of family and home.

paragon   *PA ruh gahn*
a model of perfection

In revival, led by Rex Harrison, "My Fair Lady" endures as a paragon of wit, romance and musicality. Every song is a winner. Need one add, with regret, that they simply do not write shows like this anymore?

parochial   *puh ROH kee uhl*
small in scope; narrow; provincial

> I have long since lost the parochial feeling that there is no other worthwhile cuisine in the world except that of my native France.

paroxysm   *PA ruhk si zuhm*
a convulsive or violent outburst; fit

> A little more than a decade ago, women went through paroxysms as they shortened their dresses, as much as an inch or two a month, thinking each time they did so they looked a little younger. But the search proved as futile as Ponce de Leon's, and hemlines soon came tumbling down—first to the knees, then the calf, then even lower.

parse   *pahrs*
to separate a sentence into its parts, explaining the grammatical form, function and interrelation of each part

> Mr. McKellen is an actor-scholar. He took Macbeth's "tomorrow and tomorrow" soliloquy and gave it a thick Scots burr, turning it into a comic monologue. Then he parsed the same speech for meaning, analyzing it with the erudition of an Oxford don. Finally, he spoke it, beautifully, in the context of the play, surrounded by other soliloquies.

parvenu   *PAHR vuh noo:*
upstart; a person of newly acquired wealth or power who is not fully accepted by the social class into which he or she has risen: French

> The average consumer, presented with the trim little containers and the fancy French names, might well be confused, wondering what differences, if any, there are between the parvenu yogurts and the originals. Having tasted the three new yogurts plus two yogurt drinks and having compared them with conventional yogurts, I can report that the substantive differences are minor.

patent   *PAY tuhnt*
obvious; plain; evident

> Perhaps there's nothing wrong with "Under the Rainbow" that more laughs couldn't have cured. But it also seems that Mr. Rash takes his material too seriously, so that he winds up pursuing all the plot's loose ends, instead of succumbing happily to their patent silliness.

patina   *PA tuh nuh*
a thin, outer covering, like the fine greenish crust or film on bronze or copper,
formed by natural oxidation and often valued as being ornamental: here
used figuratively

> Time can put a patina of significance and value on improbable objects: an
> Etruscan coin, an Art Deco cocktail shaker, a beer-bottle cap. Or, perhaps,
> on Leonard Bernstein's "Mass"?

patois   *PA twah*
a dialect spoken in a particular district, differing substantially from the
standard language of the country: French, clumsy speech

> The book is written in a variant of the English patois common to Guernsey,
> a British possession 30 miles west of the Normandy coast of France.

patrimony   *PA truh moh nee*
inheritance from one's father or ancestors

> German 19th-century music was a part of our universal patrimony, and
> prized as such even at the worst moments of World War II.

paucity   *PAW suh tee*
small amount; insufficiency

> The prisoners said they had been treated for wounds in the Gorazde hospi-
> tal, and assured that since they were draftees in the Serbian forces and had
> not taken part in atrocities, they would not be harmed. The prisoners' only
> complaint was of the paucity of food given to them by their captors: two
> slices of bread and a bowl of rice soup twice a day.

payload   *PAY lohd*
the cargo, warhead, bombs, etc. carried by a rocket or aircraft, having to do
with its objective but not related to its operation: originally, any cargo
producing income

> According to the space agency's plan, the payload for the second mission will
> be installed in the Columbia by June 29. The payload is an array of experi-
> mental instruments for geological mapping by imaging radar and infrared
> sensors, for observing plankton in the ocean, for optical studies of lightning
> discharges and for locating and identifying vegetation on the earth's surface.
> The Columbia carried no research payload on its first flight.

pedagogue   *PE duh gahg*
a teacher—a word with contradictory connotations, used as a term of ridicule for a narrow, petty and dogmatic educator, but also to describe a master teacher: Greek, a leader of children

Ivan Galamian, an internationally known violin pedagogue at the Juilliard School for 35 years and the teacher of many of today's best-known violinists, died, apparently of heart failure, yesterday morning in his Manhattan apartment. He was 78 years old and had been active until the end, having given his normal schedule of lessons on Monday.

pedantic   *pi DAN tik*
teacherish, in the negative sense of the word—that is, adhering rigidly to rules without regard to common sense; stressing minor or trivial points; showing off scholarship

"The Complete Book of Pastry" is admirably detailed and scholarly without being pedantic.

pedestrian   *pi DE stree uhn*
ordinary and dull

The books ranged from the profound to the pedestrian. Under the same canvas roof as Proust and Shakespeare were entire tables devoted to Cliffs Notes, the outlines used by students who procrastinate, and Reader's Digest condensed novels.

pejorative   *puh JAH ruh tiv*
a word with a traditionally neutral meaning that has taken on a negative meaning or negative connotations

The New York Zoological Society, deciding the word "zoo" had become an urban pejorative with a limited horizon, announced yesterday that it was dropping the word from the Bronx Zoo, the Central Park Zoo, the Queens Zoo and the Prospect Park Zoo. They are to be called Wildlife Conservation Parks beginning Monday, said William Conway, president of the society, who concedes he risks greatly bestirring much of the urban menagerie beyond the 10,000 creatures of the, uh, zoos. But he says he must do something about the little word. "I've been here 37 years and it's like changing my father's name," he said. "But it's about time."

penchant *PEN shuhnt*
a strong liking or fondness; inclination; taste

Retirees have always been big travelers, of course. What is new is their penchant for high-adventure travel more typical of those half their age. These days, many older people, even octogenarians, can be found riding elephants in India, horseback riding in Costa Rica and bungee-jumping in New Zealand. And the adventure-travel industry is rushing to accommodate them. While many tour operators still offer typical retiree fare—lengthy bus tours of Europe and the United States—they now also have offerings like river rafting, hiking and mountain climbing.

penultimate *pi NUHL tuh mit*
next to the last: Latin, paene, *almost*

The film's penultimate sequence, about Tony, now a junkie-bum, and his illegitimate son, Pete, is grimly funny, sad and scary.

peregrinations *pe ruh gri NAY shuhnz*
travels from place to place; wanderings; journeys

Mr. Bodkin easily fields requests for almost any type of music, a result of his own piano-playing peregrinations that have brought him to hotels in Amsterdam, Teheran, Tel Aviv and other far-off lounges.

perennial *puh RE nee uhl*
continuing for a long time; happening again and again; perpetual; everlasting

"The Catcher in the Rye" is perennially banned because Holden Caulfield is said to be an unsuitable role model. Well, Holden Caulfield isn't meant to be suitable. He's meant to be adolescent, to show you at 16 that the fun house of your own psyche is not aberrational.

perfidy *PER fi dee*
treachery; a breaking of trust

That morning, he [Balanchine] had led a one-hour company class, where he had warned the dancers about the perfidy of the mirror. Dancers always stare in mirrors; it is their preoccupation. Balanchine, however, had told them, "The mirror is not you. The mirror is you yourself looking at yourself."

perfunctory   *per FUHNGK tuh ree*
done routinely, with little care or interest; without real concern; indifferent

Service is best when the restaurant is least crowded—week nights and afternoons—when waiters and managers offer patient explanations and show a desire to please. Friday and Saturday night and all day Sunday can be hectic and customers may be treated perfunctorily.

perimeter   *puh RI muh ter*
the outer boundary of an area

A year ago, the Moroccans began building a 280-mile wall of sand, six feet high and sprinkled with mines and barbed wire, enclosing what is called the "useful Sahara." Initially ridiculed by some, this perimeter, known as a berm, was finished early this year and seems to have hampered the rebels' ability to flee across the desert after striking isolated Moroccan positions.

peripatetic   *pe ruh puh TE tik*
moving or traveling from place to place; not staying in one place for long; itinerant

Skeptics, be quiet. George Washington not only slept at the Roe Tavern in East Setauket, L.I., on April 22, 1790, he even gave it a review. "Tolerably decent, with obliging people in it," was how the peripatetic overnight guest put it in his diary, according to the Society for the Preservation of Long Island Antiques.

✦ *Peripatetic* derives from the Greek word *peripatein* (to walk around) and was first applied to the philosophy or followers of Aristotle, who is said to have walked about as he taught his students in the outdoor covered walk (*peripatos*) of the Lyceum, a gymnasium in Athens. Aristotle's system of philosophy came to be called the Peripatetic School.

pernicious   *per NI shuhs*
causing great injury or destruction by slowly undermining or weakening; exceedingly harmful; deadly

From Virginia to Massachusetts, extending as far west as Ohio, a stagnant high-pressure system stubbornly lurking over the southeastern United States has caused a dearth of rain this summer, the National Weather Service said.

The arid weather follows almost a year of low precipitation, resulting in pernicious cumulative effects like trees falling ill, with some beginning to die.

perpetual   *per PE choo: uhl*
unceasing; unchanging; endless

From the thunderous torrent at Niagara Falls to the perpetually rainy coast of British Columbia, Canada is awash in more fresh water than almost any other place on earth.

persevere   *per suh VEER*
to continue toward a goal in spite of difficulty

The world's No. 1 player showed his greatness in memorable fashion today, winning the American Express Championship and becoming the first PGA Tour player to win four consecutive starts since Ben Hogan in 1953. Woods did it the hard way, prevailing in a one-hole playoff against Spain's Miguel Angel Jimenez, and persevering through a final round that featured terrific golf, drama and heated emotions.

persona   *per SOH nuh*
the outer personality or facade presented to others by an individual

I don't think the nation ever hung on the words of Walter Cronkite. He is not exceptionally insightful or witty. Primarily, he brought a reassuring presence and persona to whatever the news happened to be that day. And I suspect even Mr. Cronkite would wince at his works being called a "heroic service."

persona non grata   *per SOH nuh nahn GRAH tuh*
a person who is not acceptable or welcome: Latin

In a fresh sign of the tensions that have grown between the United States and Russia since the war in Kosovo, Moscow has ordered an American military attaché to leave the country, American officials said today. The American officer, Lieut. Col. Peter Hoffman, the assistant Army attaché at the United States Embassy in Moscow, was declared persona non grata and left Russia Thursday evening, officials said. The American Embassy declined to say why the officer had been expelled. But some American officials suggested that he might have been caught up in tit-for-tat accusations of spying.

✦ Among the Latin phrases that were adopted into the English language with little or no change in their spelling or meaning are: *pro bono, ad infinitum, ad lib, mea culpa, alter ego, bona fide, caveat emptor, ipso facto, non sequitur, quid pro quo, tabula rasa, vox populi, ad hoc, a priori, sine qua non, de facto, status quo, per annum, per capita, sub rosa, terra firma, terra incognita, vice versa, alma mater, in loco parentis, in toto, in utero, magnum opus, rara avis, sui generis, carpe diem, in memoriam, modus operandi, antebellum, reductio ad absurdum* and *viva voce*.

personify   *per SAH nuh figh*
to represent an abstraction in the form of a person; embody

Dated Feb. 1, 1981, the unpublished memoir says: "I was 22 years old when we began filming 'Gone With the Wind.' The role of Melanie meant a very great deal to me, for she personified values very much endangered at the time. The source of her strength was love. For a little while, as I lived her life, I felt her love, felt her trust, felt her faith, felt her happiness."

pervasive   *per VAY siv*
widespread; saturating; spreading through

How pervasive is Berra's influence? In the last week, an article about a chess tournament in Oregon, an article about a fight over a new law school in Florida and a critique of an abstract art exhibit all used Berra's "déjà vu all over again" quotation. Senator Bob Smith of New Hampshire used a Berra line: "When you come to a fork in the road, take it." A story about congestion in the Hamptons recalled Berra's 1959 gem about a popular restaurant: "Nobody goes there any more; it's too crowded."

petrifaction   *pe tri FAK shuhn*
a turning into stone; a benumbed state

Part burlesque sketch, part gospel service and all silly, this play is remarkable mainly for its ability to reduce any reasonably adult onlooker to a state of instant and total petrifaction.

phalanx   *FAY langks*
a compact or closely massed body of people or things

Even before the Columbia had stopped its landing roll, a convoy of 21 service vehicles whose operators had been training for that moment for almost three months, was moving in a phalanx toward the craft, stirring up a cloud of dust like a battalion of tanks moving over the Sahara before battle.

✦ The phalanx was an ancient Greek military formation of infantry in close and deep ranks, with shields joined together and spears overlapping.

phantasmagoric *fan taz muh GAW rik*
dreamlike; magical

Since the eighth-century poet Li Po celebrated the phantasmagoric beauties of Huang Shan, a mountain of oddly-shaped peaks, pines and clouds, the Chinese have considered it one of the wonders of nature.

philistine *FI luh steen*
a person lacking cultural interests or values and interested in material and commonplace things; boor

San Francisco is on something of a cultural tear lately, cementing its position as the West Coast's cultural capital, although Los Angeles is by no means the pothole full of philistines many San Franciscans see when (if) they take the plane south.

phoenix *FEE niks*
in Egyptian mythology, a solitary bird that lived in the Arabian desert for 500 or 600 years and then consumed itself in fire, rising renewed from the ashes to start another long life: it symbolizes resurrection, renewal or immortality

This is a city well named. It may not have arisen, like the fabulous bird of Egyptian mythology, from its own ashes, but, like the original phoenix, this one sprang to life in a desert. It owes its existence to modern technology. Without large-scale irrigation and without air-conditioning, Phoenix as it now exists—the sprawling, verdant, dynamic center of a metropolitan area of more than 2.8 million people—would have been utterly unthinkable. With temperatures exceeding 100 degrees on more than 90 days a year, with an average high temperature in July of 106 degrees, God's own ungentled climate in the Sonoran Desert is better suited for cacti and Gila monsters than human beings.

picayune *pi ki YOO:N*
trivial or petty: French, picaillon, *small coin, halfpenny*

Robert S. Kane, who is revising his "A to Z" guidebooks with a new publisher, Rand McNally, avoids specifics, such as prices, but categorizes hotels and restaurants as luxurious, first class or moderate. "I don't go into picayune details that change all the time," he said, "and that people can get from their travel agents."

pièce de résistance *pyes duh ray zi STAHNS*
the principal dish of a meal; the main item or event in a series: French, piece of resistance

The world's rarest and most valuable stamp, the British Guiana 1856 1-cent black on magenta, was the pièce de résistance of last year's Rarities of the World sale and many highly knowledgeable figures were predicting that it would bring a million dollars.

pinnacle *PI nuh kuhl*
the highest point; acme

The British invented summer pudding, a ruby-red molded dome made with currants, blackberries and raspberries that is the pinnacle of their summer desserts.

pittance *PI tuhns*
a small or barely sufficient allowance of money: from the Old French pitance, *the portion of food allowed a monk or a nun, so called because it was provided through the* pietas *(piety) or* pité *(pity) of the faithful*

Her budget on "Sophisticated Ladies" was $175,000. Like other successful theatrical designers, she now has assistants who worry about getting the shoes and accessories. The "Sophisticated Ladies" budget, however, seems a pittance when compared to that of "42nd Street," which had a costume budget of over $500,000, the highest on record for a Broadway show.

pivotal *PI vuh tuhl*
crucial; central

Electronic detection and tracking devices played a pivotal part in the Battle of Britain, and since then, the rapid development of radar and antiradar technology has come to dominate human warfare.

placate   *PLAY kayt*
to stop from being angry; appease; pacify

Finland, the tiny Nordic neighbor of the vast Communist empire, kept its hard-won independence after World War II by pledging a friendship for the Soviet Union that it never really felt. Forced by geography and the cold-war balance of power to placate Moscow, Finland called itself neutral. The world called its precarious condition Finlandization. When the Soviet Union collapsed in 1991, Finland eagerly sought to join the European Union, shaking off its allegiance to Moscow and carving out a new identity for itself as a loyal partner of the West.

placebo   *pluh SEE boh*
a substance having no pharmacological effect, but given to a patient who supposes it to be a medicine; a substance used as a control in testing the efficacy of another, medicated substance

Fully a third of pains can be relieved by a placebo, or sugar pill, if the patient believes it to be an active pain-killing drug. Recent studies suggest that placebos work by triggering the release of the body's own morphine, endomorphine.

> ✦ *Placebo* (meaning "I shall be acceptable") is the first word sung in response to the priest's words in the Roman Catholic Church's vespers for the dead. The full line is *Placebo Domino in regione vivorum* ("I will walk before the Lord in the land of the living"), and is from Psalm 116. Because people who sought favors from relatives of the departed sometimes made sure they were seen singing this line at vespers, *to sing placebo*, as early as the fourteenth century, came to mean to play the flatterer. The earliest citation in *The Oxford English Dictionary* of *placebo* as we use the word today is from Hooper's *Medical Dictionary* of 1811. It defined *placebo* as a name "given to any medicine adapted more to please than benefit the patient."

placid   *PLA sid*
calm; tranquil; quiet

Some Chinese parents worry that the tough regimentation of nursery school and kindergarten tends to make their children too placid and uncreative. A professor at Peking University said he was concerned that his 5-year-old son, whom he boards in kindergarten, just sits quietly and doesn't speak when he comes home.

plastic   *PLA stik*
capable of changing or adapting

"Heredity, shmeredity! You have to do something," says Dr. Reuven Feuerstein in answer to the endless argument over whether disadvantaged children do poorly in school because of inherited traits or because of their environment. The human organism, he says, "is an open system, very plastic. It can be changed and modified." The question is whether educators have the will, the confidence and the instruments to "do something."

plebian   *pli BEE uhn*
characteristic of the common people: the plebians were members of the ancient Roman lower class

Where oysters are posh, and summon up images of costly elegance, clams are plebian and suggest a more casual, less self-conscious if no less rapturous pleasure.

plenary   *PLEE nuh ree*
for attendance by all members

The theme of the gathering of the N.A.A.C.P., "A dual society is an unequal society," was addressed in dozens of workshops, plenary sessions, committee meetings and speeches.

plethora   *PLE thuh ruh*
overabundance; excess

Noting that last-minute cancellations "never panic me at all," Mrs. Buckley went on to say that she does try to avoid either "a plethora of men or a plethora of women" at large dinners. "We always try," she said, firmly. "I know there are people who say it's ridiculous to worry about having an equal number but I happen to think it's important."

ploy   *ploi*
a deceptive maneuver or stratagem

The maker of Beanie Babies announced that "all Beanies will be retired" as of Dec. 31. Whether a marketing ploy or not, the announcement created a frenzy.

"We got a frantic call from a C.E.O. who said he was desperate for porterhouse, he was unable to get a reservation in our Minneapolis restaurant, and he was landing his jet soon at Teterboro, so could we fit him in," said Seth D. Bromberg, maître d'hotel for four years at Morton's of Chicago on East 45th Street, which caters to many captains of industry. "I thought, 'Who would make up a story like that?' and gave him a table," Mr. Bromberg said. "A few minutes later he came in with his wife. I asked, 'How did you get here so quickly?' and they sheepishly admitted that the story was a ploy. But I was charmed. I think he deserved the table, and he's become a good customer."

pluck *pluhk*
courage to meet danger or difficulty, or to continue against odds; stubbornly brave

In the Florida Straits, where so many Cubans have lost their lives trying to make their way across the last cold-war barrier to the United States, another small, overloaded boat has sunk, apparently drowning a young woman and casting her 5-year-old son adrift. For two days after the 17-foot boat went down, Elian Gonzalez clung to an inner tube before fishermen on Thanksgiving morning found him and two adults who had survived. His pluck kept him alive, and brought him to the country his mother and stepfather may have died trying to reach. Their bodies have not been found.

plumb *pluhm*
to examine closely; probe into: originally, to measure the depth of

When Hannah Green wrote her 1964 bestseller, "I Never Promised You A Rose Garden," she plumbed her own early life experiences as a mental patient to describe how schizophrenia tormented Deborah Blau, the book's young heroine.

pluralism *PLOO ruh li zuhm*
the existence within a society of groups distinctive in ethnic origin, religion, cultural patterns or the like

The president of Yale University attacked the Moral Majority and other conservative groups yesterday as "peddlers of coercion" in "a radical assault" on pluralism, civil rights and religious and political freedoms in the United States.

pogrom *puh GRAHM*
an organized persecution and massacre, often officially prompted, of a minority group, especially of Jews in Czarist Russia: Russian, destruction

Most of Argentina's Jews are second- and third-generation descendants of those who arrived around the end of the last century after fleeing the pogroms of eastern Europe and Russia. They found a young country rich in opportunity and similar in geography and culture to Europe.

polyglot *PAH li glaht*
composed of or speaking several languages

Just a few feet from the boulevard, however, is a newer face of Los Angeles. Tens of thousands of immigrants, most of them from Asia and Latin America, are crowded into what city planners call the Wilshire Corridor, and these polyglot neighborhoods are stunning evidence of the relatively recent waves of refugees from abroad that have turned this city into the nation's new melting pot.

polymath *PAH li math*
a person of great and diversified learning: Greek, polymathes *(knowing much), from* poly *(many)* + manthanein *(learn). The second part of this word is also the root of mathematics, which means "inclined to learn."*

You can call him director, writer, actor, filmmaker, photographer, professor or doctor. But call Jonathan Miller polymath or Renaissance man and he will gag. Ask him for the common thread running through his varied interests, and he will reply that if he knew, he would be in desperate trouble.

polyphonic *pah li FAH nik*
the simultaneous sounding of different notes in harmony

Bach being Bach, it should surprise nobody that his Cantata No. 50, though the briefest piece on the program, also was the best. This polyphonic jewel for eight-part double chorus, only one movement of what probably was meant to be a longer work, is a miracle of intricate design but simply irresistible.

ponderous *PAHN duh ruhs*
massive; bulky; heavy

For so huge a creature, the California gray whale is ponderously graceful, erupting from the Pacific swells in easy arcs, so big the sea itself bulges as it lifts to the surface, breaking the blue-green water with an audible cascade.

popinjay   *PAH pin jay*
a person given to vain displays and empty chatter; fop: from an old Arab name for a parrot, signifying grand plumage and empty squawking

France, for Liebling, was Western civilization. His account of the removal of its popinjay Government from Paris to Tours as the Nazis advanced makes Jean-Paul Sartre, in his "Roads to Freedom" trilogy, sound sanguine.

portent   *PAWR tent*
omen

It was a nervous moment. Nine fractious 2-year-old colts were circling the walking ring in Belmont Park's paddock. Hundreds of undecided bettors crowded the rail of the ring, looking for some portent of how to wager on a race full of first-time starters. Several edgy trainers carefully watched each step taken by their young horses.

poseur   *po ZAYR*
a person who practices an affected manner to impress others or to be noticed by them; a phony

Nancy LaMott is a model of unaffected sweetness in a cabaret field crowded with poseurs, and her spare, intimate Christmas album projects the same aura of cleancut nostalgia as her live performances.

Ibsen's women are complex, tough-minded realists, capable of looking a fact in the eye and freezing it on the spot; and they are usually right. His men, on the other hand, are obtuse, wooly-headed idealists, pompous poseurs who must be babied by their wiser wives unless they are being abandoned altogether. Ibsen's men are a laughing matter; if the world is ever going to be straightened out, his women will have to do it.

posh   *pahsh*
luxurious and fashionable; elegant

Mrs. Fenwick spoke up, loud and clear. She is a remarkable woman, slimly elegant, her blue-gray hair perfectly groomed, a picture of what I imagine in the poshest New Jersey country clubs, until she puffs thoughtfully at her pipe a moment and then raises her voice.

✦ *Posh* is widely believed to have originated in the middle of the nineteenth century as the initials P.O.S.H. stamped on steamship tickets of passengers traveling between England and India, and who were favored with staterooms that would not face the sun on that hot journey. The initials stood for "port out, starboard home." The story is interesting, but apparently untrue. *The Merriam-Webster Book of Word Histories* says that no ticket bearing the P.O.S.H. stamp has ever been found and that there is no evidence that *posh* was used as an adjective before 1918.

posit   *PAH zit*
to set down or assume as fact; postulate

People are not always kind to the beluga whales at the New York Aquarium. Sometimes they throw pennies into their pool, as though Amy Lou and Blanchon were marble fish on the Trevi Fountain, not mammals that some scientists posit may have intelligence greater than that of the average tourist.

posterity   *pah STE ruh tee*
all future generations

Arriving in Guyana shortly after the story of the mass suicide and murder stunned the world, Mr. Reston discovered the existence of some 900 hours of tapes, made for posterity because Jim Jones always considered himself a historic figure.

posthumous   *PAHS choo muhs*
published or presented after the creator's death

Sounding like a character in one of his autobiographical short stories, Mr. Saroyan called The Associated Press five days before his death to leave a posthumous statement: "Everybody has got to die, but I have always believed an exception would be made in my case. Now what?"

potable   *POH tuh buhl*
drinkable

AKRON, Ohio, Aug. 17—Thousands of residents in the southwestern part of Akron have not been able to draw potable water from their faucets for a week, and the end is not in sight. The water has been contaminated with harmful bacteria, and city officials have been unable to find the source of the problem.

a liquid suitable for drinking; beverage

Mr. Dutond downed three pounds four ounces of Maroilles, arguably France's smelliest cheese, in 10 minutes. Half the contestants were eliminated in the first round by proving unable to consume a pound of the cheese in five minutes, unaided by bread, water or wine. During the second half potables were permitted, dispensed by a gendarme enlisted to insure the moral tone of the event.

potboiler   *PAHT boi ler*
a piece of writing or the like, usually inferior and uninspired, done quickly for money: so-called because it brings in money for food and other necessities

Mr. Crichton, age 38, is not only that rare combination of successful novelist and screenwriter, he is also that rare writer who made the leap from writing potboiling paperbacks to literary respectability.

potpourri   *poh puh REE*
a mixture; miscellany: French, rotten pot

Music critics have often taken a dim view of the Three Tenors concerts, with their potpourri of hummable arias, folk songs and musical-comedy favorites boomed out over banks of loudspeakers. But admirers of the tenors have argued that these concerts have helped introduce millions of people to the sound of opera and, as such, have done a favor to classical music.

✦ *Olla-podrida* (OH luh puh DREE duh) is the name of a traditional Spanish meat and vegetable stew. It translates literally as *rotten pot*, and is called that probably because the stew is slow-cooked. When the French adopted this Spanish dish, they gave it their own name for *rotten pot: potpourri*. In English, both *potpourri* and *olla-podrida* mean an incongruous or miscellaneous mixture of any kind. In English, a potpourri is also the name of an aromatic blend of flower petals and spices stored in a jar.

precept   *PREE sept*
a rule or direction

The first precept in instrument flying is to ignore the body's sensations. The delicate mechanism of the inner ear that provides a sense of balance can also provide false cues. A pilot who feels that the plane is level, for example, may in fact be diving to the left.

precious   *PRE shuhs*
overrefined or affected, as in language or behavior

The point is this: The drinking of wine in America, particularly American wine, is on the brink of becoming inbred and precious. Wine enthusiasts, including we writers, who should know better, ape the jargon of the trade and feel special when we exchange arcane trivia about grape crushers, red spiders and who is opening next week's winery.

precipitate   *pri SI puh tayt*
to bring on; cause

Instead of expressing these feelings openly and constructively and thus dissipating them, they tense their head and neck muscles, precipitating a headache.

precipitately   *pri SI puh tit lee*
rashly; impetuously

When Mary Larkin decided to give up her job at the Mercer Rubber Company in Trenton, effective July 31, she was hardly acting precipitately. Miss Larkin, who is 93 years old, went to work for the company in 1905 and was continuously employed there for 76 years.

precipitous   *pri SI puh tuhs*
steep, like a precipice

From the beginning, there has been difficulty in recognizing toxic shock syndrome, which is commonly characterized by the acute onset of high fever, as in some cases of influenza; scaling or peeling of the skin, as in scarlet fever; and a precipitous dropping of blood pressure.

preclude   *pri KLOO:D*
to make impossible by previous action; rule out in advance; prevent

With her vivid blue eyes and her casual, outdoorsy attractiveness, Dr. Tilghman looks like the recovering jock she is. In her youth, she rode horses, skied, was on the track team and played basketball, volleyball, tennis and golf, which precluded her from being labeled a nerd for her obsession with mathematics.

precocious   *pri KOH shuhs*
developed or matured beyond what is normal for the age

Mozart, one of the most precocious composers in history—the others were Mendelssohn and Saint-Saëns—had completed 13 symphonies by the time he was 12.

> ✦ *Precocious* and *apricot* are etymological cousins. Precocious comes from the Latin, *praecoquere*, to boil beforehand, created from *prae*, before + *coquere*, to mature. In a sense, that's what precocious people do. Because the apricot ripens before the peach, the Arabs applied the Latin word *praecoquere* to the apricot, calling it *al-birquq*, early ripe. From the Arab word, the Portuguese derived *albricoque*, the French made it *abricot*, and it was absorbed into English as *apricot*.

precursor   *pree KER suhr*
forerunner; predecessor

Delmonico's was a precursor and a shaper of today's restaurant culture. It was the first American restaurant to print its menu in French, to present a wine list, to welcome women in the dining room and to be a meeting place for the city's power brokers. The restaurant gave its name to the rib eye steak and it was where lobster Newburg was invented. In the early to mid-1800's, the Delmonico family owned a farm in Queens that supplied the restaurant with fresh produce.

predilection   *pree duh LEK shuhn*
a preconceived liking; partiality or preference

At bottom, Brendan Behan was an entertainer, a performer whose notoriety, as well as much of his charm, was based on a lethal predilection for bringing out the worst in himself. Early in life he wrote awfully well; later in life he became everyone's favorite drunk. He died at 41, his public decline attended by enchanted journalists and other voyeurs, and he left behind him not so much a body of work as a reputation for being what he most certainly was not. For all the posturing about life, he was in love with death.

predisposed   *pree di SPOHZD*
inclined to something in advance; made receptive beforehand

There are composers and performers who become cultural heroes or villains by virtue of their political stance. When we hear the music of Hindemith or Schoenberg or the conducting of Toscanini, we cannot help being predisposed toward them, partly because Hitler was not.

premise   *PRE mis*
a proposition from which a conclusion is drawn; basis

It is an idea whose time came thousands of years ago, went out for Western civilization two centuries ago and now seems on the verge of a comeback. The premise: that women were intended to give birth sitting or squatting and not lying down as they have done ever since 1738 when François Mauriceau, obstetrician to the Queen of France, proposed facilitating the physician's task by having patients recline for delivery.

premonition   *pree muh NI shuhn*
a forewarning; foreboding; presentiment

When the Nazis closed in on Berlin's Jewish community in 1939, Charlotte Saloman, a 21-year-old artist, fled to the home of her grandparents in Ville-franche-sur-Mer, in the south of France. There, with a premonition of doom, she furiously began to paint the story of her life just as Anne Frank in Amsterdam had written intimately about herself in the famous diary. In late summer 1942, Miss Saloman was picked up and sent to Auschwitz, where she died the next year.

prenatal   *pree NAY tuhl*
before birth

A baby who would probably have died because of a genetic defect in its ability to use the vitamin called biotin was diagnosed early in its prenatal life and was treated successfully by giving the mother large doses of the substance daily for the final three months of her pregnancy.

primeval   *prigh MEE vuhl*
relating to the earliest times or ages, particularly before the appearance of human beings

BIALOWIEZA, Poland, Aug. 22—In one of the paradoxes of nature, the last fragment of the primeval forest that stretched from the Atlantic to the Urals, from the Mediterranean to the northern seas, remains intact here on the eastern border of Poland, one of modern Europe's most polluted countries.

primordial   *prigh MAWR dee uhl*
existing from the beginning; primitive; primeval

Clamming is a primordial experience. All it involves is walking slowly in the ocean at low tide, bending over and groping in the sediment in search of a hard, slightly rounded shape. Clamming requires no equipment, except maybe a bucket. It demands no talent, except a notion of where the clams are. Like fishing, trapping and hunting, it is one of the most ancient ways to gather food.

pristine   *PRIS teen*
untouched; unspoiled; pure; original; in its natural state

Nestled in the San Juan National Forest here in southwestern Colorado are a small rectangle of mountains and a valley that straddles the meandering East Fork of the San Juan River. For now, the rectangle's 2,780 acres are indistinguishable from the surrounding landscape, a dream scene of 1.8 million pristine acres at the Continental Divide, where the only sounds are the water rushing over rocks, the wind and the occasional cry of birds high overhead.

procrastinate   *proh KRA stuh nayt*
to put off to a future time; postpone habitually

On the topic of lunch, artists are sharply divided. There is a group for whom it is an irritation, a waste of valuable time that is to be dispensed with as quickly as possible. Others seize upon the meal as a clever way to procrastinate; ideas may still come as cucumbers are sliced or as bacon hisses in the frying pan.

procreation   *proh kri AY shuhn*
the producing of young; reproduction

SAN FRANCISCO, July 2—The hardy, prolific and devastatingly destructive Mediterranean fruit fly appears to have survived a $22 million eradication program south of the Bay area, which included extensive stripping of fruit trees, ground spraying of insecticide and the release of millions of sterile males to thwart their procreation.

prodigious   *pruh DI juhs*
enormous; huge

After the defeat of the French in Canada at the hands of the British in 1759, the French population in Canada increased so prodigiously in the 19th and early 20th centuries that the phenomenon came to be called "the revenge of the cradle." But since the end of World War II, the birth rate of French Canadians has dropped precipitously, and English-speaking Canada has grown much faster.

prodigy   *PRAH duh jee*
a child of highly unusual talent or genius

A hockey prodigy who began playing the game at the age of 5 and entered the N.H.L. as a heralded 18-year-old, Orr lived up to his extravagant notices, dazzling elder competitors and teammates with his skating, his puck control and his sense of the game.

profligate   *PRAH fluh git*
extremely wasteful; recklessly extravagant

For sheer, profligate waste of energy, it's hard to beat "Louis," the new musical in a workshop presentation at the Henry Street Settlement's New Federal Theater. This show, an ostensible account of the early career of Louis Armstrong, boasts more talented, hard-working performers than some Broadway musicals—and not one of them is put to good use.

profuse   *pruh FYOO:S*
in great amount

One of the last scenes in the movie shows an Elvis so bloated he's almost unrecognizable, sweating profusely and so obviously drugged that he can't remember song lyrics; he's in a huge arena, but he barely seems to know the audience is there.

progenitor   *pruh JE nuh ter*
an ancestor in a direct line; a source from which something develops

He's not considered a member of Britain's Royal family, but like the Queen, Walter Lee Sheppard Jr. claims direct descent from Edward III and other royal progenitors.

Just as human parents produce children of very different character, pinot and gouais turn out to be the progenitors of 16 very different wine grapes. Three are known throughout the world. Chardonnay is perhaps the leading variety of white wine. Gamay is the grape from which all Beaujolais is derived. And melon, a third pinot-gouais offspring, is the source of all Muscadet.

progeny   *PRAH juh nee*
children; descendants; offspring

The captured salmon are being removed—gently, for they are a hypersensitive fish—to a holding facility in Barkhampsted, Conn. During the natural spawning time in November, the eggs of the females and the milt of the males will be removed for artificial spawning, and the progeny will later be returned to the rivers.

There are at least 5,000 varieties of wine grape in the world, several of which have been grown at least since Roman times. All are the progeny of the wild grape Vitis vinifera but the puzzle of how they may be related to each other has long been left to wine historians and ampelographers, an obscure guild of experts who pronounce on a vine's ancestry by minutely examining its leaves.

proliferate   *proh LI fuh rayt*
to multiply rapidly; increase profusely

More and more women are playing as well as singing rock-and-roll, and bands that consist entirely of women are proliferating.

prolific   *pruh LI fik*
producing in large quantity

Mr. L'Amour, said to be one of the most widely read writers in the world, is so prolific that he can't remember whether his latest book is number 78 or 79. "I do about three a year by writing practically every day of my life," he said.

prolix   *proh LIKS*
overly long; tiresome; long-winded: usually with reference to writing

"The Firebird" is the one of Stravinsky's "big three" early ballet scores that is probably better heard in the form of a suite than in its rather prolix complete version.

prophylactic   *proh fuh LAK tik*
protecting or guarding against disease

Worldwide, 30,000 people a year die from rabies, mostly in developing countries where dogs are not vaccinated and treatment is not available for bitten people. Prophylactic treatment is recommended for travelers to those countries.

proponent   *pruh POH nint*
an advocate; supporter: opposite of opponent

Dr. Jack Kevorkian, who claims he has helped more than 130 people commit suicide, was convicted today of murder for giving a fatal injection to a man with a terminal illness. It is a verdict that people on both sides of the assisted-suicide debate believe will have a profound impact on the discussion of this contentious, emotional subject now that its most visible proponent could spend much of the rest of his life in prison.

proscribe   *proh SKRIGHB*
to forbid the practice or use of

Modern governments have a muddled record when it comes to legislating against sin. Killing, proscribed by the Commandments, is punishable by law if undertaken as a private enterprise, but not if done professionally—as a soldier or an executioner, say—in the service of the state.

proselytize   *PRAH suh li tighz*
to try to convert to one's religion, beliefs, way of life, etc.

The Baha'is have also infuriated the Islamic clergy because they are one of the few religious groups that attempt to proselytize among the Moslems.

prostitute   *PRAH stuh too:t*
to sell for unworthy or degraded purposes

The actor [Philip Bosco] says he refuses to do television commercials. "I hate to sound pompous and holier-than-thou," he explained, "but I feel very strongly as an artist that this is not the kind of thing I want to do, because it's not acting. It's being a salesman. I choose not to use the word prostitute because it's too strong. But I think that's essentially what it is. It's being dishonest, being less than true to what you hold dear."

♦ *Holier-than-thou* is a phrase from Chapter 65 of the biblical book of Isaiah. God has been provoked to anger at the sight of Jews who are sacrificing animals, burning incense and eating swine's flesh, and who say to others: "Stand by thyself, come not near to me; for I am holier than thou."

protean   *PROH tee uhn*
very changeable; quickly taking on different shapes and forms

What helps make the choreography of Dana Reitz so remarkable is its protean nature. Just as one thinks one has perceived the basic shape of a movement, that movement immediately becomes something else. Miss Reitz's choreography is a choreography of perpetual metamorphosis.

♦ Proteus was a sea god of Greek myth who could change his form at will. He would tell the future to those who could seize him, but when grasped he would change himself into anything from a lion to a tree. When held fast, though, he would return to his usual form of an old man and tell the truth.

protocol   *PROH tuh kahl*
the forms of ceremony and etiquette observed by diplomats and heads of state

New social aides are given tours of the White House to familiarize themselves with its history and background, and they are supplied with a manual that spells out the formalities of diplomatic protocol, the customs of different countries and the rules governing formal introductions.

providence   *PRAH vuh duhns*
divine guidance; fortune; luck

"And to me it has been providential to be an artist, a great act of providence that I was able to turn my borderline psychosis into creativity—my sister Rose did not manage this. So I keep writing. I am sometimes pleased with what I do—for me, that's enough." [Tennessee Williams]

provincial   *pruh VIN shuhl*
limited in perspective; narrow; unsophisticated

German 19th-century literature had a token status even among people who had never read a word of it. But German 19th-century art was thought of as provincial, second-rate, secondhand and altogether beneath discussion.

proviso   *pruh VIGH zoh*
a condition or stipulation

If you want to go up to Broadway, says the brain, it's okay by me, but I've got one proviso. No shows about show business. "Well," say I, after scanning the theater ads, "that rules out 'A Chorus Line,' 'A Day in Hollywood/A Night in the Ukraine,' 'Ain't Misbehavin,' 'Amadeus,' 'Barnum,' 'Dancin,' '42nd Street,' 'They're Playing Our Song,' 'Sophisticated Ladies'...."

provocateur   *pruh vah kuh TER*
a person hired to join a labor union, political party, demonstration, etc. in order to incite its members to actions that will make them or their organization liable to penalty: the full French term is agent provocateur

Two leaders of the Socialist Workers Party have testified that Federal agents used false charges, anonymous letters and undercover provocateurs to disrupt their political activities.

proximity   *PRAHK si muh tee*
nearness in place, time, order, occurrence or relation

Stephen Gillers, a professor at the New York University Law School and an expert on ethics and public officials, said familiarity and proximity did not always breed contempt. Strong personalities can maintain political support locally and "allay people's ethical qualms in a way that a distant figure of power can't." Rogues are often charming up close, he said, pointing as an example to Gov. Edwin Edwards of Louisiana, who was elected in spite of being indicted and acquitted twice of taking bribes.

✦ The proverb, "Familiarity breeds contempt," appears as early as Aesop (sixth century B.C.) and Thomas Aquinas (1225-1274), who wrote, "*Nimia familiaritas parit contemptum.*" Its original meaning is not that the better you get to know people the less you like them, but that one grows unappreciative of what is too easily had, or that one grows careless when familiarity with something leads to overconfidence. Winston Churchill took his turn with the proverb when he said, "Without a certain amount of familiarity, you will never breed anything."

proxy   *PRAHK see*
someone with authority to act for another; deputy

The United States has been deeply concerned about Libya's international activities for some time. It has been worried that the Libyans were serving as an indirect Soviet "proxy" in Africa by interfering militarily and politically in various countries.

prudent   *PROO: duhnt*
showing good judgment; cautious or discreet in conduct; not rash

But the casinos want much more freedom than a prudent state would grant. They would like the state to ease its rules on the size of each casino's staff and on "junkets"—organized gambling excursions. They also want to operate around the clock, and seek relaxation of other rules.

puckish   *PUH kish*
full of mischief; impish

Injury or no, Danny Kaye, at 68, could still be mistaken for Hans Christian Andersen or Merry Andrew—older perhaps, but the traces of puckishness lurk nonetheless behind the sober manner.

✦ Puck, also known as Robin Goodfellow, was a merry prankster of English folklore, an elf who delighted in tricking and confounding people. He was Shakespeare's model for Puck in *A Midsummer Night's Dream*, and lent his name, in a slightly changed form, to the breed of dog known as the pug.

puffery   *PUH fuh ree*
exaggerated praise, as in advertising or chamber of commerce boosterism

Some who have seen the new museum might consider it a work of art in its own right. Texas Monthly, a magazine not generally known for puffery, wrote of the museum that "it will undoubtedly be celebrated as one of the most original architectural projects ever undertaken in Texas," and said its design "creates some stunning effects."

punchy   *PUHN chee*
groggy, dazed or dizzy: originally from punch-drunk, a condition resulting from numerous blows on the head, as in boxing

Like most people at Cannes, Miss Burstyn said she was a bit punchy from seeing two films a day.

punctilious   *puhngk TI lee uhs*
very exact; scrupulous

On this day in New York, Danny Kaye was not feeling very funny. Maybe it was because he had expected his visitor to arrive earlier and he is punctilious about keeping appointments.

punctuate   *PUHNGK choo ayt*
to break in on here and there; interrupt

As directed by Richard Loncraine, "The Haunting of Julia" is virtually scareless, and the camera angles provide advance tipoffs to the few frightening episodes that punctuate the dull ones.

pundit   *PUHN dit*
a person who has or professes to have great learning, usually in a particular field: Hindi, pandit, *learned person*

When the Soviet Union invaded Afghanistan, pundits agreed that guerrilla resistance would be more difficult than in, say, Vietnam. Why? Without jungle ground cover, insurgents have no place to hide. It would be a piece of cake for Soviet helicopters to pick off the rebels.

pungent   *PUHN juhnt*
sharp to the taste or smell

For many people, though, working at American Chicle has not been just another job. Most of the employees say they like the place, the pay and the supervisors. They even like the smell—a pungent, sinus-clearing blend of peppermint, cinnamon and sugar.

> ◆ The Aztecs chewed chicle, a gumlike substance made from the milky juice of the sapodilla tree, centuries ago. In 1836, General Antonio Lopez de Santa Anna, of Alamo fame, while a prisoner of General Sam Houston in the United States, brought a lump of it to New York City. He tried to interest an inventor, Thomas Adams, in its possibilities as a rubber substitute. Experiments with it in that respect failed, during the

course of which Santa Anna returned to Mexico under amnesty. Adams, however, having noticed that Santa Anna also chewed the chicle, began experimenting with it as a chewing gum. The results were America's first commercial chewing gum. Today, most chewing gum is made from polyvinyl acetate, a synthetic plastic.

purist   *PYOO: rist*
a person who will not deviate from the original or traditional form of something; one who insists on strict observance of usage or rules, as in language or art

Corner groceries now carry bottled and canned iced teas in every shape, color and flavor. To front-porch purists who believe iced tea needs no more than lemon and sugar, some of the zany new combinations seem farcical at best. Strawberry iced tea? Cranberry iced tea?

> *I give you now Professor Twist,*
> *A conscientious scientist.*
> *Trustees exclaimed, "He never bungles!"*
> *And sent him off to distant jungles.*
> *Camped on a tropic riverside,*
> *One day he missed his loving bride.*
> *She had, the guide informed him later,*
> *Been eaten by an alligator.*
> *Professor Twist could not but smile.*
> *"You mean," he said, "a crocodile."*
> — Ogden Nash, "The Purist"

puritan   *PYOO ruh tin*
a person regarded as extremely or excessively strict in matters of morals and religion, as America's seventeenth-century Pilgrims were said to be

Pete Seeger has always described himself, and has been described by his friends, as a puritan: he doesn't smoke, he doesn't drink, he disapproves of gambling and there is every reason to believe that he was innocent of sex until he married Toshi Ohta, his wife of 40 years.

purple patch   *PUR puhl PACH*
a passage of obtrusively ornate writing that stands out from the style of writing around it and reveals the author's attempt at being impressive or poetic

The most powerful segments of "Anatomy of a Volcano" are, of course, the mountain in eruption, the landslides, floods and the scarcely credible flattening and stripping of mature Douglas firs many miles away. It ends with an exploration of the wasteland that shows the restoration of animal, insect and plant life has already begun. The narration, written by Stuart Harris of the BBC and spoken by Frank Donlan, wisely does not try to match this extraordinary event with purple patches, but is a model, by and large, of low-key lucidity.

purported   *per PAWR tid*
suspected of being; reported; rumored

WELLFLEET, Mass., Dec. 6—Treasure hunters say they have located the pirate ship Whidah, wrecked in a storm in 1717, purportedly carrying a fortune in gold, silver, ivory and jewels. Salvage operations are due to begin next spring.

putative   *PYOO: tuh tiv*
reputed; supposed

The production is at the scrappy collegiate rather than the professional workshop level. While all the principals sing and dance well, some of them go wildly and noisily out of control during their putative comic or dramatic moments.

quixotic

Guitarists and flutists were once considered quixotic for

wanting to build solo careers, but there

are now small armies of

each, touring as recitalists.

see page 300

quack   *kwak*

a fraudulent or incompetent medical doctor; anyone who pretends to have knowledge or skill in a field but does not; charlatan: short for quacksalver, *one who quacks, or boasts, as snake oil and liniment vendors did about their products at fairs*

The nutritional quack often cloaks his information in scientific language, supported by references in the scientific literature. Most people are in no position to check the accuracy of the claims against the original references. More often than not, they are distortions or unwarranted extensions of the true findings.

✦ *Quack* is a clipped form, a word formed by clipping off the front or back of an older word. Clips are the natural result of people wanting to say or write something in a shorter way. Clips like *mod* (ern) and *demo* (nstration) will probably always be colloquial, while others, like *zoo* (logical park) and (omni) *bus* are standard usage and rarely thought of or used in their original forms. Among the more recent clips are *stereo* (phonic), *limo* (usine), *condo* (minium), *disco* (thèque), *sit* (uation) *com* (edy) and *narc* (otics detective). More traditional clips are *ad* (vertisement), *vet* (erinarian), *coop* (erative), *lab* (oratory) and *pro* (fessional). Students are traditionally prolific clippers, as witness *dorm* (itory), *math* (ematics), *gym* (nasium), *eco* (nomics), *psych* (ology), *bio* (logy), *poli* (tical) *sci* (ence) and *grad* (uate) school. Back clips are far more numerous than front clips, probably because of the practice of retaining the most important part of the word and dropping the suffix. Two of our most common words, however, (air) *plane* and (tele) *phone*, are front clips. One popular clip gets snipped from back *and* front— (in) *flu* (enza).

qualm *kwahm*
an uneasy feeling or pang of conscience; misgiving

Ivan Fisher is a successful lawyer who defends major narcotics dealers, earns large fees for his work and makes no apologies for it. He has no moral qualms about handling drug cases, Mr. Fisher said, expressing vehemently a view shared by several other New York lawyers who were interviewed about their defense of narcotics traffickers. "Personally," he said, "I find some white-collar defendants more reprehensible—at least a drug dealer takes money from a drug user or from another drug dealer."

quandary *KWAHN duh ree*
a dilemma; perplexing situation

As the bull market ages, many investors worry that a downturn is imminent and that their profits may quickly turn to dust. On the other hand, they don't want to miss out on the fun if the market keeps rising. It's the eternal quandary of investors: Hold or sell?

quantitative *KWAHN tuh tay tiv*
capable of being measured

By running roaches on a treadmill, three scientists at the State University of New York at Buffalo have performed what they believe is the first quantitative study of energy consumption and efficiency in a running insect, and only the second such study of an invertebrate of any kind. (The first examined the energy budget of a big land crab.)

quarry *KWAW ree*
something hunted or pursued; prey

Blanda was a quarterback, and the quarterback is the marked man on any team, the quarry of 350-pound pass-rushers hungering to pluck him off his feet and ram his head into the ground.

quash *kwahsh*
to quell or suppress; put down

The Detroit office of the Internal Revenue Service is moving to quash a burgeoning tax revolt reported among 3,500 Michigan workers, many in the automobile industry, who have avoided having income taxes withheld by claiming as many as 99 dependents.

quasi   *KWAY zigh*
seemingly; in a sense; resembling; in part: Latin, as if

The particular charm of North Carolina's mountain stream trout fishing is the wilderness or quasi-wilderness backdrop. One meets few anglers on most streams and none on others, and I, for one, would rather catch a nine-inch trout under such conditions than a *five-pound*, hatchery-reared fish on a crowded river or reservoir.

✦ *Quasi* takes a hyphen when joined to an adjective (quasi-public); used with a noun, it should remain a separate unit (quasi corporation). *Quasi* is an element in only a small number of established English terms: *quasi contract* and *quasi-judicial*, for example. But it has a sound and sense to it that, when joined with most words, makes the combination seem standard usage, as in these *New York Times* examples: *quasi-operatic* rock singing; a play with a *quasi flashback* structure; a *quasi-religious* society; from *quasi Cockney* to indeterminate mid-Atlantic; information of a *quasi-classified* type; the *quasi-private* Corporation for Public Broadcasting; a general atmosphere of *quasi-sexual* horror. The combinations are limitless, and the results are almost always genuine aids to expression.

queue   *kyoo:*
to form in a line or file while waiting to be served; wait in—or on—line: the use of "up" following "queue" is optional

Miss Horne opened at the Nederlander Theater on Tuesday night, and for the last two days people have queued outside the box office to buy tickets.

quintessence   *kwin TE suhns*
the most perfect embodiment of something

The use of fire is the quintessence of the human condition, even more so than the use of tools, since some animals at least use sticks as primitive tools but only man uses fire.

✦ *What a piece of work is a man! how noble in reason! how infinite in faculties! in form and moving how express and admirable! in action how like an angel! in apprehension how like a god! the beauty of the world, the paragon of animals! And yet to me what is this quintessence of dust?*

— Shakespeare, *Hamlet*, Act II Sc. 2

quixotic   *kwik SAH tik*
idealistic and utterly impractical; having improbable goals from noble motives: after Don Quixote, the hero of Cervantes' 1605 novel, who set out to correct the wrongs of the world

Guitarists and flutists were once considered quixotic for wanting to build solo careers, but there are now small armies of each, touring as recitalists.

restorative

To give up clams would be to give up the food that is most

symbolic of childhood summers, when, after being parched

by salt and sun of Brooklyn

beaches, we crossed the

footbridge over Sheepshead

Bay and swallowed clams more

rapidly than they could be shucked at Lundy's open-air bar.

The saline clams, as coolly restorative as an ocean breeze,

satisfied both thirst and hunger, and stand in memory for

the best and most carefree summers of my life.

see page 309

raconteur *ra kahn TER*

a person who excels at telling stories and anecdotes: French

The late Francis Robinson, that amiable raconteur who ended up his many years at the Metropolitan Opera as tour director and consultant, used to have a lovely Milanov story. Zinka, he said, came to the Met to hear Mirella Freni as Adina in "L'Elisir d'amore." No competition there. Freni was a light lyric. (With dramatic sopranos Milanov could be merciless.) Anyway, said Robinson, Milanov came to his office at the end of the second act, dissolved in tears. "Francis," she sobbed. "Francis, Francis, she's beautiful. She sings like a young me."

ramifications *ra muh fuh KAY shuhns*

consequences or outgrowths of a problem, plan or statement: in botany, a ramification is a branch or offshoot growing from a main stock

A Federal jury has ordered New York City to pay $5 million to a woman who was strip-searched by jail guards, a verdict that could have broad financial ramifications for the city as it faces a class-action lawsuit filed on behalf of 63,000 people who say they were illegally strip-searched. It was the first decision against the city for its policy of strip-searching all people arrested and arraigned on minor charges in Manhattan and Queens over a period of about 10 months in 1996 and 1997.

rapport *ruh PAWR*

a close or sympathetic relationship; harmonious feeling

Learning to identify and harvest wild edibles is not, for nearly all of us, a way to reduce the food budget or a passport to survival. It is, if it appeals, another passageway to a deeper rapport with the natural world and with the dwellers of a less sophisticated time.

rapprochement   *ra prawsh MAHN*
an establishing, or especially a restoring, of harmony and friendly relations:
French, rapprocher, *bring together*

What development of recent years has done the most to assure Israel's long-term security? The answer surely is the rapprochement with Egypt. The most important of Israel's Arab neighbors is no longer an enemy.

rapt   *rapt*
completely absorbed or engrossed

Row G, on the aisle, at the National Theater for the exuberant opening night of "Evita." Alejandro Orfila, an Argentine who is Secretary General of the Organization of American States, and his German-born wife, Helga, sat rapt, watching the musical on the rise of Eva Perón. Mr. Orfila served as Juan Perón's last ambassador to the United States, from 1973 to 1975.

raucous   *RAW kuhs*
harsh, grating and loud

To the raucous sputter of a chain saw, the elm branches were falling in Riverside Park this week, sinking almost lazily to the ground from 45 or 50 feet up as a few joggers and passers-by craned their necks.

raze   *rayz*
to tear down completely; level to the ground; demolish: used almost invariably about buildings

SAR CHESHMA, Afghanistan, Oct. 24—In a country where at least 10,000 villages have been bombed, shelled and burned into rubble, the razing of one more hamlet can pass almost unnoticed. For hundreds of thousands of Afghan families who have lost their homes, the anonymity of the loss only adds to the pain.

recalcitrant   *ri KAL suh truhnt*
resisting authority or control; not obedient; difficult to manage

The film has some choice bits of comic business that no one else could have invented, for example a scene in a Chinese restaurant where Mr. Matthau argues philosophy with Jill Clayburgh while trying to snare a recalcitrant dumpling with a pair of unwieldy chopsticks.

recant   *ri KANT*
to formally or publicly renounce one's beliefs or former statements

SAN FRANCISCO, Feb. 25—A Roman Catholic priest who is a homosexual has been notified that he will be expelled from his religious order unless he resigns or recants his criticism of the vow of priestly celibacy.

recapitulate   *ree kuh PI chuh layt*
to restate briefly; summarize

In the den two teen-agers, one a boy with only one leg and the other a girl walking with crutches, were recapitulating the week's action on "General Hospital."

reckoning   *RE kuh ning*
the settling of an account

El Salvador has long been a violent society. Before the war, some 2,000 people died each year in political or personal blood reckonings.

recluse   *RE kloo:s*
one who lives a secluded, solitary life

CORNISH, N.H., Oct. 23—Not even a fire that consumed at least half his home on Tuesday could smoke out the reclusive J.D. Salinger, author of the classic novel of adolescent rebellion, "The Catcher in the Rye." Mr. Salinger is almost equally famous for having elevated privacy to an art form.

recoup   *ri KOO:P*
to get back an equivalent for; make up for

At first glance "Electra" looked like a money loser par excellence. The subject matter was grim; the cast had no naked Hollywood stars, and the playwright hadn't written a play in 2,400 years. But this week, the producers of Sophocles' revenge tragedy proudly announced that they had recouped all of the show's initial $600,000 investment at the Barrymore Theater. "I'm stunned," said Eric Krebs, one of the producers. "It's probably more money than the entire community of Greek playwrights made in 450 years."

rectitude   *REK tuh too:d*
correct conduct according to principles; uprightness

Since he has always had a reputation for moral rectitude, it may come as no surprise that Roger Staubach, who retired last year as the Dallas Cowboys' quarterback, has lent his name to a fund-raising drive for an organization [Morality in Media, Inc.] that fights what it calls smut on television.

redolent   *RE duh luhnt*
smelling [of]; suggestive or evocative [of]

Although Sidney Lumet's "Prince of the City" has an atmosphere deeply redolent of crime and corruption, very few specific misdeeds are ever shown on the screen. They don't have to be. Mr. Lumet's film offers such a sharply detailed landscape, such a rich and crowded portrait, that his characters reveal themselves fully by the ways they move, eat, speak, listen or lie.

redundant   *ri DUHN duhnt*
needlessly repetitive; superfluous

Q. You often specify corn or vegetable oil in your recipe. To me this sounds redundant. Corn is a vegetable and is, therefore, a vegetable oil. Why do you indulge in such a redundancy?

A. This has been pointed out to me on numerous occasions. I repeat "corn or vegetable" oil because some jars of oil are labeled corn and others vegetable. It is to simplify things for readers, to reassure them, in other words, that the oils marked corn or vegetable are interchangeable.

redux   *REE duks*
brought back; revived; restored: redux *always follows the word it describes*

An unexpected result of the Beetle phenomenon is that a car intended for the average person ended up crossing all class lines. The same is true for Beetle redux; the new car has been snapped up by celebrities, commoners and college students.

refurbish   *ree FER bish*
to renovate; polish up; brighten

In Connecticut, New York and New Jersey, the high price of oil is leading to the refurbishing of small, abandoned, vandalized hydroelectric stations.

They are once again becoming commercially feasible installations and making small dents in the nation's foreign payments for oil.

relic   *RE lik*
something surviving from the past that has historic or personal interest; a trace of some past or outmoded practice, custom or belief

Elio J. Ippolito is a relic as rare and obsolete as a Philco radio, and as cherished. He is a doctor who makes house calls.

remiss   *ri MIS*
negligent; careless or slow in performing one's duty, business, etc.

"I would feel guilty and remiss if we took a trip without Louis," William A. Spiegler, director of communications for the C.W. Post Center of Long Island University said of his 12-year-old son. "I couldn't take a trip that I knew would be fun and educational without him."

renaissance   *RE nuh sahns*
revival; rebirth

Alligators were once in a dramatic decline in Louisiana, the result of unrestricted killing. Now, with the help of state and Federal regulations, the animal has made a strong comeback, and signs of its renaissance are conspicuous in busy canals, bayous and rivers, in cypress swamps and residential districts and in the soup, potage alligator au sherry, at Antoine's.

render   *REN der*
to cause to be or become; make

The John C. Mandel Security Bureau once sent a karate-trained female to protect a former Olympic male wrestling champion rendered temporarily defenseless by a racing car accident.

reparations   *re puh RAY shuhnz*
the paying of compensation for some wrong or injury

Since the end of World War II, the German Government has paid out about $80 billion in war reparations and aid, most of it to Jews who survived concentration camps or fled.

repertoire   *RE per twahr*
the entire range of things in a particular field or art: French, catalogue, inventory

Pitching machines that cost around $1,500 have been refined to the point where they can deliver any of the pitches in a major league pitcher's repertoire—including a devastating knuckle ball—at varying speeds and in different locations around the strike zone.

replete   *ri PLEET*
well-filled or plentifully supplied

When "Lolita" opened its pre-Broadway tryout engagement in Boston, some reviewers and theatergoers were outraged by other, non-Nabokovian touches added by Mr. Albee. For one thing, the stage version of "Lolita" arrives replete with four-letter words in its vocabulary. There are none in the novel.

requisite   *RE kwuh zit*
required, as by circumstances; necessary; indispensable

At a party the poet and anthologist Oscar Williams was introduced to the wife of the actor George Segal. She was wearing a remarkably low-cut dress and had the requisite figure. After acknowledging the introduction, Mr. Williams unbuttoned his shirtfront and pulled it open. "I too," he said, "have a perfectly hairless chest."

rescind   *ri SIND*
to revoke, repeal or cancel

In 1954 a general meeting of the Duke faculty voted 61 to 42 to rescind the offer of an honorary doctor of laws degree to Mr. Nixon, who was then the Vice President.

resolute   *RE zuh loo:t*
firmly resolved or determined; showing a fixed, firm purpose

But it is difficult to witness anybody doing anything resolutely in sweltering Peking, with the possible exception of kissing, snoozing and trying to buy beer.

resplendent   ri SPLEN duhnt
gleaming; splendid

King Juan Carlos, a military man by training and Commander in Chief of the armed forces, appeared on television after the sprawling studio complex was retaken by loyal troops. Wearing full-dress uniform resplendent with medals, he denounced the seizure of Parliament and pledged his faith in democracy.

restorative   ri STAW ruh tiv
capable of restoring or renewing health, strength, vitality

To give up clams would be to give up the food that is most symbolic of childhood summers, when, after being parched by the salt and sun of Brooklyn beaches, we crossed the footbridge over Sheepshead Bay and swallowed clams more rapidly than they could be shucked at Lundy's open-air bar. The saline clams, as coolly restorative as an ocean breeze, satisfied both thirst and hunger, and stand in memory for the best and most carefree summers of my life.

resurrect   re zuh REKT
to bring back into notice, practice or use

Armed with a steel harpoon, a .50-caliber rifle and permission to conduct the first legal hunt for a gray whale in American waters in more than 50 years, members of a small Indian tribe gathered today on a beach on the rugged Olympic Peninsula of Washington to start an adventure intended to resurrect the glory and traditions of their whale-hunting forefathers.

retrenchment   ri TRENCH muhnt
a cutting down or reducing; curtailing

DENVER, July 4—Protecting gains made by blacks in a conservative atmosphere of Government retrenchment was the major task set before the 72d annual convention of the National Association for the Advancement of Colored People, which ended here last night.

retrospective   re truh SPEK tiv
a representative exhibition of the lifetime work of an artist or of a particular period of art

Beginning Saturday, the museum will celebrate its birthday with a retrospective honoring artists who have contributed to the growth of American crafts since World War II.

reverberate   *ri VER buh rayt*
to re-echo or resound

KOUROU, French Guiana, June 19—Western Europe's Ariane rocket rose from its jungle launching pad here today, the reverberations rolling across the wild coastal savanna, and successfully boosted two satellites into orbit around the earth.

revulsion   *ri VUHL shuhn*
extreme disgust; loathing

President Clinton said tonight that his decision to authorize military strikes against Serbia was derived from moral revulsion at the killing in Kosovo and a calculated assessment of American interests in the Balkans.

rhapsodic   *rap SAH dik*
extravagantly enthusiastic; ecstatic

Reviews of the massive book were generally rhapsodic, with one reviewer saying, "The three best novels I read this year were 'Gone With the Wind.'" J. Donald Adams, in The New York Times Book Review of July 5, 1936, wrote: "This is beyond a doubt one of the most remarkable first novels produced by an American writer. It is also one of the best. I would go so far as to say that it is, in narrative power, in sheer readability, surpassed by nothing in American fiction."

ribald   *RI buhld*
characterized by coarse or vulgar joking or mocking, especially dealing with sex in a humorously earthy or direct way

Angel Cordero, often screams and sings, and the other jockeys hurl ribald but friendly insults at one another. But Vasquez sequesters himself in front of his locker or beats his valet at backgammon in the jockeys' lounge, as he did yesterday while waiting for the Wood Memorial at Aqueduct.

rife   *righf*
commonly occurring; abounding

Most of the American musical idioms that preceded and shaped rock-and-roll were regarded "the Devil's music" at one time or another—especially the blues. Early blues lyrics are rife with satires on preachers, who are depicted as hypocrites with their minds on adultery and financial gain, and often the most uncompromising blues have suggested their own pragmatic value system as an alternative to Christian values.

riffle   *RI fuhl*
to thumb through

For the first time, women interested in making their own clothes did not have to buy a magazine, then send off for a pattern that might cost as much as 25 cents. Instead, they could riffle through an open-top box on the counter of a local store, pay a dime for a pattern and, as often as not, buy the required fabric in the same store. As a result, Simplicity, which started off using a single designer and relying on commercial printers, soon dominated the home sewing market. At its peak in the 1970's, the company, which went public in the 1930's, had 4,000 employees, its own paper mill and printing operations, factories in several countries, an extensive catalogue business, 20,000 retail outlets in the United States alone, and a flourishing sideline supplying patterns to fashion magazines.

a shallow stretch of swiftly-flowing water made choppy or ripply by rocks

Rainbow trout and the Madison River were made for each other. Bold and sometimes reckless, stout-hearted and acrobatic when hooked, the pink-striped rainbow is the pre-eminent native American trout, and it has long thrived spectacularly in the powerful currents and chaotic, boulder-strewn riffles of what some people consider the finest wild trout stream in the contiguous 48 states.

rinky-dink   *RING kee dingk*
small-time; not modern or up-to-date; corny: a slang term

What? Watch tug-of-war? "I thought it was going to be some rinky-dink competition," said Lynne Cox, manager of the United States women's water polo team, "but I stayed, mainly out of curiosity. And the thing really surprised me."

risible   *RI zuh buhl*
laughable, amusing

Meredith Monk's music, like nearly all the various manifestations of her art, can seem moving, exciting, beautiful and profoundly original—once one overcomes the impulse to find it pretentiously risible. Miss Monk is so earnestly strange in her precociously talented little-girl way that it takes a while to accept her premises and to appreciate her properly. But it's worth it to take that time.

rite of passage
an event, achievement or ceremony that marks the passage from one stage of life to another

The summer job is a rite of passage, a step between the indigency of teen-hood and the economic independence of adulthood.

robotic   *roh BAH tik*
robot-like or machine-like behavior; working or acting mechanically

Outside in the balmy tropical air, residents with deep tans and hefty girths like to relax beneath the palm trees that shade the long white beaches on this tiny Pacific island. Inside a nearby garment factory, rows of workers from China perform robotic motions under dull fluorescent lights all day long, sewing, ironing and packing. In fast-paced, mind-numbing sequence, they churn out box after box of shirts and skirts for American retailers like The Gap, Tommy Hilfiger and Sears, Roebuck.

roil   *roil*
to agitate; unsettle; make angry; rile

How to relate to the gay men and lesbians in their pews is a question that has deeply roiled many American religious organizations, just as it has proven highly contentious among many secular institutions, like the military.

roman à clef   *raw MAHN ah KLAY*
a novel in which real persons appear under fictitious names: French, novel with a key

In November, his [Meyer Levin's] novel "The Architect," a roman à clef about the life of Frank Lloyd Wright, will be published by Simon & Schuster. It is described as the story of a Wisconsin youth who comes to Chicago in an era of robber barons and muckrakers and reshapes the American landscape.

roustabout   *ROW stuh bowt*
an unskilled or transient laborer, as on a ranch or in an oilfield

Gulf takes 362,000 barrels of oil a day out of Nigeria. About 86 percent of its work force is Nigerian. A way had to be found to satisfy the 14 percent that is not Nigerian. The incentive that was worked out amounts to $2,000 a month tax-free for the lowest roustabout, and free flights to and from anywhere in the world that is home, in exchange for less than six months of labor a year.

rubato   *roo: BAH toh*
rhythmic flexibility within a musical phrase or measure: Italian, short for
tempo rubato, *stolen time*

"In my conducting, I try not to be exaggerated," [Klaus Tennstedt] says. "It's just not necessary. There is rubato in all music, even Mozart, but it should not affect the outer flow of the music; it should be an expression of the inner unrest of every score. A compromise between head and heart is the alpha and omega of music."

✦ Rubato involves varying the mechanical regularity of notes or phrases by lingering longer over some of them than the written music indicates, and making up the time by hurrying over others. The underlying tempo is maintained, as though a metronome were continuing to tick it off, but the musicians or singers are free to depart from the timing of notes and phrases as they have been set down in the written music. Just how rubato is employed in any performance depends upon the sensitivity and personal taste of the performer or conductor.

rubberneck   *RUH ber nek*
to stretch one's neck or turn one's head to gaze about in curiosity, as a sightseer

It is still enough to advertise a new play with little more than a photograph of Glenda Jackson's bony face. It is still enough for her merely to walk through a downtown restaurant on the way to a table to throw the entire bar into a frenzy of rubbernecking.

rube   *roo:b*
a naïve, unsophisticated person from a rural region: slang nickname of Reuben,
a rustic name

Orchard and its network of satellite streets—Allen, Ludlow, Rivington, Grand, Hester and Broome—are the closest thing New York has to a bazaar. And it is a bazaar in the real sense, for on Orchard Street there is no such phrase as "list price" and if you should fail to bargain you risk revealing yourself as some sort of urban rube.

rudiments   *ROO: duh muhnts*
fundamentals

When the Lehmans enrolled their daughter in a music program at the Henry Street Settlement on Manhattan's Lower East Side, they were encouraged to learn the rudiments of their child's instrument—the violin—to help with practice at home.

ruminate   *ROO: muh nayt*
to turn something over in the mind; meditate on: a mental chewing of the cud, as ruminant animals like cattle, goats, deer and camels do

"I am working, not at the pace I used to take, but at a pace. Now is the time to ruminate, assess. I have more time with my children. And I have more time with Marian. Getting reacquainted with your wife is a nice thing to have happen to you." [Jacob K. Javits]

rupture   *RUP chuhr*
break apart; burst

Nearly 20 years after the 1979 Iranian Revolution ruptured relations with Washington and installed a fundamentalist Islamic Government in Teheran, Ms. Albright said it was time to find ways to bridge the gap between the two nations and the civilizations they represent.

ruse   *roo:z*
a stratagem; trick

A New York City traffic-enforcement agent and a man who resigned as an agent last year were arrested yesterday and charged with fabricating traffic tickets, in a ruse to cover up times when they should have been working but were not, the Department of Investigation said.

S

salmagundi

The 30's, keyed to songs from or about movies, leans on

warm nostalgia—Fred Astaire, George Gershwin,

"Gone With the Wind"—and the 40's is

a mixture of wartime sentimentality and

the emergence of Latin music from

south of the border. This musical

salmagundi is carried off by a

versatile and tremendously

hard-working cast of two women and three men who are

simultaneously waiting on tables while they are performing.

see page 318

saccharine   *SA kuh rin*
too sweet or syrupy: Latin, saccharum, *and Greek,* sakharon, *both meaning sugar*

Audiences flocking to the Martin Beck Theater for the revival of "The Sound of Music" couldn't care less that many critics find the musical irredeemably saccharine. With its famously tuneful score, this 1959 show, the last Rodgers and Hammerstein collaboration, is comfortingly familiar. People watch dazed with happiness, bobbing their heads, along with the Von Trapp children as they learn their do, re, mi's, smiling with recognition as Maria lists her favorite things.

sacrosanct   *SA kroh sangkt*
very sacred, holy or inviolable

"Judges are not sacrosanct," the Mayor said yesterday in an early morning WNYC radio broadcast. "They believe they are above any kind of criticism by the Mayor. They are not."

salacious   *suh LAY shuhs*
erotically stimulating, pornographic

Condemned as salacious trash by some critics but praised as a masterpiece by many others, Nabokov's "Lolita" became an instant best-seller and soon gained wide recognition as one of the classics of modern literature—a brilliant evocation of one man's obsessional search for paradise lost amid the wilderness of roadside America.

salad days *SAL ad DAYZ*
one's fresh, vigorous, early years of life

In my salad days, I used to fasten my speared fish to a line at my waist and keep on swimming. Now I go ashore with each fish.

+ "My salad days, when I was green in judgment" is spoken by Cleopatra in Shakespeare's *Antony and Cleopatra*. Shakespeare created dozens of other phrases and expressions still used today. Among them: led by the nose, wear the heart on the sleeve, the naked truth, eat out of house and home, flaming youth, fancy free, too much of a good thing, at one fell swoop, forever and a day, play the fool, it was Greek to me, itching palm, die a slow death, truth will out.

salmagundi *sal muh GUHN dee*
a mixture: originally, of minced veal, chicken or turkey; anchovies or pickled herrings; and onions, all chopped together and served with lemon juice and oil

The 30's, keyed to songs from or about movies, leans on warm nostalgia— Fred Astaire, George Gershwin, "Gone With the Wind"—and the 40's is a mixture of wartime sentimentality and the emergence of Latin music from south of the border. This musical salmagundi is carried off by a versatile and tremendously hard-working cast of two women and three men who are simultaneously waiting on tables while they are performing.

salvo *SAL voh*
a simultaneous discharge of firearms

The opening salvo in the bidding war for Conoco Inc. was fired on Thursday, June 25, when Joseph E. Seagram & Sons, the American subsidiary of the huge Canadian liquor company, offered $73 a share in cash for 35 million shares, or 40.7 percent, of Conoco's 86.8 million shares.

sanctimonious *sangk tuh MOH nee uhs*
pretending to be pious or righteous

Needless to say, most treatments of sex-and-violence subjects are couched in the rhetoric of noble motivations. The film or news report is always offered as an exercise in consciousness-raising, designed to alert the country to some festering social problem. In fact, television seems to have entered what might be called an era of sanctimonious sensationalism.

sartorial *sahr TAW ree uhl*
pertaining to clothing or dress, especially men's

If a player who last played tournament bridge half a century ago returned to the fray today he would be struck not so much by the improvement in bidding conventions as by the deterioration in sartorial conventions. Black ties have given way to T-shirts and blue jeans.

> ✦ Jeans are made of jean, a cotton cloth of great durability, which got its name from Genoa, where it was first woven in the fifteenth century. It became the fabric of choice for sailors' trousers and the sails of the Nina, Pinta and Santa Maria. Genes, the Old French name for Genoa, was the French name for the fabric, which was adapted as "jeans" in America when it was first used in the 1850s by the Levi Strauss company to make sturdy pants for California gold rushers. Serge de Nimes, the name of another tough blue sailcloth, was woven in the French town of Nimes. It is now known as denim.

savage *SA vij*
to attack in a violent way

A 3½-hour version of "Heaven's Gate" was withdrawn last November after it was savaged by critics. The new 2-hour 25-minute version received equally negative reviews.

savoir-faire *sa vwahr FAIR*
knowledge of how to act in any situation: French, knowing how to do

Then the lights dimmed and Connie Cook, the fresh-faced model with the short blond hair, sauntered down the runway with the savoir-faire of Fred Astaire. Like the dancer, she wore white tie and tails.

savvy *SA vee*
shrewd; in-the-know; discerning: Spanish, sabe usted, do you know?

A savvy, middle-class Warsaw resident mapped out the city like a battle zone: On this side of Marszalkowska Street you can usually find bread; over here the meat lines aren't so long; vegetables are better here.

saw
an old saying, often repeated; maxim; proverb

The old saw that it is easy to stop smoking—as Mark Twain said, "I ought to know because I've done it a thousand times"—is all too familiar to millions of smokers who would like to kick the habit.

scapegoat   *SKAYP goht*
a person, group or thing upon whom the blame for the mistakes or crimes of others is thrust

The Baha'i faith originated in Iran in 1844 and has evolved into an independent world religion. Its adherents believe that a single God has been revealed in progressive revelations. Because it has roots in Islam, it has been viewed as heretical by the Islamic clergy. What has made Baha'is more vulnerable is their relative prosperity and professional success—tempting scapegoats in a revolutionary country with a floundering economy and an aimless war.

◆ *Scapegoat*, meaning *the goat that escapes*, was coined in 1530 by the English biblical translator William Tyndale (1494-1536), whose translations formed the basis of the Authorized Version of the Bible and thus one of the foundations of modern English. He was imprisoned in 1535 for his professed Lutheran beliefs and his attacks on papal supremacy, and, condemned for heresy, was burned at the stake.

◆ The scapegoat was a goat over whose head the high priest of the ancient Jews confessed the sins of the people on the Day of Atonement, after which it was allowed to escape into the wilderness.

scatological   *ska tuh LAH ji kuhl*
obscene; dirty

"The Choir Boys," a lousy movie, was a wonderful novel, and almost impossible to review in a family newspaper. The language of cops who have seen too much of the corruption of the world, and have done some corrupting themselves, is necessarily scatological.

schism   *SI zuhm*
a split or division in an organized group, especially a church, as the result of a difference of opinion or doctrine

Dr. Hobbs served two terms, from 1961 to 1963, as president of the Southern Baptist Convention and leader of 10 million Baptists. It was a contentious time when his church seemed headed for open schism between fundamentalists and a more liberal wing over just how literally the Bible must be interpreted. The convention avoided the split by not bringing the most divisive issues to the floor.

schlep   *shlep*
to move, drag or carry with effort: Yiddish

Eda Cawthon reclined on a plastic chaise longue, her eyes obscured by sunglasses and her toes wriggling and pointing at the Atlantic Ocean as she waited for her husband, Craig, to schlep back half a mile from the parking lot.

schlock   *shlahk*
anything cheap or inferior; trash: Yiddish

If you ask Samuel Klein what Klein's of Monticello, 105 Orchard, specializes in, he'll tell you, "We don't have any bottom-of-the-line children's schlock here." And he hasn't. This is a children's wear store with piles of Izod, Cardin, John Weitz, Gant and Quoddy.

schmooze   *shmoo:z*
to have a friendly, gossipy, prolonged, heart-to-heart talk: Yiddish

"Idle time is something he's never learned to live with," his close friend John Trubin once said. "He has an agenda for everything—even relaxation. He's not a guy who can sit around and schmooze."

scion   *SIGH in*
a descendant; child; heir; usually applied to one whose family is prominent in some way: also—and originally—a shoot or bud of a plant used for planting or grafting

Angier Biddle Duke, scion of two aristocratic American families who served as Ambassador to El Salvador, Denmark, Spain and Morocco and who was chief of protocol for two Presidents, died yesterday near his home in

Southampton, L.I., after being struck by a car while Rollerblading. He was 79. Mr. Duke's brother, Anthony, said that no charges had been filed against the driver.

scourge   *skerj*
a cause of serious trouble, affliction or calamity

Epidemic typhus, the scourge of many of the armies of World War I, has been a rarity in this country since the early 1920's.

seamless   *SEEM luhs*
with no noticeable separation; perfectly cohesive

One of the unusual things about Mr. Matthau's performance in "First Monday in October" is that he blends comic and serious moments seamlessly. In one scene he delivers a eulogy over the grave of a dead justice, and yet he also includes many comic flourishes.

seethe   *seeth:*
to be violently agitated or disturbed; boiling

Mr. Sands, who spent a third of his life in jail for terrorist crimes, had joined the I.R.A. at the age of 18. And the teen-agers of Twinbrook, seething with a hatred that passes from generation to generation, still provide a pool of potential talent for the illegal organization.

segue   *SE gway*
to proceed without pause from one musical number or theme to another, or from one scene into another, as in film or radio drama

"Kent State" opens with a documentary collage of 1960's images—John F. Kennedy and hula hoops, Martin Luther King and the Beatles, moon walks and Woodstock, the Vietnam "living room war" and peace marches, all of which segue into the Thursday, April 30, 1970 television speech in which President Richard M. Nixon announced the secret bombings of Cambodia.

self-dramatizing
behaving in an exaggerated way for dramatic effect or as an attention-getting device; presenting oneself dramatically

Ms. Haran may not have the most physically commanding voice among cabaret singers, but she brings an unparalleled naturalness, taste, emotional balance and overall musicality to a field awash in self-dramatizing narcissists. Her singing is buoyed with a steady pulse of swing and deepened by a lurking poignancy that is all the more compelling for its being so understated.

self-effacing   *self uh FAY sing*
keeping oneself in the background and minimizing one's own actions, accomplishments, fame or importance; modest

For performers, musical and otherwise, ego is usable if not necessary capital, and any overabundance tends to flow indiscriminately into their personalities. Emanuel Ax is a famous exception, an acclaimed concert pianist who sheds the grand manner as quickly as he doffs his concert tails, becoming to any and all simply Manny, the guy next door. Is this just another studied persona in a profession rife with them? Repeated encounters with the pianist suggest not. Indeed, it becomes hard to imagine a performer more genuinely and spontaneously self-effacing than Mr. Ax.

seminal   *SE muh nuhl*
like a seed in being a source

Professor Longhair, the New Orleans pianist and singer who played a seminal role in the development of rhythm and blues and, later, rock-and-roll, died of a heart attack in January 1980, but his music lives on.

semiotic   *se mee AH tik*
pertaining to signs

In "Family Photographs: Content, Meaning and Effect," Julia Hirsch teaches us to read, semiotically, the expressions, groupings, activities, gestures and relationships in such photographs. She observes that the formal family photograph is based on Renaissance portraiture filtered through 19th-century sentimentality, which leaned toward the "romantic agony" look of generalized longing.

send-up   *SEN duhp*
a parody; takeoff; spoof: originally, British public-school slang meaning to send a boy to the headmaster to be punished

In Blake Edwards's movie "S.O.B.," most of the actors give portrayals that are devastating send-ups of people connected with the Hollywood film industry. Perhaps none is more devastating than that of Loretta Swit, who plays Polly Reed, a powerful, ruthless, screeching, foulmouthed gossip columnist known as "the mouth of Hollywood."

sentient   *SEN shuhnt*
conscious; capable of thinking or feeling

Politicians up and down the state have been venting their outrage over the heavyweight championship fight at Madison Square Garden last weekend, the one that the judges called a draw even though most spectators thought that Lennox Lewis had cleaned Evander Holyfield's clock. What is shocking is that any sentient politician could be shocked. For as long as men have been punching out one another for cash, it has been axiomatic that the only thing in boxing guaranteed to be square is the ring.

sequester   *si KWE ster*
to keep separate, secure or secluded

State Department officials said Colonel Qaddafi, who once freely walked the streets of Libya, playing soccer with children, had virtually sequestered himself. His barrack in the Tripoli suburb of Aziya is ringed with antiaircraft artillery, machine guns and tanks.

seraglio   *si RAL yoh*
harem

A television audience confronted with quality goods is as unnatural as an archbishop in a seraglio. The natural instinct is to run.

seraphic   *suh RA fik*
angelic

What needs to be established right away—for those still afflicted with the image of Mr. Shankar as some seraphic guru for the millions—is that he is not only the greatest living master of the sitar, but also one of the most masterly instrumentalists of any sort in the world today.

serendipity   *se ruhn DI puh tee*
an aptitude for making fortunate discoveries accidentally: coined by English writer Horace Walpole about 1754 after reading The Three Princes of Serendip, *a Persian fairy tale whose title characters make such discoveries. Serendip is an old name for Sri Lanka.*

In 1977, when American scientists traveled to the Indian Ocean to observe the occultation of a star by Uranus, they made a serendipitous discovery.

They saw that Uranus had at least six faint rings around it. Later observations detected nine rings.

♦ Occultation, in astronomy, is an eclipse in which the apparent size of the eclipsed body is much smaller than that of the eclipsing body.

serrated   *SER ray tid*
having sawlike notches along the edge

Few animals have the power to frighten people into the cold terror of being eaten alive. But the great white shark does so effortlessly. Its reputation for blood lust is rooted in images of jaws gleaming with rows of razor-sharp teeth, their edges nicely serrated to ease the job of tearing through bone and flesh.

shoal   *shohl*
a large school of fish

Riding the tides of summer once again are great shoals of jellyfish, which flourish in the warm coastal shallows through the brief season of their maturity.

short shrift   *SHAWRT SHRIFT*
little attention or consideration to a person or matter: originally, the brief time allowed a condemned prisoner to make a confession and receive absolution just before execution

The World Series, with games that stretch past Letterman and Leno, has played havoc with the New York region's schoolchildren. Students have stayed up past their bedtimes, homework has been given short shrift, classroom concentration has been blurry and morning showers have been skipped for extra time under the covers.

showboat   *SHOH boht*
to show off; be an exhibitionist

"It was during the N.I.T. at Madison Square Garden," Auerbach said. "His talent for dribbling caught my eye—behind his back and between his legs, an extraordinary feat for someone 6-8. I'll tell you this, the kid was not showboating, I know showboating when I see it. He had great body control, quickness and very fluid moves."

showcase *SHOH kays*
to exhibit or display

WIMBLEDON, England, June 28—On the same day that John McEnroe threw a temper tantrum on the No. 1 court, a woman sat in the umpire's chair for the first time on center court at the All England Club. No place showcases the shifting, unsettled world of professional tennis better than Wimbledon.

shtick *shtik*
a gimmick, act or routine, especially in a show or performance: Yiddish, a piece

The walk-around is the little routine done twice, maybe three or four times, as the clowns parade around the three rings between the acts, such as a shtick that involves a slip on a big banana peel repeated for each side of the house.

sine qua non *SIN uh kwoh NOHN*
an essential condition; indispensable thing: Latin, without which not

Living in the desert for 8,000 years, one must develop some skills with which to cope. The Bedouins, a declining 700,000 people in Saudi Arabia who live in the deserts of the Arabian Peninsula, have mastered their environment. They can predict the weather, the sine qua non of an outdoor existence, and tell from footprints a person's size and sex and, if the footprints' owner is female, whether she is pregnant.

sinuous *SI nyoo uhs*
bending, winding or curving in and out; serpentine

At its center is the Paseo del Rio, or Riverwalk, a cozy, old-world collection of restaurants, sidewalk cafés, nightspots and hotels strewn like jewels along the sinuous San Antonio River as it flows through the downtown area 15 feet or so below street level.

skulk *skuhlk*
to move or lurk about in a stealthy, craven or sinister manner

British rock bands make New York debuts frequently these days, but most of them sort of skulk into town, victims of record-company austerity and the new wave's own antipretensions. Not so Spandau Ballet, which gave its New York first local performance Wednesday night at the Underground with a full, nostalgically old-fashioned blast of hype, complete with a London vanguard fashion show and a disco full of exotically costumed trendies.

And until early today, the alligator, called Albert by the local news media after the creature in the Pogo comic strip, skulked about the shallow 500-foot-long pond, feeding contentedly on carp and an occasional water bird and frustrating its pursuers while becoming a celebrity of the first rank.

◆ The satirical comic strip "Pogo" was set in Georgia's Okefenokee Swamp, where Pogo, a possum, dwelled with his animal friends. It ran from 1948 until the death of its creator, Walt Kelly, in 1973, and then off and on until 1993. In a 1953 cartoon panel, Pogo spoke a line that has become a classic American expression, "We have met the enemy and he is us." It was a variation on the message sent by Capt. Oliver Hazard Perry (1785-1819) to General William Henry Harrison during the War of 1812 announcing the American victory at the Battle of Lake Erie, Sept. 10, 1813: "We have met the enemy and they are ours—two ships, two brigs, one schooner and one sloop."

smorgasbord   *SMAWR guhs bawrd*
a wide variety of appetizers and other tasty foods served buffet style: Swedish; here used figuratively

With little fanfare, a few major insurers have been experimenting with group auto coverage in the expectation that it will eventually take its place on the corporate smorgasbord of employee benefits.

sobriquet   *SOH bri kay*
a nickname

When the building opened, it was only 25 percent rented, earning it the sobriquet of the Empty State Building. It did not really begin to fill up until after the Depression.

◆ A sobriquet is a nickname so closely attached to a person, place or thing as to be understandable when used in its place. Examples:

Eternal City (Rome)	Redcoats (British soldiers)
Empire State (New York)	Big Apple (New York City)
Emerald Isle (Ireland)	Frisco (San Francisco)
Great Emancipator (Abraham Lincoln)	Yankees (Americans)
Great White Way (Broadway)	Uncle Sam (U.S.A.)
king of beasts (the lion)	Dixie (the South)

sodden *SAH din*
heavy or soggy

It's fashionable and fun to put down British cooking. Americans love to make jokes about sodden brussels sprouts and dishes with names like Toad in the Hole.

soigné *swah NYAY*
carefully or elegantly done, operated or designed; dressed and groomed with great care and elegance: French

Not many years ago it was hard to imagine a sharper contrast than Manhattan and Secaucus, N.J. On one side of the river stood the gleaming towers, marking the very latest in soigné sophistication. On the other side were the swine, 250,000 of them in 55 Secaucus piggeries. Manhattan had That Look. Secaucus had That Smell.

solipsistic *soh lip SIS tik*
self-involved, as though no other feelings, thoughts or attitudes exist or are important but one's own: from solipsism (Latin, the self alone), the philosophical theory that nothing exists but one's own consciousness

Once again, we have a garrulous narrator (in this case, Brodkey himself) taking inventory of his life, reviewing and re-reviewing his feelings, his memories and his feelings about those memories. In his earlier books, this technique, combined with a seeming reluctance to edit out even the most trivial, abstruse remark, often resulted in windy, self-indulgent narratives that were solipsistic to the point of parody. "This Wild Darkness," in comparison, is downright succinct: death, sadly, not only seems to have focused Brodkey's mind, but also, in providing that most unforgiving of deadlines, seems to have acted as a kind of editor.

Ms. Dyson assumes that "the glitz and artificial stimulation offered by the electronic world will ultimately cause people to value human company and attention more," rather than encourage them to spend more time in isolated and solipsistic on-line worlds.

somber   *SAHM buhr*
gloomily dark; depressed, as though under a shadow

David Wells emerged from the elevator at Legends Field today after a final meeting with and a hug from George Steinbrenner, a somber look on his thick face and a softer quality to his booming voice. The man who loved being a Yankee so much that he once wore one of Babe Ruth's caps in a game had been informed that he had been traded back to the Toronto Blue Jays. It hurt.

sommelier   *suh muhl YAY*
the person in a restaurant responsible for buying the wine, assisting patrons in selecting it, and serving it; wine steward: French, originally a person in charge of pack animals

Mr. Rowan knew which wine he wanted to order, but the process took far longer than it should have. Finally the bottle arrived, and the sommelier uncorked it with a flourish and presented the cork for inspection, whereupon Mr. Rowan put it in his mouth and chewed it up. He sagely nodded his head, indicating that the cork had been approved, and motioned for the horrified sommelier to pour the wine. As the glasses were filled, Mr. Rowan kept spitting out bits of cork and nodding his head in approval. "The guy never even smiled," he said, but the others at his table were practically falling off their chairs.

sonority   *suh NAW ruh tee*
full, deep or rich: said of sound

Mr. O'Riley likes big sonorities, and attacks the keyboard energetically. When he played the Brahms F-minor Piano Quintet, he all but made a little concerto out of it. He is a pianist with temperament and a big style.

sophomoric   *sah fuh MAW rik*
self-assured, intellectually pretentious and opinionated, though immature and superficial: Greek, sophos, wise + moros, foolish

Some of the people who make pop music just want to be entertaining and to make money, but even the ones with the loftiest ambitions, the ones who want to make art, want to make popular art. Any discussion of the vitality of popular music has to take the vitality of what's popular into account, and when what's popular is mostly sophomoric, played-by-the-book hard rock, along with the usual smattering of sentimental pop ballads, popular music just could be in trouble.

soupçon *soo:p SOHN*
a tiny amount; slight trace: French, a suspicion

The staggeringly high prices are staunchly defended by Mr. Tannen. The famous "21" hamburger, for example, which is priced at $13.50, contains only the finest sirloin and tenderloin, with a soupçon of celery, he says, all of which is lovingly hand-mixed and hand-patted.

spartan *SPAR tin*
having only the bare necessities; austere: the people of the ancient Greek city-state of Sparta were noted for their frugal, highly disciplined and rigorously simple way of life

Barbara McCabe, proprietor of the Park Hotel, a cheap place for transients in downtown Helena, said Mr. Kaczynski had stayed the night off and on for many years, taking a spartan, $14 room with a sink and bed. "He was very quiet," she said. "He'd just take his key and go to his room."

spawning ground *SPAW ning GROWND*
a place where fish or other water animals lay their eggs or produce their young; figuratively, a place where an idea or movement is born

Berkeley, the spawning ground of the Free Speech Movement, student revolt and the antiwar movement, has in recent years become something of a laboratory for leftist municipal government. The city passed an initiative against police enforcement of marijuana laws, offered asylum to draft resisters and sent its mayor on trips to Cuba, Mexico City, Vienna and Madrid in pursuit of leftist causes.

spew *spyoo:*
to flow or cause to flow plentifully; gush

The disabled tanker that was swept onto the rocks in the Shetland Islands on Tuesday spewed oil into the storm-whipped waters of the North Sea, fouling miles of coastline as officials scrambled to contain what they said could be an environmental disaster.

sporadic   *spaw RA dik*
happening at irregular intervals; scattered; appearing singly or apart from
each other

The eerie nighttime howls that are being sporadically heard more and more often near suburban homes in the eastern United States are signs to wildlife biologists that the coyote, which once freely roamed eastern America in the Pleistocene Epoch and later was driven out, has returned.

spurious   *SPYOO ree uhs*
not genuine; false; counterfeit

Note: I've just eaten a large plate of crow. I am now satisfied that the document on El Salvador discussed in my column last Friday, which I believed was an official paper, was indeed spurious, as the State Department later said. Many of the facts checked out, but it wasn't a Government paper. I'm abashed.

> ✦ *To eat crow* is to undergo embarrassment or humiliation by having to retract a statement or admit an error. During a brief armistice near the end of the War of 1812, we are told in Brewer's *Dictionary of Phrase and Fable,* an American soldier hunting for game strayed across enemy lines and shot a crow. Hearing the shot, and angry at the trespass, a British soldier accosted him. Being unarmed himself, a reprimand was out of the question, so he flattered the American, admiring his aim and asking to examine the fine weapon. You can tell something about the nature of British-American warfare by the fact that the American actually handed him his gun, whereupon the Britisher pointed it at him, scolded him for trespassing and ordered him to take a bite out of the crow. Anglo-American civility continued when the Britisher returned the gun, whereupon the American aimed it at *him* and ordered him to eat the rest of the crow.

spurn   *spern*
to reject with contempt or disdain

Herbert J. Miller, Richard M. Nixon's criminal defense lawyer, said today that the former president had at first spurned a pardon from President Gerald R. Ford in 1974, saying he wanted to fight any charges that might be brought against him by the Watergate special prosecutor. Mr. Miller, speaking publicly for the first time about the pardon at a forum held here at the Duquesne University Law School, said that in late August 1974, Mr. Nixon's "initial reaction was that he did not want a pardon." He said that the former president, a proud man, "felt that if he had done something wrong, let him be indicted and go to trial."

squander   *SKWAHN duhr*
to spend or use wastefully

In case you are not familiar with baseball, Mr. Rose was one of the all-time greats, with more hits (4,256) than anyone in the history of the game. He was called Charlie Hustle. Day after day, he showed what a gung-ho attitude can do—a lesson seemingly lost on proud underachievers of the Bart Simpson generation. But by most accounts, Mr. Rose was also one of the all-time great jerks, squandering his considerable reputation on an insatiable desire to gamble.

staid   *stayd*
settled and steady

In midlife, Paul Gauguin left his wife, family and a staid bank job to live in the South Seas and paint.

stanchion   *STAN shuhn*
an upright bar, beam or post used as a support

In old comic books it was simple: When Clark Kent needed to turn into Superman, he stepped into a phone booth. But in the 1978 Superman movie he pauses at a pay phone only to find that, alas, it offers no privacy: It's mounted on a stanchion, and below waist level it's completely open to public view.

state of the art   *STAYT uhv thee AHRT*
the level of scientific or technological development in a given field or industry at the present time

The quaint and cramped 425-seat Old Globe is being re-created as a 580-seat, $6.5 million, state-of-the-art theater with removable walls, dressing-room space for 52 actors and a thrust stage that can convert to a proscenium.

stentorian   *sten TAW ree uhn*
very loud: Stentor, a Greek herald in the Trojan War, is described in the Iliad *as having the voice of fifty men*

Sometimes Mr. Jagger reaches for notes that aren't there, but the Rolling Stones have never been a letter-perfect band. The current vogue for stentorian quasi-operatic rock singing, as exemplified by performers like Pat Benatar or Meat Loaf, is foreign to their idea of what rock-and-roll is supposed to be.

stereotype   *STE ree uh tighp*
a fixed or conventional notion or conception of a person, group, idea, etc., held by a number of people, and allowing for no individuality or critical judgment

"A significant number of the Miami rioters were not poor or unemployed or members of the criminal class," the study contends. "Many held jobs and did not otherwise fit the stereotypical image of a 'rioter.'"

stigma   *STIG muh*
a mark of disgrace or reproach; a stain, as on one's reputation

He stressed that going to a vocational college apparently still carried a stigma, despite high salary possibilities for experienced machinists. "Many kids are downplayed—pushed down—by advisers and parents saying that, if they don't do well in English and math, they can go to a vocational college," he said.

stipple   *STI puhl*
to dot or fleck

It was 5:30 A.M. when Mr. Wood, in hip waders and yellow suspenders, and John Bartow, in a plaid shirt and jeans, navigated their skinny gray clam boat through the maze of marshes stippling Hempstead Bay.

stipulate   *STI pyuh layt*
to require as an essential condition in making an agreement

Salmon was once a cheap fish, as prevalent as chicken today. It was so plentiful that servants in Colonial America had clauses in their contracts stipulating that they could not be served salmon more than a certain number of times a week. Two centuries before, Elizabethan servants had objected to too many oysters. No wonder you can't get help these days.

stoic *STOH ik*

unemotional; impassive; not outwardly reacting to physical or emotional pain

Unfortunately, Mr. Santiago said, police officers confronting alcoholism or marital or other domestic problems are often unwilling to admit their problems and share emotions with peers or counselors. "We're trained to be tough, be stoic and handle crises unemotionally," he said. "But police officers are people at the core. We suffer the same kind of stresses as average people."

stoicism *STOH i si zuhm*

impassiveness under suffering, bad fortune, etc.

Besides discussing the comforting of dying people and their families, Dr. Kübler-Ross also brings up the often-neglected question of the hospital staff and their emotional needs. Their professional stoicism, she says, is just another one of the masks we put on to hide from death, and they ought to be free to grieve too, in their special ways.

✦ Zeno of Citium (c. 335-263 B.C.) was the founder of the school of philosophy known as Stoicism, called that because Zeno taught his followers in the *Stoa Poikite*, or Painted Colonnade, a building at the foot of the Acropolis in ancient Athens. Stoicism stresses virtue as the highest good, and the strict control of the passions and appetites. Indifference to the external world and to passion, Zeno taught, leads to an inner happiness and self-mastery.

stolid *STAH lid*

unemotional; impassive

In firm and clear English, the Pope spoke in generalities that nevertheless plainly applied to Mr. Marcos's decision to suspend civil rights and rule under martial law from 1972 until last month. "Even in exceptional situations that may at times arise, one can never justify any violation of the fundamental dignity of the human person or of the basic rights that safeguard this dignity," the Pope declared as Mr. Marcos sat stolidly on one of the thronelike gilt chairs on the stage.

stringent *STRIN jint*

tightly enforced; strict; inflexible; uncompromising; severe

China's population reached 1.248 billion at the end of 1998, according to the State Statistics Bureau, marking the first time the rate of population growth has been held below 1 percent. The figures reflect the impact of the country's stringent birth-control campaign, which includes a one-child-per-couple policy in urban areas.

Stygian   *STI jee uhn*

dark or gloomy: like the hellish region of the river Styx, in Greek mythology. The shades of the dead were rowed across the Styx to their eternal home in Hades, the underworld.

Just west of the Hilton Hotel's northern wall is Eddie Condon's, a reincarnation in name of the old Condon's of 35 years ago on West Street. This Condon's is a long, narrow and dark, but not Stygian room at No. 144, just a few doors east of the block's other jazz retreat, Jimmy Ryan's.

stymie   *STIGH mee*

to present difficulties that discourage or defeat any attempt to resolve a situation; to block; thwart; frustrate: Scottish, from a situation on a golf putting green when an opponent's ball lies directly between the player's ball and the hole, blocking it

He declined to be more specific, and mystery still shrouded the identity and motives of those behind the blast that killed five people, injured 1,000 others and rocked the city's largest building complex. But it appeared that the authorities were far from stymied. "We have plenty of leads—I'm feeling much better tonight," Mr. Fox said.

subservient   *suhb SER vee uhnt*

submissive; obedient; compliant

Instead of advising the women who are listening to them to "Stand By Your Man," as a more traditional country singer like Tammy Wynette would do, Miss Cash and Miss Carter encourage them to be true to themselves. They challenge the decorous and often subservient roles women have traditionally played in country music by singing songs that assert their independence and that are relatively explicit sexually, and by mixing their country music with jolting rock-and-roll.

substantive   *SUHB stin tiv*

having practical importance; having real substance and meaning

The leaders of the sharply divided Greek and Turkish sectors of Cyprus have agreed to begin "substantive" talks next month on reunification of the

Mediterranean island, the United Nations announced yesterday. The Greek and Turkish Cypriots, unable to live together since violence first erupted in the 1960's, have defied previous efforts to draw them into serious negotiations.

subterfuge   *SUHB ter fyoo:j*
a plan or action used to hide one's true objective or evade a difficult or unpleasant situation

When we were recognized, it became impossible to order the duck or pheasant pâtés. On three attempts we were told they were not fresh, yet both were on display and both were being served to other guests. Finally, through a bit of subterfuge, we did manage to try both. Though the duck proved acceptable, the pheasant was indeed stale.

succès de scandale   *suhk SE duh skan DAHL*
notoriety gained by something scandalous, as a shocking play, movie, novel, etc.: French, success of scandal

Over the years, many of Mr. Malle's films have proved controversial indeed. His second feature film, "The Lovers," which brought him early fame at the age of 26, created something of a succès de scandale when it won a special prize at the Venice Film Festival in 1958. Portraying a woman who leaves her husband for a young lover, it was condemned by censors for what were then regarded as dangerously explicit sex scenes.

succès d'estime   *suhk SE de STEEM*
an artistic work receiving acclaim from professional critics, often without being a financial success: French, success of esteem

Though the benefit was a succès d'estime, its financial intake was something less than the $20,000 hoped for.

succinct   *suhk SINGKT*
clearly and briefly stated; terse

At an awards luncheon at the Harvard Club, Mr. Steig was succinct. "I'm a writer, not a talker," he said. "Thank you."

succumb   *suh KUHM*
to yield or submit; die

Post-mortem studies of birds that lived on such rivers as the Thames, Trent and Avon showed that more than 50 percent of the birds had succumbed to lead poisoning after ingesting lead fishing weights. The rest had up to three times the normal amounts of lead in their blood.

Where desserts are concerned, almost everyone I know is guilty of succumbing to one alluring vice or another.

suffuse   *suh FYOO:Z*
to spread over or through, as with a color, light or liquid

Standing at the edge of the jagged cliffs that run along Highway 1, you can hear the violence down below, the powerful Pacific shattering itself on the rocky shoreline. But what you feel is gentleness, a light briny mist that suffuses the air.

Since the tall Gothic church was built over a century ago, it has been the center of the quiet village, and within its walls the lives of the people have been suffused with the rituals and teachings of the Roman Catholic faith.

sully   *SUH lee*
to soil or stain by disgracing or dishonoring

There are boxing people and fans who feel that passing scandals cannot seriously smirch a sport that has thrived in a state of sullied reputation for as long as punches have been thrown for pay in this country. A man enjoying a mudbath is intrepid when threatened with mudslinging.

summarily   *suh MAI ruh lee*
promptly and without formality

At least two dozen of Mr. Bani-Sadr's aides were detained. About 40 people who demonstrated in his support last weekend were arrested and summarily killed. A poster at the Justice Ministry offered "a place in heaven" to anyone with information leading to Mr. Bani-Sadr's arrest.

sunder   *SUN duhr*
to forcefully separate; break apart; split

Peace has never come easy to India. At independence in 1947, the blood of more than a million Muslims and Hindus was spilled as colonial India was sundered into India and Pakistan. India has since endured decades of caste wars and sectarian strife.

superannuated   *soo: per A nyoo: ay tid*
discharged from service, especially with a pension, because of old age or infirmity; antiquated

One striking thing to be noticed in this biography is the qualitative change over the years in Miss Callas's circle of associates. Increasingly, her days and nights were spent in the company of the world's silly people: the Elsa Maxwells, the superannuated princes, the dress designers, the perfume heiresses.

superficial   *soo: per FI shuhl*
on the surface; shallow

The whale had first tried to beach itself on Coney Island Wednesday night, but it was nudged back out to sea by a police launch. Early the next morning, it was discovered off Oak Beach. A gash on the side of the whale was found to be superficial, apparently caused when it scraped against the ocean bottom.

supernumerary   *soo: per NOO: muh rai ree*
a person considered extra; someone superfluous

Until Mr. Hoffa tapped him as his temporary stand-in when he left for prison, Mr. Fitzsimmons, a chubby, rather inarticulate man, was something of a figure of ridicule in the teamsters' hierarchy. He was known as Mr. Hoffa's "gopher," the supernumerary who would go for coffee or hold chairs.

supersede   *soo: per SEED*
to replace because a new thing is better, more modern or more effective than the old; supplant

In some Hispanic communities, the Quinceanera, a traditional coming-of-age party celebrated when a girl is 15, has been superseded by the Sweet 16 party. "Some Latina girls are choosing Sweet 16's," said Tracy Houseman, a math teacher at Mother Cabrini High School in Washington Heights, adding that many girls in her classes had had them. "In some cases, it may be an attempt to become more Americanized."

supple   *SUH puhl*
easily bent; flexible; pliant

A strong contender for the niftiest new hat in town is made in England of soft brown felt, has a pigskin band, is supple enough to stuff in an attaché case and is $39.50 at Paul Stuart, Madison Avenue at 45th Street.

surfeited   *SER fuh tid*
filled to excess or overflowing

The Pope had been shot—a consummate act of terror in a world surfeited with it.

surreal   *suh REEL*
dreamlike; fantastic; grotesque: from surrealism, a movement in art and literature that attempts to portray the workings of the unconscious or dreaming mind. Salvador Dali (1904-1989) is the best known painter of the Surrealist movement.

The river, normally about 50 feet wide at Laredo, sluggish and shallow enough to walk across, was a 100-yard-wide chocolate-colored surge early this evening, oozing across the low-lying parklands, inching up the bridge pillars and carrying past a surreal array of flotsam: telephone poles, huge tangles of mesquite trees, lampposts, sagebrush, dead animals and a garbage Dumpster.

    ✦ *Dumpster* is among the brand names and trademarks that have become so popular that people use it as a generic term, applying it to all similar products. Through advertisements in trade journals, manufacturers continuously implore the media to either capitalize the names of their products that have achieved this status, to indicate that they are specific brands, or use a generic name when the specific brand name is not intended. *The Times* capitalizes Dumpster to indicate that it is a trademark name. The difficulty with maintaining a separation between brand name and generic terms is that the brand name is often the quickest way to describe a product. Dumpster denotes an immediately recognizable object; its generic description would take several words.

    The words in the following list are brand or company names that have reached generic status. Those beginning in lower case have lost all identification as discrete brands and are treated as common nouns everywhere, including *The Times*. Those beginning with capital letters are listed in *The New York Times Manual of Style and Usage* as requiring them.

aspirin	Jell-O	shredded wheat
Band-Aids	kerosene	Styrofoam
Bubble Wrap	Kitty Litter	tarmac
canteen	Kleenex	Technicolor
cellophane	lanolin	thermos
corn flakes	linoleum	touch-tone
dixie cup	Mace	trampoline
dry ice	nylon	Velcro
escalator	Ouija board	windbreaker
Formica	Ping-Pong	yo-yo
Frisbee	Rollerblade	zipper
granola	Scotch tape	

surreptitious   *suh ruhp TI shuhs*
acting in a secret, stealthy way

The video pirates would take portable video cameras into movie theaters and surreptitiously tape the feature films being shown, Ms. Pirro said. She said they would then return to their base of operations and, using hundreds of conventional videocassette recorders, mass-produce copies of the movie.

surrogate   *SER uh git*
substitute

Lord Mountbatten, who was killed by Irish republican terrorists in 1979, was a cousin of the Queen and a kind of surrogate grandfather to Prince Charles.

suzerainty   *SOO: zuh rin tee*
control over something, in the manner of a suzerain, or feudal lord

Some date the current travails of the city's subway system to 1971, a period when Dr. William J. Ronan's suzerainty over the Metropolitan Transportation Authority was total. That year the voters rejected a $2.5 billion transportation bond issue, an act, according to these historians of our decrepit system, that hastened the decline and stall of the wholly Ronan empire.

swan song   SWAHN SAWNG
the last act or final creative work of a person: from the false belief that the swan sings beautifully just before it dies. Various species of swan do honk, croak or emit a whistle-like sound, while others never utter a note. But none sing.

It was Judge William Hughes Mulligan's final decision before leaving the United States Court of Appeals in Manhattan. The case involved smuggling rare swans from Canada, and so, in what he called his "swan song," Judge Mulligan filed a 12-page decision this week peppered with painful puns and other attempts at judicial humor. Calling the appeal a *rara avis*, Judge Mulligan said the two suspects had worked "hand and claw" in what he called a nefarious practice.

> ◆ A *rara avis* (Latin, rare bird) is an unusual or extraordinary person or thing; a phenomenon; a rarity. The Roman poet Juvenal first applied the term in the first century to the black swan of Australia.

sweatshop   SWET shahp
a shop or factory where employees work long hours at low wages under poor working conditions

While sweatshop conditions vary, there is a grim sameness to the basic appearance: rows of women bent over sewing machines, separated by narrow aisles often made impassable by dress racks and piles of piece goods.

sybaritic   si buh RI tik
fond of luxury and self-indulgence; hedonistic: the people of Sybaris, a Greek colony in southern Italy, were known for their love of luxury and pursuit of pleasure

A few years ago ready-to-wear boutiques were opening so fast that even the most inveterate shopper could not keep track of them. Now it is lingerie shops. Not corset shops. Not hosiery shops. Simply places where women can indulge their Sybaritic urges for lace teddies, silk nightgowns, satin negligees and marabou bed jackets.

symbiotic   sim bee AH tik
interdependent, as in an association of two forms of life to their mutual advantage—for example, some species of birds feed on the insects they find on the backs of rhinoceroses and other wild animals

Movies and electronic games have a symbiotic relationship. Theater owners make extra dollars by installing two or three games in the lobby.

synergism   *SI ner ji zuhm*
the simultaneous action of separate agencies that, together, have greater total effect than the sum of their individual effects

In an interview, Dr. Lewin said that the combination of alcohol, which is also a depressant, with other sedatives or hypnotic drugs often created a synergistic effect that could cause a collapse of the central nervous system, with resulting coma and respiratory or cardiac failure.

synonymous   *suh NAH nuh mis*
equivalent; alike; the same

Founded during the California Gold Rush of the 1850's, Levi Strauss, based in San Francisco, eventually grew to be the largest maker of blue jeans in the world. And as jeans evolved from miners' gear into the outfit of movie star rebels and then suburban youth, Levi's became synonymous with American style. Now that style, which had once been manufactured entirely in the United States, will be stitched together largely overseas.

tableau

Dolls have been making a whimsical journey in a fantasy world at the Museum of the City of New York, Fifth Avenue at 103d Street. They don't actually move, but in a series of tableaux they are to be seen waking up, packing their trunks, traveling through forests, a jungle and a desert to an ocean, and finally arriving at their destination: the museum itself.

see page 345

343

tableau   *ta BLOH*

a representation of a scene, picture, etc. by a person or group in costume,
posing silently without moving: French, short for tableau vivant, *living picture.*
Tableaux *is the plural.*

> Dolls have been making a whimsical journey in a fantasy world at the
> Museum of the City of New York, Fifth Avenue at 103d Street. They don't
> actually move, but in a series of tableaux they are to be seen waking up,
> packing their trunks, traveling through forests, a jungle and a desert to an
> ocean, and finally arriving at their destination: the museum itself.

tabula rasa   *TA byoo luh RAH suh*

the mind before impressions are recorded upon it by experience: Latin,
scraped tablet

> A tabula rasa is what I'm after, and if that sounds as though I were simply
> trying to dodge an honest day's labor before betaking myself to the play-
> house, so be it. Call me truant, say I'm goldbricking. My vote still goes to the
> man who doesn't prepare himself for the theatrical experience he's about to
> have. He's the man most likely to have it.

tacit   *TA sit*

not expressed or declared openly, but implied or understood

> Few gestures are taken as personally as the acceptance or rejection of food,
> most especially if it has been prepared by the giver. By overtly or tacitly reg-
> istering dislike for food served in a home, one invariably, if unintentionally,
> expresses at least a certain amount of disapproval of the cook and often of
> an entire family and its way of life.

taciturn   *TA suh tern*
almost always silent; not liking to talk; uncommunicative

Until now, Mr. Mubarak has been the butt of popular jokes in Egypt, pictured as a smiling and silent nonentity at the right hand of the President. But his taciturnity has been viewed by some as a survival tactic in a country where overly popular military figures are often quickly shuffled off to posts away from the centers of power.

tangible   *TAN juh buhl*
able to be touched; having form and substance; real or actual, rather than imaginary

VERKHOYANSK, U.S.S.R., Dec. 30—Whatever the temperature, Siberians are loath to admit it's cold. But here they have no choice—there simply aren't many colder places on earth. Dawn is still far off at 9 A.M.; it's 60 degrees below zero. The cold hits the nostrils first, an anesthetizing stab that stiffens the lining of the nose. The eyes begin to sting, and soon the cheeks start to tingle and turn pallid. Rub them quickly, say the anxious hosts, but then the diverted breath coats eyeglasses with an unyielding crust of frost. At this temperature the cold is tangible. Spoken words hover in a shimmering cloud of frozen vapor before sinking slowly to earth. Jeeps, with their engines permanently running, stand enveloped in clouds of dense exhaust vapor. Passing cars squeak loudly against the dry, sandy snow. Freezing sap snaps trees with reports like rifle shots.

tantalize   *TAN tuh lighz*
to tease by keeping out of reach

But the most tantalizing issue remaining from the settlement of the 50-day strike was exactly what manner of season will be resumed one week from Monday. Will the schedule simply be picked up after a loss of 713 games? Or will the remaining eight weeks constitute a miniseason, with second-half pennant races of its own?

✦ *Tantalize* derives from Tantalus, a son of Zeus, whose punishment after death was eternal hunger and thirst. In Hades, he was placed in a pool of water that would recede whenever he lowered his head to drink. Above Tantalus's head hung luscious fruits, which a breeze would sweep beyond his grasp whenever he reached for one. The crime for which he suffered so is variously given as his attempt to serve to the gods a banquet of his own son's flesh, his theft of nectar and ambrosia from the table of the gods, and his divulging of secrets entrusted to him by Zeus.

tantamount   *TAN tuh mownt*
equivalent

Mr. Lippman said his articles had not identified many of the people he quoted or associated with because "it would be tantamount to having them arrested."

tautology   *taw TAH luh jee*
needless repetition of an idea in a different word, phrase or sentence;
redundancy: for example, necessary essentials

"A Stranger Is Watching" is about a crazy murderer (if you excuse the tautology) who keeps a television newscaster imprisoned in the catacombs under Grand Central.

✦ Past history openly reveals the true fact that redundant tautologies recur again and again when individual persons join together similar synonyms. Here, then, is a varied mixture of word pairs, each of which the reader is invited to reduce down to one single word: free gift, present incumbent, invited guests, final conclusion, complete monopoly, temporary recess, personal friend, past experience, original source, attach together, hoist up, necessary requisite, return back and swallow down.

tchotchke   *CHACH kuh*
an inexpensive souvenir; bric-a-brac; knickknack: Yiddish

Dickens, the Rockettes, Tony Kushner—anything on a large New York stage, it seems, is fair game for the tchotchke industry. "A Christmas Carol," the new musical at the Paramount in Madison Square Garden, is selling an array of Victorian-inspired knickknacks, like Christmas ornaments and cloisonne pins, at a shop in the theater, as well as at a booth at F. A. O. Schwarz. Radio City Music Hall has just opened a freestanding shop, the Radio City Avenue Store, that markets everything from Radio City T-shirts to coffee cups adorned with the likenesses of the theater's renowned kick line.

teetotaler   *TEE toh tuh ler*
a person who abstains completely from alcoholic drinks

Susan B. Anthony was a teetotaler spinster, raised in a strict Quaker home in which toys were not allowed. In photograph after photograph she displays the stern features and cranky expression of a woman who never had fun.

◆ *Teetotaler* was first used during the temperance movement of the 1830s in England and America. Repeating the initial "t" in "total" emphasized a nondrinker's abstinence not just from whiskey but from beer and wine as well. In *The American Language*, H.L. Mencken calls teetotaler a characteristically American "stretch form," like "yes-indeedy" and "no-siree."

telescope   *TE luh skohp*
to slide one into another, like the concentric tubes of a small, collapsible telescope; condense

For his birthday, they bought him one of those small, expensive telescoping umbrellas to tuck into his briefcase.

temerity   *tuh ME ruh tee*
reckless boldness or rashness that often results from underrating the possible consequences of an act

'SHAKESPEARE IN LOVE' — Mischievously literate Elizabethans, hilarious backstage farce and the sultry teamwork of Joseph Fiennes and Gwyneth Paltrow (as passionate prototypes for Romeo and Juliet) made this the most enchanting entertainment of the year. With a sparkling screenplay by Tom Stoppard and Marc Norman, John Madden's film had the temerity to speculate about Shakespeare's life on the basis of his work. Rarely has such presumptuousness paid off so shamelessly well. Amid a splendid supporting cast, the stars shone even more brightly than Sandy Powell's spectacular costumes.

temper   *TEM per*
to bring to the proper texture, consistency, hardness, etc., by mixing with something or treating in some way

Writings found in Asia Minor said that to temper a Damascus sword the blade must be heated until it glows "like the sun rising in the desert." It then should be cooled to the color of royal purple and plunged "into the body of a muscular slave" so that his strength would be transferred to the sword.

temporal   *TEM puh ruhl*
of this world; worldly, not spiritual

I interviewed Neil Armstrong some 10 years after his Moon walk. He said he was disappointed that mankind seemed no more united after the Moon landing than before. "I had hoped the Moon shot would take our minds away from the more mundane and temporal problems that have faced us," he told me. "But we still appear to be tied up with today's problems."

tenacity   *ti NA suh tee*
firmness in holding fast; persistence

A blue crab's tenacity is often the cause of its demise. A fish head or carcass or a chicken neck attached to a string and tossed into the water sooner or later will be seized by a crab. If one retrieves the line slowly, the crab will often hang on until a net is slipped under it.

tendentious   *ten DEN shuhs*
showing or having a definite tendency, bias or purpose

Lucy S. Dawidowicz's "The War Against the Jews, 1933-1945" was indispensable reading. Her "Holocaust Reader" was a scar that glowed in the dark. "The Holocaust and the Historians" is a peculiar and—to use one of her favorite words—tendentious essay, creating more confusion than it dispels. She believes that the Holocaust, in which two-thirds of Europe's Jews were murdered, has for the most part been neglected or ignored by contemporary historians.

tenet   *TE nit*
a principle or belief held as a truth

It may seem curious that an American black woman with a degree in social work from Columbia has embraced Rastafarianism, the religion that is adhered to by most reggae musicians. Among other things, Rastafarianism teaches that women should serve their men and look after their homes; its tenets are not very compatible with feminism.

tensile   *TEN suhl*
capable of being stretched

Mr. Breuer's Cesca and Wassily chairs truly changed the way our century looked at furniture. Before Mr. Breuer began bending tubular steel and adding some leather slings to it to make seats, we thought of furniture as massive, voluminous, heavy; the Wassily chair made it suddenly clear that furniture could be something tensile and light and alive.

tenure   *TE nyer*
status granted to an employee, usually after a probationary period, assuring permanence of employment

"We have no security; tenure is unknown," said Dorothy Ozog, a fourth-grade teacher in a Catholic school in Detroit.

tepid   *TE pid*
lukewarm

I can race through two or three smutty novels and a half-dozen gossip magazines and hear the Top Forty playing on the stereo in the background while the television viewer is wasting three hours and getting nothing but the tepid, watered-down stuff afforded by three or four sitcoms and an evening soap opera.

terse   *ters*
to the point; concise; succinct; free of superfluous words

Down and almost out of her 1999 French Open final, Steffi Graf narrowed her eyes, squared her shoulders, stalked to her changeover chair at the tennis tournament and gave herself a terse pep talk. "This is the last time you'll sit in this chair, so you better make her earn it," the German star told herself that Saturday in early June. Within minutes, she reignited her heavy, powerful strokes and reduced Martina Hingis, her top-ranked opponent, who had once said Graf was past her prime, to a sobbing runner-up.

testy   *TES tee*
irritable; peevish

The current issue of Harper's contains a testy article on our current literary biggies, people like Joyce Carol Oates, William Styron, Norman Mailer, John

Updike and so on and on, the burden of which is that they are only 13th-raters whose skill at promotional flimflam has persuaded the world and themselves that they are a new race of Tolstoys.

> ✦ A *flimflam* is any trick or deception of a con artist, ranging from a single shortchanging, to the switching of a fake gem for a real one when the store owner's back is turned, to schemes in which victims invest money in a nonexistent company. The term has been used in the United States since the 1870s and in England since the mid-seventeenth century.

theocracy   *thee AH kruh see*
the rule of a state by God, whose laws are interpreted by ecclesiastical
authorities; government by priests claiming to rule with divine authority

Fundamentalist religion is gaining strength in the United States. But I do not believe it follows that religious Americans want a theocracy as their form of government. Many, even of the strongest personal beliefs, would hold to the country's tradition of diversity in faith and separation of religion from government.

theorem   *THEE ruhm*
a general statement or rule, not self-evident, that cannot be proved to be true

Halston continued to build the Halston mystique, which boils down to an uncomplicated theorem: clothes should be simple by day, extravagant by night.

threshold   *THRESH hohld*
the point at which a stimulus is just strong enough to be perceived or produce
a response

Age and sex affect the perception of pain: As you get older your sensitivity to pain is likely to decline; women tend to have a lower pain threshold than men.

thwart   *thwart*
to prevent from accomplishing a purpose; frustrate; defeat

Kudzu, a Chinese vine that has grown rampant in the South since its introduction in the 1920's to thwart soil erosion, has swallowed houses and acres of roadside in Florida, as it grows a foot a day.

time warp   *TIGHM wawrp*
the condition or process of being displaced from one point in time to another, as in science fiction

"You have to remember that Philadelphia politics are caught in a time warp," said a Philadelphian familiar with the city's politics. "In voting on Congressional races people here don't vote for national issues, they vote for constituent services. They vote on who can get their potholes fixed."

titillate   *TI tuh layt*
to excite or stimulate pleasurably

One of the demands we properly make on our political leaders is that they amuse and entertain us. Without such titillation, our spirits would be overcome by subway fires, gridlocks and blackouts, and we would fall into profound melancholy.

titular   *TI chuh ler*
existing only in title; in name only; nominal

After the embassy luncheon, Prince Charles, who will someday be titular head of the Church of England, participated in services at the National Cathedral, where the primates of the Anglican Communion are meeting.

topiary   *TOH pee ai ree*
the art of trimming and training shrubs or trees into ornamental shapes

The topiary gardens, with 80 figures of lions, camels, giraffes and other forms carved out of California privet and golden boxwood, was begun more than 60 years ago and is operated today by the nonprofit Preservation Society of Newport County.

torpor   *TAWR per*
a state of being dormant or inactive; sluggishness; apathy

Some relief from the torpor inflicted by desert air, which makes you taste sand when you lick your lips, came Wednesday night when a young Egyptian soccer team won the Africa Cup by beating Cameroon, 2-0.

torrid   *TAW rid*
passionate; ardent

It seems only yesterday that Mayor Fiorello H. La Guardia, cleaning up Times Square, ran burlesque out of 42d Street, clear to Union City, N.J. Actually that happened more than 40 years ago. It is something of a commentary too that Ann Corio, once a supreme practitioner of the torrid striptease art, has brought her stage memoir, "This Was Burlesque," back to Times Square, to the Princess Theatre, and it has an almost uplifting effect on the neighborhood.

tour de force   *toor duh FAWRS*
an unusually skillful or ingenious creation, production or performance: French, feat of strength

In something of a tour de force for an actress making her starring-role debut, Miss D'Obici plays Fosca with shrewd, merciless consistency, without an ounce of pity, which is as it should be and is the major strength of the film.

tract   *trakt*
a propagandizing pamphlet, especially one on a religious or political subject

Several of the songs on "Wild Gift" (Slash records), X's new album, champion monogamy. "White Girl" is a kind of tract on the pitfalls of sexual temptation, and "Adult Books" is a caustic indictment of pornography, swinging singles and other examples of contemporary sexual mores.

trajectory   *truh JEK tuh ree*
the curved path of something hurtling through space, such as a bullet, a rocket or a plane: used here in its figurative sense of a path or line of development

Few African countries have followed a more disappointing trajectory over the past two decades than Zimbabwe. Once a model of democracy, law and tolerance, this nation of 13 million people is becoming a fearful, militarized autocracy. President Robert Mugabe's latest diatribes against journalists and judges are particularly troubling. Zimbabwe's foreign friends, including the United States, must press Mr. Mugabe to halt this sad slide into tyranny.

transcendent   *tran SEN duhnt*
going beyond ordinary limits; exceeding; supreme

As it happened, about a dozen of the club's elderly members had gathered around the television to watch the last match of the cricket series between England and Australia, an event of transcendent interest, to be compared with the Super Bowl or the last game of the World Series.

transgression   *tranz GRE shuhn*
a breaking or overstepping of a law or rule; sin

FORT LAUDERDALE, Fla., March 1—When Reggie Jackson arrives in the Yankee camp, he will learn that inflation has hit the cost of reporting late to spring training. Jackson reported late a year ago, and the transgression cost him $500 a day. He is late again, but this year, George Steinbrenner announced, he will be fined $2,500 a day.

transient   *TRAN zee uhnt*
staying for only a short time; temporary; passing through

Pain can be sharp, throbbing or dull, mild or severe, transient or prolonged, continuous or intermittent.

transmogrify   *tranz MAH gruh figh*
to transform, especially in a strange or grotesque manner

Turning a good book into a bad movie is child's play. Any fool can do it; many have. But it has lately become commonplace to find awful novels transmogrified into movies that are even worse, and surely this is a phenomenon worth looking into.

trappings   *TRA pingz*
the outward signs of something; adornments; accessories

For all of the religious trappings, the cult primarily offered a curious mixture of socialism and blasphemy. By the time of the move to South America in the summer of 1977, critics and investigators were beginning to close in on Mr. Jones.

travail   *truh VAYL*
hardships; suffering; anguish

Legions of soap opera fans tuned in to the travails of Stella Dallas, the beautiful daughter of an impoverished farmhand who had married above her station in life.

> ✦ *Travail* comes from the Latin *tripalium*, an instrument of torture composed of three stakes: *tri*, three + *palus*, stake. In addition to its meaning hardship, suffering and anguish, as in the passage above, *travail* also means labor or childbirth pains, toil or intense pain.

traverse   *truh VERS*
to travel across, over or through

The four carriage processions that will carry the royal family on the wedding day will traverse a route laden with history.

travesty   *TRA vi stee*
a crude, distorted or ridiculous representation of something

Of all the dishes we tried none was so dreadful as choucroute garni. The sauerkraut itself was acceptable if a little greasy, but the real travesties were the meats: a skinless, supermarket variety frankfurter; a dark, dried-out, paper-thin slice of ham, and a piece of meat that was probably some form of pork, but was almost too hard to pierce with fork or knife.

tremolo   *TRE muh loh*
in music, a tremulous or quivering effect produced by the rapid reiteration of the same tone

The eerie call of the loon is one of earth's most unearthly cries. Its wailing and tremolo calls are regarded by many as the most thrilling and distinctive symbol of the northern wilderness.

trenchant   *TREN chuhnt*
keen; penetrating; incisive

Mort Sahl is back, at least for two weeks, at Marty's and at the age of 54 his humor is as it ever was—highly political, trenchantly topical, occasionally venemous, equally savage toward Republicans, Democrats, liberals, conservatives and all ideological stops between.

trepidation   *tre puh DAY shuhn*
fearful uncertainty; anxiety

Although for years I watched my mother, a terrific cook, entertain with apparent ease, I approached my own first dinner party with trepidation.

tropism   *TROH pi zuhm*
a movement or action in response to a stimulus

BONN—This is the time of year when Germans, as if seized by a communal tropism, are drawn into the woods to gather wild mushrooms. Again and again, they are told to be careful. Again and again, it seems, an extraordinary number of people do not listen. Since the mushroom hunting season started in the middle of August, nine persons have died from eating a poisonous variety called the death cup.

truism   *TROO: i zuhm*
a statement the truth of which is obvious and well known; commonplace

It is a truism that all stars were once sidemen and all sidemen want to be stars. An equally accurate but less widely recognized truism is that stars are musicians who have made clever career moves or been lucky, and that sidemen are often equally talented musicians who haven't had the breaks.

trundle   *TRUHN duhl*
to push or propel on wheels; roll; wheel

Every Tuesday and Friday, Giovanna Conti trundles her old-fashioned shopping cart, a bulging basketwork container on two wheels, to the outdoor market on the Via Trionfale near her home and fills it with potatoes, fresh vegetables and fruit.

tryst   *trist*
a secret meeting between lovers

A tryst with Lira sends Bobby escaping the jealous husband by dashing home in nothing but Lira's angora sweater, fluffy slippers and tight jeans.

turpitude   *TER puh too:d*
baseness; vileness; depravity: the word is usually preceded by "moral"

Under immigration law, convicted felons or those convicted of a crime of moral turpitude, such as prostitutes, embezzlers and petty thieves, cannot be admitted to the United States and must be returned "to the country whence they came."

tutelage   *TOO: tuh lij*
instruction; teaching

School begins promptly at 7 A.M. as dozens of budding Escoffiers don their tall white hats and spotless aprons, ready to peel, wash, chop and simmer under the tutelage of master chefs.

tweak *tweek*
to make a minor adjustment; to improve; refine; fine-tune

The Campbell Soup Company has found a way virtually to guarantee a run on its slow-selling classic soups—at least temporarily. The company is retiring the classic red-and-white Campbell's Soup label raised to iconic status by the pop artist Andy Warhol's famous silkscreen renderings. Although subtle, the label tweaking is sure to create a frenzy at stores, as consumers rush to hoard the classic soup—or the cans, anyway. The new label, which is also red and white but includes modern graphic elements, is the most significant change ever made to the classic soup can, which has lined grocery shelves for more than a century.

✦ *Tweak* has a long history, going back to at least 1601, when it meant to seize and give a sudden twisting pinch to someone's ear, nose or cheek. In his "O, what a rogue and peasant slave am I!" soliloquy (Act II, Scene 2), Hamlet says:

> *Am I a coward*
> *Who calls me villain? breaks my pate across?*
> *Plucks off my beard, and blows it in my face?*
> *Tweaks me by the nose? gives me the lie i' the throat,*
> *As deep as to the lungs? who does me this?*

The figurative use of tweak—to tease, to needle or to intentionally get someone's goat with a remark, often in a mischievous way—arose in the eighteenth century and remains popular. A 1997 *New York Times* article described how a Russian television program starring life-size puppets modeled on political figures "mercilessly tweaks the authorities on such issues as privatization and the fall of the ruble." Tweak did not arise as a term for a minor adjustment—a slight twist—until the late 1980s, when it became jargon for making a minor improvement to a computer system.

Type A
a behavior pattern associated with a tendency to develop coronary heart disease, and characterized by total involvement in one's job, a constant striving for achievement, inability to relax, impatience and tenseness: coined in 1972 by Meyer Friedman and Roy H. Rosenman, American cardiologists

The Type A behavior pattern, an aggressive, struggling, rushed action-emotion complex that is associated with heart disease, may also be associated with superior scientific work, according to Karen A. Matthews, assistant professor of psychiatry at the University of Pittsburgh.

ubiquitous

Many a hostess would love to have one or two, and the

White House has 36: white-gloved military social aides who

help smooth the way at the White

House social occasions. Quietly

ubiquitous, they direct the flow of traffic,

help greet guests at state dinners and

luncheons, move people along receiving lines

at receptions, make small talk at teas and dance with any

guest who appears to be stranded.

see pages 361

ubiquitous *yoo: BI kwuh tuhs*
present, or seeming to be present, everywhere at the same time; omnipresent

Many a hostess would love to have one or two, and the White House has 36: white-gloved military social aides who help smooth the way at White House social occasions. Quietly ubiquitous, they direct the flow of traffic, help greet guests at state dinners and luncheons, move people along receiving lines at receptions, make small talk at teas and dance with any guest who appears to be stranded.

ukase *YOO: kays*
an authoritative order or decree; an edict: Russian, ukaz, edict—originally, in Czarist Russia, an imperial order or decree having the force of law

Conversations at a [men's] club may wander from the disturbing situation in Poland to the Jets' need to get back into the National Football League race, but in most two subjects are barred: women and professional matters. The late Peter Fleming, an amateur of social history, held that this rule was an extension of the Duke of Wellington's ukase against discussion of these subjects in an officers' mess on the grounds that they were the most likely to lead to violent argument and ultimately a duel.

umbrage *UM brij*
offense or resentment taken at a real or perceived insult or slight. One either takes umbrage or gives it, but the latter usage is very rare.

During her husband's 1996 Presidential campaign, Elizabeth Dole showed up, right on time, to tape a commercial for him. She read the spot once off the prompter, thanked everybody and got up to leave. Professional actors can go through a dozen takes just warming up, but when Mrs. Dole was asked to try once more, she seemed not to understand the request, then took umbrage at the implication that her presentation had been other than perfect the first time.

unabashedly   *uhn uh BA shid lee*
unashamedly

Mr. Sinatra is not an opera singer. He uses a microphone and his stylistic idiom is unabashedly popular. But for a man of 65 years his technique is remarkable; in fact, every time this writer has heard him in recent years, his voice has seemed more secure and wider in range both for dynamics and pitch.

unassuming   *uhn uh SOO: ming*
modest; unpretentious

> Though Mr. Rush's folk baritone isn't powerful, he has an unassumingly authoritative manner that works nicely in a small club like the Lone Star.

unbridled   *uhn BRIGH duhld*
unrestrained; uncontrolled

To be sure, the Italian campaign in Libya remains as an example of unbridled imperialism beside which the operations of the British in India and the French in Morocco seem like nursery tales.

underling   *UHN der ling*
a person in a subordinate position; inferior: usually contemptuous or disparaging

Federal workers who thought they had seen everything in the bureaucracy are now being shown Government films that dramatize how right-thinking civil servants are expected to behave. One film urges underlings to track their supervisors' comings and goings and to speak out—"blow the whistle" is too hard-core a term for this Federal cinéma vérité—when the boss takes three hours for lunch.

Why, man, he doth bestride the narrow world
Like a Colossus; and we petty men
Walk under his huge legs, and peep about
To find ourselves dishonorable graves.
Men at some time are masters of their fates:
The fault, dear Brutus, is not in our stars,
But in ourselves, that we are underlings.
                    – Shakespeare, *Julius Caesar*

unflappable   *uhn FLA puh buhl*
not easily excited or disconcerted; imperturbable; calm

Lemon, who failed as an infielder and an outfielder with Cleveland before becoming a pitcher in 1946, is a secure, unflappable man who seems not to have an enemy in baseball. "I've had a hell of a life," he said during his first term as Yankee manager. "I've never looked back and regretted anything. I've had everything in baseball a man could ask for. I've been so fortunate. Outside of my boy getting killed. That really puts it in perspective. So you don't win the pennant. You don't win the World Series. Who gives a damn? Twenty years from now, who'll give a damn? You do the best you can. That's it."

ungrudging   *uhn GRUH jing*
without resentment

Still, the Norway maple does have redeeming values. An alien, it has made itself very much at home over here and is often mistaken for its American cousin, the sugar maple. If it is not sweet, however, it is sturdy, growing ungrudgingly in poor soil and shrugging off the city's grime.

unmitigated   *uhn MI tuh gay tid*
out-and-out; absolute

Helen Lawrenson, in the March issue of The Dial, the public television magazine, writes of Miss Hepburn: "A personality? Yes. An actress? No. On the set she was an unmitigated pain in the neck."

unobtrusive   *uhn uhb TROO: siv*
not calling attention to oneself; inconspicuous

During the general audiences that Pope John Paul holds in St. Peter's Square during the warm months, plainclothes agents of the Italian carabinieri and state police unobtrusively mingle with the multilingual crowds to keep an eye out for pickpockets and possible troublemakers.

unpalatable   *un PA luh tuh buhl*
having an unpleasant taste; inedible

Some of what Mr. Pyle has to say will be familiar to even the most casual butterfly aficionado: that the species' host plant is the milkweed and that the bitterness of milkweed milk makes monarch larvae and adults unpalatable to most birds. He also tells us, however, that a few species of birds have learned how to consume monarchs by picking out the tasty, nutritious bits and leaving the rest behind.

unprepossessing   *uhn pree puh ZE sing*
unimpressive; nondescript

Consider the ratfish. Plagued by unprepossessing looks and a name that invites universal ridicule, his is a woeful life. The ratfish's misery is assuaged only by the company of other equally disadvantaged deep-sea acquaintances, such as the grunt, the gag, the hogsucker and the lizardfish.

unremitting   *uhn ri MI ting*
ceaseless; without letup; never relaxing

Isaiah Thomas (1749-1831) was the leading publisher of his day and an unremitting foe of British rule.

unseemly   *uhn SEEM lee*
not decent or proper; unbecoming

GREENWICH, Conn., March 3—Practically every town in America pines for Federal money to enhance its appearance, and local politicians campaign on their success in corralling grants. But the political leaders here have decided to thumb their noses at $500,000 in Federal money that would have brightened this town's main shopping street. The money was there for the asking. But most of the town's leaders said they decided it would be unseemly for a town as wealthy as Greenwich to accept scarce Federal dollars for luxuries like wrought-iron benches, quaint street lamps and potted plants when there are far poorer towns in need of basic commodities like decent shelter.

upbraid   *uhp BRAYD*
to rebuke severely; censure sharply

The editors and their friends overflowed the 600-seat main hall, however, for a session entitled "Sex, Sexism and the Sexes," at which they were upbraided for the fact that their organization has only 34 female members.

upscale   *UHP skayl*
in the upper levels of a particular category, especially one relating to the standard of living: coined in the late 1960s to refer to people in the upper levels of income, education and social standing

"Unlike Kentucky Fried Chicken, the distinct leader, Sisters is an upscale fast-food experience. It's going after the dining-room market as well as the carry-out business."

ursine   *ER sighn*
bearlike

To begin with, Gianfranco Ferre was in town, which caused enough hub and bub to get everyone going. Mr. Ferre, who is 36 years old, Milanese and appealingly ursine, has been producing clothing under his own name for only three years, and is currently one of the few fashion talents intent on exploring new ideas in clothing design.

utilitarian   *yoo: ti luh TAI ree uhn*
made for usefulness rather than beauty or other considerations

Not many New Yorkers looking for artistic inspiration turn to manhole covers. But those who do so tend to be as passionate as, say, lovers of British shock art. Where other people see only a utilitarian metal disc and think only of pipes or cables, the cognoscenti see beauty, history, symbolism and wide-open design possibilities. "It's a little niche," said Michele Brody, who is trying to raise money to manufacture a series of covers she has designed.

✦ Utilitarianism encompasses two related doctrines: one, that actions are right in proportion to their usefulness or their tendency to promote happiness; and two, that the purpose of all action should be to bring about the greatest happiness of the greatest number. The English philosopher Jeremy Bentham (1748-1832) coined the term and promoted this philosophy along with James Mill and his son John Stuart Mill. Bentham himself remains useful to this day: his skeleton, dressed in his clothes and with a model head, stands at University College, London. It was his wish.

vaunted

By the time of the first spacecraft encounter with Mars,

however, no one seriously believed any more in the vaunted

Martians who were said to have built

a global system of canals. These

turned out to be figments of the

imagination of astronomers of the late 1800's.

see page 370

vacuum   *VA kyoo uhm*
a state of being sealed off from external influences; isolation

No amount of planning and preparation by the Secret Service, no bulletproof car, no armed bodyguards can guarantee the safety of a public figure if an assassin is willing to risk capture or death. Especially in America, the occupant of political office cannot survive in a vacuum. He has to mingle with the electorate and take his chances.

a space left empty by the removal or absence of something usually found in it; void; emptiness

One of the most basic human instincts is the need to decorate. Nothing is exempt—the body, the objects one uses, from intimate to monumental, and all personal and ceremonial space. It is an instinct that responds to the eye, for pure pleasure; to the rules of society, for signals of fitness and status, and to some deep inner urge that has been variously described as the horror of a vacuum and the need to put one's imprint on at least one small segment of the world.

> ✦ *Vacuum* is among the hundreds of Latin words adopted into English unchanged. Some others are: *acumen, affidavit, alibi, aorta, bonus, cornea, elixir, emporium, explicit, gratis, genius, inertia, innuendo, item, memento, minutia, panacea, recipe, requiem, tarantula, status, stimulus, verbatim, veto* and *vim.*

vagary   *vuh GAI ree*
an unpredictable occurrence, course or instance

Sitting back after lunch, Mr. Sommers commented on the vagaries of the 5,000 foot altitude, which require a sensitive—and patient—cook: More flour may be needed than a recipe calls for; steaks take 20 minutes to broil —rare—and eggs require six minutes to soft boil.

variegated   *VAI ree uh gay tid*
having variety in character or form; varied; diversified

As it did a few years ago when it focused on "classics in action," Lord & Taylor has gathered together the variegated strands of current fashion, added some notes of its own and dubbed the package "the new heroines."

vaunted   *VAWN tid*
boasted or bragged about

By the time of the first spacecraft encounter with Mars, however, no one seriously believed any more in the vaunted Martians who were said to have built a global system of canals. These turned out to be figments of the imagination of astronomers of the late 1800's.

vector   *VEK ter*
an animal, as an insect or mite, that transmits a disease-producing organism from one host to another

Dog ticks can be vectors of Rocky Mountain spotted fever, a usually mild but sometimes serious infection that is now prevalent throughout the country, particularly in suburban and rural areas.

veer   *veer*
to swerve; shift; alter a course

By now, he is as familiar a figure on the city landscape as the souvlaki vendor. He—and the sense here is that men are more the issue than women— is the fellow you see behind the wheel of a Lexus or some other car of suitable status, trying to negotiate New York traffic while talking on a cellular phone. You know him well. He veers erratically from lane to lane and brushes back pedestrians as he turns into a crosswalk, jabbering nonstop, one hand on the wheel and half a brain on what he is doing. The sinking feeling in your stomach tells you it is only a matter of time before the self-absorbed clod does serious harm.

✦ Souvlaki (soo VLAH kee) is a Greek dish consisting of lamb chunks marinated in olive oil, lemon juice, oregano and other seasonings, then skewered (sometimes with vegetables such as green peppers and onions) and grilled. Shish kebab is its Turkish, Afghan and Arab equivalent.

vehement   *VEE uh muhnt*
characterized by forcefulness of expression or intensity of emotion, passion or conviction; emphatic; fervent

Someone had written to Shaw asking for his autograph to which, Mr. Lowe said, Shaw replied with vehemence that he did not give autographs, doesn't believe in autograph hunters nor autograph collecting, a pastime he described as "despicable." He concluded with both a flat refusal to give his autograph and a threat—if he ever bothered Shaw again, the playwright wrote, he would regret it. "Very sincerely yours. G. Bernard Shaw."

vehicle   *VEE uh kuhl*
a play, role or piece of music used to display the special talents of one performer or company

It may have taken a long time for her to get to Broadway, but she has arrived in high style. In Lillian Hellman's "The Little Foxes," Elizabeth Taylor has found just the right vehicle to launch her career as a stage actress.

velleity   *vuh LEE uh tee*
a wish, ambition, desire or promise accompanied by so little will that it is assured of never being acted upon

Croatia briefly mouthed velleities about inviting the Serbs to return.

veneer   *vuh NEER*
an attractive but superficial appearance, hiding the true nature of what lies beneath it

The veneer we call social order is a very thin membrane indeed—it is the mutual contract we make with our neighbors to respect each other's place and space.

venerable   *VE nuh ruh buhl*
worthy of honor or respect because of age combined with character, achievement or position

Christiane Amanpour made her "60 Minutes" debut last night with a solid 13-minute report from the Afghan capital of Kabul on the fundamentalist Islamic Taliban whose forces now control three-quarters of the country. Ms. Amanpour brings to the venerable news magazine program the reputation and authority she earned during years of covering the world's misery spots for CNN.

venture capital   *VEN cher KA puh tuhl*
funds invested or available for investment at considerable risk of loss in potentially highly profitable enterprises

Coca-Cola will establish a $1.8 million venture capital fund to help develop black-owned companies and investment groups set up to buy into existing bottling franchises or to purchase wholesale distributorships. The funds will be lent with interest; thus Coca-Cola will make money on this aspect.

verisimilitude   *ve ruh si MI luh too:d*
the appearance of being true or real

WILLIAMSBURG, Va., May 2—Prince Charles and a royal entourage of embassy officials, personal aides and security personnel swept into town for about three hours today to pick up an honorary fellowship at William and Mary College and tour the reconstructed Colonial buildings. During an address at the college, Prince Charles joked about being a "genuine Redcoat" who had come to Williamsburg "to add a little verisimilitude to your proceedings."

✦ *Verisimilitude* is usually used to describe the quality in a work of fiction that makes its events, characters and setting seem possible or believable to the reader. Daniel Defoe's *Journal of the Plague Year* (1722) is a prime example. Written in the form of a narrative of a Londoner during the Great Plague of 1664-65, the supposed eye-witness story is so vivid, forceful and accurate that some modern librarians and bookstore owners, either reading or scanning the book, have placed it in their nonfiction sections.

vermiform   *VER muh fawrm*
wormlike

Few magazine articles have transfixed so many readers as Jacobo Timerman's prison memoir in The New Yorker of April 20. Understandably. There is no more devastating account of Argentine repression, and no more vivid depiction of the vermiform creatures who inhabit that country's murderous security forces.

vernacular   *ver NA kyuh ler*
the style of architecture and decoration peculiar to a specific culture

Fans of 20th-century Americana should not miss John Margolies's color photographs of vernacular architecture, such until recently unappreciated structures as diners and filling stations, which can be seen at the Hudson River Museum (511 Warburton Road, Yonkers) through Sept. 13.

vestige   *VE stij*
a trace, mark or visible evidence of something that is no longer present or in existence

One fine day this summer, wreckers toppled six towering smokestacks along the Monongahela River. Once part of a huge coke works but long idle, they were the last vestiges of Big Steel left within the Pittsburgh city limits. The mills that once employed tens of thousands of workers and made a third of the world's steel have vanished like ghosts at dawn. Iron City, a k a Steeltown U.S.A., is no more.

vet
to examine, investigate, evaluate or verify in a thorough or expert way: at first the short way to say veterinarian, it became also a verb for a vet's general checkup, which was later applied to a doctor's checkup of a person, and eventually to this sense

Since 1980, after a horse was killed by a dynamite explosion in "Heaven's Gate," the Screen Actors Guild contract has required that the American Humane Association vet any scripts involving animals. Representatives visit film sets to insure that even rats and spiders are not mistreated.

viable   *VIGH uh buhl*
physically fitted to live; capable of living

To be viable, frog eggs must be fertilized immediately after laying, so a scientist will squeeze the frogs, causing them to eject their eggs, and quickly apply frog sperm.

workable and likely to survive

What is left to be said about Caruso? His name, even now, is synonymous with opera, and there has never been a time over the past 80 years when his records were not before the public. He was the first big record-seller—a good case could be made for the fact that Caruso singlehandedly turned the phonograph from a mechanical toy into a commercially viable artistic medium.

vicarious   *vigh KAI ree uhs*
shared in or experienced by imagined participation in another's experience

Getting students to develop reasoning abilities early is considered vital and Mr. Lipman's approach for elementary school pupils permits youngsters the security of vicarious reasoning. They read about characters their own age in works of fiction in which reasoning concepts are strewn lavishly through the pages.

vicissitudes   *vi SI suh too:dz*
unpredictable changes; ups and downs

His current success notwithstanding, the 34-year-old actor is also resigned to the inevitable vicissitudes of the theater business. "I've been 'discovered' an awful lot. What happens? Nothing," he says with a rueful smile. "I think you have to be discovered around nine times before you start to make a living at this."

vie   *vigh*
to compete

One competition has youngsters vying in a mannequin-modeling contest, with models striking poses for 15 minutes without moving—no blinking, smiling, twitching or stretching.

vignette   *vin YET*
a short literary or dramatic sketch

Mr. Bergquist's play, which he described as a series of satirical vignettes about contemporary life with an emphasis on the popularity of various schools of psychotherapy, has been playing on and off in Stockholm for the last six years.

vindication   *vin duh KAY shuhn*
a clearing from criticism, blame or suspicion; the evidence that serves to justify a claim or deed

> WASHINGTON, April 14—To the millions of citizens who watched the space shuttle Columbia glide to its flawless landing today, the newest space exploit was sweet vindication of American know-how. The automobile industry may be beset by Japanese competition and the military establishment may feel that Moscow has gained the advantage of momentum in the strategic arms race, but the nifty two-wheeled touchdown in the Mojave Desert provided a quick, jubilant lift for a nation that has been suffering from technological self-doubt.

vindictive   *vin DIK tiv*
vengeful in spirit; inclined to seek vengeance

> Yesterday Mrs. Montenegro said: "We want the judges and all to know that we do not come to the courts for vindictiveness or vengeance. We want only justice. We ask that the victims also be heard in the court. We are tired of being nonpersons in the courtrooms."

vintage   *VIN tij*
being of a past era

> A special Art Deco display will highlight this weekend's semiannual exhibition for collectors of vintage posters and postcards. Appraisals of antique cards and postcards will be offered.

> ✦ The term *Art Deco* derives from the *Exposition Internationale des Arts Decoratifs et Industriels Modernes*, held in Paris in 1925. The Art Deco style is characterized by geometric forms, strong colors and a streamlined effect in art and architecture. New York City's Chrysler Building and Radio City Music Hall are major Art Deco creations, both built during the height of the style's popularity, the late 1920s and early 1930s. Art Deco saw a revival in the late 1960s among artists, architects and industrial designers that is still flourishing.

virtuoso   *ver choo: OH soh*
a person displaying great technical skill in some fine art, especially in the performance of music

Jascha Heifetz, who died on Dec. 12 at the age of 86, was unforgettable in every way. It was not only that he was the greatest virtuoso after Paganini, and that he set all standards for 20th-century violin playing. Rather it was that everything about him conspired to create a sense of awe. His platform mannerisms, for instance—or, rather, lack of mannerisms. He would stride out, handsome, impeccably groomed, dignified, remote, unsmiling, and play with hardly a body motion. But the effect was awesome.

virulent   *VIR yoo: lint*
actively poisonous or injurious; deadly

Joe Camel may be gone and the Marlboro Man may be breathing his last, but those crafty tobacco company executives are as committed as ever to their life's work, which is the spread of their virulent product to as many people on the planet as possible.

visage   *VI zij*
face; aspect; appearance

The manager said that Mr. Monberg could be "one of the guys" in a social setting, but in public he adopts a stern, investment-banker type visage.

viscera   *VI suh ruh*
the internal organs of the body: here used figuratively

Mr. Rushdie, whose other novel, "Grimus," I haven't read, was born in Bombay and now lives in London. Bombay is the viscera of this novel, as Danzig was for Günter Grass in "The Tin Drum."

visceral   *VI suh ruhl*
emotional or instinctive, rather than intellectual; earthy

It is still possible to buy a White Mountain ice-cream maker that is hand-cranked. Then you can have the enjoyment—and I really do think it gives some people a good, visceral feeling to do things the hard way—of cranking the dessert for about 25 minutes.

vista   *VI stuh*
a distant view

The Negev, which encompasses 60 percent of the area of Israel proper, is an arid and barren stretch of wilderness with quiet vistas of hills and mountains and canyons in some places.

vitriol   *VI tree awl*
bitterness of feeling in speech or writing; acidlike criticism

Of the many things American shoppers dislike about retail stores, few inspire vitriol like poor customer service. "I find the norm is absolutely *no* service," said Mrs. Cohen, a freelance writer. "When I do get good service, it absolutely boils down to the individual and not to the corporate culture of the store."

◆ Vitriols are mineral salts called sulfates, among them copper, zinc and iron sulfate. If a sulfate is heated, vapors are given off, which when cooled and dissolved in water, produce sulfuric acid, an extremely corrosive liquid. The date of *The Oxford English Dictionary's* first citation of vitriol used figuratively is 1769, although the word had been used in chemistry since the fourteenth century.

vociferous   *VOH si fuh ris*
loud, noisy or vehement in making one's feelings known; clamorous

After decades of often vociferous hostility toward the environmental movement, Ford Motor and the rest of the auto industry are beginning to show some interest in improving their records on pollution.

vogue   *vohg*
the accepted fashion or style at any particular time; general favor or acceptance; popularity: French, a fashion

Chèvre, that tangy, aromatic cheese formed from pure goat's milk, is suddenly in vogue. As if out of nowhere, a staggering and mysterious variety of chèvres have appeared on the scene, replacing Brie as *the* imported cheese in demand.

volatile   *VAH luh tuhl*
vaporizing or evaporating quickly

Hundreds of people were forced out of their places of work and traffic was backed up for miles on major roadways near Newark International Airport early this morning after a railroad tank car containing 26,000 gallons of a volatile toxic chemical caught fire at the Oak Island Conrail freight yards.

likely to shift quickly and unpredictably; unstable; explosive

In "Girl Interrupted," Ms. Ryder (who served as an executive producer) digs hungrily into the role of a neurotic young woman who, in today's therapeutic parlance, "acts out" with a vengeance. In conveying her character's volatile emotional life, Ms. Ryder gives her most penetrating screen performance, one that deserves extra credit for not pleading for our love.

voluminous   *vuh LOO: muh nuhs*
enough to fill volumes

But Jefferson kept voluminous records of anything that could be measured. He designed and commissioned the building of several elaborate hodometers, which were instruments attached to carriage wheels to measure distance. He measured miles, paces, degrees, hours and even the number of shovels of earth required to fill in the grave of a friend.

voracious   *vaw RAY shuhs*
having a huge appetite; very greedy or eager in some desire or pursuit; insatiable

To call the bearded dragon lizard a voracious eater would be an understatement. It happily consumes most any insect, no matter what the defense mechanism of the prey.

vulgar   *VUHL ger*
lacking taste; coarse; crude

When the new Bonwit Teller store on East 57th Street was still a-building, it was covered by a seven-story-high billboard bearing the store's celebrated trademark of purple violets. Such a huge sign might ordinarily seem to be a vulgar commercial intrusion on genteel 57th Street, but somehow this sign was special—it was a breath of fresh air and color on the street, a surprise element at enormous scale that enlivened its entire block.

vulnerable   *VUL nuh ruh buhl*
liable to succumb to persuasion or temptation; susceptible to injury or attack; insufficiently defended

Advocates for the elderly have contended that they are particularly vulnerable to the sophisticated mailings and look-alike documents used by the sweepstakes industry.

wane

This has been, in my own case, a banner year for growing

tomatoes and, of all the things that come from my garden, it

is one of the only vegetables of

which I never tire. My enthusiasm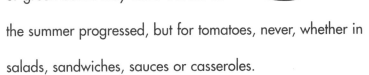

for an overabundance of zucchini

or green beans may have waned as

the summer progressed, but for tomatoes, never, whether in

salads, sandwiches, sauces or casseroles.

see page 381

wag *wag*
a comical or humorous person; joker; wit

It wasn't long after Richard Thomas, who used to play John Boy Walton on television, became the father of triplet daughters Wednesday that wags started calling the new arrivals John Girl I, John Girl II and John Girl III.

wane *wayn*
to grow gradually less; fade; decline; weaken

This has been, in my own case, a banner year for growing tomatoes and, of all the things that come from my garden, it is one of the only vegetables of which I never tire. My enthusiasm for an overabundance of zucchini or green beans may have waned as the summer progressed, but for tomatoes, never, whether in salads, sandwiches, sauces or casseroles.

wanton *WAHN tuhn*
sexually loose or unrestrained

Survivors of childhood's rainy afternoons will recall the hours passed looking up racy words in the dictionary. The same parents who'd hidden "Tropic of Cancer" from innocent eyes never seemed to have grasped the wanton possibilities of a walk through Webster.

> ◆ *Dictionary: A malevolent literary device for cramping the growth of a language and making it hard and inelastic.*
> — Ambrose Bierce, *The Devil's Dictionary*, 1911

senseless, unprovoked or unjustifiable

> Capt. Roy Baughman of the Green Brook police said that vehicular homicide charges in New Jersey require proof that a driver "operated a motor vehicle carelessly and heedlessly in a willful or wanton disregard for the rights of others."

war-horse   *WAWR hawrs*
a symphony, play, opera, etc. that has been performed so often as to seem trite and stale: an allusion to a horse that has been in battle many times and is trotted out again and again for its dependability

> Back in the old days, 25 to 30 years ago, the City Opera was a haven for the adventurous. But after its move to Lincoln Center in 1966, the company began more and more to stage the same war-horses that dominated the repertory across the plaza at the Metropolitan Opera.

wastrel   *WAY struhl*
an idler or good-for-nothing

> "Stripes" stars Bill Murray, who says his achievements make his mother happy "not because I'm successful, but because I didn't turn out to be a complete wastrel."

wean   *ween*
to withdraw someone gradually from a habit, occupation or object of affection, especially by substituting some other interest

> Drugs are regarded as only a temporary solution to tension headaches. For some patients, weaning from heavy doses of strong pain killers, such as those containing narcotics, is the first crucial part of treatment, since prolonged use of the drug can result in a reduced tolerance to pain and may cause other health problems.

whet
to sharpen; stimulate

> Virgil's smells great, as any barbecue place should, and the enormous menu, a paean to regional barbecue from the Carolinas to Kansas City, also whets the appetite.

✦ *Barbecue* originated among the indigenous Caribs and Arawaks of the Caribbean Islands. So did *caiman, canoe, hammock, hurricane, maize, manatee, mangrove* and *papaya*. All were adopted first by the Spanish and then borrowed from Spanish into English between 1550 and 1700.

whipsaw   WIP *saw*
to subject to two opposing forces at the same time: from a saw with a long, curving blade and a handle at each end, used by two people

As children across the United States swarm back to school, principals from Washington to Palm Beach County, Fla., and from Houston to Los Angeles say they are struggling through the worst teacher shortage in recent memory. They describe being whipsawed by swelling enrollments and a push to reduce class sizes at a time when more teachers are retiring.

white elephant   WIGHT E *luh fuhnt*
a possession unwanted by the owner but difficult to dispose of and expensive to keep or maintain

"Just last month I was on the Norway, which used to be the great French liner France—the grande dame of the twilight years of the North Atlantic runs. She sat for five years, a big white elephant, and the Norwegians took her and she's completely rejuvenated."

✦ Many centuries ago in Siam, now Thailand, each white or albino elephant captured or born in captivity was considered sacred. It became the property of the king and was not allowed to work. If the king wanted to punish someone he didn't like, he would present the unlucky person with a white elephant. One could not refuse a gift from the king, and it wouldn't be long before the white elephant had brought its new master to financial ruin, eating him out of house and home.

white lie   WIGHT LIGH
a lie concerning a trivial matter, often one told to spare someone's feelings

Social Security was sold to the public as the alternative to depending on children or charity. The truth, though, is subtly different. Social Security is not considered a handout only because society winks at the resemblance. It is a system of white lies. Social Security payroll taxes have never paid for more than a small fraction of the benefits promised. The system only muddles through by taxing today's workers to pay for today's retirees.

windfall   *WIND fawl*

any unexpected acquisition, gain or stroke of good luck: like something blown down by the wind, as fruit from a tree

When the Speaker of the House, Representative Thomas P. O'Neill Jr., emerged from a White House meeting today with President Reagan he denounced the President's tax proposals as "a windfall for the rich" and said the Democrats were concerned with "the working class."

wiseacre   *WIGHZ ay ker*

an offensively self-assured person; smart aleck: Dutch, wijssegger, *soothsayer*

In the beginning, Joe De Filippis considered calling his clothing shop for men 5 feet 8 inches and under the Short Stop, the Small Shop or the Little Store. One tall wiseacre even suggested the Masculine Munchkin.

wistful   *WIST fuhl*

full of melancholy yearning; longing

One of the most wistful of Brooklyn dreams—the return of the borough's baseball Dodgers to their home turf—received a daylong elaboration in parties and proclamations yesterday. By order of Governor Carey, a statewide Brooklyn Dodger Day was designated.

wolf   *woolf*

to eat ravenously

Having fasted since the previous midnight, they wolf down the chicken soup and crackers, cookies and hot chocolate that they are offered.

woo

to try to persuade; appeal to: from the earlier sense of to try to get the love of or seek as a spouse

Under intense new pressure to compete for patients, New York area hospitals have jumped into the business of wooing patients. In the last year to 18 months, hospital administrators say, most local institutions have begun advertising either for the first time or more aggressively than ever before.

Many have hired consultants, and some are considering celebrity spokesmen and women.

workhorse WERK hawrs
a person who works tirelessly or assumes extra duties: from a horse used for labor, rather than for riding or racing

Although she set high standards for her students, Dr. Wakin, who was just as demanding of herself, was a popular teacher. A workhorse who cheerfully accepted administrative tasks others shunned, Dr. Wakin never became a full professor. Her friends attributed the slight to the internecine world of academic politics.

wrangle RANG guhl
an angry, noisy dispute or quarrel

After an angry political wrangle, the board of the Metropolitan Transportation Authority voted 8 to 6 yesterday to pave the way for a probable July 1 fare increase. Board members shouted at each other across a conference table before they reached their decision.

wrath rath
intense anger; rage; fury

Martin, who has often demonstrated his wrath against umpires by screaming obscenities, kicking dirt and hurling his cap, went into that act in the fourth inning of a game that the A's lost to the Blue Jays, 6-3.

wry righ
drily humorous, often with a touch of irony

Betsy Cronkite, discussing the wry sense of humor of her husband, Walter, recalls in an interview in the February issue of McCall's that after a national magazine asked Mr. Cronkite to write his own obituary for it, he sent one in immediately. The obituary read in full: "Walter Cronkite, television and radio newsman, died today. He smothered to death under a pile of ridiculous mail which included a request to write his own obituary."

wunderkind VOON der kint
a child prodigy, or one who succeeds at something at a relatively early age: German, wunder, *wonder* + kind, *child*

Prince, the 21-year-old Minneapolis-bred wunderkind of black music, put on an electrifying performance at the Ritz last Sunday night. Four months ago, when Prince played the same club, it was half-empty. But word of mouth and widespread critical acclaim for his third album, "Dirty Mind," insured that the show would be sold out.

X·Y·Z

Xanadu

His [Robert Moses'] first great achievement was the erection

of Jones Beach, for which he took an almost unused

sandbar and at vast expense transformed

it into an elaborate seaside

Xanadu for the masses,

complete with bathhouses,

restaurants and a tower inspired by a Venetian bell tower.

see page 389

Xanadu   *ZA nuh doo:*
a fabled city built during the 13th century by Kubla Khan, the Mongol emperor of China, and depicted in Samuel Taylor Coleridge's poem, Kubla Khan

His [Robert Moses'] first great achievement was the erection of Jones Beach, for which he took an almost unused sandbar and at vast expense transformed it into an elaborate seaside Xanadu for the masses, complete with bathhouses, restaurants and a tower inspired by a Venetian bell tower.

◆ Samuel Taylor Coleridge (1772-1834) fell asleep one afternoon in the summer of 1797 while reading about Xanadu in a travel book, and dreamt, he said, a 200- to 300-line poem. Upon awakening, he began to write it down, but after 54 lines he was interrupted by a visitor and could never again recall more of the poem. Its opening lines are: *In Xanadu did Kubla Khan/A stately pleasure-dome decree:/Where Alph, the sacred river, ran/ Through caverns measureless to man/ Down to a sunless sea.*

xenophobia   *zee nuh FOH bee uh*
a fear or hatred of strangers or foreigners: Greek, xenos, *strange or foreign +* phobos, *a fear*

Sealed off from the rest of the world first by its ruling theocracy and then by its xenophobic Chinese occupiers, Tibet was long inaccessible to Western visitors without lots of ingenuity or money. Once the Chinese opened the area to snare the tourist dollar, it was inevitable that a guidebook would follow.

yahoo   *YAH hoo:*

a rough, coarse or uncouth person: in Swift's 1726 book, Gulliver's Travels, *the Yahoos are a race of beastly human creatures; their masters are the Houyhnhnms, a race of horses of the highest intelligence and rational thought*

"Beatlemania," which opens today at the Ziegfield and other theaters, is even more about its audience than it is about the Beatles, who of course were not willing participants in this venture. While the four Beatle stand-ins launch perfunctory versions of Beatle hits, the extraneous footage recalls the viewer's lost youth. In the purest yahoo spirit, the audience is encouraged to cheer for the things they used to dig, and boo the things they didn't. Richard M. Nixon gets boos, which isn't surprising. And there are cheers for Dustin Hoffman, Janis Joplin, marijuana and LSD.

zany   *ZAY nee*
comical in a wild, ludicrous or slapstick manner

On "Seinfeld," Jerry's apartment door wears an impressive array of hardware, but he never seems to put the locks to use. This is probably for the same reason that other series leave apartment doors unlocked: so the zany next-door neighbor can barge in, without tempo-slowing buzzers and bells.

zeal   *zeel*
intense enthusiasm, as in working for a cause

Day and night on France's windy western coast, Radio Kerne transmits a bright mix of music sprinkled with local news. It is a new station run by young people for a young audience—but with a difference. Most of Radio Kerne's operators are volunteers, working with the zeal of missionaries. Their preferred music comes from bagpipes and flutes. And they broadcast only in Breton, a Celtic language spoken for more than 2,000 years that until recently seemed doomed to disappear. "Saving the culture of Brittany is very much on people's minds," said Isig Flatres, who is the manager of the station. "This generation is no longer embarrassed about speaking or being Breton."

zealot   *ZE luht*
a person zealous to an extreme degree; fanatic: when spelled with a capital Z, a member of a radical political and religious sect among the ancient Jews who openly resisted Roman rule in Palestine

At 9 o'clock on Sunday, ABC begins presenting its eight-hour, multimillion-dollar "Masada," which will be shown over four consecutive evenings.

Filmed on location in Israel, this is the story of how, in the year A.D. 73, 960 Jewish Zealots killed themselves rather than surrender to the 5,000 Roman soldiers who were invading their fortress.

zenith   *ZEE nith*
the highest point; culmination; peak; summit: Arabic, path above the head. In astronomy, the point in the sky directly overhead. Its antonym is nadir.

A political climb and a zeal for Republican Party activism that began when he was a teen-ager reached its zenith today when Attorney General Peter G. Verniero was confirmed by the State Senate as a justice on the New Jersey Supreme Court.

More masterly ways with words

Giving Language Life
Verbs of Action

Nothing animates and invigorates one's written or spoken expression more than well-chosen verbs, the heartbeat of every sentence. Nothing can *be,* nothing can *do,* nothing can *happen* without a verb.

But forceful, vigorous and vivid verbs are probably the most underused and underrated words in the language. They take a back seat to adjectives in the work of many writers, who think that the number of adjectives one uses is a mark of good writing. Yet adjective-loaded writing can be overdone and underwhelming. Verb-loaded writing is vital and animated.

No aspect of journalistic writing is more impressive than the talent for selecting verbs that bring a scene or an idea to life—as in this passage from *The New York Times*:

> Furious, brick-busting winds—which some witnesses said
> looked like a tornado—twisted down over Jersey City and
> Staten Island yesterday afternoon, uprooting trees, whipping up
> garbage cans and ripping off roofs, one of which whizzed across
> a block before it smashed down onto three empty cars.

Whew! Did you see that? Did you hear that? You just witnessed a windstorm that may well have been more vivid in your mind's eye than film of it would have been to your real eyes.

Here are more examples from *The Times* of how reporters skillfully use verbs to place their readers at the scene.

> All along the road, entire families trudged in both directions
> throughout the day, balancing large packages on their shoulders
> or lugging sacks of rice and beans.

> Performing a mesmerizing spiral sequence, in which she leaned
> backward and touched her head to her skate, then bent forward
> and grabbed one ankle while lifting her other leg in the
> 12 o'clock position as she glided across the ice, Cohen won first
> from five of the nine judges.

The slate roof was burned and torn, the sanctuary gutted, the organ and its pipes ruined, the stained glass shattered, and the painting of Our Lady of Guadeloupe, donated to the Hispanic parishioners who succeeded the parish's Italian and Irish immigrants, was lost.

The floodwaters carried off whole barns, toppled silos, destroyed farmhouses and transformed the grassy valley into a rocky, muddy mess. Dozens of trees, uprooted by the swift currents and stripped of bark, lay in piles where the waters left them. Acre after acre of cornfields resembled rice paddies, with corn stalks plastered flat to wet ground scored by little streams of water.

A car that careered out of control after colliding with another vehicle slammed into a Morningside Heights bakery cafe yesterday, pinning a Columbia University student against the building and injuring three other pedestrians, the police said.

Among the most active verbs are those derived from nouns—to *carpet* a room, *shoe* a horse, *cycle* to town. These verbs are particularly animated because they describe the action and the object in one word, and *that* is powerful imagery. *Cycle* calls to mind both the action of riding a bicycle and the bicycle itself. Let's use another example: you can put wallpaper up, or you can paper the wall. In the first instance, there is an unmoving object, *wallpaper*, accompanied by a plain verb, *put*. In the second instance, paper becomes the object and the action, and you've eliminated the plain verb.

The following words can be used as both nouns and verbs. In addition, they are all examples of onomatopoeia—words that sound like the object or action they signify. This gives each of them three dimensions: the word *represents* a thing, it conveys the *action* of that thing, and it *sounds* like that thing. Heavy-duty for one word, and it shows how even the shortest, simplest words can superbly serve the person who knows how to use them. Try devising your own sentences for these words, first as nouns and then as verbs. (An example would be this pair: *There was a splash below. Something splashed below.*) And note the additional punch each word has when you use it as a verb.

bang	chirp	growl	snap
bark	clang	hiss	splash
blare	clatter	murmur	whack
blast	crackle	roar	whisper
boom	crash	scratch	
buzz	creak	sizzle	

Back-formations

While many verbs created from nouns are now everyday words, accepted by even the most censorious protectors of the language—*donate* made it through a gantlet of nineteenth-century criticism—newer ones continue to raise dander among grammarians, teachers and others sensitive to new forms of old words. Most of the time, the reaction results simply from the fact that the new verb from the old noun *is* new—its strangeness, its appearance as an interloper, its unfamiliar sound make it look, sound and feel wrong.

And yet, the same people who may avoid *enthused* and *impacted* may be perfectly happy with *diagnosed* and *donate*. All four verbs evolved through back-formation, the creation of a new verb from an old noun. Thus, we have *televise* from *television*, *peddle* from *peddler*, *edit* from *editor*. More proof that back-formations are normal linguistic constructions: *automate* from *automation*, *bulldoze* from *bulldozer*, *commute* from *commuter*, *escalate* from *escalator*, *loaf* from *loafer*, *sightsee* from *sightseer*. All were formed from the nouns that preceded their invention.

So why the continuing fuss about *enthused*, over which a fuss has been made since at least the mid-nineteenth century? Many still consider it to be overly informal to the point of sounding slapdash, as jarring as a kerchief worn with an evening gown or work shoes with a tuxedo.

Prioritize has been a real bugaboo, a back-formation of *priority* that gained a foothold in the 1960s but has nevertheless been loathed by many. But do its critics fulminate over *jeopardize* and *deputize*? Those who criticize a new back-formation are merely reacting against the new and unfamiliar and are expressing, above all, a personal taste. While a newly back-formed verb may, indeed, sound strange—even ugly—as *prioritize* does to many people, its true offense is almost always its newness. *Categorize* and *stigmatize* aren't very pretty either, but who complains?

This is not to say that every new back-formation should be welcomed with open arms into the language or assumed to be here to stay. The noun *interface*, a computer term meaning a point where two or more systems meet or connect, gained some popularity in the 1970s as a verb meaning *to communicate* (*they interfaced across the conference table*), although it was consistently denounced as an atrocious application of a mechanical function to a human relationship. Either the condemnation worked or people just got tired of the novelty, for in its verb form, *interface* is rarely heard or seen today.

To use or not use any particular back-formed word really comes down to personal taste and peer pressure. If you don't like a back-formed word, don't use it. If you like it but worry about what others will think if you say it or write it, either don't use it or take the plunge proudly and let the chips fall where they may. And if you are a critic of a back-formed word, check out the word's history before you banish it from your writing.

Less Is More
Allusions

"I love the Metropolitan Opera," said Leontyne Price in *The New York Times* when she was among the Met's stars. "For me, it's a total Shangri-La." All we have to read is the name of that utopian Buddhist community in James Hilton's 1933 novel *Lost Horizon*, and we know how perfect a place Ms. Price considered the Met. She reminded us of something we already know and can compare the Met to.

Indirect references like this are called allusions, and they play an important part in creating images for readers. Allusions link what we are reading with what we have read, heard or seen in the past, enhancing new material with old associations. Shangri-La is a word with a meaning of its own, a fictitious Himalayan paradise that most people know the significance of even if they haven't read *Lost Horizon*. But for those who have read the book the image is far more evocative. The whole place seems to appear before the mind's eye.

This is the way of an allusion, getting us to experience a word on two levels at once. Mythology, literature, the Bible and history are the major sources writers draw from when they want us to associate new material they are presenting with what we have read or experienced in the past.

Allusions also help to colorfully emphasize a notable quality about a person or thing, as in this opening passage of an article in *The New York Times* about the proliferation of Indian restaurants on a single block in Manhattan:

> In the beginning was Shah Bag. And Shah Bag begat Kismoth. And Shah Bag also begat Romna. And Shah Bag and Kismoth begat Nishan. And Nishan begat Anar Bagh and Shamoly, which in the course of time begat Mitali and Bangladesh. And East Sixth Street looked upon all this Indian cooking and saw that it was good.

Biblical and mythological allusions abound in Shakespeare's plays and poems. Today we need footnotes to help us understand many of them, but the Elizabethan audience probably had little difficulty in understanding what Mark Antony meant when he referred to "Caesar's spirit, ranging for revenge, with Ate by his side." Shakespeare's audience would have known *Ate* (AY tee) to be the goddess of revenge.

Shakespeare's works have themselves been the major source of literary allusions for hundreds of years, with expressions like "star-crossed lovers" and "Et tu, Brute?" adding richness and significance to writing and speaking. The name Romeo is an allusion unto itself, used to describe a young man ardently in love.

Allusions appearing in books tend to derive from traditional sources because books are written to be read not only now but next year, a decade from now, or far into the future. Journalists writing for tomorrow's paper, however, are free to reach for contemporary allusions. Thus, reporters allude to culturally transient creations, as a sportswriter did when describing the figure skater Tara Lipinski as an "Energizer bunny of a jumper." A reporter alluded to a television program whose outstanding feature is guests fighting onstage when he wrote: "in Woody Allen's movie 'Celebrity,' the most telling and amusing scene involves a Jerry Springeresque free-for-all."

Here are other passages from *The New York Times* with allusions ranging from the classical to the contemporary.

When we last left the Cinderella tale of Polytechnic University in Brooklyn, it was celebrating a bequest of $175 million from one of its former chemistry professors and his wife and grappling with the pleasant problem of how to spend it.

The Dalai Lama simply states and restates his belief in the essential goodness of human nature, but that seems a touch Panglossian after this bloody century.

"E.R.," the Mona Lisa of contemporary television, is about to be put up for auction—and every network in America wants this work of prime-time art hanging on its wall.

What most people remember about the Monitor and the Merrimac is that, like the gingham dog and the calico cat, or Tweedledum and Tweedledee, the two of them fought each other.

Leading with his famous chin, Kirk Douglas (who turned 83 yesterday) gleefully devours the scenery in "Diamonds," a simmered-in-schmaltz comedy about a grumpy older man determined not to go gentle into that good night.

Ever since the apple episode, delving into secret knowledge has been a risky business.

Now, without being quite ready to lie down like the lion and the lamb, these top business and labor leaders say they want to work together for the national interest.

Show Me the Mummy! Internet Offers a Home to Archaeology

Headline writers for *The New York Times* have a penchant for allusions to popular songs—"popular" meaning anything from Stephen Foster to Stephen Sondheim and later. Headlining a story about tired commuters with "I've Been Sleeping on the Railroad" may have been a cinch, but imagine the copy editor's grin after reading a story about the Giants ending a 6-10 football season and coming up with "A Disgruntled Team That Got No Kick From Campaign."

Here is a selection of *New York Times* headlines containing allusions to songs. (To identify the ones you don't know, ask someone older—or younger.)

A museum exhibit of jewelry that belonged to a Russian dynasty:

Diamonds Are a Czar's Best Friend

Brides-to-be slim down for their wedding dresses:

Get Me to the Gym On Time

A review of a concert of Jimmy Van Heusen songs:

Up There, Where the Air is Rarefied

Offbeat publications for Civil War buffs:

Mine Eyes Have Seen the Coming of a Lot of Wacky Stuff

Computer-based slot machines in Las Vegas:

Luck, Be a Microchip Tonight

Reviews of six Queens, N.Y., restaurants:

Over the River and to the Food

A new minor league baseball team's first game in its Newark, N.J. home stadium:

A Home Team to Root, Root, Root For

A review of singer KT Sullivan's cabaret show of Jerome Kern songs:

The Music Is Sweet, the Words Are True

A review of a film about rehearsing for *Hamlet*:

There Is Nothing Like a Dane

A review of a television movie about Frank Sinatra's Rat Pack:

Extremes With Impossible Schemes

A greenhouse manager and his family living in the New York Botanical Garden:

A Cunning Cottage 3 Could Share (Public Invited)

Caring for rooftop gardens in New York City:

On City Roofs, It's Not Easy Being Green

The cleaning and restoration of the flag that inspired Francis Scott Key:

New Dawn for Flag That Was Still There

A reporter's queasy experience on a trapeze:

The Greatest of Unease

Two fashion designers talking about the latest designs:

Everything's Coming Up Froufrou

Sidney Blumenthal, a White House adviser, being deposed before members of Congress:

A Very Model of a Modern Gentleman

Photo headline of a man rapelling down the face of the Old Man of the Mountains, in Franconia Notch, N.H.:

Cheek Bone's Connected to the Jaw Bone

A summer day camp specializing in rock music:

Hello Fender, Hello Gibson

A company that makes custom-made shoes:

These $2,000 Boots Are Made for Walking

The excavation of a seventeenth-century pleasure garden across the river from the Taj Mahal:

What a Little Moonlight Can Do

The demise of a radio station devoted to popular standards, and of a well-known cabaret:

The Memory of Love's Refrain

Meet halfway (and go no farther)

The allusion is one of the most effective literary devices writers can employ because with a single word (Hercules) or phrase (a thumbs-up verdict), they double the impact of their message. But there's another, more subtle reason why allusions are so affecting: they create intimacy between writer and reader. Allusions ask the reader to meet the writer halfway, not only understanding the allusion, but filling in what has been left unsaid. Often, there's a little nod of recognition within us, a response to the fact that the writer has shared our literary or cultural experience.

Part of the fun and intellectual stimulation of an allusion is that the person, place or thing alluded to is not explained. Readers are expected to know it. The passage below, for example, missed being a true allusion because the part after the dash explained what the reference was to—thus giving readers a direct, rather than an indirect, reference:

> In fact, as the leading whistle-blower and campaigner for a union, Ms. Saumier has earned a reputation among blue-collar workers and middle-class churchgoers as the Norma Rae of Syracuse—a reference to the heroine of the 1979 film that starred Sally Field as a union organizer.

The writer who says, "As Charles Dickens wrote in *A Tale of Two Cities*, it is the best of times and the worst of times," weakens the statement by giving us too much information. In writing, as in so many other things, less is more, and suggestion often strikes deeper and more memorably than direct statement.

The Lowest Form of Wit, Says Who?

Puns

Puns have traditionally been called the lowest form of humor, but the tradition is carried on only by people without the talent for making puns. They're jealous.

A pun is a play on words. Sometimes the play is on a different sense of the same word, as when, in *Romeo and Juliet*, the dying Mercutio (who can't resist a pun even in his last moments) says, "Look for me tomorrow and you will find me a grave man." Sometimes the play is on a similar sense or sound of different words, as when a traffic reporter for a New York City radio station described an expressway notorious for its traffic standstills as the Long Island Distressway, and a *Times* reporter began an article about his whale watching experience off Montauk, Long Island, with "Call me a schlemiel."

Punning is a natural act of people who like to play with words and who have the verbal dexterity to make unusual associations from plainly spoken statements. Their minds work like one-armed bandits in gambling casinos, with plums and cherries and oranges spinning madly upon someone's utterance, searching for the right combination to connect on a pun.

Many people groan when they hear a pun. But this is a learned response. They feel it's expected of them, and they would rather appear sophisticated than give the punner the satisfaction of laughter.

Those who do laugh at puns appreciate the mental gymnastics required to create a play on words. Unlike jokes, which may take time to devise and can be retold, a pun is a one-time thing, manufactured in an instant, suiting only the present occasion, and rarely recycled. It is the most evanescent form of wit.

Puns in literature, however, can become classics. In the *Odyssey*, composed about 800 B.C., a sea goddess, seeing the shipwrecked Odysseus adrift on a raft, says (in Homeric Greek, but translatable into English as the same pun), "Poor Odysseus! You're odd I see, true to your name!"

The New York Times Manual of Style and Usage cautions against obvious puns (which may, indeed, deserve a groan), like "Rubber Industry Bounces Back"; the overuse of puns; and puns on people's names, such as "a player named Butcher carved up the opposing team."

Pun intended

In the following selection of puns and other wordplay that have appeared in *The Times*, note that in addition to being humorous, the wordplay advances the story, and that even if readers don't catch the pun, the sentence still makes sense.

Even those who prefer smooth peanut butter are now faced with a crunch.

Natick Lab's recommendations, if accepted, would allow full-scale fish testing to begin as early as this fall.

The presence of Prince Charles will add a fillip to an evening-long celebration of the Royal Ballet's 50th anniversary at Lincoln Center.

After two and a half slow-gaited years, the "horse licensing and protection measure" galloped through the City Council on July 21, passing 40-0.

A racy sitcom called "Soap" once sent Baptists and other church groups into such a lather that several sponsors pulled out.

Balloons have become a high-flying business and sell at inflated prices.

When it comes to scented fragrance advertisements, The New Yorker has decided the noes have it—because readers have declared, in no uncertain terms, that their noses have had it.

E Pluribus Unum
The Melting Pot of English

English has always been a blend of tongues. In 1066, the year of the Norman Conquest, England's language was Anglo-Saxon (or Old English), a blend of tongues introduced by the Angles, the Saxons, and other Germanic and Scandinavian tribes that settled in England during the fifth century.

The Lord's Prayer in its Anglo-Saxon form gives you an idea of how different that language was from modern English.

Faeder ure thu the eart on heofonum, si thin nama gahalgod.
Father our, thou art on heavens, be thy name hallowed.

Tobecume thin rice.
Become thy rich.

Gewurthe thin willa on eorthan swa swa on heofonum.
Worth thy will on earth so so on heavens.

Urne gedaeghwamlican hlaf syle us to daeg.
Our daily loaf sell us today.

And forgyf us ure gyltas, swa we forgyfath urum gyltendum.
And forgive us our guilts, so we forgive our guiltings

And ne gelaed thu us on constnunge
And not lead thou us on temptation

Ac alys us of yfele. Sothlice.
But free us of evil. Soothlike.

Different, yet similar. The strange spellings and archaic sounds of the words cannot mask the fact that there is much familiar to an English-speaking person in that Anglo-Saxon prayer—especially when you read it out loud.

The Norman Conquest ushered in the next major period of English, Middle English, with Norman French the new ingredient added to the blend.

Here is the Lord's Prayer again, this time in its fourteenth-century form. A translation is no longer needed.

Oure fadir that art in hevenes, halwid be thi name.
Thi kyngdom cumme to.
Be thi willa don as in heven and in erthe.
Gif to us this day oure breed over other substaunce.
And forgeve to us oure dettis, as we forgeve to our dettours.
And leede us nat into temptacioun
But delyvere us fro yvel. Amen.

The new words are French, many of them derived from Latin, such as *substance*, *debt*, *debtors*, *temptation* and *deliver*.

By 1450, Anglo-Saxon and Norman French had mixed so inextricably that together they had formed one language. The period of modern English had begun.

Two languages become one

The Anglo-Saxon language may have contained as many as 100,000 words, but 85 percent of them fell into disuse in the two centuries following the Norman invasion. Because the Normans were the ruling class, their language dominated the church, the courts, the government and the military—all of England's important and vital institutions. In fact, the most telling proof of the influence of French on the English language is that almost every important term associated with England's institutions is of French derivation.

From the church come *saint*, *clergy*, *miracle*, *mercy* and *faith*; from the courts, *jury*, *judge*, *crime*, *arrest*, *accuse* and *bail*; from government, *crown*, *state*, *country*, *tax*, *nation* and *parliament*; and from the military, *war*, *peace*, *battle*, *arms*, *soldier*, *navy*, *enemy*, *spy* and *assault*.

It is popularly thought that the one-syllable words of modern English derive mostly from Anglo-Saxon, the language of a relatively simple-living people. That is only partially true. While *man*, *wife*, *child*, *house*, *bench*, *meat*, *grass*, *leaf*, *good*, *high*, *strong*, *eat*, *drink*, *sleep*, *live*, *fight* and *love* are, indeed, Anglo-Saxon in origin, many other everyday words are not. The Normans contributed *air*, *sound*, *large*, *poor*, *real*, *cry*, *please*, *pay*, *quit*, *wait*, *age*, *face*, *use*, *joy* and *pen*.

It took centuries for Anglo-Saxon and Norman French to blend into a common tongue. It takes time for languages to fuse, and most Anglo-Saxons were resistant to learning the language of their conquerors. As new generations were born, however, old memories died. By the middle of the fifteenth century they were no longer Anglo-Saxons and Normans: they were the English, a distinctive people with a distinctive language. During the hundreds of years when Anglo-Saxon and Norman French were fusing into one language, the slow blending process caused the words of both languages to take on a uniquely English sound. That's why we detect no difference between words of

Anglo-Saxon origin, such as *eat* and *sleep*, and those of Norman origin, such as *face* and *pen*.

May we borrow that word, please?

In the centuries following its emergence as a modern language, English adopted thousands of words from other languages, especially as England became a nation of international merchants, traders, explorers and colonizers. Most of these words don't look or sound particularly foreign to us because their sounds and spellings were Anglicized. *Yacht*, *booze*, *easel* and *pickle* may hint slightly of their Dutch origin, but *nap*, *leak*, *toy*, *snap* and *kit*, also Dutch, don't seem at all foreign.

From Arabic (either borrowed directly or via Italian, French or Spanish) come *cotton*, *orange*, *sugar*, *almanac*, *alcohol*, *algebra*, *giraffe*, *magazine* and *zero*. From German we have *noodle*, *seminar*, *bum*, *nix*, *halt*, *poker*, *swindler*, *stroll* and *sleazy*. From Italian are derived *balcony*, *bandit*, *miniature*, *umbrella*, *cartoon*, *bank*, *cash*, *concert* and *attack*. From Spanish come *cask*, *cargo*, *chocolate*, *guitar*, *plaza*, *tomato*, *patio* and *ranch*.

Smaller contributions have come from Hebrew (*amen*, *jubilee*, *cherub*, *sabbath*); Hindi (*bungalow*, *pajamas*, *cot*, *loot*, *thug*, *jungle*, *shampoo*); Persian (*bazaar*, *caravan*, *magic*, *rice*, *rose*, *tape*, *tiger*); Portuguese (*albino*, *molasses*, *pagoda*); Pacific Island languages (*bamboo*, *taboo*, *tattoo*, *gingham*); West African languages (*banana*, *jazz*, *banjo*, *tote*, *gorilla*, *yam*); and American Indian (*moose*, *raccoon*, *skunk*, *moccasin*, *mackinaw*).

Many words have come into English more as contributions than adoptions. They were brought to the United States, or created here, by settlers and others who needed new words to describe their new environment and way of life. In this way English was enriched by the French (*gopher*, *pumpkin*, *chowder*, *bayou*, *butte*, *rapids*, *depot*, *shanty*, *toboggan*, *apache*, *lacrosse*, *levee*), the Spanish (*armadillo*, *corral*, *lasso*, *rodeo*, *stampede*, *bonanza*, *vigilante*, *canyon*, *mesa*, *tornado*), the Dutch (*cookie*, *waffle*, *sleigh*, *boss*, *caboose*) and the Germans (*delicatessen*, *frankfurter*, *pretzel*, *semester*, *pinochle*, *loafer*, *ouch*, *phooey*). Each word is Anglicized just enough to make it comfortable English, yet each retains some of the flavor of its original language.

Thousands of other adopted words, however, have fully retained their foreign look and sound, and these are properly called foreign loan words. Even though *avant-garde* has been used by English-speaking people since the fifteenth century, it still looks and sounds French. *Postscript*, by contrast, is a foreign word that has become fully Anglicized through the dropping of a few letters and the combining of two words. As a sixteenth-century Latin loan, it was *post scriptum*; if it had stayed that way it would be as genuine a Latin loan today as *ad infinitum*, *per capita* or *sub rosa*.

Sometimes, instead of adopting a foreign word, we find as close a literal translation for it as we can. The result is called a *calque*, a French word meaning *imitation*. *Masterpiece* is a calque from the German *meisterstück*. Other calques from German are *superman* (*Übermensch*), *chain-smoker* (*Kettenraucher*) and *academic freedom* (*akademic Freiheit*). *Gemütlichkeit* has remained in its German form because a suitable calque has not been found for it.

Thousands of foreign words and expressions are currently in use in English, from commonly understood expressions like the Latin *ad lib* and the French *faux pas* to the less used *tabula rasa* and *chef d'oeuvre*. While some loans have been an integral part of English since the Middle Ages, such as the French *adieu* and *bon voyage*, others, like *ombudsman* (Swedish) and *karaoke* (Japanese) have been well known only in the past few decades. The foreign entries in *Words That Make a Difference* range from the erudite (*succès d'estime*) to the slangy (*bubkes*), but they have this in common: they fill a need that no English word satisfies.

The Americanization of language

Word borrowing isn't a one-way street. Many English words and phrases—especially American ones—have gained worldwide currency, thanks to the pervasiveness around the world of American culture since the mid-twentieth century. Their pronunciation, however, is often adapted for the borrower. Japanese teenagers listen to a *disuku jokii* (disk jockey) and play a *shidi* (CD); Spaniards may have a *coctel* before dinner and mix their whiskey with *lleneral* (ginger ale); an Italian will wear a *pulova*, play *futbol* and tell a friend to *tegidizi* (take it easy). In France, moviegoers will see a *trilleur*, in which a *sexi* woman in *des shorts* falls in love with a *teuf* gangster during *le holdup*.

Americanisms (called *Franglais* by the French) are anathema to the French Academy, which assiduously keeps them out of the Academy's dictionary, the country's major language arbiter, and discourages their use on radio and television. But while the Academy continues to purge Franglais, millions of French citizens are buying *les blugines* and lunching at *le snacque-barre*, where you will find them eating *le cheeseburger* and drinking *le milk shake*. As they say in Spanish-speaking countries, *que sera*....

Franglais is an ocean away. Closer to home, Spanglish is taking hold. Spanglish is the blending of Spanish and English by some Spanish-speaking people living in America. You speak or write Spanglish by giving English words a Spanish pronunciation and then spelling them accordingly (*fafu* for fast food); using a shorter English word for a longer Spanish equivalent (*parquin* instead of *estacionamiento* for parking); mingling Spanish and English words in the same sentence ("Ponte los red shoes" for "Put on your red shoes"); and literally transposing English expressions into Spanish. An example would be a store clerk saying "¿Como puedo ayudarlo?" for "How can I help you?," rather than the traditional Spanish "¿Que desea?"

Some experts embrace Spanglish as a colorful and dynamic fusion of two languages; others lament it as a debasement of Spanish that is diluting the integrity of both Spanish and English. Is Spanglish a phase that will dissipate, or will it flourish and become a new American form of Spanish that will also influence spoken English?

Tiempo will tell.

The Outer Edge of Language
Slang

The most fertile, creative and restless part of our language, slang is often the most forceful and expressive way to communicate. When we are excited, upset or outraged we tend to reach for slang, sometimes even surprising ourselves when we come out with a word we have never uttered before. In the early 1970s, *rip-off*, *uptight* and *hang-up* were the possessions of the Woodstock generation; the same adults who spoke disparagingly of men's ponytails and earrings then, and would never use "rip-off" and "uptight" in conversation, do so today. To people born since the 1970s, those words are nothing less than standard English vocabulary. As a high school student said to me when I asked her if she considered *rip-off* and *uptight* to be slang: "They're just compound words, right?"

In fact, while the verb *to rip off* and the noun *rip-off* are labeled "slang" in some dictionaries and "informal" in others, the labels may eventually be removed—just as *mob*, *joke*, *nowadays*, *workmanship* and *downfall*, once slang, became mainstream English.

It's not hip to be mainstream

Slang is language born out of the mainstream, the product of subgroups of people, among them teenagers, students, racial, religious and ethnic minorities, rock and jazz musicians, prisoners, soldiers and gangsters. Each is a group whose members spend a lot of time in each other's company, living lives often isolated or filled with turmoil, uncertainty, tension, innovation or rebellion. Slang is the group's verbal distinction. Members develop words and terms that are their special language, often taking pleasure in their inventions but later abandoning them when their private slang comes into mainstream use. *Hippie*, a 1940s African-American word for "a person who tries without success to be hip," fell largely into white use in the 1960s as it took on its counterculture meanings. The evolution signaled its demise as a word among most African-Americans.

Slang has a way of working itself into our psyches. Through repetition in newspapers, magazines, radio, television and the movies, many slang words eventually take hold on the general population. Time appears to be slang's arbiter, as it is of all language, and if what we once thought was coarse and inappropriate shows us that it can fill a gap in our communication, we make it ours (sometimes against our better judgment).

A slang word that has taken a firm hold in recent years is *dis* or *diss*, meaning to show disrespect for someone verbally or through slighting behavior. It originated in the early 1980s among African-American teenagers, was popularized in rap music and has been so thoroughly mainstreamed that speakers and writers, including newspaper columnists, use it unabashedly. As a clipped form of *disrespect*, *dis* is in the same family as *mob*, which is the clipped form of *mobile vulgus*, Latin for "movable crowd," and *taxi*, which is short for *taximeter cabriolet*.

Samuel Johnson's toolbox

No one can kill a slang word, nor can the concerted efforts of teachers, parents, editors or dictionary makers. Slang does, however, wither away and die from disuse or overuse, or because it held the flavor of an era that has passed. *Hooch* was fine in the 1920s for cheap booze, but when Prohibition ended, so did the word's aura; *groovy* was jazz slang in the 1930s, and counterculture slang in the 1960s. It's gone, and you'd sound silly saying it today, except jocularly.

Slang words die when they have lost their usability—never because there are restrictions placed against them, despite the efforts of influential people to prevent them from taking hold. Samuel Johnson, who intended his 1755 dictionary to be the final word on what was pure in the English language, raged against such barbarous slang as *wobble, dodge, flippant, fop, frisky, fuss, simpleton, banter, swap, budge, coax, touchy, stingy, fib, chaperon* and *fun*—obviously unsuccessfully. Johnson's original intent in publishing the first dictionary of the English language was to create a sort of toolbox of words to which no other new tools would be admitted; English would be sufficiently supplied with all the tools it needed. But he came to realize that language cannot be fixed and that changes must take place. No lexicographer could assume, Johnson said, "that his dictionary can embalm his language, and secure it from corruption and decay. Sounds are too volatile and subtle for legal restraints."

Here are conversational slang words and terms, new and old. Some of them may be a part of your everyday vocabulary; others may be completely unknown to you. Some you may have hated when you first encountered them but find yourself quite cozy with now; others you may have embraced immediately. Some you are absolutely certain you will never say and would be mortified to have someone else hear you utter. If some of these words aren't recognizable to you as slang, no sweat!

a drag	cop out	funky
airhead	crash	grungy
blew my mind	dude	gut reaction
boss	duh	hack it
bro	dweeb	hairy
bummer	flipped out	hang up
cool	freak	'hood

humongous	peachy	vibes
kinky	phat	wannabe
knockout	pig out	wimp
natch	scuzzy	wonk
nebbish	shrink	wuss
off the wall	turn-on	zit
on the fritz	twerp	
out of it	twit	

Beyond the Comma
The Semicolon, Colon, Dash and Parenthesis

The skillful handling of punctuation is as important to precise, clear and lively communication as the skillful employment of words. The comma, of course, is the most useful and necessary internal punctuation mark, but if it has been the only punctuation mark you use, you have been placing unnecessary limits on the way you express yourself in writing.

There is no mystique to the semicolon, colon, dash and parenthesis. Familiarity with them comes simply from observing the way other writers use them, and then beginning to incorporate them into your own writing.

The semicolon

The semicolon can be intimidating. People tend to avoid it; they think only accomplished writers and grammar experts know how to use it. But once the five major uses of the semicolon are understood, the mark should lose its forbidding reputation.

1. *Use the semicolon when you must have a stronger break in a sentence than a comma but feel a period would be too strong.*

> I don't think we need any more firewood; we already have
> enough for the winter.

In this case, a comma would be incorrect; the result would be a run-on sentence (also called a comma splice). A period would be correct but too strong; the writer wants to show a closer connection between the two parts. We see, then, an important use of the semicolon: it indicates closer connections between thoughts than a period does. Another example:

> That filter-down theory hasn't worked in India; rich people just
> don't spend money to help the poor.

Again, the second part of the sentence could have been a separate sentence, but the writer wanted to show its close relationship to the first part.

2. *The semicolon replaces coordinating conjunctions, such as* and, but *and* because *for the purpose of tighter writing.*

> Gina wouldn't admit that she had sent me the letter; neither
> would she deny it. (The semicolon replaces *but*.)

Slocum took the train and was home by 9 P.M.; Hadley took the bus and didn't get home until midnight. (The semicolon replaces *but*.)

Only rarely has the okapi been sighted by people; its secretive nature keeps it deep within the jungle. (The semicolon replaces *because*.)

Whenever two sentences seem so closely connected in thought that you don't want to separate them, but also don't want to use a conjunction, you can join them with a semicolon.

3. *Semicolons are the perfect midpoint between two balanced statements.*

All that is positive about his children he credits to his effect on them; all that is negative, he credits to his wife.

I don't see frustration with the president; I see frustration with Congress.

It's a beginning, but nothing is resolved yet; you don't become cured after just one meeting of Alcoholics Anonymous.

4. *Ordinarily, a comma appears between sections of a sentence that are joined by a coordinating conjunction* (and, but, for, nor, yet, or).

Bill Finn was first in line for the manager's job, but he was passed over after his division lost the B.L.T. account.

But when a coordinating conjunction joins sections that themselves have commas, a semicolon helps to distinguish the sentence's major divisions.

Bill Finn, one of our sharpest salespeople, was first in line for the manager's job; but when his division lost the B.L.T. account, he was passed over.

5. *The semicolon separates elements in a series when the elements contain commas.*

The high scorers were Bob Anker, 24 points; Ralph Monti, 20 points; Al Marcus, 14 points; and Richard Grayson, 12 points.

We spent a week in Berne, Switzerland; two weeks in Milan, Italy; and a week in Dusseldorf, Germany.

In these sentences, the semicolon has neatly separated items that commas would have thrown together confusingly.

The colon

The colon is an introducer. Many of us probably used it for the first time when we learned how to write the salutation of a business letter (*Dear Mr. Stewart*:).

1. *The colon is among the most sophisticated and helpful punctuation marks. Those two dots say the equivalent of* for example, as follows, this is what was said, *or* this is what is meant.

I remember how he looked when we left him: downhearted and frail.

Costa Rica's condition can be tersely summed up: worthy, democratic and broke.

Nevertheless, Mr. Boas observed: "These people manage to subsist on an income that permits only the barest necessities."

Clara has a heavy but stimulating schedule in school this term: physics, chemistry, algebra, French and psychology.

Flanagan was dumbfounded: Wherever he went, bad weather seemed to follow.

The mayor's present stance goes something like this: If he can get both the parkway and an equivalent amount of money for mass transit, then he will take both.

Note that the first word after a colon is not capitalized if what follows the colon is not a complete sentence. If a colon is followed by a complete sentence, that sentence may or may not be capitalized: that choice is up to the writer or the editor. (*The Times* prefers it; my editor does not.)

2. *The colon introduces quoted material of more than one sentence or paragraph.*

In the normal flow of journalistic and other prose writing, quotes are introduced by commas, as here:

The governor said, "I will not be a candidate this year."

A colon, however, should be used when a quote will be several straight sentences or paragraphs of direct quotation, as here:

> In outlining his reasons for not seeking re-election, the governor said: [followed by five paragraphs of direction quotation].

The dash

Dashes can be lively, brash or dramatic. Like colons, their major function is to introduce, but they do it in a more spirited and informal way. A colon is a momentary stop; a dash is a momentary skid.

The colon is a rather sedate and formal introducer that implies *This is what I mean* or *For example*. A dash quite often seems to say *Get this!*, *Are you ready for this one?*, or *This may surprise you*. The dash, almost always, suspends you for an instant—then throws the rest of the sentence in your lap.

> For Costa Rica to borrow so heavily was surely unwise—but it was encouraged by Washington and eager commercial banks.

> What bothered him most, though, was that the thief turned out to be the person he had the greatest trust in—his partner.

> Frank's the kind of guy who'll do anything for a friend—and never stop talking about it.

1. *A dash may replace a colon when you're looking for an informal air. Some sentences would be too solemn or stiff with a colon.*

> The trip wouldn't have been as enjoyable without our poodles—Muffy, Quincy and Ralph.

> We covered a lot of territory in two weeks—Spain, Italy, France, Germany and Switzerland.

2. *Dashes in pairs function much the same way as parentheses. But parentheses usually enclose supplementary information or asides, while dashes set off material that is more central to the meaning of the sentence.*

> France is not obsessed—as America now is—with the need to act always in concert with her allies.

> Mrs. Milligan—even though she was my mother she required me to call her Mrs. Milligan—was rather formal for a parent.

Mr. Sartre's points of view were less heeded—although still respected—in the 1970's as he became a maverick political outsider on the extreme left.

In these sentences, the material between the dashes speaks just as loudly as the rest of the sentence, which was precisely the writers' intention. Were parentheses used instead, they would have muted the material within them.

3. *Use dashes instead of commas to avoid confusion when the elements of a sentence would run into each other.*

The boats—catamarans, runabouts, sunfish and dinghys—were thrown high onto the beach by the storm.

If a comma were used after boats, it would at first seem to the reader that boats and catamarans were being talked about. But in this sentence, *boats* is the category under which catamarans, runabouts, etc. fall. Although the reader would quickly catch on, it would have been an unnecessary hitch in the reading. In addition, that comma and its partner after dinghys would have resulted in a five-comma sentence—something to avoid. Dashes gave us a clearer sentence with a clean, crisp look.

These examples further illustrate the clarity and crispness you can get when you replace commas with dashes.

The cafeteria food—the hot plates as well as the sandwiches—was awful.

However, two familiar faces—Walter and Adele Pollack—did not attend the mayor's dinner, explaining a week ago that they would be in Albany.

4. *Dashes also indicate a break in thought.*

Oh, no, I forgot to bring my—oh, wait, here it is.

What I dislike most about Ferdy is—but why should I burden you with my problems?

He began: "Dearest Felicia, I suppose you've been wondering—" but crushed the paper in his hands and threw it away.

Use the dash sparingly. It's a versatile mark, and one so meaningful it comes close to being a word itself. But like the exclamation point, it has a tendency to be overused by its biggest fans. Overuse dilutes its effect, and readers begin to find it an intrusion rather than an aid. Precisely because it is so expressive, it should be reserved for the times when it will do the most good.

The parenthesis

Readers approach a parenthesis expecting to hold the sense and structure of the first part of the sentence in abeyance until they are past the closing parenthesis, at which point they're ready to resume the original flow. For that reason, parenthetical material should be as short and clear as possible, with few or no punctuation marks.

1. *Parentheses enclose material that is not essential to understanding a sentence but in some way enhances it. They may contain an illustration, explanation, definition or additional piece of information. But we have all come to expect that parentheses will not contain information vital to a sentence—only supplementary or incidental material.*

   Ms. Nguyen (pronounced Win) was born in 1975 on the day Saigon fell.

   Fifty varieties of sausage are available (from $2 to $12 per pound).

   Mrs. Henderson left the courtroom saying only "c'est la vie" (that's life) to the waiting reporters.

2. *A parenthetical statement within a sentence, even though it is a complete sentence in itself, does not take an initial capital letter or a final period. That's because every sentence can begin only once, and parentheses and their contents are really part of a sentence-in-progress.*

   Spaghetti and meatballs (my mother's always tasted better on the second day) is still my favorite dish.

3. *The parenthetical statement does take a capital letter and a period, however, if the parenthesis begins an entirely new sentence. When parenthetical material comes at the end of a sentence and is part of it, place the period outside the closing parenthesis.*

   Spaghetti and meatballs is my favorite dish. (My mother's always tasted better the second day.)

   He called to me from his new car (a blue Datsun with a yellow side-stripe).

Use parentheses, like the dash, sparingly. Each parenthesis is, after all, an interruption, and the fewer for the reader, the better.

The Good, the Bad and the Awful
Usage

For more than 300 years, the French Academy, a group of eminent scholars and writers, has kept a sharp watch over the French language. The Academy is there, in the words of its statutes, to "give definite rules to our language, render it pure, and establish a certain usage of words." Members have succeeded in preventing thousands of words and phrases from gaining a foothold in the French language, first by condemning them in speeches and journals, and then by denying them entry in the Academy's dictionary, a work of scholarship equivalent to *The Oxford English Dictionary* and the final word in acceptability. Few French writers have dared to ignore the Academy or challenge its standards.

The historian Will Durant, in *The Age of Louis XIV*, suggests that the reason France never produced a Shakespeare was that the Academy discouraged the kind of inventiveness with words and language that was one of the marks of Shakespeare's genius. Shakespeare either coined or used in writing for the first time about 1,500 words, contributing more words to the English language than any other person. A selection of those words appears under the entry for *intransigent*.

Although no academy like France's has ever existed in England or the United States, John Dryden and Jonathan Swift strongly advocated one, and Queen Anne showed some interest. But she died in 1714 and was succeeded by George I, a German, who showed little interest in English (he never even learned to speak it), and the Academy movement died.

It has fallen to individual English and American writers, teachers and scholars to act as self-appointed guardians of our language. And while the educational establishment in both countries has been generally successful in maintaining standards of grammatical correctness among educated people, those individuals who have attempted to screen words from the language, in the fashion of the French Academy, have knocked their heads against a brick wall.

Take the sixteenth-century English dramatist Thomas Nash, for example. In 1592, he called *ingenuity*, *notoriety* and *negotiation* "pathetic" words. Thomas Wilson, whose *Art of Rhetorique* (1553) was read by Shakespeare, termed *capacity*, *celebrate*, *native*, *fertile*, *relinquish* and *confidence* "affected" and "outlandish." He also condemned *splendidious* (splendid), *fatigate* (to cause fatigue) and *adnichilate* (to annul). But the last three didn't become obsolete because of Wilson. They died from disuse: they lacked serviceability, while *relinquish*, *confidence* and others were useful.

Closer to our time was Ambrose Bierce, who wrote a little book on usage titled *Write It Right* (1909). In it he called *tantamount* an "illegitimate" and "ludicrous" word and deemed *gubernatorial* "needless and bombastic." He also said that because *dilapidated* comes from the Latin word for stone (*lapis*), it "cannot properly be used to describe any but a stone structure"; that *laundry* is "a place where clothing is washed" and cannot mean "clothing sent there to be washed"; and that we must say "asylum for the insane" and not "insane asylum," for an asylum cannot be insane.

Ever hopeful

If this last stricture of Bierce's is hard to take seriously today, consider what is happening with *hopefully*, as in "Hopefully, the rain will soon stop." That use of *hopefully*, which is understood by everyone who hears it or speaks it to mean *it is to be hoped*, has been the object of great scorn by usage experts who say *hopefully* may only mean *in a hopeful manner*, as in "We waited hopefully for the rain to stop." How, they ask, can one say, "Hopefully, the rain will stop"? Rain can't be hopeful. But the use proved too popular, and many of its one-time detractors—among them William Safire, *Times* consultant and language maven, and the late Theodore Bernstein, a *Times* assistant managing editor—eventually changed their minds and accepted it.

Hopefully, *hopefully* will eventually be accepted by all but the most puristic of writers. After all, if it is perfectly good usage to say, "Luckily, the gun misfired" or "Happily, autumn is here," it should be no less acceptable to say, "Hopefully, the rain will soon stop." Whether the syntax of those three sentences is logical is less important than whether their meanings are clearly understood. We cannot condemn a word simply because it is taking on a new function. We must allow our language to breathe—in the name of dilapidated log cabins, gubernatorial elections and dirty laundry.

"For the fact is English is a growing language, and we have to let out the tucks so often," wrote the American humorist Gelett Burgess in 1915. "English isn't like French, which is corseted and gloved and clad and shod and hatted strictly, according to the rules of the Immortals. We have no Academy, thank Heaven, to tell what is real English and what isn't. Our Grand Jury is that ubiquitous person, Usage, and we keep him pretty busy at his job."

While many controversial issues regarding usage have resulted from the persistence of fallacies, differences in taste, idiosyncrasies and resistance to the new, most rules and distinctions of usage and style are there for good reason: to maintain clarity, correctness and readability in writing and speaking, and to achieve a uniform understanding among those who speak and write the language. Here are some of those rules and distinctions of usage and style.

accept/except

Accept is always a verb meaning to take or receive: *Cyril would not accept the blame. Jill was accepted into Yale.* As a verb, *except* is uncommon, and means to omit or exclude: *Please except me from your plans; I'm busy that day. Cordelia was excepted from her father's will. Except's* common use is as a preposition meaning but: *No insect except the praying mantis can swivel its head.*

affect/effect

Affect is always a verb (except for one noun use in psychology) and usually means to influence: *Tornadoes always affect my sinuses. Affect* also means to pretend: *Mel affected a limp in order to get our sympathy. Effect* is usually a noun meaning result: *Knaggs's "Not guilty" plea had no effect on the jury. One effect of the transit strike was an increase in foot traffic. Effect* is sometimes a verb meaning to bring about: *The mediator effected a quick settlement of the strike.* As a plural noun, *effects* can mean property: *Charlie's personal effects were stored in the prison safe.*

afterward/afterwards

In the United States, *afterward* is preferred; in Great Britain, *afterwards. Hey, buddy, let's meet at Times Square afterward. I say, old chap, shall we meet at Grosvenor Square afterwards?*

aggravate

In its formal and strict sense, *aggravate* means to intensify or make worse: *Hot foods aggravate the pain of an abscessed tooth. Racial tensions were aggravated by the sit-ins.* When it is used to mean annoy or irritate, *aggravate* is considered informal or colloquial: *Get out of this kitchen and stop aggravating me, you rotten kid!* Some usage experts would banish that use of *aggravate* altogether. Most of them probably don't have children.

a lot/allot

A lot is a phrase that means many, and it is incorrect to write it as one word (alot): *Buzzy ate a lot of oysters. A lot of people wondered who she was. Allot* means to distribute in shares: *Buzzy allotted ten oysters to each guest. We can allot only ten gallons of gas to each car.*

all right/alright

There is absolutely only one correct way to say *all right*, and that's it. *Alright* is always all wrong.

already/all ready

Already is an adverb and means earlier or previously: *By the time the bus arrived I was already soaked through. Marc has already decided to retire.* *All ready* is an adjective meaning completely ready: *Plotkin's crew was all ready by 3 P.M.*

although/though

Although and *though* may be used interchangeably. *Though*, however, is more commonly used in the middle of a sentence and is preferred at the end of one: *Although it was still drizzling, the ball game began. It was an exciting, though wet, game. We stayed the full nine innings, though.*

altogether/all together

Altogether means entirely, on the whole, or in all: *It's altogether too hot in here. That was an altogether rotten remark, my dear.* *All together* means everyone together, in a group, or all at once: *All together, there were ten of us. Roy gathered his chisels all together and brought them in from the rain.*

alumna/alumnus alumnae/alumni

An *alumna* is a woman graduate: *Rachel is an Emory alumna.* An *alumnus* is a male graduate: *Bob is a Brooklyn College alumnus.* *Alumnae* are women graduates: *Lisa and Jill are Yale alumnae.* *Alumni* are male, or mixed, graduates: *Ruth and Chuck Madison are alumni. The alumni committee meets each winter.*

amiable/amicable

Amiable means friendly, pleasant or good-natured, and refers to people's dispositions: *Rebecca's cheerfulness makes her an amiable classmate.* *Amicable* means friendly in feeling, showing good will or peaceable, and is used in connection with human relationships: *What had begun as a tension-filled meeting ended amicably.*

among/between

In general, *between* applies to two things, and *among* to more than two. *Stashu skied between the fir trees. Stella and Martha divided the chocolate malt between them. Among the eight of us, Sparky had the largest nose. Granofsky swam gingerly among the jellyfish. Between* also refers to three or more things when each is considered in relation to the others as individuals: *Rivalry is great between the Ivy League football teams. José had to choose between Tel Aviv, Pago Pago and Tijuana as the location of his new novel.*

and/but

There's no reason why a sentence cannot begin with *and* as long as it is a complete thought or an effective piece of writing. In the first chapter of Genesis, thirty-three out of thirty-five sentences begin with *and*. Our teachers told us never to begin a sentence with *and* or *but* because they wanted us to avoid writing incomplete thoughts. But the rule should never have been an absolute one. Sentences beginning with *and* or *but* are found in virtually every book; newspapers print dozens of sentences every day beginning with the words, usually to break up long sentences for easier comprehension. *Most shrimp are frozen and then sold thawed. But the Maine shrimp are so fresh they are often sold with their heads on. And now is the time to try them, seafood dealers say.*

angry at/angry with/mad

Use *angry at* with things, and *angry with* with people: *Germaine was angry at having missed the train. Gert was angry with Gladys for ruining the fudge. Mad* is acceptable as an informal or colloquial alternative to angry, but inappropriate in formal use: *Boy, was I mad when the waiter dropped the quiche in my lap. Mad* is properly used when it means insane or frenzied: *You think me mad, don't you, simply because I collect old light bulbs.*

because

Many people are under the impression that one must never begin a sentence with *because*, yet a glance at any book or newspaper will reveal how mistaken that notion is. True, *because* is often the first word of a sentence fragment that belongs with the preceding or following sentence: *Because it was hot. Because it wouldn't do any good.* Those, of course, are sentence fragments and incomplete thoughts. But this isn't: *Because it was raining, Willie parked his cycle under an overpass.* We have simply begun the sentence with the dependent clause. The test is to switch the clauses around—in this case, beginning the sentence with *Willie.* If it works that way, it is all right to begin it with *because.*

bring/take

Bring denotes movement toward the speaker or writer: *Please bring me back an order of fried wonton. Take* denotes movement away from the speaker or writer, or any other movement that is not toward him or her: *Let's take this extra wonton over to Febo's place. San Francisco can be quite cold in August, so take warm clothes.*

canvas/canvass

Canvas is a kind of cloth; to *canvass* means to solicit votes, opinions or sales from door to door, or person to person, without a prior appointment. *Molly canvassed the neighborhood selling magazine subscriptions.*

capital/capitol

A *capitol* is always a building. *Capital* is used in every other sense.

carat/karat/caret

Gemstones are weighed by *carats: We priced a 2-carat diamond at Ludlow's.* The fineness of gold is measured in *karats: Pure gold is 24 karats.* A *caret* is an editing symbol (^) that indicates something missing such as a letter or word:

for

It's time a change.

^

careen/career

Careen means to lean sideways, as a sailing ship before a high wind, or to lurch from side to side while moving rapidly. *Waves slapped the deck of the careening yacht as it turned in the wind.* To *career* means to move at high speed, to rush madly. *Pedestrians scattered as the ambulance careered through the intersection.*

climactic/climatic

Climactic refers to a climax: *Four major characters die in* Hamlet's *climactic scene*. *Climatic* refers to climate: *Climatic conditions make the Napa Valley ideal for grape growing.*

complement/compliment

To *complement* is to complete or make perfect: *Sara's pearl necklace complemented her black gown. Adele's photos complemented Walter's writing, and the result was a beautiful book.* To *compliment* is to praise: *The judges complimented Inez on her apricot marmalade.* The words retain the same sense when used as nouns: *Sara's pearl necklace is a complement to her gown. Inez appreciated the judges' compliments.* A *complement* is also a group or set: *The president sent a complement of Americans to the prime minister's funeral.*

could of/should of/would of

All these are incorrect constructions when the writer means *could have*, etc., as in "*I could have danced all night.*" The error springs from the contraction *could've* sounding as though it should be written *could of.* But there's simply no such grammatical construction. *Of* is not a verb; *have* is.

delusion/illusion

Delusions are more serious than *illusions*. A *delusion* is a false belief that is wholly accepted as true and guides one's actions. Under *delusions*, people spend years seeking the fountain of youth, trying to turn lead into gold, or expecting gasoline prices to return to thirty-nine cents a gallon. Such *delusions* obviously contradict rational thinking. *Illusions* are basically false impressions that tend to dissipate or shatter with experience. Commonly shattered illusions are the belief that one's parents are perfect, that crime never pays and that "I'm not the marrying type."

disinterested/uninterested

Disinterested and *uninterested* may look like two of a kind, but they have quite different meanings. *Disinterested* means objective, unbiased, impartial, fair and unprejudiced. It's the kind of attitude expected of a judge and the members of a jury, a labor arbitrator, a referee or an umpire, a news reporter or a parent when each child claims the other one started something. *Uninterested* means bored, uncaring, indifferent, apathetic. A disinterested judge may take notes; an uninterested student may not.

elicit/illicit

To *elicit* is to call forth or invite: *The mayor's speech elicited both boos and cheers. The lawyer elicited conflicting testimony from the witnesses. Illicit* means unlawful, improper or prohibited: *The judge's illicit involvement in the casino operation made the morning headlines. Illicitly sold cigarettes cost the state millions in taxes.*

emigrate/immigrate

To *emigrate* is to leave one country to settle in another. To *immigrate* is to enter a new country after leaving another: *Boris Vilensky emigrated from Russia in 1998. Boris Vilensky immigrated to the United States in 1998.* To Mr. Vilensky's friends in Moscow, he is an emigrant. To his friends in the United States, he is an immigrant.

empathy/sympathy

Empathy is feeling someone else's situation deeply because you have undergone similar experiences or because you are putting yourself in that person's place. *Sympathy* is pity or compassion for another's troubles, without necessarily sharing deeply in their feelings.

ensure/insure

Both words mean to make certain or to guarantee, but only *insure* may be used to mean to guarantee payment for loss or damage: *This cushioned package will ensure safe delivery of the china, but I'll insure it for $100 anyway.*

etc.

Etc. is often a cover-up. The writer can't think of anything else, and *etc.* is added to give the opposite impression: *New York City's major problems are street crime, dirty subways, high rents, etc.* That's not fair to readers. How are we to know what the writer would have added? Use *etc.* only to avoid an unnecessarily long and obvious list: *Our camping gear was the usual: tents, sleeping bags, cooking utensils, etc.* This use of *etc.* is more acceptable because the unlisted items can, indeed, be assumed by most readers. (*Etc.* appears in several of this book's definitions to indicate that the few words preceding it are part of a well-understood category.) But for clear, precise writing, avoid *etc.* altogether. If you want to indicate that a list is partial, use constructions such as: *He had many pets, among them a dog, a cat, gerbils and turtles.*

explicit/implicit

Explicit means clearly stated, with nothing implied; distinctly expressed; definite: *On Ralph's desk was an explicit memo from the boss: "Clean off your desk. You're fired."* *Implicit* means understood without being plainly stated: *Implicit in my mother's memo to me ("Your room is filthy") was the message that I'd better clean it up, or else. Implicit* also means without reservation, absolute: *I have implicit faith in my surgeon's skill.*

farther and further

Farther should be used only for physical distance, *further* in the sense of additional or continued. *Farther* has *far* in it, and that helps remind one of physical distance. *We couldn't drive any farther that night. Further changes are out of the question at this time.*

fewer/less

Use *fewer* when talking about countable things: people, animals, trees, houses, wishes, phone calls. Use *less* in reference to quantity or bulk: noise, hostility, sand, oxygen, money. Note: *less* water, but *fewer* gallons of water; *less* time, but *fewer* hours; *less* sugar, but *fewer* lumps of sugar; *less* anger, but *fewer* angry words. Use *less* when the number is only one: *Today I received one less card than yesterday.* Use *less* for quantities of time, distance, weight and money: *less than five minutes ago; less than five miles to go; three less ounces in this box; less than $40 a day; $40 less than I earned last week.* Use *number* where you would use *fewer*, use *amount* where you would use *less* (*the number of hours; the amount of time*).

flaunt/flout

To *flaunt* is to show off proudly, defiantly or gleefully; to display in a defiant way: *The football team flaunted their victory by wearing their uniforms in school the next day. Flaunting his passes at the security staff, Joe walked backstage after the concert to meet the stars.* To *flout* is to show contempt for, scornfully disregard, or ignore: *Gruber flouted every surf-fishing rule and still caught more fish than anyone else. Thousands of New Yorkers are flouting the traffic laws by going through red lights, double parking and ignoring stop signs.*

flutist/flautist

Americans write and say *flutist*; the English write and say *flautist*. *Flutist* has been a word since 1603, *flautist* since 1860.

forbidding/foreboding

Forbidding, an adjective, means looking dangerous, threatening or disagreeable: *Children kept far away from the forbidding shack. Income-tax forms have always looked too forbidding for me to try to compute my own. Foreboding* (note the *fore*, meaning *ahead*), a noun, means a portent or presentiment, especially of something bad or harmful: *With a sense of foreboding, Norman opened his report card. An unexplainable foreboding kept Anna from boarding the plane that night.*

foreword/forward

A *foreword* is part of the introductory material in a book, as distinguished from *forward*, meaning in front or ahead.

forgo/forego

Forgo (sometimes spelled *forego*) means to do without, give up: *I think I'll forgo dessert tonight. Mike and Saulo spoke civilly to one another, forgoing their usual gibes. Forego*, meaning to go before, precede, is rarely used and archaic: *The soup course will forego the fish.* But its gerund *foregoing*, meaning just past, previously said or written, is common: *The foregoing was a paid political announcement.* Thus, it's *forgo* and *forgoing* when you mean doing without, and *foregoing* when you mean previous.

graduate from

You can *graduate from high school* or *be graduated from high school*, but you can't *graduate high school*. *To graduate* means to raise a step. Therefore, you can't graduate high school; it has to graduate *you*. The *from* is always needed, unless the school also is left out, as here: *We graduated in 1981. We were graduated in 1981.*

hanged/hung

People are *hanged*, pictures are *hung*.

healthful/healthy

Healthful means helping to produce good health: *You're not eating enough healthful foods like fruits and vegetables. Healthy* means in good health: *Mike has been feeling healthy since his surgery.*

imply/infer

To *imply* is to state indirectly; to hint or suggest: *By checking my figures, are you implying that I can't add? Addie implied that she wanted to be invited by saying she had nothing planned for the weekend.* To *infer* is to draw a conclusion from facts or evidence: *From her smile, I inferred that she was pleased with me. Her rumpled clothing led me to infer she had slept on the couch all night.*

in/into

In indicates location or motion inside something: *Gabriel swam in the pool. There's something in my eye. There's a mouse in the kitchen. Into* indicates movement from one place to a point within another place: *Gabriel dived into the pool. I got into bed, but lay awake for hours.*

its/it's

Use *it's* only as the contraction for *it is: It's hot.* Use *its* (no apostrophe) for everything else. Many people habitually place an apostrophe in the possessive pronoun *its*, but it has no more business being there than it does in *hers, his* or *theirs*, which are also possessives.

jibe/gibe/jive

A confusing trio. *Jibe*, a colloquial or informal word, means to be in harmony, agreement or accord. *His court testimony did not jibe with the statements he made to a police officer just after the collision.* A *gibe* is a jeer, a taunt or a teasing remark. *After knocking the ball into the opposing team's basket, the player endured the gibes of his teammates.* Although *jibe* and *gibe* are often used interchangeably, *jibe* should be used when you mean "agreement," and *gibe* when you mean "taunt." *Jive* is sometimes used for *jibe*, as in *Their testimony didn't jive*, but that usage is incorrect. *Jive* is an outdated word for jazz or swing music, and slang for deceptive, nonsensical or glib talk. *Man, are you jiving me, or what?*

lie/lay

Lie is used when a person or thing sets *itself* down. *Lay* is used when a person or thing sets *something else down*. *I will lie down. I will lay the book down.* *Lie* has no object. *Lay* does—book. Some more examples: *If you're tired, lie down. If you're tired, lay down the cartons.* For the past tense of *lay*, always use *laid*: *Jim laid down the cartons. Jim has laid down the cartons.* For the past tense of *lie* you have two choices. The first—and this is the most confusing part of the whole lie/lay mixup—is *lay*: *Yesterday, I lay in bed all day. The lion lay in wait for the zebra.* The second choice is *lain*, which is used with *have, has* and *had*: *I have lain around for hours. The house had lain in ruins for a century.* *Lying* is a form of *lie*: *I am lying down. We were lying in the sun.* *Laying* is a form of *lay*: *Stop laying your tools on the furniture. I'm laying the tile tonight.*

loan/lend

Although *loan* used as a verb (*I loaned him my pen*) is acceptable to many writers and language authorities, others prefer to use only *lend* as a verb, and reserve *loan* for noun use (*a $500 loan*). Others use *loan* as a verb only in financial contexts: *The bank loaned Apex $3 million.* Whatever your choice, keep the tenses parallel: the past tense of *loan* is *loaned*; the past tense of *lend* is *lent*.

loud/loudly

Although *loudly* is the true adverb of the pair, *loud* (which is ordinarily an adjective) is optional after such verbs as laugh, sing, scream, say, talk, roar and sneeze. (See also *slow/slowly*.)

masterly/masterful

Masterly means skillful or expert. It connotes talent, being a master at something. *Masterful* (not as kind-sounding a word) means domineering, imperious, overpowering. It connotes force, one person's will over another's. Arturo Toscanini was a *masterly* conductor, but he often treated his musicians in a *masterful* way. A chef may be *masterful* toward his kitchen crew but turn out *masterly* creations. And the San Quentin warden may run his prison with a *masterful* hand, while in Cell Block D someone is picking his cell lock with a *masterly* hand.

may/can

May and *can* are commonly used interchangeably for permission, but *may* is still considered the correct choice in formal speaking or writing: *May I leave the room? May I have a cup of tea, please? You may call me tomorrow if you wish. Can* should be limited to statements of power or ability: *Can I use the chair, or is it still broken? Can I see you a minute, or are you on your way out? You can use the stairs now; the paint is dry.*

oral/verbal

Verbal applies to all language, written and spoken, so it is somewhat ambiguous to refer to a nonwritten contract as *verbal*, when you should be talking about an *oral* contract: *Our oral agreement was sealed with a hand-shake. Verbal,* however, is used in relation to spoken language in these instances: *First they fought verbally* (the idea being that they fought with words), *then they took swings at each other. Emma is quite verbal* (proficient with words) *for a two-year-old.*

practicable/practical

Practicable means capable of being done or put into practice; feasible; possible. *Practical* means capable of being done usefully or in a worthwhile fashion. It might be *practicable* (possible) to construct a mile-high building, but would such a skyscraper be *practical* (useful or worth building)?

preposition at the end

In 1672, the English poet John Dryden, who knew Latin, got the notion that since a Latin sentence cannot end with a preposition, neither should an English one. But there is no foundation in English grammar for the rule that says one shouldn't end a sentence with a preposition, and language experts no longer subscribe to it.

presently/at present

Presently means soon or before long: *The train will arrive presently. Presently, it began to rain. At present* means now or at this time: *At present, no tickets are available. He's living alone at present.*

preventative/preventive

Preventative and *preventive* both mean the same thing. *Preventive* is preferred.

regardless/irregardless

Always use *regardless*. *Irregardless* is a meaningless word and never correct.

slow/slowly

Slow usually serves as an adjective (a slow train), but it may also be used as an adverb in place of *slowly* (go slow). Used as an adverb, *slowly* will never sound wrong, although *slow* may: *I'm catching on slow*. Your best guide, then, in using *slow* in place of *slowly* is your own sense of what sounds right. (See also *loud/loudly*).

split infinitives

The rule against splitting an infinitive is based on a fallacy. There is nothing grammatically wrong with doing it. Virtually no professional writer thinks it's wrong any longer to split an infinitive, but most people avoid doing it because they are aware that those who don't know that a split infinitive is not wrong will be critical, and who needs the aggravation? Editors at *The Times*, for example, tell reporters that while there is nothing wrong with the split infinitive, it should be avoided because "we get letters." You may wish to compromise by splitting only when you feel that if you don't, the sentence will not read as smoothly or as clearly. So go ahead, split that infinitive proudly. (But be aware that by doing so, you may be criticized by people who don't know any better.)

stationary/stationery

Stationary means standing still. *Stationery* is writing paper. One way to remember which one has the *ery* is to remember that a person who sells *stationery* is a stationer. Another way is to associate the *e* in *stationery* with envelope.

teeter/totter

Although *teeter* and *totter* both refer to unsteady movement resulting from insecure balance, *totter* implies an impending fall that will be no farther than the base on which something stands (*he tottered homeward*), while *teeter* implies an impending fall from a height to a lower position than one on which the object is standing. (*The car teetered on the edge of the cliff.*)

used to/use to

Although it sounds as though we're saying "I *use* to hate broccoli," we're really saying, "I *used* to hate broccoli." It's simple: We're speaking in the past tense, so we need the *d* after *use*. Because the "d" gets lost in the "t" in "to," many people drop it in their writing. Don't do it.

Bibliography

Agnes, Michael, ed. *Webster's New World College Dictionary.* 4th edition. New York: Macmillan, 1999.

Asimov, Isaac. *Words of Science.* New York: New American Library, 1969.

Ayto, John. *Dictionary of Word Origins.* New York: Arcade Publishing, 1990.

———. *20th Century Words.* New York: Oxford University Press, 1999.

Barnhart, Clarence L., Sol Steinmetz, and Robert K. Barnhart. *The Barnhart Dictionary of New English Since 1963.* New York: Barnhart/Harper & Row, 1973.

———. *The Second Barnhart Dictionary of New English.* New York: Barnhart/Harper & Row, 1980.

Bartlett, John. *Familiar Quotations.* Boston: Little, Brown and Company, 1955.

Beckson, Karl, and Arthur Ganz. *A Reader's Guide to Literary Terms.* New York: Noon Day Press, 1962.

Bernstein, Theodore M. *The Careful Writer.* New York: Atheneum, 1966.

———. *Do's, Don'ts & Maybes of English Usage.* New York: Times Books, 1977.

Bierce, Ambrose. *The Devil's Dictionary.* N.p.: Albert & Charles Boni, 1935.

———. *Write It Right.* New York: Charles L. Bowman & Co., 1934.

Bliss, A.J. *A Dictionary of Foreign Words and Phrases.* New York: E.P. Dutton & Co., Inc., 1966.

Bremner, John B. *Words on Words.* New York: Columbia University Press, 1980.

Brewer, Ebenezer Cobham. *Brewer's Dictionary of Phrase and Fable.* New York: Harper & Row, 1970.

Bullock, Alan, and Oliver Stallybrass. *The Harper Dictionary of Modern Thought.* New York: Harper & Row, 1977.

Burgess, Gelett. *Burgess Unabridged.* Hamden, Conn.: The Shoe String Press, 1986.

Campbell, Oscar James, ed. *The Reader's Encyclopedia of Shakespeare.* New York: Thomas Y. Crowell Co., 1966.

Cerf, Christopher, and Victor Navasky. *The Experts Speak.* New York: Pantheon Books, 1984.

Ciardi, John. *A Browser's Dictionary.* New York: Harper & Row, 1980.

———. *Good Words To You.* New York: Harper & Row, 1987.

Clarke, Joseph F. *Pseudonyms: The Names Behind the Name.* Nashville: Thomas Nelson, Inc., 1977.

Copperud, Roy H. *American Usage and Style.* New York: Van Nostrand Reinhold Co., 1980.

Crowell, Thomas Lee Jr. *NBC Handbook of Pronunciation.* New York: Thomas Y. Crowell, 1964.

Cuddon, J.A. *A Dictionary of Literary Terms.* London: Penguin Books, 1982.

Cummings, Park., ed. *The Dictionary of Sports.* New York: A.S. Barnes and Co., 1949.

Davies, Christopher. *Divided by a Common Language.* Sarasota, Fla.: Mayflower Press, 1997.

Dickson, Paul. *The Dickson Baseball Dictionary.* New York: Facts On File, 1989.

———. *Slang.* New York: Pocket Books, 1998.

Dillard, J.L. *American Talk.* New York: Random House, 1976.

———. *Black English.* New York: Vintage, 1972.

Elliot, Stephen P., Martha Goldstein, and Michael Upshall, eds., *Webster's New World Encyclopedia.* New York: Prentice Hall, 1992.

Finegan, Edward. *Attitudes Toward English Usage.* New York: Teachers College Press, 1980.

Flexner, Stuart Berg. *I Hear America Talking.* New York: Touchstone, 1979.

———. *The Random House Dictionary of the English Language.* New York: Random House, 1987.

Flexner, Stuart Berg, and Anne H. Soukhanov. *Speaking Freely.* New York: Oxford University Press, 1997.

Follett, Wilson. *Modern American Usage.* New York: Avenel Books, 1980.

Fowler, H.W. *A Dictionary of Modern Usage.* New York: Oxford University Press, 1950.

Funk, Charles Earle. *2107 Curious Word Origins, Sayings & Expressions.* New York: Galahad Books, 1993.

Gilman, E. Ward, ed. *Merriam-Webster Dictionary of English Usage.* Springfield, Mass.: Merriam-Webster, 1989.

Glazier, Stephen. *Random House Word Menu.* New York: Random House, 1997.

Gove, Philip Babcock, ed. *Webster's Third New International Dictionary.* Springfield, Mass.: G. & C. Merriam Co., 1976.

Grambs, David. *The Random House Dictionary for Writers and Readers*. New York: Random House, 1990.

Hastings, James, ed. *Dictionary of the Bible*. New York: Charles Scribner's Sons. 1963.

Hayakawa, S.I. *Use the Right Word*. The Reader's Digest Association, Inc., 1968.

Hendrickson, Robert. *The Dictionary of Eponyms*. New York: Stein and Day, 1972.

———. *The Literary Life and Other Curiosities*. New York: Viking, 1981.

Hopkin, Daniel J., ed. *Merriam-Webster's Geographical Dictionary*. Springfield, Mass.: Merriam-Webster, Inc.,1995.

Jones, Barry, and M.V. Dixon. *The Rutledge Dictionary of People*. New York: Rutledge Press, 1981.

Knowles, Elizabeth, ed. *The Oxford Dictionary of New Words*. New York: Oxford University Press, 1998.

Kohl, Herbert. *From Archetype to Zeitgeist*. Boston: Little, Brown and Company, 1992.

Kolodin, Irving. *The Musical Life*. New York: Alfred A. Knopf, 1958.

Labensky, Steven, Gaye G. Ingram, and Sarah R. Labensky. *Webster's New World Dictionary of Culinary Arts*. Upper Saddle River, N.J.: Prentice Hall, 1997.

Major, Clarence. *Dictionary of Afro-American Slang*. New York: International Publishers, 1970.

Matthews, Mitford M. *Americanisms*. Chicago: The University of Chicago Press, 1966.

McHenry, Robert, ed. *Merriam-Webster's Biographical Dictionary*. Springfield, Mass.: Merriam-Webster, Inc., 1995.

Mencken, H.L. *The American Language*. New York: Alfred A. Knopf, 1962.

———. *The American Language, Supplements I and II*. New York: Alfred A. Knopf, 1962.

Metcalf, Allan A., and David K. Barnhart. *America in So Many Words*. Boston: Houghton Mifflin, 1997.

Mish, Frederick C., ed. *The Merriam-Webster Book of Word Histories*. New York: Pocket Books, 1976.

———. *Webster's Ninth New Collegiate Dictionary*. Springfield, Mass.: Merriam-Webster, Inc., 1985.

Morris, William. *The American Heritage Dictionary*. Boston: Houghton Mifflin, 1978.

Nash, Ogden. *I Wouldn't Have Missed It*. Boston: Little, Brown and Co., 1972.

The New York Public Library Desk Reference. New York: Macmillan, 1998.

Nicholson, Margaret. *American-English Usage.* New York: Oxford University Press, 1957.

The Oxford English Dictionary. Oxford: Oxford University Press, 1971.

Partridge, Eric. *A Dictionary of Clichés.* London: Routledge & Kegan Paul, 1985.

———. *A Dictionary of Slang and Unconventional Usage.* New York: Macmillan, 1970.

Pei, Mario. *Glossary of Linguistic Terminology.* New York: Doubleday Anchor, 1966.

Reader's Digest. *Family Word Finder.* New York: The Reader's Digest Association, Inc., 1975.

———. *Success with Words.* New York: The Reader's Digest Association, Inc., 1983.

Rodale, J.I. *The Synonym Finder.* Emmaus, Pa.: Rodale Books, Inc., 1961.

Rohman, Chris. *A World of Ideas.* New York: Ballantine Books, 1999.

Rosten, Leo. *The Joys of Yiddish.* New York: McGraw-Hill Book Co., 1968.

———. *The Joys of Yinglish.* New York: McGraw-Hill Publishing Co., 1989.

Safire, William. *On Language.* New York: Times Books, 1980.

———. *Safire's Political Dictionary.* New York: Ballantine Books, 1980.

Scholes, Percy A. *The Concise Oxford Dictionary of Music.* London: Oxford University Press, 1964.

Serjeantson, Mary S. *A History of Foreign Words in English.* London: Routledge & Kegan Paul, 1935.

Shakespeare, William. *The Complete Works of William Shakespeare.* Edited by William Aldis Wright. New York: Garden City Books, 1936.

Shepard, Richard F. *The Paper's Papers.* New York: Times Books, 1996.

Siegel, Allan M., and William G. Connolly. *The New York Times Manual of Style and Usage.* New York: Times Books, 1999.

6,000 Words: A Supplement to Webster's Third New International Dictionary. Springfield, Mass.: G&C Merriam Co., 1976.

Tocqueville, Alexis de. *Democracy in America.* Edited by J.P. Mayer. New York: Doubleday & Company, 1969.

Toussaint-Samat, Maguelonne. *A History of Food.* Malden, Mass.: Blackwell, 1992.

Tulloch, Sara. *The Oxford Dictionary of New Words.* Oxford: Oxford University Press, 1991.

12,000 Words: A Supplement to Webster's Third New International Dictionary. Springfield, Mass.: Merriam-Webster, Inc., 1986.

Uvarov, E.B., D.R. Chapman, and Alan Isaacs. *The Penguin Dictionary of Science*. London: Penguin Books, 1979.

Wentworth, Harold, and Stuart Berg Flexner. *Dictionary of American Slang*. New York: Thomas Y. Crowell, 1975.

Zijderveld, Anton C. *On Clichés*. London: Routledge & Kegan Paul, 1979.

Sources

Day after day, I read with wonder the words and sentences of *New York Times* writers. Journalism may be history in a hurry, but the writing in *The Times* never seems to have been hurriedly written. And yet we know that much of it is written on deadline, some of it under stressful and even dangerous conditions. A combination of craft and art, *Times* writing is not just informative but enjoyable to read, and often eloquent and deeply touching. Credit goes not only to the writers but to the copy editors, for their skill in insuring the economy, clarity and grace that are a mark of *New York Times* style.

Here now are the names of the *Times* writers whose work is presented in this book. Some of the passages are from articles that had no bylines. While I do not know who their authors were, I suspect—and hope—that many of their names appear below anyway, because most of these articles were written when *The Times* had a one-byline-per-day policy (which no longer exists). Several passages in the book are from editorials, written by members of *The Times* editorial board, but of course unsigned. Because many editorial board members have written bylined articles outside the editorials column—before, during or after their tenure on the board—their names will appear here for that reason.

To those unnamed writers whose contributions to this book come only from their unsigned work, my special thanks.

Jill Abramson
Andrea Adelson
Ron Alexander
Lawrence K. Altman
Neil Amdur
Dave Anderson
Jack Anderson
Susan Heller Anderson
Natalie Angier
R.W. Apple Jr.
Harvey Araton
Karen W. Arenson
Eric Asimov
Charles Austin
B. Drummond Ayres Jr.
Russell Baker
Josh Barbanel

Isadore Barmash
James Barron
Ann Barry
Barry Bearak
Elizabeth Becker
Pam Belluck
Leslie Bennetts
Joseph Berger
Ira Berkow
Robert Berkvist
Richard Bernstein
David Bird
Jayson Blair
Mary Kay Blakely
Eleanor Blau
Ralph Blumenthal
Raymond Bonner

William Borders
Sarah Boxer
Keith Bradsher
Rick Bragg
Ben Brantley
Kenneth A. Briggs
William J. Broad
Fred Brock
John M. Broder
Jane E. Brody
Ethan Bronner
James Brooke
Clifton Brown
Ken Brown
Malcolm W. Browne
Anatole Broyard
Nadine Brozan
Nelson Bryant
Tom Buckley
John F. Burns
Marian Burros
Fox Butterfield
Vincent Canby
Dana Canedy
Deirdre Carmody
Maurice Carroll
Bill Carter
Chris Chase
Chass Murray
Lydia Chavez
Craig Claiborne
James F. Clarity
Dudley Clendinen
Francis X. Clines
Adam Clymer
Roger Cohen
Glenn Collins
Michael Cooper
John Corry
Holland Cotter
Edward Cowan
Alan Cowell

John M. Crewdson
Steven Crist
Ann Crittenden
Barbara Crossette
Judith Cummings
Jack Curry
Suzanne Daley
Lee A. Daniels
James Dao
John Darnton
Peter G. Davis
Anthony DePalma
Sam Dillon
E.J. Dionne Jr.
Philip H. Dougherty
Maureen Dowd
John Duka
Georgia Dullea
David W. Dunlap
Jennifer Dunning
Joseph Durso
Erik Eckholm
Richard Eder
Thomas W. Ennis
Steven Erlanger
Gerald Eskenazi
Harold Faber
Florence Fabricant
Geraldine Fabrikant
Seth Faison
M.A. Farber
Stephen Farber
William E. Farrell
Joan Lee Faust
Barnaby J. Feder
James Feron
Fred Ferretti
Robin Finn
Ian Fisher
Lisa Foderaro
Henry Fountain
Elizabeth M. Fowler

Pierre Franey
Ben A. Franklin
Lucinda Franks
Douglas Frantz
C. Gerald Fraser
Alix M. Freedman
Samuel G. Freedman
Howard W. French
Milt Freudenheim
Jonathan Friendly
Dorothy J. Gaiter
Barbara Gamarekian
Edward A. Gargan
Anita Gates
William E. Geist
Henry Giniger
Grace Glueck
Carey Goldberg
Paul Goldberger
Sam Goldpaper
Erica Goode
George Goodman Jr.
Walter Goodman
Michael Goodwin
Michael R. Gordon
Denise Grady
Laurel Graeber
Jerry Gray
Linda Greenhouse
Steven Greenhouse
Paul Grimes
William Grimes
Jane Gross
Pranay B. Gupte
Mel Gussow
Bernard Gwertzman
Clyde Haberman
Katie Hafner
Richard Haitch
Robert Hanley
Aljean Harmetz
Fred M Hechinger

Chris Hedges
Donal Henahan
Melinda Henneberger
Diane Henry
Bob Herbert
Raymond Hernandez
Hubert B. Herring
David M. Herszenhorn
Amanda Hesser
Gladwyn Hill
Michael deCourcey Hinds
Moira Hodgson
Eva Hoffman
Paul Hofmann
Warren Hoge
Stephen Holden
Bernard Holland
Pamela G. Hollie
John Holusha
William H. Honan
Marvine Howe
Allen Hughes
Ada Louise Huxtable
Molly Ivins
Andrew Jacobs
Caryn James
Michael Janofsky
Donald Janson
Anne Jarrell
Gregory Jaynes
Dirk Johnson
Kirk Johnson
Laurie Johnston
Nadine Joseph
Michiko Kakutani
Henry Kamm
Jonathan Kandell
Michael Katz
Leslie Kaufman
Michael T. Kaufman
Shawn G. Kennedy
Walter Kerr

John Kifner
Peter Kihss
Peter T. Kilborn
Seth S. King
Wayne King
N.R. Kleinfield
Judy Klemesrud
Verlyn Klinkenborg
Gina Kolata
Allan Kozinn
Hilton Kramer
Albin Krebs
Nicholas D. Kristof
Carl H. Lavin
Carol Lawson
Christopher Lehmann-Haupt
Joseph Lelyveld
John Leonard
Anthony Lewis
Flora Lewis
Paul Lewis
Robert Lindsey
Frank Litsky
Steve Lohr
Jere Longman
Elaine Louie
Arnold H. Lubasch
Sarah Lyall
Rick Lyman
Neil MacFarquhar
Gene I. Maeroff
Andrew H. Malcolm
David Margolick
James M. Markham
John Markoff
Peter Marks
Douglas Martin
Janet Maslin
Edwin McDowell
Robert D. McFadden
Jesse McKinley
Donald G. Jr. McNeil

Karl E. Meyer
Drew Middleton
Bryan Miller
Judith Miller
Herbert Mitgang
Paul L. Montgomery
Wendy Moonan
Gretchen Morgansen
Bernadine Morris
Alfonzo A. Narvaez
Enid Nemy
Gustav Niebuhr
Evelyn Nieves
Floyd Norris
Bernard D. Nossiter
John J. O'Connor
Molly O'Neill
James R. Oestreich
Buster Olney
Norimitsu Onishi
Eric Pace
Robert Palmer
John Pareles
Peter Passell
Robert Pear
Jane Perlez
Iver Peterson
Ann Powers
Julia Preston
Frank J. Prial
Todd S. Purum
Anna Quindlen
Howell Raines
Deborah Rankin
Nick Ravo
Wendell Rawls Jr.
Vivien Raynor
Ruth Reichl
Rita Reif
Robert Reinhold
Andrew C. Revkin
William C. Rhoden

Frank Rich
Lynda Richardson
Alan Riding
Sara Rimer
Teresa Riordan
Terry Robards
William Robbins
Selena Roberts
Nan Robertson
Ruth Robinson
John Rockwell
Thomas Rogers
David Rohde
Larry Rohter
Lynn Rosellini
David E. Rosenbaum
Elisabeth Rosenthal
Jack Rosenthal
A.M. Rosenthal
Sheila Rule
John Russell
Susan Sachs
Kevin Sack
William Safire
Sandra Salmans
Agis Salpukis
Richard Sandomir
Wolfgang Saxon
Sydney H. Schanberg
Ann-Marie Schiro
Harold M Schmeck Jr.
Serge Schmemann
William E. Schmidt
Eric Schmitt
Harold C. Schonberg
Edward Schumacher
Tony Schwartz
Katharine Q. Seelye
Somini Sengupta
William Serrin
Richard Severo
Philip Shabecoff

Joe Sharkey
Richard F. Shepard
William G. Shepherd Jr.
Nathaniel Sheppard Jr.
Mimi Sheraton
David K. Shipler
E.R. Shipp
Marlise Simons
Margot Slade
Barbara Slavin
Suzanne Slesin
Alison Smale
Hedrick Smith
Red Smith
Ronald Smothers
Dava Sobel
Alessandra Stanley
Jacques Steinberg
Jennifer Steinhauer
James P. Sterba
James Sterngold
Damon Stetson
William K. Stevens
Barbara Stewart
Henry Scott Stokes
Sheryl Gay Stolberg
David Stout
Neil Strauss
Stephanie Strom
Reginald Stuart
Ronald Sullivan
Walter Sullivan
Eric Taub
Philip Taubman
Angela Taylor
Stuart Taylor Jr.
Kathleen Teltsch
Jo Thomas
Robert McG. Thomas Jr.
Anthony Tommasini
Samuel A. Tower
Joseph B. Treaster

Alan Truscott
James Tuite
Wallace Turner
Patrick E. Tyler
Lawrence Van Gelder
Vartanig G. Vartan
George Vecsey
Sam Howe Verhovek
John Vinocur
Nicholas Wade
Matthew L. Wald
Amy Waldman

Ray Walters
Bayard Webster
Bernard Weinrub
Benjamin Weiser
Patricia Wells
John Noble Wilford
Lena Williams
John S. Wilson
Carey Winfrey
Christopher S. Wren
Monique P. Yazigi
Paul Zielbauer

About the Author

Robert Greenman is a consultant to *The New York Times* Newspaper in Education program and the author of many of its curriculum guides. He is a frequent workshop presenter on the topic of newspapers as a teaching tool, addressing conferences of the National Council of Teachers of English, the International Reading Association, the Journalism Education Association and the Columbia Scholastic Press Association. He is the author of *The Adviser's Companion*, a guide for school newspaper advisers.

Mr. Greenman has taught more than 10,000 high school and college students the value, power and pleasure of using language effectively. He has received many national awards for his contributions to journalism education, including the Charles R. O'Mally Award for Excellence from *The Times's* Newspaper in Education program. He is a graduate of Emerson College.

Mr. Greenman and his wife, Carol, live in Brooklyn. They have three daughters and three grandchildren, whom he is teaching to appreciate words that make a difference.